T

Suhash Chakravarty was born in Maihar (Madhya Pradesh). He graduated in History from St. Stephen's College, Delhi and went on to do his doctorate from Selwyn College, Cambridge.

He returned to teach History at St. Stephen's College and later became a reader at the Delhi University. His other books include, *From Khyber to Oxus: Imperial Expansion* and *Anatomy of the Raj.*

Suhash Chakravarty is married with a son and lives in Delhi.

Suhash Chakravarty

The Raj Syndrome

A Study In Imperial Perceptions

PENGUIN BOOKS

Penguin Books India (P) Ltd., B4/246 Safdarjung Enclave, New Delhi 110 029, India
Penguin Books Ltd., Harmondsworth, Middlesex, England
Penguin Books USA Inc., 375 Hudson Street, New York, New York 10014, USA
Penguin Books Australia Ltd., Ringwood, Victoria, Australia
Penguin Books Canada Ltd., 10 Alcorn Avenue, Suite 300, Toronto, Ontario M4V 3B2, Canada
Penguin Books (NZ) Ltd., 182 – 190 Wairau Road, Auckland 10, New Zealand

First published by Chanakya Publications 1989

Revised and updated edition published by Penguin Books India (P) Ltd., 1991

Typeset in Times Roman by J.S Enterprises, 8/39, Kirti Nagar Industrial Area, New Delhi 110015
Made in India by Ananda Offset Private Ltd., Calcutta

Dedicated to the memory of my mother who inspired me.

Contents

Preface

I am happy that a new edition of *The Raj Syndrome* is being brought out by Penguin India. For this edition, I have systematically revised the references and corrected and updated the text wherever it seemed necessary. In view of the extensive notes and references in the book I have not thought it prudent to attempt a separate bibliography.

The book is primarily a study in imperial sensibility. I have sought to examine the nuances of British perceptions of India during the period covered, roughly, from the imperial assemblage of the Delhi Durbar of 1877 to the replacement of the Union Jack on the Red Fort by the Indian tricolour in 1947. However, these dates have not been strictly adhered to owing to the compulsions of historical analysis. I am aware that the genesis of imperial perceptions must be traced much before the assumption of the title of the Empress of India by Queen Victoria and that the hangover of the self-images, illusions and stereotypes of the Raj still continues to condition and influence the discourses of independent India.

In a sense the book seeks to sketch the outlines of imperial perceptions *per se*. The Raj was central to the formation of British imperial ideology and the syntax of imperial prose in India was candid and unambiguous. The imperial *lingua* of George Nathaniel Curzon and Rudyard Kipling was confirmed by Evelyn Baring Cromer in Egypt, Frederick John Dealtry Lugard in Nigeria and Duncan MacDonald in Arabia. Kipling's outburst against Mr Paget M.P., was an expression of the pent-up feeling of imperial politicians and statesmen in Britain and administrators in India and elsewhere in the empire and echoed by poets, publicists and novelists alike. In due course, even the liberal assimilation of imperial ethos and commandments was complete. In examining the impulses of imperial Britain in relation to India I have disassociated myself, as far as possible, from the romantic and idealized image and role of civil servants, politicians, generals, missionaries, reformers and reconciliers sustained by historians and conserved by laymen.

I leave the rest to the readers.

New Delhi — *Suhash Chakravarty*
June 1991

1

The Omphalos of the Empire

Of late there has been an effulgent intellectual output induced by a fresh spurt of interest in the Raj. Researchers, writers, retired civil servants and army-men have mused over the diverse contours of the imperial psyche and sensibility. This literary fluorescence consists of, among other things, a study of the racial vanity, social pique and sexual susceptibilities of a small British power-elite. A substantial number of works dwell on the intrigues and rivalries of this alien community and a good deal are nostalgic discourses on a remarkable variety of themes that include exotic culinary techniques, the drift and bent of contemporary fashions and designs, the fascinating appeal of Indian photography in its infancy and the stately values of imperial aesthetics. Besides, they accommodate reviews of expansive impulses from the North-West Frontier and tales from the verdant hill stations, sun-baked district headquarters and snooty bungalows of the Civil Lines. The Raj has also formed the *mise-en-scene* of a grim collection of selected epithets from the gravestones in the cemeteries of India.[1]

The accent in these publications has been conspicuous. One is presented with warm accounts of the high noon of the Empire as well as soulful descriptions of the interplay of light and shadow during its twilight hours. There are Pharisaic exaltations as well as some sensitive reminiscences. Together they have sought to portray a charming panorama of British India.

From this pot-pourri one gets an impression of the joys of life in a wonderful land of pukka sahibs, burra mems and punkah-wallahs. It is an image of British India etched nostalgically. It is one of crows, rust sunsets, of dinner parties that ended with little glass bowls full of water and curious herbs to wash fingers in, of shining rivers and beautiful women and of cane chairs on gymkhana verandas. It recalls the small talk indulged in by the 'white ranis' and is almost oblivious of the arrogant social aloofness of the community. It idealizes the controversial political positions adopted and affirmed by its self-centred leadership and glosses over the consequent racial bitterness. These lonesome yearnings and gaudy gasconade, nevertheless, have a compelling appeal and they serve to create an illusion that obscures a complex reality.[2]

In reality, the Empire in India had a surly and unpleasant image. A sense of disciplined conformity, an intemperate bearing, a cheeky swagger, pert claims to racial superiority, the elaborate rituals of a European mission and an extravagant indulgence on the part of a public school aristocracy furnished British rule with its singular distinctiveness. As a result, a pretentious hauteur blissfully insulated a ruling minority from an India immediately beyond the various layers of *khidmutgars*. It may not be injudicious, therefore, to trace the faded lines of imperial perception somewhere beyond those simple formulations woven around the exploits of a so-called 'exile race in action' or the nursery rhymes hummed in a curious Anglo-Indian patois by the native ayahs for the *babalog: umti dumpti gir gia phut.*[3]

*

By the turn of the twentieth century, the Empire meant, for an average Englishman with a moderate income and modest intelligence, a fundamental faith. It swayed the whole nation which turned ecstatic about the expanding colonial world. A popular wall-hanging entitled *Following the Flag* portrayed a typical upper middle class family at the breakfast table around fragrant cups of Darjeeling tea with a tight-lipped papa in a smoking jacket, a namby-pamby mama in a frilled muslin bodice, a flippant daughter with ribboned hair and a frisky son in his Eton blazer. While the grumpy papa read out *The Times* reporting the current campaign, the sportive children periodically moved the Union Jacks pinned on a map on the table and sought to assess the fluctuating military positions thus stimulating the fascination of the half-witted mama. For this family, and for all those who were placed above them and many who were placed below them, the Empire had become the leitmotif of their daily lives.

James Morris in *Farewell to Trumpets* exemplified this ebullient national preoccupation.[4] From the spirited editorials in *The Times* to matchbox lids, from children's fashions to parlour games, from music-hall lyrics to parish-church sermons and from Woolwich to Sandhurst[5] the imperial *chanson de geste* was relentlessly chanted. The Empire was the plot of novels and flavoured the dialogues of plays, it set the rhythm of ballads and constituted the inspiration of orators. Lipton's slogan 'From tea garden to tea pot' typified the force of the psychological propaganda for the Empire. The new vehicles of imperial propaganda included almost every item of normal human consumption. The Empire Exhibition at Wembley in 1924–25 officially advertised that its primary object was to discover new sources of imperial wealth and to open fresh world markets for dominion and home products. The organizers of the Exhibition sought to demonstrate to the people of Britain the almost infinite 'possibilities of the Dominions, Colonies and Dependencies Overseas'.[6] It was meant to be a stock-taking of the entire resources of the Empire. If the Empire meant 'preferential treatment', 'commerce' and an 'organic growth' of different races, the Exhibition at Wembley offered at a single site a veritable attraction of imperialism actualized. The official guide stated: 'There the visitor will be able to inspect the Empire from end to end. From Canada it is but a stone's throw to Australia, from Australia a short step to India and the Far East, from Hong Kong a few minutes' walk to New Zealand or Malaya. In a single day he will be able to learn more geography than a year of hard study would teach him.'[7]

Wembley and other imperial exhibitions left a deeply engraved impression on the popular imagination of an Empire dedicated to order and decency, trade and civilization and of the irresistible fascination of India. That popular culture was animated by an active theatre which was primarily devoted to the creation of racial stereotypes. The audience was given a simple formula to appreciate an Indian sunk in tropical indolence and oriental fatalism. He is caste-ridden, superstitious, a prisoner of astrologers, litigious, lustful and trapped in a number of enervating institutions. He is also shifty and treacherous. By the 1920s, cinematic dramatization of imperial classics kept up the popular cultural momentum while the British Broadcasting Corporation was given to stimulate that imperial patriotism. Imperial sensibility was not merely an upper-class affair. There was a visible line of communication between Kipling and Newbolt on the one end and the musical comedies like *The Grand Mogul* and *The Nautch Girl* on the other.[8] The culture of the street, the expectations of a slum and the prospects of the white-collared skilled workers were instilled by the vision and illusion of domestic 'under classes' becoming colonial 'over classes'. As John M. Mackenzie put it: Since 1880 imperialism became a popular culture. Setting it forth more explicitly, James Morris stated: 'It was as though the whole nation was being deliberately disciplined into the imperial fervour.'[9] Between the school saga, *vive la compagnie* and the Sunday hymn in chapel, 'Onward Christian Soldiers', valour, glamour, dominion, law, discipline and class were fused into an identifiable national cultural consciousness.[10]

The Lord Bishop of Calcutta consecrated this general euphoria when he introduced Arthur Stanley's anthology of patriotic verses which was published both for the children of the British Isles as well as for the less fortunate sons of the babus of Calcutta.[11] Alfred Tennyson's aphorism, 'the song that nerves a nation's heart is itself a deed', formed the pith and marrow of the Bishop's exhortations. What was more disturbing was that patriotism and the imperial inheritance were alloyed into an orthodox social creed which touched and shaped every aspect of British life. G.A. Henty's tales of 'robust British adventures' in a bizarre and variegated India,[12] Rider Haggard's series of 'honest encounters' in pagan and primordial Africa, [13] C.R. Low's chauvinistic apologies in *Cracy to Tel-el-Kebir*, Rudyard Kipling's 'white man's burden' and Henry Newbolt's pseudo-poetry[14] exalted the imperial consciousness, making it reverberate ceaselessly. The British middle class moved round and round this imperial mulberry bush. Its eyes were focussed on the various imperial stadia in remote lands and its mind was charged with an inspired mission together with its struggles, triumphs and tragedies. India stood at the centre of this physical and emotional experience.

A giant among boys' story writers, Henty wrote books which were popular and welcomed everywhere. Hailed as 'the king of story-tellers', Henty was much admired by his juvenile audience. What would the boys do without Henty? asked the *Journal of Education*. Ever fresh and vigorous, the *Journal* claimed, his books had at once 'the solidity of history and the charm of romance'. Those who knew something about India would be most ready to thank Henty, the *Academy* reviewed, for giving their children the instructive volume *With Clive in India*.[15] In *The Tiger of Mysore*, for example, Henty wove fact and fiction so skilfully that the reader could not help acquiring a warped and contorted view of the 'blood-thirsty tyrant' Tipu Sultan, who, the young boys were informed, revelled in acts of the most abominable cruelty, massacred for his own perverted pleasure and tortured simply to gratify his lust for murder.[16] Henty was prolific in his 'Book for Young People' series of Blackie and Sons. His hero invariably followed a military career, excelled in reckless adventure, and was usually portrayed like a haughty Roman character with indomitable courage, sternness and discipline. Henty's hero exposed the deceitful nature of the natives of India in all their vivid variety, fought in Virginia during the Civil War and was also to be found with Wolfe in Canada and Gordon in Khartoum. Henty's hero was ubiquitous through the ages and across the continents of the world. He was full of vigour and heroic inspiration for impressionable minds. He tenderly nursed 'the birthright of the just and the noble' to conquer the wild people of the world.[17] On these themes Blackie and Sons supplied hundreds of titles by lesser known writers in its 'Three Shilling Series' and 'Half-Crown Series'. The Seeley Service and Co. supplemented Blackie's series with its own 'Library of Adventure', 'Heroes of the World Library' and the 'Pink Library'. These were stories of intrepid bravery and stirring adventure, of British knights and bishops in their encounters with uncivilized men, wild beasts and the forces of nature. Pennell of *Pennell of the Afghan Frontier* was, for example, an inspiring figure—a self-effacing missionary devoted to sports, childlike in simplicity, fearless in crisis and who also happened to be a saint.[18] Jesse Page's *Judson, The Hero of Burma,* Dowson's *Missionary Heroines in India,* Edward Gilliat's *Heroes of Modern India, Heroes of Modern Crusades* and *Heroes of the Indian Mutiny,* to name a few, were historical romances filled with pride at British achievements in far-off lands.[19] Amy Carmichaels' *Raj, Brigand Chief* carried a foreword by the Bishops of Madras, Tinnevelly and Travancore, which asserted that this was the true story of a sensitive Indian Robin Hood driven to dacoity by religious and social persecution and who was rescued from that life of self-torture by his sincere conversion to Christianity.[20] *Captain Courageous,* with all its great sea-adventure stories, retained its fascination for children as well as grown-ups. Kipling's heroic conception of life and his admiration for bravery and courage, wherever he might find them, never dimmed. In the tough Gloucester fishermen in search of cod and halibut he sought elements of glory while in the schooner's skipper, Disko Troop, he portrayed an admirable and kind man. A soft young boy was regenerated, Kipling continued to harp, by his very contact with a brave hero. Boys, Kipling suggested, ought to be tough, and hardy and learn to obey orders.[21]

Osbert Sitwell, endowed with a reputation for aristocratic eccentricity, recollected in a fine evocation of the England of his own childhood days: 'How exciting were those romances, chiefly the novels of Rider Haggard, which reflected to perfection the Cecil Rhodes-Boer War materialism, tinged with both idealism and I.D.B. of that strange epoch, just as Rudyard Kipling supplied the inspired part of it. . . .' A feeling of imperial romance filled the classrooms and playgrounds. 'If only one could find', Sitwell recalled his childhood fantasies, 'those hidden kingdoms, at present wasted on the natives and guarded from their rightful owners, the British, by occult and deathless enchantresses; if only one could find them, and open the country up!'[22] Colonials returned home with quaint gifts from the queer East. Cecil Sitwell, a cousin, was one of them and the children of the family gazed at him admiringly and envisioned him against the backdrop of a host of lion cubs 'playful as kittens'. The adults remembered him as a singularly fearless man who went out unarmed to quell a dispute 'while violent human savages' turned on him.[23] These new heroes were presented as adventurers. They encountered physical danger, pitted themselves alone against fate and lived in an unfamiliar land. It was claimed that they were only trying to help a black man lead a happier life or increase the sum of England's geographical knowledge. Undaunted by problems, they forged ahead, leaving behind the homes they loved. If two of them met in the Himalayan snows, the nursery rhymes of British adventures underlined, it was not strange that in five minutes they would be talking of Piccadilly![24]

Charles Dilke had inseminated the minds of educated Britons with a near paranoid swagger to look upon themselves as a master race. Dilke's *Greater Britain* had become a proverbial adage. It signified intellectual dynamism, political expansion and the extension of the rule of law. John Seeley, the celebrated Cambridge historian, moulded that illusion into a passionate worldview and studded it with the myths and parables of imperial expansion. He distinguished between the colonial empire of British settlements and India where a native population was to be governed for its own welfare. He visualized that the British colonies would eventually form a fraternal confederacy of Greater Britain. India, on the contrary, he prescribed, would be held in trust. Seeley's *Expansion of England* meant more than a greater pride in the Empire or 'a larger patriotism'.[25] It was hailed as a remarkable cultural achievement of the British nation. Those who watched India most impartially, Seeley vaunted in 1833:

> see that a vast transformation goes on there, but sometimes it produced a painful impression upon them; they see much destroyed, bad things and good things together; sometimes they doubt whether they see many good things called into existence. But they see one enormous improvement, under which we may fairly hope that all other improvements are potentially included; they see anarchy and plunder brought to an end and something like the *immense majestas Romanna pacis* established among two hundred and fifty millions of human beings .... The transformation we are making there may cause us some misgivings, but though we may be led conceivably to wish that it had never been begun, nothing could ever convince us that it ought to be

broken off in the middle.[26]

The extension of *Pax Britannica* was greeted unfailingly as an unavoidable commitment and it was presented as a hallowed obligation which constituted a spiritually ennobling exercise as well.

Thomas Carlyle, John Ruskin, Benjamin Disraeli, Cecil Rhodes, Alfred Milner and Joseph Chamberlain among many others carefully developed the emotional, romantic and pragmatic areas of imperial sensitivity. Carlyle tore apart the utilitarian scruples against expansion as he romanticized courage, strength and valour. His doctrine of work reinforced imperialism with a fallacious claim of moral obligation. People, it was asserted, had a duty to develop the lands they occupied and if they did not they had no exclusive right to them.[27] Ruskin urged the youth of England to make their country the centre and omphalos of the world and to promote the power of England by land and by sea.[28] The Primrose League with its Disraelian motto, *imperium et libertas*, together with his famous Crystal Palace speech of 1872 seeking to strike a national consensus around a happy combination of old institutions, the Empire and reforms,[29] moulded imperialism into a powerful material force in a period characterized by a drive to 'occupy, fortify, grab and brag'.[30]

The Empire and chivalry were hitched together in 1872 with Tennyson's *Idylls of the King*. As an ideological flourish, imperialism highlighted the significance of a national obligation. William Steed, the editor of *The Times*, endorsed that bounden duty when he put it in no uncertain words: 'The English speaking race is one of the chiefs of God's chosen agents for executing coming improvements in the lot of mankind'.[31] Cecil Rhodes and Alfred Milner had already determined the way to that promised land. The *Big Hole* of Kimberley transformed the fantasies of nursery rhymes into cruel realities with the alluring prospect of a diamond destiny. To Rhodes, the Empire was bread and butter as well as an untouched arena inviting the initiative of men of character and leadership. To Milner, it was an organic community of interests and a common civilization. It was organization, power, authority and devotion. To Chamberlain, India and the Empire constituted a prosaic essential: it was commerce. To the Government Committee of 1917, India was the most stable beam of the imperial nexus.[32] The imperial idea had found its towering proconsul in George Nathaniel Curzon, its wandering Evangelist in George Robert Parkin, its swashbuckling Don Quixote in George Taylor Denison, its Poet Laureate in Rudyard Kipling and its empyrean citadel in New Delhi. To an average Briton, Cecil Rhodes' maxim, 'Philanthropy plus five per cent', offered Dei gratia, an enticing prospect and he simply fell for the half-crazy flamboyance of this enigmatic imperial Goliath: 'I walked between earth and sky and when I looked down I said—"this earth shall be English" and when I looked up, I said—"the English shall rule this earth"'.[33] L.S. Amery described these men as Elizabethan. The suggestion behind the appellation was that they combined patriotism and vision with a love for power, wealth and a reasonable lack of scruple with regard to the methods adopted.[34]

It may be true that British diplomacy of the last quarter of the nineteenth century appeared somewhat defensive. The totality of expansive impulses nevertheless offered a spectacular sight.[35] The annual parliamentary reports on the moral and material progress of India generated a feeling of unquestioning superiority of British hegemony in India in sharp contrast to the shaky Russian breastworks in Central Asia stoutly defended by her pioneers and generals.[36] There was no dearth of Social Darwinists to draw up an argument from the natural sciences and to belabour the basic inequalities between the European and non-European peoples.[37] Karl Pearson, for example, idealized imperialism as an essential part of 'natural history', as the inevitable struggle between races leading to the triumph and survival of the fittest. 'The path of progress', he announced in 1900, 'is strewn with the wreck of nations; traces are everywhere to be seen of the hecatombs of inferior races ... Yet these dead people are in very truth, the stepping stones on which mankind has arisen to the higher intellectual and deeper emotional life of today.'[38] The Liberal Unionists added a further dimension. Speaking to his followers, Austen Chamberlain expressed his belief that a policy which was born of despair and dislike for obligations and responsibilities would attract no popular favour in England.[39] The question of Irish Home Rule had been associated with a slanderous campaign against an alleged wholesale surrender to lawlessness. If the movement was allowed to triumph, it was prognosticated, it might even plunge the great Indian dominion into disorder.[40]

Curzon synthesized these related ideas into an ideology with an organic unity. He was applauded when he proclaimed that he had been called upon by Providence to devote 'the whole of his working manhood to the study and service of the Empire'.[41] He maintained that the physical expansion of Europe was prompted by the law of modern nations which stated that every nation must expand. Although initially Britain had launched on historic quest, her example soon inspired other nations to follow faithfully. The United States of America, it was pointed out, had been pushing ahead towards an imperial destiny. This lesson had also been grasped by France, Italy and Germany. Japan had already been swept into the same vortex. Imperialism had become a respectable world phenomenon. As a movement of modern history, Curzon maintained, it had acquired a touch of inevitability.[42]

Curzon contested the proposition that the remarkable extension of the Empire in India should be dubbed as the product of a sudden impulse engineered by a set of buoyant buccaneers or be smudged as the result of the calculations of machiavellian cunning. He insisted that the Empire should not be interpreted either as an upshot of national vanity or as the outgrowth of territorial cupidity. On the contrary, a noble commitment, he stressed, formed the *point d'appui* of imperialism. The Roman Empire, according to him, developed its own imperial ideas: the diffusion of order amidst anarchy and of universal law in the midst of chaos. Charlemagne, Alexander, Akbar and Napoleon, he claimed, had evolved their own distinct *Zeitgeists*. The credibility of imperialism was invariably assessed in terms of its intrinsic ideas. In consonance with this hypothesis, Curzon went about delineating the significant features of British imperialism. The vital energies that had been inspiring her imperial career were identified. These historical forces, Curzon exclaimed, were the spirit of enterprise of Great Britain, the laws of political and economic gravity and the dynamic conception of a master race.[43]

In keeping with this perception, the expansion of the British frontier in India as elsewhere was presented as a spectacular march of civilization. Whether amidst the mango groves of Palasi or on the banks of the Sutlej, whether in the rugged Aravallis or in the fastnesses of the Maratha uplands, whether in the treacherous quagmire of the Irrawaddy or in Afghanistan the so-called 'land of stones and scoundrels',[44] it was drummed into the ears of a prostrate population that British diplomacy and arms desired justice. In imperial literature British rule meant law and British force signified the protection of the weak against a barbarous bully. The irresistible 'Red Line', triumphant in a hundred battlefields, once again stood fast, H.S. Cunningham proudly chronicled in his tale of Dustypore, 'against the onset of despairing fanaticism', and once again the line moved forward the boundaries of a conquering race.[45] This constituted an imposing imperial refrain. In her *On the Face of the Waters,* written against the background of the Revolt of 1857, Flora Annie Steel put her audacious stamp on this unfaltering imperial claim. Known to the contemporary British establishment of Lahore for her flurried and fidgety disposition,[46] Flora Annie Steel recounted the annexation of Awadh: 'Here and there above the trees, the dome of a mosque or the minaret of a mausoleum told that the town of Lucknow, scattered yet coherent, lay among the groves; the most profligate town in India which, by one stroke of an English pen, had been bidden to live as best it could in cleanly, courtless poverty'.[47] Cunningham chuckled as he summed up the intellectual foundation of W.W. Hunter's *Rulers of India*: 'The solid tramp of British soldiers' feet, sounded the death-knell of a rule whose hour of doom had struck and was blotted for ever from the page of the world's story'.[48]

Imperial expansion carried with it its own rationale. Edward Robert Bulwer Lytton had laid down the essential principles of imperial expansion—that a loose group of barbarous states outside the frontier of a 'civilized' Empire 'may be compared with the fresh air necessary for life'. But the space was strictly limited; and 'if it be obstructed altogether', Lytton added, 'we cease to breathe, we perish'.[49] Prince Gortchakoff's famous circular of 1864 was an imperial invocation and was adopted by Russia's rival in Asia as the essential principle of her own manifesto. Physical expansion of European powers, it maintained, could not be contained simply because it was forced on them by the unpredictable acts of aggression by restless nomadic tribes immediately beyond the settled frontiers.[50] The upshot of the imperial ukase read as follows: 'To ask a barbarous country between the two civilized nations to retain its independence is like asking water to stop at a certain point on its way downhill or like asking an egg to stand on its end.'[51]

Curzon pushed the logic forward. The British Empire, he expounded unequivocally, implied the disappearance of misery, oppression, anarchy, superstition and bigotry. It connoted the extension of peace, justice, prosperity, humanity and freedom of thought and expression. The progressive features, Curzon gloated, evoked unprecedented loyalty and enthusiasm even in the remotest corners of the earth.[52] The Raj, (this was Kipling going berserk) was blessed by the Queen's peace:

> There's a convict more in the Central Jail
> Behind the old mud wall;
> There's a lifter less on the Border trail,
> And the Queen's Peace over all,
> Dear boys
> The Queen's Peace overall. . . .[53]

It was 'law', 'regularity', 'routine', 'obedience', 'stability', and hence, 'peace' that constituted the *summum bonum* of a belauded imperialism. The concept of 'law' was given a flatulent existence in the imperial curriculum.[54] It was considered to be the supreme test of human achievement and was responsible, the imperialists portended, for the maintenance of a semblance of order amidst the jungle people. 'Law was like the Great

Creeper because it dropped across everyone's back and no one could escape'.[55] Its function was to coordinate conflicting interests. It was necessary to underwrite the sheer existence of the common folk, especially in a country known for its scarcity, drought, brigandage and 'water truce'. Law was indispensable for any ordered society and it was spelled out as common knowledge that the 'strength of the Pack is the Wolf and the strength of the Wolf is the Pack'.[56]

The Queen's peace was analogous to the Raj. It was, in its turn, typified by the Grand Trunk Road in Kipling's magnum opus, *Kim*: 'All castes and kings of men move here. Look! Brahmans and Chamars, bankers and tinkers, barbers and Bunnias, pilgrims and porters—all the world coming and going'. It was a 'wonderful spectacle', Kipling eulogized, 'of a stately corridor, all India spread out to left and right. It runs straight, bearing, without crowding, India's traffic for fifteen hundred miles—such a river of life as nowhere else exists in the world'.[57]

The relentless service of the Raj to mankind was projected in every aspect of its endeavours. It was discovered in the 'Overland Mail' 'operating from level to upland, from upland to crest, from ricefield to rock-ridge and from rock-ridge to spur'.[58] The Queen's peace was designed to reflect, somewhat uncomfortably, in the paternalistic care of a district officer who was presented as a missionary faithfully nursing the aspirations of the inarticulate millions in sharp contrast to the disquieting restlessness of a self-seeking literati in their alleged unprincipled bid for a *vakil raj*.[59] Either as a robust young man called Namgay Doola, the son of Timlay Doola, who was identified as Tim Doolan with a drop of British blood in his veins and a metamorphosed Christianity at heart, providing instinctively the necessary leadership in an inaccessible chiefdom and exhibiting 'his extraordinary behaviour bordering the western concept of honour'[60] or as an infirm district officer ensuring on his death-bed the steady flow of water to the lands of warring tribesmen,[61] Englishmen in India were depicted as the most conscientious servants of God.[62] Kipling faithfully sang these claims in his *A Song of the English*:

> Keep ye the law — be swift in all obedience—
> Clear the land of evil, drive the road and bridge the ford.
> Make ye sure to each of his own
> That he reap where he hath sown,
> By the peace among our people let men know we serve
> the Lord![63]

The elements of progress and loyalty, it was underlined, had transformed imperialism into a progressive force. This creed, systematically worked out by Richard Temple, James Fitzjames Stephen and John Strachey, was emphasized by every civilian. This was not an assertion of an egalitarian worldview as it glorified a mercantile past, rhapsodized the brutal ascendancy of an agressive military power and romanticized the liquidation of traditional societies. It indicated the prospect of an ever-widening vista for the promotion of British 'freedom' and 'law' on to the 'unknown sandhills' and 'marshy lands' by certain unauthorized actions on the part of a few sportive men on the distant live frontiers of the Empire. Curzon ranted that despite human failings the British Empire in India epitomized a happy combination of moral virtues, a spirit of humanity and a puritanical fervour. These qualities rather than those of 'filibuster or the bandit', provided the *differentia specifica* of the Raj.[64]

The Empire, in general, Curzon explained, could no more be discredited by the slur upon the character of its sedulous agents often toiling *con amore* amid political and moral upheavals than paintings or poetry could be sneered at because a few poets had been immoral or painters lax. Some physical advances on the imperial map, it was conceded, had been fortuitous. The zealous pioneers often stumbled and faltered unwittingly. Besides, there had been unfortunate cases of regrettable short-sightedness. Curzon, the primate of the Raj, however, revelled without a touch of self-reproach: 'We have often blundered into many of our greatest triumphs.'[65] It would have been churlish and even coarse to justify the 'ugly business' of war and brutal massacre especially when one was armed with a magazine rifle facing a rabble loaded with 'Lhasa-made' matchlocks. It was nonetheless noted smugly that in.Fleet Street the horror of an Eastern encounter was invariably exaggerated. Edmund Candler spun a long yarn that it was a characteristic error of an Englishman living in London to conclude that 'the Oriental mind's fighting as much as he does, and dwells on death with as great a fear'. In the East, he added with vicarious pleasure, men looked upon long life as a rare phenomenon. Candler, the man-on-the spot, seeking to explain away the situation, saw the dead lying in the garden of marigolds and hollyhocks and he remembered that 'only an hour or two before they have lost in a greater game in which he took staked his life'. The Great Game in Asia was presented before an avid crowd at home as a sublime and grotesque exercise, but still, as an imperial obligation and a sheer imperative in a savage land.[66]

*

The secular religion of 'pure imperialism', of which Curzon was an ardent votary, became an inflexible creed during the Boer War and a resolute commitment after the ascendancy of Japan as a world power. The Boer War had called for national introspection.[67] It was admittedly the bloodiest military encounter since the days of Napoleon. It lasted two-and-a-half years; and of the nearly forty-five thousand British and colonial soldiers engaged on the front, some twenty-two thousand were killed. To many, the spectacle of a big England bullying a little Transvaal was too unseemly and repellent a sight to be overlooked casually.[68] Diplomatically, Britain had been cornered and her splendid isolation was more discomforting than her solitary magnificence. There were dissenters at home. The military leadership was reprimanded and subjected to popular indictment. Britain seemed to have lost her special sense of favour and the world a sense of awe. Kipling rebuked 'the flannelled fools at the wicket' and scolded the 'muddied oafs at the goal'.[69] Curzon sneered at England's endemic fear of being great.[70] A touchy Robert Salisbury was provoked into a tart response as he wondered if he could get an opportunity to drown a testy Paulus Kruger in a bowl of turtle soup.[71] However, despite confusion, imperialism made merry in its laboured victory. Alfred Austin captured the mood of this extrovert, unrepentant England:

> Wrong! Is it wrong? Well, may be.
> But I'm going just the same.
> Do they think me a Burgher's baby,
> To be scared by a scolding name?
> They may argue and prat and order,
> Go tell them to save their breath:
> Then, over the Transvaal border,
> And Gallop for life and death.[72]

The war resulted in the creation of a reconditioned imperial idea. In the course of resolving the apparent contradictions of the Boer War, imperialism was endowed with the halo of divinity. The imperial mission had been authoritarian and was now rendered even more so than before. It sought to shuffle away the embarrassments of a popular parliamentary consent. It was proud, self-righteous, sentimental and stoked an inflated British ego:

> Winds of the World, give answer! They are whimpering
> to and fro—
> And what should they know of England who only
> England know?
> The poor little street-bred people that vapour and fume

and brag,
They are lifting their heads in the stillness to yelp at the
British flag![73]

In fact the Boer War made imperialism an effusive sentiment. Sitwell in his innocent childhood did not overlook 'the keenest sense of patriotism and rejoicing' that seemed to have inspired everyone. Englishmen in the Empire as also the Americans in the Philippines were urged to:

Take up the white Man's burden—
Send forth the best of ye breed—
Go bind your sons to exile
To serve your captives' need;
To wait in every harness
On fluttered folk and wild—
Your new-caught sullen peoples,
Half-devil and half child.[74]

The imperial adventures were composed as measures blessed by the will of God. In the *Recessional*, Kipling summarized the imperial prayer to the Maker 'Beneath whose awful Hands we hold Dominions over palm and pine':

If, drunk with sight of power, we loose
Wild tongues that have not thee in awe,
Such boastings as the Gentiles use,
Or lesser breeds without the law—
Lord God of Host, be with us yet,
Lest we forget—lest we forget. . . .[75]

The resurgence of Japan was often cited by contemporaries as a prelude of things to come. In some respects, the Russo-Japanese War was a relevant milestone in imperial history if not a determining landmark or even a crucial turning point. Already during the Boxer Uprising, Kaiser had coined for the imperial vocabulary an explosive phrase, 'the yellow peril'—denoting the danger from the Chinese and the Japanese. With regard to this alleged threat to European supremacy he had raised a clamorous outcry in the imperial citadels. It articulated a campaign for the recognition of a pretentious claim of racial superiority by all its necessary attendants. The rise of modern Japan seemed to have challenged the axiomatic supremacy of the white Christian race. Everyone foreglimpsed in it a frightening prospect. Was it desirable, Kipling, the minstrel of the

Empire muttered, to sanction the uninhibited growth of a modern Japanese State armed with dangerous striking powers and endowed with an odd political culture? The imperial mind had serious misgivings with regard to the future of Japan. It was sceptical of her endeavours and apprehensive of her designs.[76] Despite such vacillations however, all forebodings with regard to Japan spearheading a resurgent Asia against an imperial West were submerged by a vigorous assertion of self-confidence. Japan's experiments were scrupulously isolated and punctiliously circumscribed. It was dinned into the ears of a callow audience that although Japan had disproved the invincibility of Europe, she had not as yet taught Asia the discipline of character and the spirit of self-reform to which she herself owed her success. It was noted with spiteful relish that in India popular ideas betrayed little enlightenment, that the awakening of China had been following a tardy process, that the convulsions in Persia had little impact on a resurgent India and that the reforms in Turkey had resulted in an unadulterated despotism.[77] Bampfylde Fuller, along with many others, was optimistic. He was certain that there was no danger of a nationalistic steam 'overpowering us in India'. On the contrary, he adjured his contemporaries that 'we should not take our hands from the oars and drift with the steam'.[78] The Boer War concretized the imperial idea with cheerful prospects. Japan helped to fuse that consciousness into a stubborn monolith.

While the white colonies constituted imperialism's ornate cathedral cemented by common ties of race, language and religion and the black colonies its private reserve, India formed the principal rampart of the British imperial system. She was its halting place, its springboard and its central operation theatre. No one was willing to relinquish that 'divine dispensation'. The Raj meant much to the Empire. Early in 1870, Richard Southwell Bourke, the Earl of Mayo, had noted its conspicuous potential. Apprehending sinister Russian designs towards the Indian frontier Mayo declared: 'We are determined as long as the sun shines in heaven to hold India—Our National Character—Our Commerce demands it—and we have in one way or another two hundred and fifty million of English capital in this country.' Russia, he added, was ignorant of the mighty power that Britain wielded in India and of the 'moral influence we could, if we choose exercise on our borders'.[79] To that intensely practical Viceroy, India had become the conduit of British prosperity and the repository of her 'national character'. Recognizing the strategic importance of India in British imperial calculations, Lytton in 1877 sought to actualize the nebulous imperial idea in the magnificent Delhi Durbar with the assumption of the title of

Empress of India by the British queen. Lytton's grandiose scheme of imperial defence and his attempt to project the image of the Raj as the champion of Muslim interest from Turkey to Singapore, contending the imperial pretensions of Russia, underlined the commanding position of India in the imperial scheme of things.[80] Curzon's tenure as Viceroy was the high noon of the Raj. Both in terms of imperial vision and its fulfilment, 'the Jewel in the Crown' had become luminous, enterprising, domineering and extrovert. Curzon argued that the central position of India in the Far East was best demonstrated by the political influence which India exercised over the destinies of her neighbours and the extent to which their fortunes revolved upon an Indian axis.[81]

The independence of Afghanistan, Curzon contended, the continued national existence of Persia, the fate of the Bosporus and the destiny of Egypt depended in more than one sense on the decisions at Calcutta. The Indian Empire, as the powerful neighbour of China, also influenced the politics of Korea. Thus, the Raj acquired for the island of Great Britain a special say and a decisive initiative in global politics. This remarkable ascendancy of Britain in world affairs pushed France into a renewed Asian career.[82] Curzon dwelt on the theme exhaustively and his views became commonplace in imperial vocabulary. More than anyone else, it was he who contributed to the perception of the centrality of India in the imperial system and enriched the imperial information centre with his expertise. 'Just as it may be said that the Eastern Question turns', Curzon advocated, 'upon the dismemberment of Turkey, so the Eastern Question in Asia turns upon the continued solidity of Hindustan.'[83] The political and military unity of India under the British rule had ensured that domineering position and no one could ever think of walking out of India without picturing to oneself, Morley supplemented Curzon, the anarchy and the bloody chaos which would follow from such a 'deplorable step'.[84]

During the second decade of the twentieth century it was estimated that the British Empire embraced one fourth of the humanity and India contributed over three hundred million to the four hundred million subjects of the British crown. The numerical strength of the Indian subjects and the immense natural wealth of India actuated a sense of pride which came to be grafted permanently on the British imperial sensibility. The imperial pride of Britain was its chief political asset: it was both a moral and a material force. The loss of British power in India, it was believed, would have been a frank confession of Britain's moral bankruptcy in a world dominated by concession, treaty ports, extra-territorial rights, buffer zones, client states and formal empires. It would have also signalled the collapse of Britain's decisive role at the conference table.[85] Without India, the Empire would be lost. 'When India has gone, the great colonies are also gone.' Curzon admonished a faltering generation: 'Do you suppose that you can stop there? Your ports and coaling stations, your fortresses and dockyards, your crown colonies and protectorates will also go too. For either they will be unnecessary as the toll-gates and barbicans of the Empire have vanished, or they will be taken by an enemy more powerful than yourselves. . . . England from having been the arbiter would sink at best into the inglorious playground of the world.' The market for her manufacture, would wither away; her noble aspirations would be reduced to self-indulgent materialism and 'her subjects would perish in bogs and sands. . . and be lost for ever'.[86]

The strategic position of India in the Empire had become all the more sensitive in view of the awakening of Asia. Chirol presumed that the phenomenon might prove to be disastrous to the dominions whose shores were washed by the Pacific especially if the British Empire was deprived of its 'restraining' influence as the greatest power in Asia. With the loss of India, British position all over Asia, Chirol paraphrased Curzon, would be completely shattered.[87] The growth of the dominions, Chirol asserted, had enabled India to acquire increasing strategic importance for the safety of the whole Empire. Almost equidistant from Australia and South Africa, India supervised some of the vital areas of the ocean highways connecting the remotest parts of the Empire. Examining the position carefully Chirol posed the problem with his characteristic clarity:

> Ask any one who watched the course of the South African War what would have happened had we not had the resources of India to draw upon safely and expeditiously for prompt re-inforcements and for large supplies of all sorts after the first reverses in Natal? Ask any student of naval affairs what would be the effect upon naval power of the loss of India, and the answer would, I think, convince the Australians and South Africans at any rate that the problem of India is in this respect also of no less importance to the Dominions than the Mother Country. . . .[88]

Evidently, after the First World War, the maintenance of British power in India purely on economic terms had become indispensable for the Empire. British economic interest in India was enormous. Chirol thought that this aspect had not been adequately appreciated because its complexities could not be assessed either by the amount of British capital invested in India or by the intricacies of financial relationships between Britain, the rest of the Empire and India. There was a singular pattern of economic ties between them. Chirol maintained that the prosperity of the British Empire depended upon the stability of the great system of credit which lubricated every department of commerce, industry and finance. The loss of India, he wrote, would shake to its very foundations that delicate system of credit which had become essential both to the dominions and the mother country.[89] The severance of India from the Empire, Chirol argued with an air of prophetic insight, would be inopportune for 'the supremacy of the White Man' all over the world. Japan had already shaken the faith of imperialism in its own sense of invincibility. Its confidence quivered at the sight of a resurgent Asia. The publicists of the Raj shuddered at the thought of the collapse of its principal hinge on which the whole system turned. Curzon must have shared the feelings of Whitehall, the Fabians, the 'proconsuls', the 'pioneers', 'guardians' and 'politicals' alike when he asserted:

> If you were to save your colony of Natal from being overrun by a formidable enemy, if you want to rescue the White Man's legation from massacre at Peking, and the need is urgent, you request the Government of India to despatch an expedition, and they despatch it; if you are fighting the Mad Mulla in Somaliland, you soon discover the Indian troops and the Indian Generals are best qualified for the task, and you ask the Government of India to send them; if you desire to defend any of your extreme outposts or coaling stations of the Empire—Aden, Mauritious, Singapore, Hongkong, even Tien-tsing or Shanhai-kwan, it is the Indian army that you turn; if you want to build a railway to Uganda or in the Soudan, you will apply for Indian labour. When the late Mr. Rhodes was engaged in developing your present acquisition of Rhodesia, he came to me for assistance. It is with Indian coolie labour that you exploit the plantations equally of Demerara and Natal; with Indian trained officers that you irrigate Egypt and dam the Nile; with Indian forest officers that you tap the resources of Central Africa and Siam, with Indian surveyors that you explore all the hidden places of the world.[90]

It was natural, therefore, that Indian loyalty could not be allowed to evanesce. The British Empire of India was essentially based on force and it had to be maintained, if necessary, by brute force. This overriding commitment in favour of the Raj was condensed in the Victorian 1840s of unabashed ardours and unshakable religious beliefs; it survived the phase of doubt, disillusionment and shaken standards of the Georgian 1920s and persisted through the mental and moral fog that engulfed Britain through the Second World War. In 1929 it was estimated that British interests in India were extensive. A third of the British army was trained and maintained by her thus considerably relieving the British tax-payers. The Indian army, one of the largest standing armies in the world, was controlled and directed by the Britons and it guarded strategic areas including the West Asian oil fields and Malayan rubber belts. A third of Britain's overseas trade from Egypt to north China was militarily supervised by the Raj. India was Britain's largest importer of textiles and absorbed a fifth of Britain's overseas investment.[91] Many members of the British Parliament had family connections with Indian army or civil services. The family of the Molsworths, for example, spent an aggregate of one-hundred-and-thirty years of service in India and when the last of the Molsworths returned home he did so with 'sadness but without regrets' because he was convinced that 'our work has been well done'.[92]

In January 1942, Clement Attlee, L.S. Amery and Linlithgow agreed that India had been profoundly affected by the changed relationship between Europeans and Asians which had begun with the defeat of Russia by Japan at the beginning of the century. The hitherto axiomatic acceptance of the innate European superiority over the Asians had sustained a severe blow and the balance of prestige, always so important in the East, changed. The process, they believed, would be continued by the reverses suffered by France and Britain at the hands of the Japanese. The gallant resistance of the Chinese and the success of the Russians, a semi-oriental people, against the axis, they feared, would lend substance to the hypothesis that the East had been asserting itself against the dominance of the West.[93] Even the purely constitutional problems of India, they thought, had been rendered complex under the pressure of these circumstances. Linlithgow and Churchill agreed on the weighty strategic importance of India in a global war. It was this consideration that decided the political issue of the government in 1942 in India notwithstanding the uneasiness and criticism of the left wing and Liberal elements in the parliament and the press. Willy-nilly a wavering Attlee came round to appreciate a stubborn Linlithgow's assessment.[94] The following paragraph of the viceroy's letter of 21January 1942 clinched the issue and restored the balance of an indecisive war cabinet:

> What we have to decide however is whether in such circumstance, whatever the feeling of India, we intend to stay in this country for our own reasons, and whether India's place in imperial communications is so important, at any rate in war time, that we must hold on and must not relinquish power beyond a certain point. If we accept that India is too important at this stage for us to take any chances, then I would rather face such trouble as may have to face here as a result of making no concessions now in the political field than make concessions which are ill advised and dangerous and on which we might have to go back for reasons of imperial security at a later stage in the war.[95]

India's geographical position between the European axis powers and Japan invested her with a striking military importance in a trans-continental front stretching between Libya and Singapore.[96] Demands from China and Australia extended her obligation. Indian troops were required to fight in Iraq and Iran and in Malaya and Burma. India became a significant unit of the imperial defence system when Linlithgow committed the Government of India to definite proposals for the protection of West Asia and India with the approval of the cabinet. Plans for the campaign in Iran and other centres of West Asia had been worked out and Wavell expected India to undertake the entire responsibility for the area. With the formation of the Eastern Group Supply Council, India had become the fulcrum of the Commonwealth war policy.[97]

The defence of India was more than a local issue: it was recognized as a part of imperial high policy. As the international situation became increasingly gloomy in the 1930s, the defence potentialities of India assumed vital proportions. The uncompromising position of the Government of MacDonald on defence safeguards was stoutly upheld by British public opinion. In a sense, the Round Table Conference had been subverted before its inception. Thereafter control of defence portfolio became the bone of contention between the Indian nationalists and the Government. To the nationalist India, it was the indicator of British sincerity. For the Governments of India and Britain, the security of the Empire could not be tampered with by inexperienced Indian leadership. Imperial strategy and security were wrapped up in a hush-hush secrecy while strategic analysts in India acquired remarkable official recognition.

*

It was around this tropical outpost of the Raj that the distinctive features of an imperial culture sprouted and matured. For Lord Lugard, the reorganization of northern Nigeria was to be modelled after the Indian administration. It was to be the 'little India' of Africa.[98] For Hardinge of Penshurst, the Eastern vilayats of a disintegrating Ottoman Empire were to be refashioned on the pattern of the British Indian dominion.[99] For Cecil Rhodes, Rhodesia was to be turned into a profitable plantation economy with the assistance of Indian labour and India-trained engineers.[100] Whether in South Africa or in the Fiji Islands, cheap Indian labour had been encouraged to migrate so as to turn the white undertakings into economically viable units.[101] The long and languid gun-boat diplomacy in the yellow seas had to be conducted with a liberal use of Indian resources.[102]

The conquest and consolidation of Punjab, Sind, Baluchistan and the frontier areas along with Kashmir, Gilgit, Chitral, Hunza and Ladakh were closely watched by the Russian columns advancing as they were through the Kizil Kum desert over the Kizil Arvat ranges and across the Syr Daria to a threatening proximity of Amur Daria.[103] The Czar, in his turn, constantly elbowed his generals to learn from and emulate the Indian experiments.[104] Far away in Central Africa, the French and Belgian forces had been contending for the possession of the virgin, fertile and fabulous land of Congo which was hailed by their respective imperial journals as a beautiful land resembling a resplendent India.[105] King Leopold's childish fantasy of carving a glittering empire out of the magnificent African cake,[106] Charles de Freycinet's operations for integrating Algeria, Sudan and Senegal into a French commercial complex[107] and the project of the British colonial office for penetrating deep into Africa in the wake of the scramble for market were animated and buoyed up by the Raj.[108]

England's national euphoria with regard to a 'Greater Britain', France's popular slogan *la plus grande France* and *Nouvelle France*, Russia's so-called compulsive search for a natural frontier inhabited by a sedentary population and Germany's pride in the export of *Kultur* were national variations of a similar ideological formulation.[109] Without the Indian Empire as the exempli gratia, none of these positions would have been either feasible or even tenable. India was ubiquitous in British imperial sensibility. Referring to the elegant Indian Room of the Sitwell mansion, Osbert Sitwell quipped, 'Just as the Indian Room and its very name had no doubt been inspired by the most august example at Osborne, so the letters that my grandmother wrote from it, like those of the former Queen-Empress, traversed the world and reached many distant points of the Empire'.[110]

There is no doubt that India had done much to forge the idea of the Empire as the sought-for playing field of the chivalrous English gentleman whose image had been assiduously sculptured over the years by K. Henry Digby, Thomas Carlyle, Edward Fitzgerald and Charles Kingsley as the new model of the ruling class. This class, it was bluntly asserted, deserved to rule because it possessed the necessary moral traits. It was essentially elitist and strove to create within the ranks of British public schools a close fraternity alive to the cause of imperial obligations and ever ready to assert its superiority. This band of brothers was further stratified. At the summit of the social pyramid were perched selected elite groups around masterful personalities that exerted a powerful influence on imperial policies and radiated a mysterious appeal to the popular imagination. General Garnett Wolseley had his 'Ring' in India; Herbert Horatio Kitchener had his 'Cubs' in Egypt and Sudan; Alfred Milner had his 'Kindergarten' in South Africa and Arthur Balfour presided over the 'Souls' in Britain.[111]

Both the universities of Cambridge and Oxford contributed significantly towards the formation of the imperial sensibility. The Apostles, a secret intellectual society at Cambridge, having an impressive membership that included Alfred North Whitehead, Walter Raleigh, Henry Sidgwick, G. Lowes Dickinson, F.D. Maurice, the numerous Stracheys, James Fitzjames Stephen, Harold Cox, T.W. Arnold and Theodore Morison to mention but a few, deliberated primarily on India. With its appropriate Indian connections through a set of bright young men despatched on their mission to the East and backed by a somewhat intriguing Bloomsbury contact, it rendered the Indian commitment a much applauded world phenomenon.

Oxford, too, moved in intellectually. The arrival of the Rhodes scholars hastened the process, widened its purview, and extended Oxford's horizon. What had been the university of one particular country came to feel itself as the university of the entire English-speaking world. It strengthened its position as an almost exclusive recruiting ground of the 'knights' and 'bishops' of the Raj. It reviewed the changing circumstances and organized a Round Table Group around a romantic visionary, Lionel Curtis, honoured by the editors of his papers at the Bodleian Library as 'the prophet unarmed'. No one who mattered in the first three decades of the twentieth century in terms of the Indian policy was left untouched. With celebrated historians like Arnold Toynbee, H.A.L. Fisher and Ramsay Muir, eminent publicists Valentine Chirol and W.S. Steed, imperial administrators James Meston, William Marris and Malcolm Hailey and statesmen Austen Chamberlain, Edwin Montagu and George Nathaniel Curzon, the Round Table Group presented a national spectrum. Its 'moots', 'eggs' and 'omelettes' sought to outline a blue print for an organic empire.[112]

India however continued to baffle the Oxford group as it proposed to accommodate her, though somewhat uncomfortably, to an all-white combination.[113] London, the metropolis, hastened to inaugurate the School of Oriental and African Studies on imposing though pedestrian lines.[114] Over the years, the *Nineteenth Century*, the *Fortnightly Review*, the *Quarterly Review* and the *Round Table* together with *The Times* of London and the *Statesman* of Calcutta became the repository of imperial sensibility directing a popular jingo and rescuing it from being treated by the 'cockney press' as a 'penny-ha-penny' affair.

There was a firm conviction that distinguished the imperial fraternity. The imperialists were indignant at the uncontrolled industrialization and the inevitable evanescence of 'Green England'. If the Great Exhibition of 1851 denoted a definite phase in the aesthetic expression of maturing British capitalism, the incongruous Gothic structure of the British pavilion reflected the positive assertion of a conservative reaction from within.[115] The society that was visualized by this determined political backlash, was not a withdrawal to a feudal England but a paternalistic, hierarchically arrested industrial society dominated by an arrogant landed gentry opposed to an unbridled extension of democracy.[116] Eager to support technology and industry, they were reluctant to endorse Herbert Spencer's proposition that industrialization would push the society away from 'status' towards 'contract' as the determinant of social relationships.[117] Kipling adulated the machines that served the society 'four and twenty hours a day'.[118] Even so, in keeping with the retrograde social and political developments of the time, he would not welcome the fruition of a set of new social values emanating from industrialization. If the industrial infrastructure was to survive and not create social turmoil, and if the triumph of socialism was to be thwarted, the industrial society needed to be reinforced by the old values of authority, obedience and discipline. In India, and in the rest of the Empire, the ruling class devoted itself to the uninhibited improvisation of its ideas. It carefully contrived the fantasies of a modern Roman Empire and grafted the passion for unrestricted authority on to the viceroys, governors and administrators who were greeted as proconsuls and centurians. It was construed that the imperial obligation of Rome had been inherited by Britain and 'in the discharge of it, the highest features in English character have displayed themselves'. As early as 1888, Froude had shaped this aspect of the imperial idea[119] and Kipling hailed the 'Imperial Fire of Rome' as a divine dispensation that had fallen 'on us, thy son'.[120]

To the imperial culture, the doctrine of character was more engaging than considerations of intellect. The Rhodes scholarship prescribed the qualities of public school men as the essential criteria for its munificence. These included a fondness of and success in 'manly' outdoor sports, such as cricket, football and the like, a demonstration of the qualities of 'manhood', a devotion to duty, a sympathy for, and a willingness to protect, the weak; courage, honesty, unselfishness, kindness and fellowship.[121] Thus, the candidates were to be selected not merely on the basis of their intellectual attainments but also for displaying qualities of character.[122] The specific virtues of the ruling class, it was assumed, were chivalry, honour, patriotism, snobbery, sentimentality and an unmitigated faith in the efficacy of 'pluck' and 'grit' as capable of working wonders. Farming, fox-hunting, cricket and subsequently polo provided it with a permanent social backdrop. All these qualities turned it into a very special type. Diana Barrington, a typical character of a representative Anglo-India fiction,[123] summed up the virtues of the ideal Englishman in India: 'I should hate a man, who took an hour over his tie, lolled on a sofa reading poetry or sat hand in hand with me looking at the moon and criticised my dress like a milliner. I like to know that my husband is a man and not an old woman. He shoots tigers, plays polo and rides races with my full approval'. It was widely believed that the Raj would be more faithfully served by a disciplined football eleven than by an average member of parliament.[124] By teaching skill in cricket, a Harrow inscription added, the boys were taught the values of manliness and honour.[125] It was an image of a set of well-paid secular missionaries who embellished their exacting Indian commitment with a judicious selection from varied manly sports like pigsticking, shooting, fishing, riding, tennis, racquets, bridge and shikar regardless of the climate of assassinations and riots around them.[126]

The English public school was invariably looked upon as the institution for imparting precious lessons in imperial obligations. 'Of all things in the world there is nothing', Kipling wrote, 'always excepting a good mother, so worthy of honour as a good school'. It turned out men who did more real work than men who wrote about 'what other people had done or ought to do'. Its object, it was announced, was not to teach or to judge men and things 'from the narrow point of view of a specialist'. On the contrary, one was trained to look at and examine them by and large from a larger and nobler perspective. 'No book in this world', Kipling vouched, 'will teach that knack'. The motto of the British school, it was stylized, was, 'Fear God, Honour the King and Serve the Empire', and the 'Cheltenham and Marlborough and Haileybury chaps' went over, the imperial publication avowed, to Boerland and Zululand, India and Burma, Cyprus and Hongkong and 'lived and died as gentlemen and officers'.[127] Even the most 'notorious bully', Kipling boasted, returned home 'with a fascinating reputation' of having led a life of forlorn hope and behaved like a hero in a savage land. Saluting the Widow of the Windsor, a school paper pledged:

> For we are bred to do your will
> By land and sea, wherever flies
> The Flag, to fight and follow still,
> And work your Empire's destinies
> Once more we greet you, though unseen our greetings
> be, and coming slow.
> Trust us, if need arise, O Queen!
> We shall not tarry with the blow.[128]

Newbolt's 'Vitai Lampada' combined chivalry, character, sports and discipline together with public school, duty and the Empire and decked that synthetic sentiment with a mass emotion and a romantic refrain: 'Play up, Play up, Play up the Game!'[129] For the young apprentices of the 'Great Game', Robert Baden-Powell coined a ponderous but pompous apothegm: 'Be Prepared'.[130] Kipling cautioned that a cool head, an unbroken soul and an untiring body were required in a greater measure by the Empire than superfluities of wit: 'This is the Law which all laws embrace—Be fit—be fit!'[131] It was taken for granted that men followed gentlemen much more readily than they would an officer whose social position was not so well assured. No one was quicker than Tommy Atkins at spotting the 'gentleman'. The essential qualifications required of an officer were those which any gentleman might have: the habit of wearing decently cut clothes, an ability to speak without dropping his 'h's', an acquaintance with the outward manners of good society and the skill to handle a knife and a fork without exciting the disgust and reprobation of his messmates, together with some knowledge of sports, an interest in wine and tobacco and a strong feeling against the 'savages' who must be conquered. The gulf between the officers and the ranks was not to be bridged.[132]

There was no room for diffidence and doubt as to the righteousness of the imperial cause in India. The Raj overwhelmed both the romantic ideologues as well as the pragmatic administrators by its impressive mystique. Its size, its population, its variety, its unity, its strategic location and its ancient history added much to its legendary charm. Curzon professed that it was neither a military nor a feudal Empire. Its splendours could not be evaluated simply by its extensive territorial acquisitions. Structurally, the British Empire, Curzon announced, was not merely a cluster of subordinate units grouped in deferential pose around an imperial axis with India as its most luminous core.[133] His riotous imagination out-Curzoned Curzon himself as he proceeded to discover for the Empire an apposite metaphor in the planet Saturn with its concentric circles:

> Still as, while Saturn whirls, his steadfast shade
> Sleeps on his luminous wings.

India constituted, in this picturesque presentation, the cape or the dusky ring, the mysterious film of darker hue amidst the encircling belt of the planet.[134]

Meanwhile (and perhaps as a matching response to the eloquence of the statesman) the Empire created its own captains. In thousands of classrooms children were taught to prattle the story of the nine little nigger boys and the importance of being a gentleman. They were also brought up on the exploits and legends of the old and new knights, of Peter Pan, of the Lost Boys in the Never Never Land and of the adventurous prince awakening the Sleeping Beauty and slumbering civilization to life amidst an unruly people. The Empire, they were taught, was the product of every imaginable variety of heroism and valour. There was no paucity of publicists and there was no dearth of improvization. There was the 'coolness of brain', it was proclaimed, that thought out a plan at dawn and held on to it all through the 'long and murderous day'. There was the bravery of mind that made 'the jerking nerves held still and do nothing except show a good example'. There was the 'sheer reckless strength that hacks through a crowd of amazed men and comes out grinning on the other side'. There was also the 'calculated craftsmanship' of a few lonely men who would calmly wipe out every soul in an 'angry explosive rifle-pit' and there were the enduring spirits which, despite long seige, never lost heart, manner or temper'.[135]

Besides, from the crucible of war, Maud Diver boasted, many Vincent Leighs of *Desmond's Daughter* emerged having overcome inherited shyness and developed in a manner that probably surprised none more than themselves.[136] Against the background of a monotone of sand and lost in a haze of dust and the consequent uncertainties, Vincent learnt the lessons taught by the North-West Frontier. Of course, there were moments of selfishness and sheer despondency intensifying a sense of acute desolation[137] but the task had to be fulfilled and the imperial mission ensured that transformation in character, though gradual, was steady and certain. Some of them had gone to India, no more than boys; they returned from their first operation as men, tried in the furnace and 'proven sterling metal throughout'. They had become effective implements finely tempered for the larger work and deeper sufferings that still awaited them. Heroism was to take many forms. In Elder Pottinger of Maud Diver's frontier biography it took the shape of a sturdy, indomitable perseverance, and courage in the face of overwhelming odds; but there was nothing loud and impetuous about it. Presence of mind and personal demeanour of the man-on-the-spot represented his inward qualities.[138] The ascendancy of the superior race in imperial perception was complete as one was compelled to witness in that strange wilderness of the frontier, a remarkable phenomenon. The Pathan, the Sikh and the Dogra soldiers were still enmeshed in their 'unfathomable notion of pollution and purity' while a little apart from this volatile obscurantism sat eight detached Englishmen responsible for the welfare, discipline and loyalty of seven hundred odd human beings of an alien race and creed! These aliens were held together and welded into a formidable fighting machine, Maud Diver vaunted, by a threefold faith in the '*pultan*', the British officer and 'the great white Queen'.[139] In other words, Maud Diver carried the tradition of Kipling forward. To her, the Raj was the physical expression of a superior race—the embodiment of a saga of sacrifice, devotion and perseverance for the promotion of civilization in an alien and savage country.

As a corollary, the imposing collection of the lives of national heroes in school textbooks was enriched by the inclusion of a colourful imperial appendix. Thus, the images of a Horatius holding the bridge, Arthur and his romantic knights, Prince Rupert charging with his cavaliers, John Shore at Corunna and Horatio Nelson at Trafalgar were juxtaposed with the myths and realities of a Robert Clive of Plassey punishing the 'vile ruffians' responsible for the 'black hole' of Calcutta; a daring Arthur Wellesley forcing his way through the formidable defences of Seringapatam held by a 'fanatic' Tipu Sultan; an uncompromising Evangelist in William Bentinck rescuing the miserable widows from the flames of sati single-handedly against the tide of Hindu society; a precocious Thomas Babington Macaulay generously opening the gates of infinite western learning to the limited perception of the heathen mind of doubtful texture; a formidable Sir Hugh Rose caught up in fiery battles against the high-spirited and passionate Rani of Jhansi; a chivalrous Henry Havelock along with a fierce Colin Campbell sacking the city of Lucknow to the war cry of 'Cawnpore! Cawnpore!'; a valiant John Nicholson falling pluckily at the gates of Delhi; an intrepid Frederick Sleigh Roberts holding on in the ruggedness of Kandhar, the stony tribesmen capering to the tune of a diabolical Ignatief and his Cossack hordes; a 'Chinese' Charles Gordon proudly facing the screaming dervishes at Khartoum; a gritty Herbert Horatio Kitchener displaying a dramatic and daring performance at Fashoda and enacting an ingenious military programme at Khyber; the gallant regiment at Balla Hissar dying to a man, and the audacious garrison on the slopes of the Ridge of Delhi in 1857 playing cricket in the jaws of death.[140] It was espoused frequently that throughout a hundred changing years, young people from Britain continued to serve India better in some periods than others 'but always with certain bedrock qualities, that have nothing brilliant about them, though they have created and maintained the world's greatest Empire'.[141] Briefly these qualities could be summed up, in Maud Diver's idioms, as strength of character, courage, integrity and simple devotion to duty. V.A. Smith, H. Rawlinson, Edward Thompson, G.T. Garratt, W.W. Hunter, Stanley Lanepool, P.E. Roberts, H.H. Dodwell, C.C. Davies, Percival Spear and C.H. Philip, to name a few, buffed the imperial sculptures with their tutored skill and historical imagination.

The Empire called for, it was expatiated, physical expansion and a determination to defend, hold on to and consolidate territorial acquisitions against all intruders. It demanded indomitable bravery, supreme sacrifice and unflinching patriotism. It sanctioned the conviction of the Light Brigade to ride on to the Valley of Death, underwrote the credo of Tennyson to hail 'once more to the banner of battle unroll'd' and recommended W.E. Henley's prayer for a war 'righteous and true'. [142] The imperial consciousness of Britain inspired Newbolt to implore:

So shall thou when morning comes,
Rise to conquer or to fall
Joyful hear the rolling drums
Joyful hear the trumpets call.[143]

Empire-building, it was asserted, was an uphill task. There had been intense human suffering in the undertaking. India, it was alarmed to note, was infested with cholera, malaria and enteric fever. In fact the unending draw from India transformed the P & O Shipping Company in the imperial prescription into an 'Exile's Line' and it supported a continuous flow of 'the gipsies of the East' bound to the 'wheel of the Empire'.[144] The Empire, in its turn, was depicted as a hard taskmaster, oblivious of the decaying bungalows, mobile camps, dear friends and deserted houses. British graves multiplied. Death was so common a feature of Anglo-Indian life that it was viewed with near fatalism.[145] 'It's before us, an' be'ind us, an' we cannot get away'.[146] From 249 Regent Street, a London undertaker continued to advertise, well into the twentieth century, complete mourning outfits for India at a concessional rate while profusely thanking his customers for their extraordinary patronage over the years.[147] In India, a gravestone reminded, 'death is such a swift and cunning hunter that before you know you are ill, you may be ready to become its prey—where death, grave and forgetfulness may be the work of two days'.[148] Kipling italicized the situation:

> Never the lotus closes, never the windfowl wake
> But the soul goes out on the East Wind and dies for
> England's sake—
> Men or women or suckling, bride or maid—
> Because on the bones of England, the English flag is
> stayed.[149]

In memorium to one who represented thousands of those who sacrificed lives in the distant outposts of the Empire, Henry Bruce composed:

> Who were the women of your life?
> Know you Eliza? Madame Grand?
> Had you, a world away, a wife?
> Loved you the daughter of the land?
> Such things we cannot understand,
> We only know that in your span,
> Campaigning on a torried sand,
> You lived and died an Englishman![150]

Some others, like E.W. Savi's Maxwell, went to India for distraction, hiding his unheeded domestic wounds by an unpenetrable reserve. To him, London seemed too vast compared to Kaman, a pin-point in the Empire. Faced with the realities of life, he was to find his peace of mind in the white man's mission in a wild country with its surprises, mysteries and trim bungalows.[151] There was no lack of improvisation of human suffering in the imperial propaganda. Thus, birth, absence, longing, laughter, tears and death, as Kipling put it, were conspicuously overlooked. This saga of self-torture for the Empire gave rise to other imperial myths adding to its sense of pride. One is virtually goaded to think of the parents left with no option but to send their young children back to England; the resulting distortions in their personalities, and the tragic prospect of a soft young boy of Kipling's turning into a 'baa baa black sheep' of the family.[152] One is compelled to imagine the plight of the little girl who was sent over to her old-fashioned grandparents in England in Sara Duncan's *A Mother in India* and almost to share the tragedy of the unfortunate mother torn between the natural inclinations of her heart and the austere compulsions of imperial obligations in the heat and dust of an Indian cantonment![153] Charles Monoly grafted an element of melancholy monotony on this tragedy of loneliness. The two Europeans in his *Antony Vanroy* lived together as the only white men in the place for nearly five years: they had passed the stage at which the arrival of a chance comer of their own colour was a godsend; they no longer actively disliked each other's company. They reflected, in their apparently faceless demeanour, neither the exultation of any success or the depression of any failure. The European in India, it was added indulgently, might have his failings, but much of these might be forgiven if 'one takes note of the inhuman loneliness of his station', and adds to these the hazards of sudden death and severe mutilation of limbs at the hands of an unpredictable Yusufzai[154] or the penury of Yardley Orde's helpless widow passing her hat around for a meagre return-fare to England despite a lifelong service to the Empire![155] Every human sentiment, it was proudly claimed, was sacrificed at the altar of the land that was 'yet to be made'.[156]

Service in India, according to another myth, was a permanent banishment with forlorn hopes and faltering resolutions. Mr Blythe of *A Forlorn Hope* spent his lifetime in India but medical advice forbade his going home where he would not have stood even the first winter. His government service would yield an inadequate pension and he apprehended that his domestic life, with three growing daughters, would invariably pass through deep waters. Nellie had to drop the handsome young subaltern, while the younger daughter had been chasing a rich *kala admi* in search of security with the 'frightful' sequel of outcaste Eurasian children looming ahead Mr Blythe could only dream of seeing the dear old haunts again in the midst of old associations and feeling the old-home sensation in his bones.[157] For Reverend Henry Inglis, on the other hand, work meant rough travel through tracts of scrubs, jungle and heavy forest, across gullies and river beds, up and down the slopes of the hills carrying with him a few medical comforts 'to semi-savage people, jungle tribes, aborigines, poor, primitive souls and bodies as yet hardly higher than the animals, owing to the cruel barriers of castes and customs'. The author merely underlined the claims of the British mission when he wrote that Henry Inglis was indifferent to his own convenience and was eager 'to lighten the darkness of these miserable beings' and give them 'spiritual and physical aid'.[158]

It was repeated *ad nauseam* lest one forget that the real East was not quite that of the picture palaces. It was not the sensuous paradise manufactured by film producers. The real India meant for an Englishman smells and sweaty bodies, spittings of 'pan' mixed with tobacco juice, dances whose very technicalities spelt boredom and a music which was nothing but a 'wail of highpitched agony'. 'In my consciousness', Victor Dane concluded, India constituted 'a sort of semi-black interlude' full of loud noises, swearings, gleeful native stewards, naked ascetics with strange mysteries, intriguing controversies, a closed religion where even an experienced British C.I.D. remained, forever, an illiterate intruder. 'Life becomes', Dane was convinced, 'very tedious in India for the average official' and he probably welcomed the change of seeing a passionate communal riot 'which could not have been matched even in Nero's days'.[159] Miss Talbot of Alice Perrin's *For India* had been keeping the company of Indian students in England and, as a result, had formed the highest opinion 'of the Oriental's capacity for self-government'. Once in India, however, she began to appreciate, albeit reluctantly, the uncertainties of British obligation. India's duty and honour stood between John and Miss Talbot. A close observation forced Miss Talbot to conclude that no country was better managed than India, 'none in which the administration did more for the masses of the people'. She only wished things were as well conducted in England![160]

India had a special attraction for growing English girls. They sought to learn the realities of life in military stations and to absorb the glamour of Eastern habits and customs, and the atmosphere of gaiety and leisureliness that prevailed for the wives and daughters. 'They went to India to be married and seldom failed to secure husbands'. They had the time to cultivate the art of sex appeal and were 'for ever spoilt for domesticity in England'. Wives came home but they were restless to return to India not always for the sake of their lonely husbands, 'but for the good times they always had among the best types of men England bred and for the flirtations that were ready to hand', for those colourful stories of dignity and splendour of important personages, private secretaries, aides-de-camp and those avenues, buntings and pennants flying in their festoons from post to post, bands playing, receptions, durbars, dinners for weeks on end, regular gymkhanas and dances in the midst of an admiring and friendly set. They thought that they could metamorphose a bachelor abode into a veritable bower of feminine loveliness and convert a bungalow veranda into an exotic living-room with trellis screens and climbing roses to shut out the glare of the sun and furnish the enclosed corner with 'Cawnpore' druggets for the early morning *chota hazri*.[161] E.W. Savi, Alice Perrin, Sarah Jeannette Duncan and Sarah Tytler fashioned and fanned the myths of the glamcrous East.[162] This contrived image was modulated by constant reference to the experience of a real India. In a small station, a district superintendent of police, his two young assistants, the P.W.D. engineer, a forest officer and contractors of diverse commercial enterprises made up the social element of a small British settlement and they congregated every evening at the club, ('shunned by the Hindu magistrate and his deputy having sneaking sympathy for Congress agitation') to amuse themselves and to spoil the newly wedded wife of a young officer by over-attention.[163] Life was reduced, Savi sought to conceptualize the stern imperial commitments, to a colourless interlude between furloughs which were spent in Europe and responsibility turned into a formidable courage to face treachery, terrorism and discomfort with ever-smiling faces and increasing social isolation.[164] Between the illusions and realities of English society in India, the myth of the white man's burden discovered a very large and attentive audience.

British commitments in India maintained and reinforced class differentiations. But it was proudly proclaimed for the consumption of the underdogs at home that the Empire was also a great leveller in its own way. This was how the illusion of a colonial privileged class was dangled before the domestic underlings. Consider, for example, the dilemma of Patrick Malony of F.E. Penny's *Patrick*.[165] Despite Pat's cleanliness, clothes, socks and shoes, white skin and blue eyes, his Indian stepmother's cares and the absence of 'the chee-chee accent of the country born', the chaplain was apprehensive of introducing into their circle a boy who swore and who had been brought up by an old barrack-room *habitué*. The boy's use of barrack language gave away the fact that he had been brought up by parents who were of that class. If Malony had performed his duty towards his son, the minister pondered, he would have, at the end of his service, returned to his native land with the boy. The vicar soon realized that the old soldier was crippled by rheumatic gout and needed the help that could only be provided by a wife or a personal servant. An unflinching devotion to the Empire had its price and the boy was being denied his right to have 'the privileges of his birth and nationality' in spite of his father's efforts to 'keep out the rudeness of the natives till I'm big enough to kick'em'. The padre was swayed by his national pride and he resolved that Pat had to become one day Sir Patrick Malony![166]

Another imperial epithet inscribed that uncertainties were complete in India. 'East of Suez, some held, the direct control of Providence ceases', wrote Kipling as he sought to stress the horrors of life in India. Men, he argued, had been handed over there to the power of 'The Gods and Devils of Asia', and the Church of England as well as Providence exercised merely an occasional and modifying supervision in some odd cases.[167] It was also felt that in India, a man grew used to misrepresentation of his motives. Paradoxically, it was boasted that there was ample room for excitement and memorable moments of romance and adventure. In this sense, the Raj provided an opportunity for a complete life with all its ups and downs. There were the fierce Afridis of the Kurram valley, the flying bullets and the 'arithmetic of the frontier' which no formula of the textbook could have taught. Life was cheap:

> Two thousand pounds of education
> Drops to a ten rupee jezail—
> The Crammer's boast, the Squadron's pride
> Shot like a rabbit in a mud.[168]

There was also the Indian National Congress 'that squeaked', the babu who dropped 'inflammatory hints in print',[169] and the 'unwholesome' city that Job Charnock had built.[170] One longed for the Kalka hills overlooked by the Tara Devi where the lights of Simla town and the rings of the 'tonga-horn' conjured a magical world of dockets, billets-doux, files, fans, swords and office-box and, of course, the Gaiety Theatre.[171] In fact it was assumed that 'for rule, administration, and the rest, Simla's best!'[172] Even in the days of Humphrey Trevelyan, Simla life seemed not so very different from what it had been in Kipling's days—complete with a new generation of Mrs Hawksbees.[173] In sharp contrast, Calcutta, 'chance-directed, chance-erected, laid and built on the silt', where 'palace, byre, hovel, poverty and pride' coexisted side by side, exasperated the official mind.[174] Even Lutyens' Delhi, full of 'dust and monuments', was dull. The favourite habit of the officials to go for picnic-tea out on a tomb did not appeal to the Viceroy's wife. Delhi's bazaars, she thought, were aggressively non-cooperative and increasingly pro-Gandhi![175] If Simla, Ooty, Mussoorie,

Delhi, Bombay and even Calcutta meant society, gay dinner parties, dances and flirtations, the North-West Frontier meant a perilous life in a desolate district, the wild inhospitable Indo-Afghan frontier, a sort of a retreat in small forts scattered amongst disaffected tribes whose one idea was pillage, insurrection and ambuscade. In these barren and solitary mountains, Dekobra sighed, 'death lurks at night under the immutable stars'.[176]

There was the fellowship of professional soldiers, the Tommy Atkinses. These soldiers of the Empire were at once the drunken, disorderly reprobates, the heroes of romance, the storming columns of Delhi, the defenders of the Khyber and the bulwark of the Raj.[177] Some of them could have even recalled nostalgically the innocent regimental *bhisti,* Gunga Din[178]; recollected the feats of a Kamel who made the meeting between the East and the West possible[179]; remembered the Lama of Kim's heart in their relentless pursuit of the Great Game[180] and pined to see, much to the amusement of George Orwell and his ilk,[181] the love-lost eyes of the Burmese girl in her melodious refrain:

> Come you back, you British soldier,
> Come you back to Mandalay. . .[182]

The ideologues of the Empire made no bones about the economic and financial impulses of expansion. Curzon vouched 'that both our Indian and African dominions had an economic origin'.[183] Unlike some present day social scientists, he did not fight shy of this remarkable fact. The search for a potential market and the raw materials of an Asian El Dorado were far too seductive even for the most circumspect statesman. With Indian resources tamely at the command of Britain, the expansive impulses were regulated and given a direction. In his volumes on the imperial problems in Central Asia, Persia and the Far East,[184] Curzon examined in great detail estimates of trade and industries and concluded in favour of increasing prospects of the existing and potential British commerce in these areas. Ellenborough had visualized it; Auckland had been prodded on to an ill-advised action to promote it; R.H. Davies collated the necessary statistics and information in a background paper for the development of trans-Himalayan trade of an integrated economic unit composed of Punjab, Sind and Baluchistan with Karachi as its principal coastal outlet[185]; and J.S. Lumley gauged the prospects of tea and piecegoods in Central Asia with the insidious zeal of a confirmed protectionist.[186] Shakespeare, Shaw, Pundit Munphul, Faiz Bux and a score of explorers, often dressed as 'dervishes', ceaselessly moved in the busy bazaars and distant villages on the trade routes of Balkh, Badakshan, Meshed, Herat, Bokhara and Khiva, engaged in probing missions and discovering devious means of underselling competitive Russian commodities.[187] Mayo, Lytton and subsequently Curzon endorsed the attempts to open the gates of Persia. They worked out the strategies of a proxy war with the Russians as Hindu merchants were encouraged to sell Enfield rifles to the Turkoman tribes to clear the way for British commerce.[188] T.D. Forsyth was sent over to Sinkiang to make extensive surveys of its market. With a liberal supply of British arms and backed by British recognition, he propped up an independent Muslim Khanate to protect possible British commercial incursions.[189] From Irrawadi movements were set afoot to push trade into southern China.[190] The Chinese trade had been commanded for centuries by Bombay and Calcutta together with Singapore. The old bed of the Oxus had to be revitalized,[191] ran the imperial speculation, the Russians were to be checkmated at Syr Daria[192] and a three-pronged entry into the Persian Gulf, Central Asia and Sinkiang was planned with mechanical precision.[193] There was no lack of enthusiasm and energetic spirit. Curzon enriched the proceedings with an exalted imperial vision as Francis Younghusband was encouraged to make a sudden appearance before the lamas of the Hermit Kingdom[194] while the Persian Gulf came to be known in official circles as Curzon's Lake.[195] Some other projects were modified by practical considerations while some were neutralized by timely interventions and irresistible compulsions of global diplomacy.

Call this sub-imperialism or the result of unauthorized impulses on the part of a group of restless but lonely men on the frontiers in search of glory and recognition or the consequence of the unpredictable intrigues by the uncivilized people beyond the British line of defence.[196] One may even desire to push away the economic implications of expansion on to a secondary plane, dismiss the invading British army from Calcutta to Kabul as the unmindful little lambs of Mary meandering innocently across the fences, and overwhelm the trade statistics by an impressive show of foreign policy and diplomacy.[197] One may portray Gallagher and Robinson as honest 'non-Leninist Leninists', if one pleases.[198] D.K. Fieldhouse might assert that the new imperialism was 'specially a political phenomena in origin' and scholars might exhort themselves to separate economic, political and strategical considerations. But, as Barraclough puts it, the political, strategic and economic dimensions of the route to India formed a seamless whole and the recognition of this fact was essential for understanding British imperialism in India as much as in Africa.[199]

No one can possibly deny that a search for markets had become the overriding priority in imperial calculations. 'There is nothing ignoble or selfish in seeking fresh markets for our produce and manufactures', Curzon clarified. 'There is nothing wrong in establishing ourselves in an unsettled and derelict country with a view to bringing wealth to our people. Japan would never have been opened had it not been for the European and American traders and the new world would never have been occupied but for similar reasons'.[200] An American scholar, who followed the Robinson-Gallagher model closely, wrote that there were national differences in colonial policy 'but the consistent common goal was economic control even if the means varied'.[201] Curzon was conscious of the embarrassment which an undiluted economic explanation of British acquisitions might have caused to many. He would, therefore, implore that the Indian Empire should not be depicted as an exclusive commercial concern. Its genesis should not be defined, he emphasized, in standards and prescriptions dictated by obvious financial considerations. He entreated that imperialism must adopt a lofty vision. It must don a gorgeous apparel.[202]

It was in this context that one of the principal epigraphs of the Raj was written and preserved for more than a century. The overriding consideration that seemed to have agitated the minds of the politicians, administrators and generals, was the prospect of a coterminous European frontier in the sandhills of Asia. It unnerved men in authority, cutting across political affiliations. It was both the realities and fantasies of a potential market that drew the Europeans into the so-called no-man's lands and the British Government found itself in an odd position of stoutly defending the right of its citizen 'to get his throat cut wherever he found it necessary'.[203] The Central Asian contest was fierce. The spoils were rich and enticing as the Chinese Empire, despite occasional spasms, lay inert and moribund. All eyes were set on the Frontiersmen, 'the living embodiments of the imperial idea'.[204] The incertitude of the Russian designs in Central Asia caused an endemic fear, and after 1917 the threat of Bolshevism was superimposed on a revitalized Russophobia.[205] The North-West Frontier was synonymous in imperial history with fortitude, grit, courage, wisdom and romance. Herbert Hayens in his tale of the Khyber pass underlined, 'The events which I have here attempted to chronicle have long since passed into history. But the British spirit displayed by the men who fell bravely fighting in the Afghan passes still survives, and many a gallant lad since then has echoed with his latest breath poor Charlie Durant's dying words, "They will say in England we have tried to do our duty"'. Hayens' Clevely Sahib epitomized in himself the romance of the frontier for a century -and a-half.[206]

It is small wonder that the imperialists had no patience for some 'pseudo-moral' issues raised by the critics of the Empire. Curzon dismissed them as the 'hypocritical ideologues of opportunism'. John Morley, in particular, was singled out as the target of his bitter vituperations. The pressures of parliamentary politics often compelled Morley and his political associates to espouse conflicting positions in public giving rise to irksome suspicions especially in the minds of the Big Englanders. They derided the Liberals as being soaked in 'the spirit of Birmingham' and 'smothered under the cotton bales' of Manchester and apprehended that the Little Englanders might be goaded by the logic of their own arguments to allege that the Empire-builders were, as a rule, commandment-breakers and proconsuls were, in general, a particularly dangerous type. Morley was taken to task for his imprudent impudence in designating the foundation of British rule in India as a long 'train of intrigues and crimes'. 'Crimes hover over', Curzon disclaimed, 'the birth of liberty, equally that of despotism and small states have produced their own villains with unabated regularity as the larger ones.'[207]

There were many die-hards who shared Curzon's anxiety. They were appalled by the flighty Parliament and its insouciant attitude towards India. Some of them were discomposed to find that the Empire-builders were invariably reprimanded by it, 'first for the sin of blood-guiltiness' because they were by profession soldiers, next for 'murder' because they had fought great battles and finally for 'extravagance' because they saddled the British tax-payers with the enormous expense of the conquest and administration of a given territory.[208] An irate Kipling, a romantic Lytton, an erudite Curzon, a stolid Minto, a diplomatic Hardinge, a determined Reading, a flexible Irwin, a prudent Linlithgow and an uncertain Wavell groused, remonstrated and sought to persuade an obdurate audience that the maintenance of the acquisitions would not cost the tax-payers much. But they were shaken to discover that despite relentless persuasion, some of their listeners chose to remain cheerfully unconcerned.

Curzon, Kitchener and Kipling were echoed elsewhere as well. A contributor in the *Fortnightly Review* evaluated the new imperial consciousness and emphasized its historic mission. He castigated the policy or the lack of it in India under the succession of unimaginative proconsuls resulting in an awkward drift on the part of the governing power and a state of apathy in the country towards it. The power-elite, it was complained at various levels, couched itself in Simla for six to eight months in a panoply of official armour and hibernated at Calcutta for the rest of the year.[209] A sharp decline in the prestige and authority of the viceroy was clearly perceptible: 'No Indian—not even the elite who surrounded the viceregal throne—believed that the viceroy was anything more than a gold-gilt dummy'.[210]

An 'onlooker' commented that the image of a silent, unfeeling authority had been projected paradoxically in the land of eternal paternalism. The birth of the Indian National Congress, he claimed, was viewed by many as a revolt against the agonizing aloofness and indifference of Britain represented by the viceroy and the parliament.[211] Curzon's arrival on the scene, he argued, stalled the political paralysis of the Government. As Curzon surrounded himself with processions, ceremonials and the Durbar, the British illusion of permanence in India was further cushioned. It was felt that the Raj had been given another shot in the arm and buttressed by a reinvigorated moral fibre. As a result it regained confidence in the righteousness of its causes and Curzon came to be revered as *rara avis*. Following Curzon's departure, the author complained, *Pax Romana* came once again, under the spell of a spiritless administration, marked by an unconscious relaxation of authority. A writer in the *Quarterly Review* saw in Morley's *Indian Speeches* and in Minto's public pronouncements almost a design to expose the darkest side of the Indian Empire to the view of Britain. The Indian questions whose echo reached England, the author charged, were plague, famine, waves of malaria, the wrongs of South African emigrants and anarchy. The intelligent foreigner, he wrote, would carry away the impression that 'we had been on the verge of a cyclone vortex. . . '.[212]

The *Nineteenth Century* was particularly dismayed by the readiness on the part of British political parties to laugh off a well-established convention not to toss about Indian feelings towards England in public. It had been acknowledged by all that the Indian questions ought to be reserved for the scrutiny of the official experts. There was a general consensus with regard to British commitments and responsibilities in India. But much to the discomfiture of the *Round Table*, Indian affairs were being handled as part of stock-in-trade in party politics.[213] Flimsy public opinion, it grumbled, replaced expert opinion. An analyst cogitated that in that altered political climate the choice between reticence and frankness had been displaced by a nettling option between ingenuousness and misrepresentation.[214]

A writer in the *Quarterly Review* dreaded the vision of a popular Indian viceroy putting himself at the head of an Indian movement against the parliament, against the self-governing dominions and even against the public services. He scoffed at the tendency to play-off one section of Indian subjects against another and the expediency of appeasing the noisier one. There was, he argued, no scope for political bargaining between India and Britain because there was no inherent equality between the two. The fact that the Sikhs and Gurkhas fought in Flanders was a ludicrously irrelevant reason for supposing that the essential basis of the relations between the countries had been suddenly subverted. This was a popular accord. The office of viceroyalty of India was not a political one and it could not be expanded into a 'trusteeship' of the people. 'If India were to force politics upon Britain', it was asserted, 'she could not expect a continuance of political impartiality here'.[215] It was maintained that since no concession would bring peace in India it was natural to infer that the most rational course would be to pursue a just policy based on experience. That the aspiration of the Congress for self-determination on colonial lines would probably never be viewed with favour was widely acknowledged. 'We must, therefore, make our minds', the *Quarterly Review* declared, 'to pursue the old, grim, thankless task of ruling, heedless of praise or blame, expecting no permanent diminution of our difficulties, content if we have done justice according to our light'. It was a call for a resolute determination to keep British interests inviolate and for affirming afresh a firm faith in the 'exalted character of our work'.[216]

Bampfylde Fuller, himself a victim of the timorous policy of an unresponsive Minto, had sought to restate the position. He believed that the existing political troubles in India stemmed from a change in British perception of Indian loyalty. He advocated that the basic assumption of British rule had so far been fairly simple. It was artless and somewhat inane. 'We are obeyed', it was plainly avowed, 'because we deserved obedience'. That assumption, Fuller maintained, had been founded upon a frank admission of British authority which was valued without hesitation as superior in character. He dismissed the new stance of the administration which emphasized that loyalty could only be secured by political negotiations. This stand was based, he argued, on a misleading notion with regard to the potentialities of a few educated Indians clamouring for concessions.[217] Even at the height of the national agitation, following the massacre at Amritsar, Maud Diver pooh-poohed Indian nationalism as an evanescent sentiment. It was dismissed as an abnormal mass hysteria triggered off by the unscrupulous Gandhian politicians who were singularly inept to sustain it, while the ignorant and illiterate people fluttered about without a sense of reason and a consistent loyalty to any cause.[218]

Thus, while the national movement was cast aside as a transient affair, the experts in the administration were entreated to opt for an inflexible political posture.

In the past, it was held, the loyalty of India had been presumed as axiomatic because of her respect for the courage and fortitude of the Englishmen and for their commitment to justice and fairplay. India, by and large, had been reconciled to the British rule despite displaying an occasional delinquency for she was convinced, the publicists assumed, that the British connection had ensured for her a more honest, stronger and a more humane government than what she had herself developed and organized over the centuries.[219] Evidently the writers, by and large, lent their unqualified support to the views of the Indian civil services on the higher objectives of British rule in India. A high standard of public duty, a wholesome sense of responsibility and the 'general trend of policy towards liberality and humanity', it was flaunted, compensated human failure in India.[220]

The skilful portrayal of an Englishman engrossed in his concern for the welfare of the victims of his military might was attempted to render the imperial character attractive. There was, it was pointed out with much fanfare, an element of childlike simplicity in his quest; an unbiased devotion in his concern. It was proclaimed in a spirit of self-indulgence, that 'Allah created the English mad—the maddest of all mankind'.[221] As a consequence, respect for the government, it was avowed, was retained despite periods of trials and difficulties. 'We have educated though education obviously increased our difficulties', Fuller bragged as he enunciated the stupendous task of Britain in India, 'we have allowed free speech in press and on platform, though that freedom was often used to attack us; in times of famine, we have fed the hungry on a scale to amaze the socialist enthusiasts; we have done our best to protect the poor by land laws which anticipated the dreams of Land Reform'.[222] 'Customs', Fuller boasted, 'have begun to support us'. This sentiment of acknowledging that the British had actually done some good for the Indians, he blustered, though somewhat fragile at birth, gained fibre from the habits of half-a-century.

The political situation, however, portended continual tensions. The optimistic views entertained in some quarters were dampened by a feeling of diffidence. Many members of the exalted civil services in India deplored the gradual but almost inevitable extinction of Indian loyalty. They whined as they helplessly watched its impact on their proverbial confidence.[223] They ascribed the erosion of faith in the Raj to the new creed of the administration. Loyalty was no longer considered, they carped, as the spontaneous manifestation of gratitude to which the British rule was legitimately entitled. On the contrary, loyalty was being interpreted, they mumbled, as a sentiment which ought to be won by indulgence, insured by negotiations and retained by compromises and concessions. It was unfortunate, they complained, that the Government of India and public opinion in England had imparted to the Indian nationalists the lessons of mutual advantages and the notions of political bargainings.[224]

The process of parliamentary democracy and the demands of popular elections, they argued, might have worked well in Britain, but that political perspective could not be recommended to the Government of India and to the erratic passions of an 'Oriental people'. Under no circumstances, a startled Valentine Chirol expostulated, could the authority of the State be exposed to the Indians as a commodity 'for sale or barter'.[225] Following the Rowlatt Satyagraha and the massacre at Amritsar, E.Bruce Mitford urged the Government not to waver, falter or conciliate. 'In such a country as India agitation feeds on weakness. That is the diet which the Government has supplied'. As a consequence, he argued, they have in the Indian intelligentsia a spoilt and unhealthy child. 'Now that the challenge has been thrown down, there can be no dallying with treason. The Raj must govern or get out'.[226]

It was emphasized that the Government had certain inherent obligations to this society and on these delicate but indispensable issues one could not afford to entertain any compromise. 'It does not', Al Carthill made no bones about the amoral determination of the administration, 'of course, in the slightest degree matter whether the things it believes in are true, probably no faith was ever wholly true—but it must believe in them. Faith it is said can move mountains, it can at least put a decisive end to political agitation, because people will not eternally, or even for very long, dash their heads against an unshakeable rock'. Al Carthill argued that men despised an impotent authority. They venerated power, even malignant power. In fact, they loved power coupled with beneficence. Those who thought, Al Carthill averred, that severity would increase civil disorder and that 'imbecile' weakness would allay it, knew little of crowd psychology. 'We are indeed babes terrified by painted devils; men who know their cause is just heed not the clamours of the mob'.[227] In 1934, Yeats-Brown decided to stand by the anamorphosed Raj against the wavering pacifists then being impelled by 'selfish reasons' to opt for concessions, negotiations and compromises. He had no faith in hypocrisy or falsehood. The Empire was a mission which in a savage country, he pronounced, was to be discharged with adequate doses of force and brutality. He did not share the optimism of the 'Olympians in the cool offices in Simla' that the army was loyal, the peasants contended, and that the action of General Dyer had been unwarranted. This represented, Yeats-Brown chastised, the view from the mountain tops. Things looked, he asserted, different on the plains. General Dyer did not know, he wrangled, on that torrid morning when he marched through Amritsar that that very afternoon he would be firing into a crowd in Jallianwala Bagh. Dyer had proclaimed in every *mohalla*, Yeats-Brown vouched, that all assemblies were illegal and yet the people assembled. Considering the argument that a lesser use of force would have achieved the vital purpose, Yeats-Brown raised a loaded question: 'But how could Dyer, how could any man, always strike a just mean, achieve the right balance between severity and compromise in the asphyxiating dust and heat of India?' Too often, he argued the imperial case, decisions were to be taken in split seconds in the face of imminent, deadly peril as a momentary weakness of today in Lahore might lead to a hundred deaths tomorrow in a faraway Kanpur or Delhi. Force was a necessary element of imperial statecraft, the author reminded his irresolute readers, and violence and injustice could only be met by swift action and disciplined strength. There was, he held without any inhibition, no room for compromise and, abstract theories. Such philanderings with treason meant a straight road to ruin.[228]

It was a sturdy resolution and it reflected a clear-cut ideological position. The Liberals, who had allegedly initiated the race for the application of Western concepts to Indian realities, were accused of failing to grasp the difference between races and countries.[229] The ideologues of the Empire thought that the panacea for Indian problems was to be traced in a political concord in which India ought to stand outside the clash of party politics and that the fluctuations of political opinion in Britain should not unsettle the continuity of a consistent Indian policy. The *Nineteenth Century* called for a renewed effort. It was unconcerned with the antics of a few obstinate Indians. It called for a fresh endeavour to reinforce the foundations of Indian loyalty.[230]

The Liberals, however, did not overlook the interests of the Empire despite puerile political pressures to the contrary. They were not lukewarm about the inconveniences caused by an unwholesome depiction of the Raj. John Morley was a practical man of the world and he knew his game far too well to be seduced by the temptations of fleeting popularity. So was his astute disciple Edwin Samuel Montagu. They concurred with Curzon in maintaining that the Raj constituted an indispensable ingredient of British character. Edmund Burke's conservatism, based on a spontaneous reverence for ancient institutions and a resolute aristocratic restraint, had a profound impact on the former's social and political outlook.[231] Montagu carefully cultivated Curzon, his most imperious contemporary.[232]

There was a sanctimonious air in the fatuous exhortations of the Raj. A divine will, the social obligations of a superior race, the central position of India in the economic and strategic map of the Empire and the existence of a well-synchronized elite corps both in India and Britain in tune with the much-publicized British mission had inaugurated an imperial paranoia.[233] As a consequence, it perpetrated a false consciousness of unflagging confidence. 'Why should we, alarmed by the difficulties which may only be passing', Fuller asked, 'jeopardise the peaceful continuity of a dominion which the determination of our ancestors has won for us, which we have preserved and elaborated to the credit of our race, and which conduces to the happiness and improvement of millions of people. Let our motto be, as it has been *sursum corda*'.[234] The situation seemed dangerous though not desperate. India, it was feared, was being either swayed away by the 'slippery' Bhadraloks or threatened by an *émeute* led by the 'reactionary' Arya Samajists or subjected to the wishful glances of the 'treacherous' Chitpawan Brahmins longing for the return of a Baji Rao![235] In response, 'Lift up our hearts' was the imploration of the imperialists to the valiant men on the various fronts. It was a battle cry for many.

India, according to British statesmen, was a geographical expression, inhabited by various ethnic stocks and held together by British imperial hegemony. 'For a score of centuries', Morley had amplified, 'the Hindus were bribed and had taken bribes, and corruption has eaten into their national character so deeply that those who are the best judges declare that it can never be washed out'.[236] Experts, irrespective of party affiliations, agreed with him. They all believed in the importance of the Empire as a necessity at certain stages of civilization and the world's progress. A Christian sense of superiority was grafted on to that imperial mission. Thus, one was faced with a paradoxical situation. While the exercise of despotism over the Christian and 'civilized' people of Cyprus was to be resisted, such a form of government was safely recommended to the people of India, Egypt and Singapore. Christianity and progress, according to the imperial ideologues, were interdependent as a 'universal law for all times, all states and all societies'. This perspective was confirmed by the Simon Commission and the Lindsay Commission and largely adhered to by the Conservative and Labour parties during and after the Second World War.[237]

The centrality of the Raj in the Empire rendered the Indian undertaking very attractive. Its possession reinforced British culture with a renewed interest in militarism, royalty, national heroes, cult of personality, racial ideas of superiority and a contrived sense of Christian mission. The Raj became an essential part of British social history. It helped to develop the 'core culture' of imperialism and fashioned the 'dominant ideology' of British society. The determination to hold on to India at all costs led to the improvisation of a series of imperial myths and legends. The providential character of British mission in India was upheld on grounds of lofty moral principles. Mastery of this enormous territory conferred on British character an inflated imperial pride as also a set of prejudices. Maintenance of an arbitrary rule over India, despite professed British traditions of freedom and justice, was sought to be cushioned by widely circulated racial stereotypes. Kipling gave the Raj a wide ideological umbrella which sheltered a whole range of self-righteous exaltations, romantic images and contorted visions wrapped up in a seductive phrase: 'white man's burden'. The rulers would have, of course, condescended to throw a few crumbs from time to time, from the hallowed constitutional confectionary to the so-called hungry nationalists, especially if such gestures could be helpful in stimulating the loyal opposition of some in their political encounters with the uncompromising militancy championed by others. That the Raj was the fulcrum of the Empire and was to be preserved at all events was an imperial consensus despite acute tactical differences conditioned by the dialectics of British parliamentary politics. The remarkable feature was that Curzon, Milner, Morley, Hardinge, Crewe, Montagu, Wedgwood Benn, Ramsay MacDonald, Irwin, Willingdon, Linlithgow and Churchill were equally committed to uphold and advance that imperial strategic accord.

2

Through the Imperial Looking Glass

That Empire-building was a demanding responsibility was repeatedly affirmed. The ideologues asserted that the task involved great risk and required sagacity, circumspection, honesty, strength of character and presence of mind. The problems confronting the Empire-builders were matters of fundamental importance and there was no opportunity for equivocation. Legislation in India, as elsewhere, had been carried out, Kipling wrote, according to the various customs of the tribes where possible and guided by common sense of the moment when there was no precedence.[1] The institution of law and order in an unknown land animated its own legends. There was no lack of flamboyance and poets and publicists were eager to extol the abounding achievements and fruitful experiments of the 'pioneers' and 'guardians'. A later-day historian immortalized them as a set of conscientious British utilitarians operating on the uneven Indian scene.[2] The pattern of imperial sensibility was thus nourished by falsified facts. Hypocrisy, which supplied this nourishment to false consciousness, found in the same consciousness its own moral justification and confirmation. To use Ernst Fischer's formulation, hypocrisy helped to obliterate the contradiction between reality and false consciousness while false consciousness furnished hypocrisy with credentials of indispensability. In the process of the self-glorification of the Raj, the nebulous dividing line between faith and casuistry, admiration and worship, conscious deception and false consciousness was blurred. The image of the Raj, as a result, was split into distinct units: into a world of sensory perceptions of visible, audible and palpable reality and into a super-world of hollow, loud and monotonous claims, dogmas, myths, pride and prejudices. Both worlds existed; but they never met on equal terms. A confused reflection of reality, distorted insights and half-truths together with an officially sponsored organization of optimism and swagger tinged the imperial looking glass.

'You will concede,' Kipling argued, that a 'civilised people who eat out of china . . . have no right to apply their standard of right or wrong to an unsettled land'.[3] Where the Queen's law did not carry, he observed ingenuously, it was a specious expectation that 'other and weaker' rules could be obeyed. Those who run ahead, Kipling thought, 'of the ears of Decency and Propriety, and make the jungle ways straight, cannot be judged in the same manner as the stay-at-home folk . . . .'[4] In short, the Empire-builders were presented as men of a special breed for the responsibility assigned to them by destiny had to be carried out in an uncivilized country where normal standards of morality could not be applied. Asserting such a position, Kipling laid down the parameters of the ideology of the Raj. It was stern, arbitrary, amoral, based on expediency and designed to create a permanent gulf of contempt and fear between the ruler and the ruled. In order to make the physical separation between the master and the bonded men conspicuous and visible, the imperial governing class was not expected to socialize with the common folk. The code of behaviour was fashioned to draw respect and not affection.

The imperial manifesto for India was candid that among the forerunners of civilization 'was Georgie Porgie, reckoned by all as the strong man'. John and Henry Lawrence, H.S. Edwardes, Mountstuart Elphinstone, John Jacob, Charles Metcalfe and Bampfylde Fuller, Lord Curzon, the Earl of Linlithgow or Maurice Hallett could not afford to be mere obsequious pupils of some irresponsible visiting members of Parliament. The conditions of India in 1915 goaded a firebrand left-winger in Ramsay MacDonald and a Tory hardliner in Ronaldshay to close their ranks and walk hand in hand much to the delight of Valentine Chirol.[5] The problem of India in 1942 forced Stafford Cripps to walk out of his Indian connections right into the heart of Churchillian orthodoxy, albeit reluctantly.[6] Guy Wint, despite his Liberal reputation, endorsed, as late as 1945, Kipling's outburst against Mr Paget, M. P. as an expression of a genuine pent-up feeling of official India accumulated over a century.[7] Penderel Moon, in 1946, sympathized with the imperious memsahib in her loneliness amidst a warm Indian summer.[8] In India, the imperial argument continued, men of a 'lesser breed' would be simply itching to take advantage of the Englishman's civility and generosity and might even adroitly use their superiors' name against all and sundry. The generous sahib might as a result, be forced to take stern action against his native retainer.[9] Asia in general, and India in particular, it was widely disseminated, were not going to be civilized on the lines of the West. 'There is too much Asia and she is too old. You cannot reform a lady of many lovers,' Kipling propounded, 'and Asia has been insatiable in her flirtations'. She would never attend Sunday school or learn to vote or render habitual obedience to law without the show of the naked sword.[10]

Evidently the problems confronting the Indian administration were invested with a significant uniqueness. The singularity of the situation suggested that the performance of the rulers was not to be evaluated by 'Western' standards of public and private morality. It was assumed that the issues of 'good' and 'self' governments had to be appreciated by specific political and administrative expediency of the time. Invariably, the basic argument was that the concepts of 'Conservatism', 'Liberalism' and 'progress' were inapplicable to the special Indian conditions as the Indian problems were too complicated and complex to be analyzed systematically. The primary object of 'imperial ethics' was to shelter imperialism behind an irrational ideological shield so that it was placed beyond a rational social analysis. Protected by this synthetic system of morality, imperialism could thus be conveniently, though not comfortably, interpreted varyingly as an act of divine mercy or as a cruel piece of humanity. It is striking that imperial offensives were similar everywhere,irrespective of geographical locations and divergent social systems. With suitable modifications, comparable arguments were advanced in the cases of Khartoum, Awadh, Delhi, Cairo and Kabul alike. Everywhere the civilizing mission of Britain, the onward march of a 'masculine' and 'scientific' Christianity and the assertion of the superiority of imperial pride were discerned in the assault of imperialism. At all places it was made to confront barbarism, superstition and tyranny and everywhere an atmosphere of lawlessness of the native society was improvised and condemned for provoking an inevitable imperial retribution. In such circumstances, imperialism would naturally be excused and condoned for all its excesses and brutalities. Imperial impulses were invariably presented as decisive steps in the march of civilization that were characterized as more or less predestined and intertwined with the idea of progress. Since the attainment of peace and an ordered life were accepted, without an iota of doubt, as the object of imperial intervention, official spokesmen were able to create a convincing case for posterity.

Kipling spelt out a well-circulated fable that the new acquisitions had been, before annexation, 'one crazy hell of murder, torture and lust'; 'a hysteria of blood and fanaticism'.[11] Maud Diver echoed Kipling when she wrote that isolated within the narrow ravines of the North-West Frontier the 'Tommies' scaled the heights and plumbed the depths through intimate personal contact with love, danger and death.[12] Kipling spitefully recalled the gory days when Sudan was being 'reduced to sanity by applied death' on an unprecedented scale. In one day and one night, he gibed, 'all those who had any power and authority were wiped out . . . till no chief remained to ask after any followers'.[13] The imperial retribution in Khartoum, as elsewhere, was savage. The followers of Mahdi were dragged in the streets and an immaculate Kitchener led the procession while the luminaries of the Empire jostled each other and elbowed their way through the frightened crowd, only to have a full glimpse of this odious display of British might.[14] The Last Post played by an army-in-occupation added an imperial solemnity to the occasion! One might also recall Lytton's instruction to Roberts, on his mission to Bala Hissar, way back in 1879, to avenge the murder of Louis Cavagnary.[15] The city of Kabul had then stood, Lytton had thundered, 'as a national culprit awaiting its sentence' and he ordered a clean sweep with a simple unfaltering stroke in order to take full advantage of the wounded pride of an incensed John Bull.[16] One is also forced to recollect the blood-thirsty *ravanche* in India following the Revolt of 1857 which had covered a wide area from Delhi to Awadh.[17] Flora Annie Steel depicted the inhuman realities of the uprising in her flamboyant novel *On the Face of the Waters* in which Kate Erlton had initially opted for moderation but as the heat of the mutiny became unbearable, she drew back unceremoniously. The 'dark incomprehensible' faces overwhelmed her and she was obliged to change her mind: 'Uncivilised, heathen, as they were—tied to hateful, horrible beliefs and customs—unmentionable thoughts!' Kate's metamorphosis was inevitable. The 'innate repulsion of the alien overpowered her dim desire to be kind'. She learnt to appreciate the assertion of her husband, Major Erlton, that he was a Christian soldier whose task was to become 'the happy instrument of rescuing his neighbour from eternal damnation' of Hinduism, 'the cult of the inevitable'.[18] The triumphant movement of the Christian power had been violently challenged and the imperial deposition fashioned, by an unholy combination of obscurantism of various forms in 1857. The Delhi Ridge with 'the history of heroism crystallized into its very dust' reflected on the imperial mind the memory of the valorous deeds of Britons at that hour of crisis which went to make up 'the finest record of pluck and perseverance the world is ever likely to see'. It was, Flora Annie Steel harangued, the symbol of chivalry, righteousness, courage and sacrifice 'under John Nicholson's wild temper, his indomitable will, his fierce resentment at everything which fell short of his ideals'. The Ridge stood in the imperial ballad of 1857 for the quaintness, individuality and wisdom of British chivalry and as the backbone of a Christian recompose and restoration.[19]

E.M. Hull cautioned that in these foreign lands 'we are outside convention and beyond the laws that govern conventional societies. Here it is only a strong hand that rules'. Equity and justice, it was maintained, had to be interpreted according to the needs of the various classes of society. For the first time in his sheltered existence, Caryll, the sensitive lad of E.M. Hull's *The Son of the Sheik*, had been brought face to face with the stern realities of ruling a 'turbulent community that was outside Civilisation'. For the first time he had seen the execution of summary justice in a land 'where retribution was swift and violence could only be met by violence' and for the first time he had been brought in contact with the law of nature that demanded an eye for an eye. There were moments of dismay at the futility of the European experiment in the East. Caryll, like many young civil servants in India, was not confident if the modern slogans of improvement and education would ever mean anything to the natives. It was only a Reverend Hubert who could comfort the unsteady Caryll that these strange and wild standards, however gruesome they might seem to him, were 'the only methods these people understand' and the boy acknowledged that this crude style and tenor would persist until civilization swept away the savages and cleared the way for modern thought and improvement.[20] Thus in the name of civilization, all human norms could be ignored.

Retribution was invariably followed by 'reconstruction', which deserved, the imperial braggadocio continued, (Sudan being presented as a representative case), 'an epic of its own'.[21] There was nothing left for the builders, Kipling puffed, not even wreckage. Even the remnants of property, title and sense of possession had vanished and the people 'stared and fumbled like a dazed crowd after an explosion'.[22] However, Kipling assured, they were gradually fed, watered and marshalled into 'some sort of order'. They were engaged in construction work and almost by physical force pushed and hauled along 'the ways of mere life'. They had to be taught 'kindergarten fashion'. Before long they learnt to mend their fences and settled down to a 'civilisation of the brick bungalows and bougainvillaea sort'[23] in keeping with Kipling's attitudes and outlook. Maud Diver concludes her *Desmond's Daughter* with a grand finale of a unique triumph: There, an amazing sight awaited them. Frank's orderly garden was overflowing with unbidden guests, the strangest that any Commanding General had ever entertained unawares. The place was a seething mass of packed turbans and wild-looking figures, in *chogas* or dust-coloured rags. Having heard the news of Desmond's imminent departure, these men had invaded that astonished cantonment to make their farewell salaam and express their admiration for the man who had fought them, fined them and yet had treated them always with scrupulous justice. The cheering crowd of Afridis went back to their hills, adds Maud Diver, quite unaware that 'for Theo Desmond, their spontaneous tribute was an unperishable memory—the finest victory he had ever won'. And, in honouring this man, Maud Diver voiced a universal British feeling of pompous exaltation, 'they honoured equally the race that breeds such men' and confirmed afresh in their simple and elementary fashion 'the unquestioning fact that England holds her supremacy in the East as much by the power of individual character as by the power of the sword'.[24] The message was clear. As militant soldiers of Western civilization, though the English faced heavy odds, physical risks and the loss of precious lives in their confrontations against the blind and fanatic superstitions of savage people of the world in encounters that were bitter and ferocious, the results were rewarding. The outcome did not indicate a stalemate or an uneasy truce. It did not reflect the survival of a savage past under the modest supervision of Christian soldiers. It was the beginning of a new life and a new civilization. Initially, British reconstruction signalled a modest inception but soon it promised remarkable possibilities. This perspective of Kipling was affirmed by politicians and statesmen in Britain, administrators in India and subsequently confirmed by historians, poets, publicists and novelists alike.

From India it was cheerfully reported back home that the white men as masters of the East possessed a sense of discrimination, understanding and decency. They had to punish the offenders but they did so according to the Eastern norms of justice. Percival Christopher Wren declared: 'White Men do not offend against the religion of others; they understand caste and respect it; they know that prisoners of war are to be honourably treated.... Yes, they understand a high-caste man, and know the difference between a dog of a low-caste negro askari of Africa, and a high-caste Kshatriya sepoy of India'. Malhar Rao, Wren's hero, was confident of the respect for social dignity entertained by the victorious Feringhee and felt assured that he would be provided with justice and fairplay by the British officers. The proud Maratha soldier captured in these thoughts a stereotyped British perception of a regimented Indian mind.[25] What Wren conveyed was that despite a conscious desire to turn the Indian world upside down, the dictates of common sense and expediency prevailed. The stratified Hindu society made sense to the British soldiers of fortune. British compromise in India was an act of statesmanship. There was no option in that vast continent but to be circumspect, at least on trivial social matters, of the inhabitants and such a sense of discrimination won for the

British, the author suggested, the applaud of the high caste Hindus who served the new masters without inhibition. But behind this assessment, Wren gave vent to his racial pride against a non-Christian and non-white people.

The Raj was the centrepiece of the British Empire and it experienced all forms of imperial experiments. Kipling's analysis of British initiatives in Egypt and the Far East applied equally to India. Together, they represented the exploits of an aggressive imperial culture. The story of Egypt had its own flavour. But it was, Kipling echoed the official opinion, once again a saga of the persistent application of human energy and skill in bringing an ordered routine out of amorphous confusion. 'Here is a country which is not a country', Kipling indulged himself in reference to Egypt, 'but a longish strip of market-garden, nominally in charge of a government', which was not a government but 'a disconnected satrapy of a dead empire', controlled painstakingly by an agency, which had been tied up 'by years, customs and blackmail' to six or seven European powers, all with rights and perquisites but none of whom was responsible to any one.[26] Kipling insulated these powers including Great Britain and disengaged them scrupulously from the conscientious British administrators devoted to a disinterested service to mankind: 'Among these conflicting interests and amusements', Kipling was eager as ever to eulogize the man-on-the-spot—, 'sits and perspires the English official', whose job is irrigating, draining and reclaiming land on behalf of ten million people, and often finds himself tripped up by 'intrigues and bafflements which ramify through half-a-dozen harems and four consulates'.[27] Kipling's pronouncement on Egypt constituted perhaps the best exposition of the strategy of an informal empire. All the way from the Aegean and the Mediterranean Sea, Salisbury had discerned as early as 1878, a vast region wherein the existing forces of government were slowly decaying. Few who were acquainted with the East, he argued, would have thought that Britain could safely look on till the process of disintegration had eaten out the inherent powers of resistance of the native societies.[28] Many would have opted for a partial or complete occupation of Persia, Afghanistan and Mesopotamia. Africa was being parcelled out among rival contenders. There were some who were inclined to demonstrate that a fresh annexation of a territory could only be recommended as an extreme remedy pressing heavily on the exchequer with an almost overwhelming weight on the recruiting machinery and a long and perilous line of communication. They were disposed to favour what Salisbury called 'the pacific invasion' by Britain. As merchants, as railway developers, engineers, travellers, later as employees like Charles

Gordon or Killop, as ministers like River Wilson or as political agents, Englishmen, it was attested, were bound to assert their domination 'not by political privilege or military force but by the right of the strongest mind'.[29] But such an exercise in intellectual imperialism was not to be equated with a philanthropic endeavour and Salisbury vouched readily that in a few years the British would govern without even drawing a sword.

In his analysis of the Far East, Kipling found that Great Britain had a limited liability. Her military commitment was marginal. Working within the ambit of the 'glorious' uncertainties of modern finance, we were told, the members of the small commercial community in Hong Kong, Shanghai, Korea and Tokyo were apprehensive of the future. They fretted and fumed as they feared that they might go to bed at night only to discover in the morning that 'all the money that was theirs yesterday is gone away, and it may never come back again'.[30] Kipling was at pains to dramatize the unpredictable twists and turns in the life of the members of what he called the Overseas Club. They were faced with people 'that are beginning to experiment with fresh-drafted and half-grafted codes which do not include juries', and were confronted by a system 'that does not contemplate a free press, and a suspicious absolutism' from which there was no let-up.[31] Justifying the hoity-toity demeanour of the British merchants and their monomania for extra-territorial jurisdictions and gun-boats, Kipling made out an agreeable case holding forth that, in view of the unstable life in the East and its portentous prospects, it was but natural that pretty, tiled bungalows with a sylvan view did not console them and even the voices of the politest people on earth jarred sorely.[32] Emotionally, the man-on-the-spot became increasingly self-centred. His loyalty to England turned into a hollow slogan. For him, the Empire meant a battleground where one had to be strong, stronger and strongest. At this altar of power and amidst angry but unarmed millions he could satisfy his personal lust while fulfilling the imperial destiny of Britain.[33]

It is remarkable that the image of the man-on-the-spot continued to linger in the imperial mind as that of one who was endowed with suavity, tolerance, statesmanship, sympathy and the 'blessed habit of not being surprised by anything whatever'.[34] These soldiers of fortune, it was projected, were relentlessly carrying the mission and message of a civilized Europe into far-off lands. The perception of unperturbed frontier men, administrators, merchants and planters living among 'strange sounds and smells' suffused the imperial sensibility with a romantic aura.[35] The world of the Empire, it was believed, was lonely, large and self-absorbed. It was a much larger slice of the universe than the Englishmen cared to admit. There were families which had served the Empire for five or six generations. Their fate had sent them to India which, it was admitted without dissent, was 'not a golden country, though poets have sung otherwise'.[36] These men could 'die with great swiftness' and those who survived might 'suffer curious things'. Fierce wars on the frontier followed by the 'boundless monotony of cantonment life', stringent subjection to the guard room for 'conduct unbecoming of a soldier', and finally, a life of responsibility according to official communications constituted an endless course of routine.[37] It was, the publicists were unanimous, a story of continual endeavours based on patience, application and discipline.

The Anglo-Indians in their scattered garrisons, Maud Diver confessed, often presented an impression of a 'mute, snobbish, not obviously clever and obviously ill-educated lot'[38]; standing as the 'stewards of great mysteries' who did not understand any race but their own. This perception of the British left Maud Diver uneasy and anxious to rescue them. Delving a few inches deeper one could detect, she wrote, 'under the surface of a muteness and officialism the sturdy self-control and the patient and persistent driving force that have made the country what it is today'.[39] Defending the aloofness of the Englishman in India, a writer in the *Quarterly Review,* dismissed the 'favourite caricature' of the Englishman in India as a hectoring, domineering, swaggering overlord, exacting salaams from every Indian who traversed his path,[40] arguing that the old conception of the district officer as a cross between a country squire and an estate agent, with a dash of the policeman and a pinch of the old-fashioned chairman of quarter sessions thrown in was a dying creed.

Public opinion in England was made to believe that with diminished initiative and curtailed responsibility, the young district officer was exposed to the subtle art of provocation of the Bengalis and the irritation of incessant criticism in England. He laboured with an oppressive feeling generated by the impossible magnitude of his task and felt frustrated under the 'overwhelming weight of the vast inertia of the East'. As a result it was probable that the comparative aloofness of the Englishman in India was one of the secrets of his success. At home, Aldous Huxley wrote, the same Englishman was lost in a nameless crowd; he did not count because he was nobody. But in the East, life satisfied the most powerful of all the instincts—that of self-assertion.[41] For example, even the young man of Kipling's *Barrack Room Ballads* who went out from a London suburb in search of a career in India found himself a member of a small ruling community surrounded by slavish servants, dark-skinned subordinates and millions of Indians from the coolie to the maharaja, from the illiterate peasant to the holder of an Oxford degree. Huxley, who shared in full measure British prejudices about India, wrote: 'Superiority in India is a question of epidermis'.[42] Robert Byron who was equally sensitive on this point, stressed the foundations of British arrogance in his *An Essay on India*. White pigmentation of skin, he wrote, 'at first only a symbol of material efficiency assumes, and is paid, the homage of a divine attribute'.[43] Thus not only administrators, judges and doctors but even merchants and salesmen were given a special status and they felt inspired by the righteousness of their cause. 'Every white man in Asia becomes an Apostle and is prepared to maintain his part in face of all opposition'.[44] The life of these men included, it was maintained cheerfully, plenty of sunshine, lots of fresh air, much insolence, frothy gossip and 'real hard work' in an atmosphere of unexpected shifts of fortune with little prospect of reward.[45] E.M. Forster, Edward Thompson and C.F. Andrews felt uneasy with this intrinsic and priggish segregation of imperialism. But then, only a few could comprehend the dynamics of the system.

Empire-building, another imperial undersong advertised, was a thankless job. It was contrasted with the somewhat pleasant irresponsibility of the members of the parliament. A young man, Kipling wrote in an attempt to etch a representative imperial portrait, might be given his 'heart's desire in the form of a raw district' where on two-third of a member of parliament's wage and under awful conditions of service he would have felt irked in his morbid isolation with the certainty of picking up two sorts of fever in the bargain.[46] Despite the rose-bushes and the best of well-maintained bungalows, despite the relaxing melody of the 'koil' singing on the *'siris'*, the squirrel's clattering speech from 'the creeper-covered trellis' and the 'blue jay screams' of the *'cheery satbhai'*, the young man would have cried out: ' I am sick of endless sunshine, sick of blossom-burdened bough.' He would have longed to get back even for a day to England in her leafless woodlands.[47]

Behind the swashbuckling demeanour and 'refreshing' arrogance of the sea-captains, consuls, district administrators, statisticians, army commanders, members of Skinner's Horse, politicals, revenue officials, agents of the export and import firms and residents and amidst the talk of tea, silk, banking, exchange and tribal customs, including those of migrant husbands and compulsory polyandry, there was, Kipling detected, an eerie feeling with regard to the inevitability of dangerous contingencies and, paradoxically, also of an unaccountable sense of cheerful preparedness to meet these situations. Violent clashes, it was maintained, were often forced on them by the 'Oriental' people who were 'embarrassingly economical of the truth' although they were, Kipling comforted as if to soften the blow, equally endowed with a 'sharp human instinct for valour and respect'.[48] Confrontation with these people was their daily bread. It might have been owing to the 'want of any fixity of commitment' in the native system which, in turn, Kipling reckoned, could have been the consequence of the manner 'in which the climate has affected, and rulers have ruled these men for untold centuries'.[49]

Kipling was corroborated by many who raised their voice in defence of the discretionary powers of the unrewarded men on the imperial frontiers.[50] Maud Diver was keen to pay tribute to the initiative and drive of the unknown soldiers who built without rancour, roads, railways, canals, bridges and the great irrigation schemes and who conquered the uncertainties of the Khyber Pass and waged war, as she put it, against famine and disease in the face of a strange combination of bigotry, ignorance and superstition. Everywhere, they exhibited, Maud Diver fluttered her imperial pride, 'that zealous and disinterested service which has become recognised as a primal quality of the race—the hall-mark of the gentleman'.[51] They were the 'unsung' heroes of British India. There were Alex Taylor and 'Buster' Browne consuming their flaccid vigour on the Grand Trunk Road[52]; there were Frederick Mackeson, Henry Lawrence and Robert Warburton taming the Khyber and Victor Bayley pushing a railway through the difficult pass as Mrs Bailey or the 'Lady Sahib' greeted the moment when 'the grimy train clattered, whistling madly, into Landi Kotal station'[53]; there was John Pennycuick, quick in decision but unyielding in perseverance, with his picked staff of the Young Cooper Hill engineers applying himself on the Periyar project, 'a plain tale of a unique engineering triumph, seldom, if ever, excelled'.[54] The imperial mind often moved away in an untutored excursion to a world of fantasy. Flora Annie Steel's Craddock is a patterned character of imperial literature—one who stood for unrewarded but unrepented service. He and his superior were engaged in the wilderness like another Moses and Aaron in preparing the railway across the desert, thus trying to prevent 'a survival of the past ages from being in the permanent way of civilisation'.[55] These imperial craftsmen, artists, pastors and messengers did, Maud Diver exclaimed, 'more than build—a word that suggests dead brick and stone. They created between them a living Indian Empire that contained within itself the elements of growth; and growth is all'.[56] They were rewarded, it was modestly though firmly added, by a simple spiritual satisfaction as they noted that much suffering had been alleviated and many lives had been saved in a country where 'the God Climate unceasingly brands and burns his nothingness into man'.[57] Governments and gunboats, Kipling had anticipated, might have opened a land, but 'it is the men of the Overseas Club that keep it open'.[58]

Flora Annie Steel compared the British experience in India with the repressive frustrations and exacting obligations of Babur, the Empire-builder of the sixteenth century. The founder of the Mughal Empire, she thought, must have found the Indian countryside 'ugly and detestable' and must have wondered, as did the British general subsequently, if he had better left India undisturbed only to allow it 'to stew in its own juice'. There was no denying, Steel held firmly, that the country had few pleasures to recommend itself. The people, she indicted, were not handsome and had no idea of the charms of friendly society or of social intercourse. They had little 'comprehension of mind', no 'politeness of manners' and no 'fellow feeling'. The very thought of the beauty of the 'Garden of Fidelity', she conjectured, must have made Babur feel sick. He, however, stayed on for 'there was duty as well as beauty to be considered'. The state of mind of Babur, Steel blazoned, 'has the sympathy of thousands upon thousands of others; since there is scarcely an Anglo-Indian who has not felt the same on a hot, breathless May morning when the dull eyes, seeking for some object on which to rest, find none, save a wide waste of sand, an indeterminate *kikar* tree and an aggressive crow bent on showing you that he is as black inside as he is outside'.[59]

Thousands of Englishmen in India seemed to share the familiar apprehensions of Babur. Like him, Flora Annie Steel vouched, they were also divided in their minds between a longing to see their native country and their ideals of self-denial and responsibility. They hesitated but stayed on. 'In truth', Flora Steel professed, 'Babur could be the patron-saint of the Indian Services'. For them, like Babur, the conquest of India was not adequate. What was important was to establish with all 'vivid vitality of British nation an ideal Empire that would endure'.[60] One of the bases of this imperial obligation, it was avowed, was courage. It differed from jingoism and rash expansion. It was also remote from craven timidity. Rule of some kind was a condition for the attainment of this object and trade was its inevitable effect. Its essential element was caution which involved a spirit of conciliation. Force was its necessary foundation. But an Empire could not be governed, it was argued, if it was to be perpetually conquered. Nor could it be maintained if its stability depended on the indulgence of the neighbours. Acquiescence and habitual obedience were not inherent but had to be acquired and these were ensured, it was proudly claimed, by substantial achievements. Should England be driven out someday from India, it was affirmed, her churches, hospitals, schools, bridges, roads, navigations and reservoirs ought to exhibit to the world its genius.[61]

One may not be inclined to crib over the authenticity of the voice of the expert that one hears in the stories and verses of the Raj. One does not think it necessary to pause and ponder over the superficialities of Kipling and the more astute and less subtle observations of Steel. Their voices might not have been satisfactory. But even beyond the world of legitimate moral inquisitions, this atypical shelf of English literature on India was able to project the exploits and perceptions of the participants in a historical movement. That movement was complex, diverse and quite matter-of-fact even though it was unusually self-righteous and querulous. It appeared both queer and grotesque. Kipling, more than anyone else, captured its dominant themes and aberrant ethics. There was something more than the 'lower-middle-class snarl of defeated gentility'[62] in him. There are the responses of the barrack-room soldiers, the strife and struggle of the man-who-has-had-to-meet-a-payroll, and the encounters and involvements of the engineers, forest officers, civil servants, Simla officialdom and commanders on the front in a country of 'archaic contradictions', supernatural mysticism and 'crimes and degradation'. As 'true imperialists', Curzon, Kipling and many others were critical of official lapses. They derided inefficiency and disparaged artificial countenance. True, they often overdrew their lines, laying their colours arbitrarily, underplaying some emotions and overplaying some others. But all through his literary endeavours Kipling, in particular, portrayed and extolled the deluding false-consciousness of the British in their attempt to construct a bridge across what they decided to dub as an inscrutable land of lethargy and an opium-dulled world of the supernatural.[63] It may not be necessary here to review the characteristics of that 'inscrutable land'. One wonders if there was any attempt at all to throw a bridge between the East and the West in terms of even basic human understanding. The imperial sensibility had its foundation on hatred, contempt and exploitation. It could not have undertaken a project aimed at a true reconciliation. Bridge-building was never included in the die-hard imperial agenda. On the contrary, a myth became a superficial stereotype and a stereotype was turned into a ribald preoccupation.

To Kipling, Maud Diver, Flora Annie Steel, Sarah Duncan and even Edward Thompson, like Curzon, Milner, Rhodes and Kitchener, the imperial mission was an obsession and all of them became prisoners of their propaganda. Perturbed by the haunting prospect of these inept human agencies wrecking the 'bridge' with their uncertain, imperfect and stolid interference, they placed the Empire on a higher pedestal than the daily routine of the Government of India and the democratic uneasiness of the British Parliament.[64] Kipling's Findlayson could not entirely trust the white men engaged in bridge-building projects. Even at home, Englishmen of different callings, ignorant of India but meddlesome nevertheless, would have continued to obstruct that chivalrous enterprise but for a strict Hitchcock and his unfailing perseverance.[65] India of the 'Bridge-Builders' was so incomprehensible that it did not fail to instil a despondent mood. The image of India *In the house of the Suddhoo*, on the other hand, was illusive.[66] It closely followed the uncanny figure of Azizum, a lady of the city and a veiled woman, quite adept in both the roles. Kipling hammered his point home. In the face of the challenge presented by India there was no scope for smoking-room complacency. Unlike George Orwell's experience, Kipling's imperial obligations could not be summed up in the phrase, 'futility of the white man's dominion in the East'.[67] Kipling's 'burden' was an idealization of an aggressive and flamboyant Raj.

The true imperialists were conscious of the fact that the Empire, like everything else, was ephemeral. It was nevertheless, they averred as ideologues, a noble task delightfully conducted and hopefully concluded with full knowledge of the inevitability of death and destruction, which even 'the children of the zodiac' came to appreciate albeit reluctantly.[68] There was in them a strange mixture of an element of nagging repentance, an inflated pride and it-could-have-been-better feeling. They were not frightfully concerned about the destiny of Englishmen in the East. 'It is a hard law but an old one—Rome died learning it, as our Western civilisation may die—that if you give any man', wrote Kipling depressed as he was about the future of British rule in India, 'anything that he has not painfully earned for himself, you infallibly make him or his descendants your devoted enemies'.[69] Despite such prognostications he as well as Curzon went out of their way to applaud the Indian experiment as the highest achievement of their race.

Kipling became the barometer of British interests in India. Civilians affirmed that they served Kipling's India. W.W. Hunter, who misjudged *Departmental Ditties,* exhorted the young Kipling to present to the world, the British experiment in India which 'has never had an equal in history'.[70] In fact Kipling's perception had already become the criterion of British judgements on India. Ronald Wingate, like many others, felt the weight of the white man's burden[71]; Edwin Harward talked of the 'Kipling telescope' of the official India[72]; G.N. Molesworth detected that cult of Kipling seated heavenly on the Olympus[73]; and Edmund Candler thought that his generation of civil servants learnt everything about India from all that Kipling wrote about it. In fact, long after his departure, the Kipling hangover remained very strong.[74] Claud H.Hill found Kipling's description of the voiceless millions in India as true as ever. Maconochie confirmed the enlivening effect of Kipling on the blurred vision of a tired and confused district officer.[75] Leonard Woolf was at a loss to make up his mind whether Kipling had moulded his characters of Anglo-Indian society accurately or whether the men in the clubs and messes were consciously shaping their own characters on the image of Kipling.[76] Compiling an anthology of poetry, Field Marshal A.P. Wavell acknowledged the compelling impact of Rudyard Kipling on his impressionable mind and the remarkable resilience of that influence throughout his career. The core of the collection, he asserted, was Browning and Kipling. 'Indeed I would ask for Kipling still—"The Roman Centurion's Song", "The way through the woods", "When last picture is painted", "Our Lady of the Saeb-cloth . . . ." Whether the soldier-statesman of the Empire directed his attention to the music, mystery and magic of nature or the business of war and good fighting, or the spirit of adventure and self-sacrifice, the hymns of Kipling brought him both inspiration and comfort.[77]

The image of British India as projected by Kipling had an extensive audience.

After the announcement that the Nobel Prize was to be awarded to Tagore, Western critics sought to establish the superiority of the 'Caucasian race' over the 'Indian race'; to discover in the poet, a dreamer with a 'narrow Western outlook' and a dated Western sensibility who had been favoured by preferential treatment that was, according to them, often meted out to 'colonials' for political exigency.[78] They saw the award as something of a humiliation to which they were supposed to adjust themselves:

> It is the first time that the Nobel Prize has gone to anyone who is not what we call 'white'. It will take time, of course, for us to accommodate ourselves to the idea that some one called Rabindranath Tagore should receive a world prize for literature. (Have we not been told that the East and the West shall never meet?) The name has a curious sound. The first time we saw it in print it did not seem real.[79]

Kipling had taught them that the very essence of all things Eastern had some kind of super-personal and undefinable mystery. In fact the East, especially India, had been providing Europe with a readymade exotic formula and critics found Tagore not even sufficiently Eastern. He was a half-baked Western, an anti-climax not representing the 'real' India.[80] 'We of the West do not want from the East poetic edifices', the *Liverpool Post* declared, 'built upon a foundation of Yeats and Shelley and Walt Whitman. We want to hear flute of Krishna as Radha heard of it, to fall under the spell of the blue God in the lotus-heart of dreams'.[81] As an Oriental poet Rabindranath, the *Queen* of London pronounced, had nothing to offer the West. 'Those who wish to be impressed by glimpses of a life that is different from our own, by revelations of the Eastern mind which works in a way we can never understand, would do far better to go to Mr. Kipling for what they want . . . .'[82] Indeed critics often crossed the frontier of sanity and moved into the realm of absurdity. The *Birmingham Gazette* thought that Tagore's *Gora* merely recalled 'to many readers that of Kipling's story, *Namgay Doola*'. In fact in both the works, the reviewer added, 'the fervent patriot turns out to be not pure Indian, but half-Irish!' In the *Natal Mercury*, the critic was shocked to find in *Gora* 'a kind of inversion of Kipling's *Kim*, in which the author tries to point the opposite moral', utterly lacking the genius of Kipling. It was, the reviewer pronounced, a long, surgid, meandering plot 'continually lost sight of in a mess of side bones and irrelevances'.[83] Kipling's India and Rabindranath's India had nothing in common. Kipling provided, as A. Aronson puts it, the Western reader with all the 'glamour' and 'romanticism' of the East 'for which there was such a great demand'. That sensibility responded to India in terms of romantic idealization or in terms of either snobbish contempt or condescension.[84]

India, it was stressed with great aplomb, was a unique land. No academic appreciation or theoretical proposition devoid of practical experience could have rendered her people and institutions comprehensible to a European. India, it seemed, had been reserved for the Indian Civil Service to penetrate, fathom and grasp. A seasoned administrator of the vintage of Reginald Craddock or Claud Hill would have agreed with Kipling's description :

> From the well-ordered road we tread,
> And all the world is wild and strange;
> *Churel* and *Goul* and *Djinm* and sprite
> Shall bear company to-night,
> For we have reached the oldest land
> Wherein the Power of Darkness range.[85]

The district officer was the pivotal point of Indian administration. He shared the responsibilities of all the specialized agencies of the government. But he also stood as its local representative. The archetype of the district officer, immortalized by Kipling, was that of an omniscient and omnipotent father of his people. He managed his two thousand square miles of earth and his million human beings with little interference from headquarters. His word was law and the prescriptions of remote impersonal authority in Britain hardly added weight to his own wishes. But over the years the autocratic rule of young officers had been clipped and pruned by the demands of a developing Empire and it was only on the frontiers that civilian and military officers still ruled by personal authority that recalled the memory of Nicholson. It was conceded that there had been a marked decline in the efficiency and capabilities of the civil services since the days of Elphinstone. By the turn of the century, the district officer already had no spare time to think. 'Between the Devil—the Secretariat, asking for more information—and the deep sea—the people of a vast region shouting for justice—the District officer had not much leisure to think on the tenderness of India.' Only a few could filch a precious hour or two to look up from their office desks towards the crowded Indian horizon. It was maintained, nevertheless, by an expert of the *Round Table* , that the local officers had wide discretion over a large part of India. In adjusting the collection of taxes to agricultural conditions, in keeping peace, in settling disputes, in repressing the exactions of landlords, their stewards and the hordes of official subordinates, the head of a district retained, despite constant denudation of authority, immense discretionary powers. His burdens had increased but his position had not been greatly impaired.[86]

Educated young Indians turned out by the Indian universities in the last quarter of the nineteenth century introduced a disturbing note in the conversations of the exclusive clubs. It was resolved that the merit of these men had to be examined in practical terms. Officials concluded that these young Indians had education but lacked character. More often than not, 'the Englishman', an expert of the *Round Table*, propounded that the young Indian competition-wallah lacked the other prerequisites necessary for his career—often he came of poor stock, and was bodily unfit for a robust and exacting life; often success had turned his head or over-study enfeebled his physique or intellect and more often than not perhaps a conservative upbringing and caste prejudice had rendered it hard for him to take a broad and objective view. It was hoped that a way could be explored of encouraging Indian merit without flooding the administration with effete or conceited weaklings. If training and experience were successfully brought to bear on the right material there would be no reason, the *Round Table* was confident, to fear that Indian officials and non-officials could make common cause against the Englishman. Britain's task in India was certainly becoming more delicate and difficult than before; but despite waning confidence, it was hoped that they would live up to the expectations at home. 'England need not fear', it was announced, 'that her servants will fail her in India; if she would only believe it, they change their climate, but not their character, East of Suez'.[87]

Examining the Christian forces at work in the administration of India and the mutual relations of the British Government and Christian missions between 1600 and 1920, Arthur Mayhew, a director of public instruction in India declared: 'Often unconsciously, and sometimes with protestations to the contrary, those responsible during a century and a half for India's welfare had been concerned not only, as Kipling suggested, with the Law of the Prophet, but also with the spirit of the Gospels'.[88] This statement, the author elucidated, might embarrass a coy and unassuming bureaucracy unused to praise. He suggested that the Simla secretariat was engaged under episcopal supervision in translating the Sermon on the Mount into official jargon.

Mayhew popularized a familiar contention that Christianity in relation to Government did not imply official recognition of a system of ethics or the substitution of the Gospels for orders and regulations, but meant a particular conception of God's relation to men which impressed on the rulers a sense of respect for the dignity of every class of society. It also inspired a belief in human progress, a hopeful determination, a progressive vigour and a divine opportunity to rebuild a civilization on certain permanent values which recognized no geographical distinction. 'Our policy has been moulded by men who have come gradually to see that the distinction between Christian missionary and administrators in India was one of scope and method rather than of aim or motive power'.[89] This implied, the author argued, no flagging in the spirit or in the quality of evangelical and administrative work. Increasing readiness on the part of the Government to honour Christian obligations, educational progress and gradual enlightenment of public opinion, the author opined, transformed prophets and pioneers into men distinguished by unobtrusive and impersonal activity more anxious to gain colleagues than disciples. This was perceptible, Mayhew maintained, from the days of Charles Grant, John Shore and the Clapham Circle to a host of Christian stalwarts like the Lawrences, James Outram, Herbert Edwardes, Mountstuart Elphinstone, Robert Grant, James Thomason, Bartle Frere, Robert Montgomery, J.M. Macleod, Edward Thornton, William Muir and Henry Durand. Advancement on

Christian lines had moved apace especially during the period covered by William Bentinck and Dalhousie with John Malcolm operating in the west, Thomas Munro in the south, Alexander Duff in Bengal, John Wilson in Bombay and Jonathan Duncan in Benares. Subsequently, despite the alleged intellectual and spiritual atrophy of the English society in India, detected by many ardent missionaries, Christian ethics and morality, Mayhew asserted, were tuned to the Government's policy and Christian missions and institutions were included within the governmental infrastructure.[90]

There was no paucity in Anglo-Indian fiction of examples depicting the liberating influence of Christianity. Nora E. Karn in her collection of short stories, *The Believer and other Stories,* identified Christianity with humanity. The Christian nun of 'The Bhaktani' spoke in the warm language of the East, of 'a woman's heart, of a woman's life and of a woman's joy'. The Eastern heart listened attentively and was awakened. Basanti no longer stretched her hands vainly after the mysteries of loneliness and God. Basanti had received the light of life; she went to her husband and though she did not become a Christian, Christ's love overwhelmed her.[91] Again, it was under the inspiration of Christian love that Behari Das, a Brahmin boy found a friend in Sri Chand, the son of the *bhangi.* Reprimanded by the schoolteacher who upheld the permanence of caste exclusiveness but encouraged by Lotan Singh, the Jat, himself educated in a missionary school, the friendship between the two matured passing through plague and epidemic and they became 'the apostles of a new caste', that was created out of love.[92] Mankar and her husband, Kishan, low-caste Christians, found it difficult to comprehend that when a man became a Christian he entered an entirely different community with different social laws and grades and that the new *biradari* owed something to them. Mankar a simple Punjabi girl, remained a mystic at heart and identified herself with the sins of her husband for her own sake. He was her *parameshwar ka rooh.* For her, this was the wish of Jesus.[93] Another girl with her child in her lap became a *sadhni* of Jesus, defied a cruel Hindu society and trudged all over religious India in the garb of a mendicant with the joy of St Francis in her heart. Christianity, it was maintained, was the essence of liberty and unless a significant proportion of the whole community had become true Christians, self-government might become a sheer calamity.[94]

Maurice Dekobra started out for India with the idea that the antagonism between the West and the East was not so irreconciliable and that an understanding of the two mentalities could be fostered and moulded by mutual goodwill. But he left India with the conviction that the Isthmus of Suez separated the incompatible communities, 'as different, one from the other, as the animal kingdom is from the vegetable'. This portrayed, he stated, a fundamental antagonism: a spiritual, religious, moral and social dissonance divided them. These innumerable barriers, Dekobra emphasized, paralysed all good feelings or deep friendships. There were three thousand years of irreconciliable civilizations which provided, Dekobra expatiated, a gap between the West and the East. 'Between them and us', he underlined, 'there is, on the one side the animal that they behead every morning to appease their vindictive Goddess, and on the other side, the serum of the Pasteur Institute'. As a Christian, he affirmed confidently, he could not become a Hindu even if he agreed to accept their religion complete with 'all that gross image worship, which extends from the ever-menacing lingum to the sacred bulls with reddened muzzles'.[95] A white man, it was asserted, was a permanent *persona non grata*.

Dominance and power meant egocentric megalomania. It was reiterated time and again that the huge and remote dependency had been governed over the years with remarkable ease by a handful of Englishmen. Writing against the background of August 1942, Peter Muir emphasized and applauded this particular fact. Lonely posts, he reasoned, existed all over the country and it might have been just a matter of simple initiative to drive these officials out of their posts from one end of India to the other by really non-violent means.[96] Seventeen years earlier Aldous Huxley had almost winced when he concluded that without any violence, merely by refusing to accept the white man at his own valuation and declining to have anything to do with him, the Indian could reduce the British rule to impotence. But both Huxley and Muir were convinced that the Raj was not fragile and it had considerable resilience.[97]

*

The whole process of ensuring an ingrained political obedience to an alien power was facilitated, it was adjudged, by the vivid individuality of this ancient civilization. Valentine Chirol, for one, detected a striking feature in Indian history. He argued that while India produced during her long history, thinkers, philosophers, writers, builders, artists, warriors and even statesmen 'it created, in the main, a social and religious rather than a political system'. As a religious system, Chirol amplified, Hinduism was extraordinarily flexible. He emphasized that it had no moral codes—tolerating both polyandry and polygamy and countenancing the greatest sensuousness and the most extravagant asceticism. Its ethics, like its pantheon, had been stretched for centuries to shelter strange gods and customs which the petitioners for admission within its fold might have wished to bring with them.[98] The same code which exalted the Brahmins and the cow, Lockwood Kipling observed, 'thrusts the dog, the ass, the buffalo, the pig and the low-caste men beyond the pale of merciful regard'. This topsy-turvy morality of the Hindus would offer, Lockwood Kipling derided, a higher place to the 'levitically' clean Hindu, who would have died sooner than eat flesh and who would also rather die than touch or help a dying man of a low-caste near the door, than to an English lady whose life had been spent in active beneficence.[99]

Hinduism as a social system, on the other hand, offered essentially a rigid framework. In particular, Chirol pinpointed the impact of the startling institution of caste. It created, he underlined, innumerable dividing lines which had split up Indian society into thousands of water-tight compartments 'within which an Indian is born, lives and dies without any possibility of emerging from the one to which he was predestined'.[100] It was, therefore, remarkably convenient for Chirol and others to manipulate the opinions of distinguished Indologists. M.Senart, for example, had described the caste system as a close corporation, largely hereditary, equipped with traditional and independent organizations observing common usages with regard to marriage, diet and ceremonials and ruling its members by the sanction of severe social penalties. The Hindu mind, as a result, was obsessed by the tenacious hold of an extraordinary 'purity - pollution' syndrome sustained by a plethora of ceremonies and rituals. Following this general line of argument, Herbert Risley, an official expert on Indian anthropology, ventured to examine the process by which castes proliferated. He presented his concept of a Hindu caste, rather frivolously, in terms of an English social group, the Smiths whose infinite number of 'in-marrying' clans and 'out-marrying' genera together with an intricate pattern of sub-divisions broke the entire series of clans into a sort of ascending scale of social distinctions.Likewise the strange Hindu social hierarchy, he explained, was seated unrivalled on a system of untouchability and was led by the Brahmins who constituted, by all counts, the proudest and closest aristocracy that the world has ever seen. Walter Roper Lawrence thought that Brahmanism was the essence of the 'Hindu Octopus'. It was a gentle, easy, clutching, inevitable system for the control of a vast mankind.[101]

However complex and oppressive the system might have been and still is, it is incumbent for us to note that the political contours of caste differentiations emerged in high relief in imperial sensibility offering considerable leverage to the rulers for conditioning social forces. Thus Herbert Risley, Alfred Lyall and Valentine Chirol forcefully argued that although the caste system as a social and religious institution remained largely unbroken, it completely failed as a stable and constructive political force. Candler associated stability with conservatism. In the West, he argued, it was the expression of the attitudes of the aristocracy while in the East it was the mantle of the humblest. In the West, he added, the lower and middle social strata were unsettled with aspirations; in the East, fatalism inspired them with repose.[102]

The country also had queer customs which gave women the freedom to humiliate themselves before men. There was no concept of love between a man and a woman. Early marriage and early motherhood, it was asserted, in order to underline the detours of Indian psyche and sensibility, gave the females of that 'God-forsaken' country the occupation they required along with self-respect. The only love that was known was that which a mother felt for her young, which 'even the animals demonstrate' or the abnormal mother-fixation of the males which destroyed the germs of any healthy human love.[103]

To this was added the horrors of an abject fatalism. 'It is not to be done huzoor.' Flora Annie Steel's *khidmutgar* entreated, 'We are in the hands of fate. If death comes, it will come, but it will end in birth'.[104] It shook the Christian missionaries who, as a consequence, felt obliged to look after the needs of the lonely Hindu soul. They tried to go deep into the emotional confusion of the Hindu mind and sought to comprehend the intellectual void caused by the depressing doctrines of maya and karma. For a Hindu, a Christian missionary insisted, everything in the heavens above and on the earth beneath, every thought of mind and every act of body, whether an act of devotion or one of nameless impurity—everything was maya. It appeared to him that Hinduism destroyed responsibility because it upheld that 'in all things man acts not freely but under the compulsions of an inevitable necessity'.[105] The whole universe, a missionary summed up the Hindu view of life, 'is a gigantic lie, and the liar is the supreme Brahma'. Besides, the weight of the law of karma, it was asserted, ceaselessly oppressed the Indians without a rational way out of it. It was both an irresistible and an inhibiting force for a Hindu was led to believe, as Lockwood Kipling ridiculed, that even a stray bull might be the 'potential grand-father'.[106] There were conscious sins as well as unconscious ones relentlessly germinating evil results for the future. The cold logic of karma, it was noted with concern, offered no ray of hope to the suffering Hindu mankind.

This Hindu view of life was enunciated with remarkable finesse. It became, over the years, a significant imperial prism. In 1923, C.F. Bechhofer elaborated that to the Hindu cosmology, the world was a dream. 'The external world, the world outside ourselves', Bechhofer's Brahmin deliberated on the Hindu concept of illusion, 'is made up only of our impression of it; the visible world is the sum of what we see, and the world of sound of what we hear and so on. It is the influence of maya that makes us think it real'.[107] A bewildered Christian in Hewett was sufficiently confused by the harmonious voice of the Brahmin who quoted the mystics as well as the Hindu, Christian and Muslim authorities in order to establish this eternal dream of the universal mind. As Hewett rode around the dam with a mass of machines, materials and tools he wondered how 'a jester Maya was to delude herself with all this rubbish!' Probably, a sympathetic Hewett concluded, Hindu mystical writings were the natural expression of human impulses in a backward and unscientific environment. But even he found them remote and fantastic, viewing Hindu philosophy with a strange admixture of admiration and horror. A 'liberal' Hewett concluded that morals in India were relative, subjective, contradictory and mechanical.[108]

Sarah Tytler was struck by the deeply-rooted irrationality in Indian psychology and sociology. The ancient beliefs and customs, she wrote, were 'so full of sensuous fascination and of moral and spiritual horrors, so wonderful in their power and stability, which commanded and coloured every portion of the false social system and religion', that she almost felt an uncanny feeling around her. Superstitions, she felt, were endemic in India. British settlements were like armed forts surrounded by thousands of simple Hindu and Muslim folks whom 'we have made our enemies in trying to be their friends, as well as in riding roughshod over them'. What appeared to Sarah Tytler most disquieting was that there were not enough trustworthy men to defend these forts. Both Alice Grey and Bennet Hill had lost much of their life and happiness in this unfortunate country. But for them service in India was an 'exaltation of a fellowship with the Lord's suffering'. Alice decided to join Reverend Bennet Hill only if she could be of any service to Bennet and to God's work in India. It was to be the happiness of service, suffering and ingratitude all through.[109]

Discoursing on crimes in India, S.M. Edwards (with a distinguished career in India behind him) concluded that a direct and close linkage existed between Indian religions, traditions and mysteries and the political and other crimes of the twentieth century. 'In the peculiar circumstances and conditions of India and its huge heterogeneous population it is questionable whether the Government of the last few years has not extended its toleration of anti-social movements and disorder almost beyond the point of safety'.[110] He condemned the suicidal policy in India 'where the vast mass of the people is uncivilised according to modern standards, and where large numbers of actual and potential criminals are ever ready to seize the first opportunity for resorting to the methods of violence and forms of crime inherited from past ages of rapine and violence'.[111] Christianity, it was assumed, could not co-exist with Hinduism and missionaries often called for exclusive official patronage. Over the years the sympathies of the Government had shaped and regulated a set of firm guiding principles. Basking under the warm glow of official care, Christian propaganda turned intensely intolerant. 'If Christ is to rule over India,' wrote one of its active cadres, 'then Hinduism and all its various superstition must go. You can neither lessen His light nor illuminate its darkness by a process of assimilation'.[112]

As the prospect of Christian conversion loomed large in the eyes of the missionaries, they were often carried away by their unrestrained optimism beyond all reasonable proportion. Thus Henry Whitehead, the Bishop of Madras and G.W. Briggs of the Christian Missionary Society, reported gleefully that there existed in India enormous raw material ripe for instant conversion. Christianity, Briggs penned, was for the lower castes like the Chamars more than a social and economic gospel. Hinduism, he maintained, on its lower side was polytheistic and saturated with demonology. Therefore, the Chamars, it was held out, must look elsewhere for deliverance from superstition, the fear of evil spirits and the evils that follow in the wake of these beliefs.[113]

Bishop Whitehead endorsed this view. The first step towards any social progress in rural India, he argued, was to demolish this chaotic clutter of beliefs and practices, rites and ceremonies and clear the ground for the teaching and worship of the Christian church. He hoped that Christianity would bring to the Indian villagers, especially the outcastes the truth of the existence of an omnipotent God of infinite love, a direct access to this fountain of love and the truth of universal redemption from sin. A sense of social security, a permanent protection against mysterious devils and the liberation from passive inertia in the face of the inevitability of the law of karma were offered as the immediate fruits of conversion as the missionaries sought to reach out to the hearts of the downtrodden and the lowly.[114]

Henry Whitehead characterized Hinduism as 'a religion of fear and superstitions' finding its outward expression in mean symbols and 'in forms of worship that are to a very large extent disgusting and even immoral'.[115] The result was revolting. Jim of *The Ruined Temple* felt uneasy in the abode of a Hindu god for whom he had developed no special love. As he inspected this abandoned temple with countless niches and carved decorations, 'thrown together without any order or design' he was convinced that the Hindu mind was a riotous medley of untutored fancies and obnoxious superstitions.[116] 'There was scarcely a square foot of surface that did not display an array of fantastic figures and designs'. There were intricate patterns in zigzag work, circles and scrolls. There were figures of lotus flowers, goats, monkeys, crocodiles and elephants and an endless variety of gods and goddesses in weird, grotesque representations, 'some half-human and half-animal'.[117]

The imperial mind questioned, in utter bewilderment, the queer imagination that had conceived 'these strange creatures'. It was overwhelmed by a creepy feeling which stood between it and Hinduism with its 'ugly gods', devastating 'evil eyes' and 'sure charms'—all shrouded in mysterious forces that were beyond any rational explanation.[118] It shivered at the infinite and immense secrets of India.[119] The Jain temples at Mount Abu rattled Edmund Candler. He was amazed by 'the miracles of elaboration', the diversity of the compositions and the uncompromising 'severity of the details' of the shrines. Yet the whole effect, Candler announced, was to tease one out of thought. 'Looking at it I could understand', Candler gave vent to his sophisticated aesthetics, 'the mood of the iconoclast'. The destroyer of images 'appeared to me a man of sensibility, a man who thinks and feels too much rather than too little, who is not deceived by the public about art. I could imagine a spiritual man with a little warm blood in his veins running amok in the place with a chisel and a hammer'. Candler was convinced that Dilwara owed its preservation to its remoteness. Aurangzeb would have surely levelled the temple to the ground! Lutyens would have concurred with him.[120]

The complete subordination of the civil to the sacerdotal power in India created its own arbitrary lines of social antagonism and helped to deepen other lines of division. Antipathies of race and religion, Lockwood Kipling lamented, were calmly ignored by those who wrote of the people of India as indivisible.[121] Thc inherent tensions in society, he added, found expression in 'sayings wherein the donkey takes part'. Lockwood Kipling amused himself with these sayings quite unmindful of the English parallels such as the proverbial 'Welsh nitwit' and 'Scottish muckworm': 'A Hindustani will say of a Punjabi, "A country donkey with a Punjabi bray", and the Punjabi retaliates with, "A country donkey with an Eastern limp", while of the Bengali babu with his affected English speech and manners, they say, "A hill jackass with an English bray".'[122]

In the context of the 'unique' Indian situation, it was universally affirmed that India ought to be regarded as a continent by itself, comprising a variety of nations that differed more widely amongst themselves, both racially and linguistically, than the nations of Europe. It was pleasing for many to espy in India a spectacle of divisions, competitions and conflicts having immemorial roots. This legacy of the past, as some modern historians are inclined to characterize the phenomenon, was merely carried on to the present by a new vehicle termed euphemistically, and erroneously by the educated classes as nationalism. Old rivalries were assigned new nomenclatures while competitions and collaborations of the modern world merely switched on the traditional channels of social communications. As a result, it was vouched that the country was distinguished by the absence of horizontal loyalties and rendered conspicuous by the presence of competitive vertical allegiances. Thus the administrators in India, their spokesmen in the *Fortnightly Review* and *The Times*, as well as their present-day apologists agreed that the idioms and ideologies of modern nationalism should be dismissed as superficial veneers adopted for the sake of convenience by 'modern elite groups' still seeking to pursue the threads of traditional social rivalries.[123] The Brahmins, it was maintained, still constituted the overwhelming majority of the intelligentsia who cared not a whit for the voiceless millions. Nevertheless, this 'Brahmin democrat', wrote Bruce Mitford in 1919, anticipating the later day historians, was shrewd enough to see that the voiceless millions, organized as mobs, might 'serve his purpose admirably'. They could give force and volume to his windy oration.[124]

One-fifth of humanity, the imperialists swaggered, lived here and the British could not have held the country for even a day unless ninety-nine per cent of the people were stirred by them. The nationalist agitation, it was maintained, was carefully manipulated by that one per cent which was far from united. Education in India, Chirol elucidated, might have modified the historical divisions but it seldom obliterated the 'peculiar idiosyncracies' of the different races. The 'proud and chivalrous clans of Rajasthan', it was pointed out, differed *toto caelo* from the 'emotional and supple Bengalees'; the 'astute, hardened Maratha' from the 'patiently plodding Tamil' and the 'fierce and warlike Pathan' from the 'simple-minded jungle folk of southern India'.[125] These differences, he maintained, were visible everywhere—in the local beliefs and customs, in literature and art, and in poetry and architecture. Besides, if one added to this, the vagaries of nature and the tyranny of warring tribes, dynasties and devastating armies, he held, one might comprehend the remarkable human inertia in India. This monotonous unfolding of Indian history explained, he asserted, how individual initiative had come to be paralysed and how a sense of utter helplessness and fatalism prodded people on to accept the caste system which offered at least an element of social protection in an atmosphere of changeless stability.[126]

A circumspect academic viewed the situation in 1940 in a confidential memorandum written for the Government of India: 'We have therefore to face the fact that India is not only one society with diverse. . . political manifestations; nor it is one society with certain deep rooted economic class interests, it is a group of societies, rarely geographically distinguished, but more often superimposed one upon another, or existing side by side. Each has its special attitude to life, which is the basis of each one's scale of individual and social values, each regards its own attitude to life as something upon which it will accept no dictation and brook no interference; and each is therefore willing to accept all-India majority decisions only with large reservations. . . .'[127]

Even Islam with its uncompromising monotheism, Chirol contended, made only a marginal impact on Hinduism. As a political force, it was concluded, Islam had already become moribund and it was generally held in official circles that it owed its political existence largely to the British rulers who had resisted the political revival of Hinduism and had ever since held the balance even between all creeds and communities. In the antagonism between the two religions, it was argued, the deepest chasm in Indian society ought to be located and nursed. This fundamental difference between the two communities had to be sustained and an institutional framework was devised in order to stir up and, if necessary, convulse their ancient rivalries. A learned historian lamented that Akbar had successfully pulverized political Islam. He felt the need to rejuvenate it once again.[128] Both Valentine Chirol and E.M. Forster, men of different vintage, derided and scoffed at Akbar's attempt to reconcile Hinduism and Islam by fusing the higher 'philosophical elements of these religions into a new unitarian faith'. Akbar's policy of *sul-e-kul* and his institution of *Tauhid-e-illahi* were decried as futile political gestures. Forster's Aziz was a nationalist and a rational Muslim. When asked if Akbar's experiment was on the right lines, he demurred. Indian society, he declared, was not as simple as it had been made out to be. Its contradictions were far too complex to be glossed over by an arbitrary prescription from above.[129]

In more than one sense, it was believed that an encounter between the East and the West was destined to end in disaster. The transformation of

Abdul Karim in *Indian Dust* may be presented to illustrate the point. Coming from a society which judged thought by its 'coherence with authority' and valued life for 'its consistence with custom' and its abnegation, Abdul in Oxford was swept off his feet by the sudden wave of doubts and criticisms. Self-reliance, self-realization, emancipation, broadening the mind from tradition and rationalism were the values of the West. For Abdul and 'the young Muslim India', Oxford epitomised these virtues and qualities. As a consequence, Abdul Karim and many others found themselves misfits in their own community. They were restless and discontented. They appreciated the concept of private property, law, impartial administration, encouragement and reward. But they were at a loss to harmonize their thoughts with the demands of traditional society. This uneasiness grew into a morbid obsession to shake off the inhibiting umbilical cord of tradition. Abdul Karim's body began to show the resultant strain and his face became worn and livid. Cut off from social realities, grateful for the blessings of the Raj and depressed by the sluggishness of his own society, Abdul Karim turned into a helpless neurotic preoccupied with the quiet courtesies of the East.[130]

It may not be inappropriate here to draw the readers' mind to the remarkable tenacity of imperial perceptions which, in due course, skilfully accommodated the social, political and economic changes in Indian life and the responsive attitudes of the Indian people to the rational impulses from within. A learned commission under Professor A.D. Lindsay, master at Balliol College, Oxford, reporting on Christian higher education in India affirmed this phenomenon in 1931.[131] It maintained that although a ferment was in process within Hinduism, Vedantic philosophy still retained its control and moulded consciously or unconsciously the fundamental attitudes of a vast majority of Hindus. Politics, it contended, with its contentions, filled the air with clamour; patriotic passion swayed the life of many;superficial secularism was rampant and the higher aims of social service were being superimposed on an amoral individualism of Hinduism. These changes had been so radical, so vast and so rapid, it exclaimed, that it appeared that one faced an entirely new country. But these impulses from within were dismissed as 'the outward polish of life'.[132]

Indian nationalism, it was presumed, could not but relate itself to what was so central in India, the religion of the people. As a result, it produced primarily a return to orthodoxy which, in its turn, quickened ancient rivalries and flamed up dying religious passions. Edmund Candler and many other observers would have agreed with this assessment. Candler deprecated that a graduate of the Calcutta university was ever ready to exculpate and recommend the law of karma on the basis of genetics and heredity and the *sankhya* philosophy by a reference to the theory of evolution and yet he would not budge from the laws of Manu. Those who professed this new synthetic logic were, Candler taunted, more than hypocrites. The trite and dull explanations of modern Hinduism, if taken seriously, Candler observed, would be devastating in their effect on its own mystique. 'The terrific arm of *Shiva* would have fallen limp, the *Trimurti* become impotent and dishonoured and the effulgence of *Brahma's* God-head dimmed!'[133]

The ascendancy of a superficial secularism, typified in the Nehru plan for an Indian constitution and in the personality of the Indian leader, Jawaharlal Nehru, the Lindsay Commission declared, breathed new life into the spirit of easy accommodation of a pantheistic attitude blurring distinctions between truth and untruth and between right and wrong. This had sapped the moral strength of India through the ages, wrote the Lindsay Commission, and it continued to exercise its enervating influence. It quenched the spirit of free enquiry and 'lulled people into a slothful contentment with things as they were'.[134] With regard to the various efforts by eminent Indians to recondition Hinduism, two superficial motives were discerned. The first was the desire to give Hinduism a place in the modern world of activity and competition and the other was to render it respectable before a Western audience. Thus although the *Gita* with its call for action became a breviary of inspiration to Bal Gangadhar Tilak, Mohandas Karamchand Gandhi, Aurobindo Ghosh, Swami Vivekananda and Dayanand Saraswati, the Lindsay Commission opined that the outcome was warped, desultory and perfunctory. An apathetical demeanour in the face of a much-trumpeted unreal world, the Commission noted, reflected the indifference to the problems of life which were projected as illusion and the desire to fly from reality rather than to come to terms with it, formed the background of Indian initiatives.[135]

There had been, it conceded, some laudable attempts on the part of saints, philosophers and reformers 'to place Vedanta on horseback'. The Lindsay Commission, however, unanimously concluded that Vedanta, in that awkward position, occupied 'an uneasy seat', 'The dominant figure in the Indian landscape', the Commission pronounced, 'is still the Hindu ascetic and sceptic sitting by the Jumna's bank watching the phantasmagoria of existence with indifference mingled with contempt'.[136] The general flow of life and its orderings, the Commission noted, were still believed to be determined by forces with which one could have no relationship save that of submission. 'India is too old to resent us'. There was a familiar ring in the exasperation of Candler. 'Yet who can doubt that she will survive us? The secret of her permanence lies, I think, in her passivity and power to assimilate. The faith that will not fight cannot yield'.[137]

The city of Benaras was frequently upheld as representing the incongruity of this intriguing development. Eternal India persisted there with more ardour and enthusiasm than anywhere else despite the definite assault of Western science. The economic thought and practice, 'of which Adam Smith was the philosopher and James Watt was the exponent' co-existed in the surrounding panorama of Hinduism 'whose philosophical basis could only be the Vedanta'. The insolence and defiance of a superstitious Hinduism amazed the learned Commission. Hinduism at Benaras, the Lindsay Commission reported, still continued to unfold itself, unheeding a Muslim emperor's opposition, quite oblivious of the purifying and uplifting efforts of the Buddhist monastery of a neighbouring Sarnath and in sheer indifference to the challenge of a Western and Christian civilization symbolized by the steel bridge.[138] Although the alien forces, of which the railway was a manifestation, had been destroying the 'material foundations' of a village society 'of which Hinduism is the religion', the Commission was far from satisfied. Christianity, and along with it, Western civilization, the Lindsay Commission lamented, found Hinduism so firmly entrenched in the Indian ethos that they could only touch it marginally. The future seemed uncertain and this uncertainty released a feeling of melancholic frustration which, in turn, reinforced the claims of righteousness and dressed imperialism with a touch-me-not aloofness.[139]

Aldous Huxley had voiced a similar apprehension and had been quite harried by the prospect of an Indian democracy. 'Transplant a few medieval cardinals and dukes across the centuries into modern Europe', Huxley delighted himself in his singularly colourful metaphor, 'you might convince them that democracy was a good thing, but you could hardly expect them to forget from one day to the next their prejudices about villains and burgesses and their conviction of their own inherent nobility'.[140] Though it was an apt description of the incongruous growth of an institution in a hostile historical environment, Huxley was inclined to apply his model to India quite unmindful of the developments since the much applauded British 'Utilitarians' in India. What is intriguing is that he would have liked to see his model stretched appropriately in order to bring it on par with certain inconvenient Indian realities. Any indigenous government under Swaraj, he was keen to argue, would necessarily be in the nature of a despotic oligarchy.[141]

The problem was viewed in no less radiant terms by the *Nineteenth Century*. India, it was prognosticated, was not yet ready for democracy. She was like 'a garment woven in many colours; caste and religion are still its very warp and woof. The attempt to force the material into a new shape, designed on a western pattern, is likely to leave it a thing of shreds and patches'.[142] The writer reiterated that a natural growth was essential for an organic democracy. Popular institutions could not be grafted on to an alien constitution. 'Let us avoid', he cautioned, 'binding the feet of the infant legislator in India, like those of the girl-children of China'.[143] To the Western mind territorial representation seemed logical; but the Indian mind, it was asserted, was not troubled merely by logic. Its social and religious idiosyncracies asked for the natural development of institutions reflecting the varied texture of every gradation of caste, creed, colour and language. From a purely imperial point of view, this was a crucial factor because the proposed political transition under these conditions would necessarily be a prolonged, if not a permanent, affair and British predominance would be its decisive imperative. It was a land whose millions displayed the whole range of human passions—the vices, virtues, mental imperfections, physical qualities, secret hates, noble gestures, regrettable atavisms and intellectual gifts. 'How can we expect this conglomerate mass of humanity, this mosaic of customs, languages and beliefs', Dekobra voiced a universal imperial resolution, 'to have a common outlook, a civic unity, the preface of an approaching nationalism?' The 'incredible fanaticism of India' he added, rendered such a political synthesis illusory and 'all benevolent neutrality of antagonistic believers absolutely out of question'.[144]

Percival Spear added in his memorandum of 1940 (amidst a much talked-about constitutional concoction) that the application of a 'unitary democratic theory'[145] to India with a parliamentary system as its expression was not possible and hence inadmissible. The most significant feature of the 'budding democracy of India', Spear argued, 'was an unwillingness to accept the decisions of majority'. One was tempted, he cautioned, to explain it away as a mere temporary phenomenon resulting from the expediency of transplanting 'an authoritarian tradition into democratic soil'.[146] But during the twenty years of democratic practice, Spear emphasized, the pressure of tradition showed little signs of erosion. On the contrary, it had increased. 'The Indian democrat', Spear put it, 'like the Irishman, is apt to be against everyone, including himself'.[147] It was not a question of lack of capacity for democratic technique or any lack of experience. It was more a problem of the reality of the situation where Western political democratic theory could not be fruitfully applied. The political theories of both Mill and Rousseau, the primary educators of India, assumed a basic unity of outlook and 'fundamental belief' amongst the citizens of a democracy. In fact, Spear argued, the fundamental dissenters had been evicted from the body politic by Rousseau through a social contract thus making it homogeneous with differences only of judgement rather than of principle. Since the Lucknow Pact of 1916, the Indian National Congress had taken for granted that a similar unity would be achieved in India, transcending racial and religious considerations. Such hopes were turned illusory but the recognition of the illusion had not been openly avowed. The result of a forced adoption of a parliamentary system would be, he conjectured, to put power into the hands not of a majority of the whole society produced by a combination of interests and the working of reason, but into the hands of the majority societies. Even a marginal adjustment of the problem would not have solved the crisis. 'In such circumstances a part of the minority in one part of the country might get a share of the "official meal", Spear argued, 'but a very large minority elsewhere are sure to go hungry'.[148] The solution, according to this expert on India, should have been sought in a confederation of castes, tribes and cultural groups through the system of traditional Panchayat. The object ought to be an oligarchic rule with a durbar system supported by an authoritarian viceroy appearing from time to time either 'as a benevolent Vishnu' or as 'a destructive Shiva'. Spear was convinced that the balance was to be held , so that the opposing interests might in time come into some sort of harmonious cooperation. It could only be done, he held, by the continued rule of the Empire which, by virtue of its attitude of detachment, 'has given proof of its capacity for the task'. To surrender at that stage of India's development, the destinies of India's millions to the hands of a few urban intelligentsia, 'would be a gross betrayal of trust'.[149]

If Spear provided the philosophical hypothesis for the retention of British rule in India despite the ascendancy of an uncompromising nationalism, Maurice Gwyer, the chief justice, sought to work out an institutional frame for that political consensus.[150] The distinct tendencies which had emerged in India since the outbreak of the Second World War formed the basis of Gwyer's prescription. He discerned a struggle for power between groups as the dominant feature of the new phase. The brief tenure of popular government in seven provinces exemplified, he argued, that there was no 'unified political entity' in India qualified to hold power in case a complete transfer of authority was contemplated. The Congress

Party, he wrote in agreement with many others, was essentially Hindu and was locked-up in a life-and-death struggle with the Muslim League, the principal organization of the large Muslim minority.[151] Other minority groups had their own ideas regarding the future government of the country. In the absence of any agreement about the shape of things to come, Maurice Gwyer concluded that there was no political party or a combination of political parties which could claim with authority that it represented India. As an antidote to the remarkable diversity of the demands and the possibility of disintegration of the country, Maurice Gwyer urged that the Indians ought to make an earnest attempt to find a rational solution to their domestic problems so that the British could relinquish control to an Indian political authority which had the power to accept it. The Muslim apprehension that democratic rule would mean a Hindu Raj was a grave predicament, Gwyer argued, while the insistence of the Congress that the Muslim fears were artificial figments was merely a self-satisfying chimera. As a constructive approach, Maurice Gwyer proposed, the political scientists should recognize that the British system with all its merits might not necessarily be *comme il faut* in India and would not be gracefully accepted by a sizeable minority. The solution ought to be attained, he gave his considered opinion, in a statutory coalition executive responsive to public but not accountable to the party in majority in the legislature. This might lead to a rearrangement of governments and areas of the country including a realignment of native states with the Indian constitution. This meant that the 'undiluted nationalism' and 'political emotionalism' of the Congress ought to be supplanted by a rational approach with the primacy of viceregal veto as the crucial monitor of the whole system.[152] This was the political articulation in constitutional terms of Spear's enigmatic formulation of a 'destructive' Shiva and a 'constructive' Vishnu rolled into an ultimate and irrevocable authority playing the decisive mediatory role.

It is small wonder that Katherine Mayo ingeniously appended Indian nationalism with the superstitions of a ritualistic Hinduism and fused them into a powerful anti-Indian demonstration.[153] The life of the village of Sita in 'The Widow' was 'pre-ordained in immemorial law' which was ostensibly amoral but essentially very cruel. So was that of Ram Singh of Maud Diver's 'The God of the East'. Desert-born and desert-bred, the silence and lifelessness of Ram Singh's surroundings did not oppress him. He was completely absorbed, we are told, 'in the secret communions of his soul with the great unknown Soul of Things', to one whose countless manifestations 'the grotesque red shrine by the well' was dedicated.[154] An air of dignity, a stoic acceptance of life's vulgar inevitables and a

Brahminical self-righteousness were carefully manipulated by Maud Diver as she underlined a religious horror that embraced every aspect of Hindu life including petty financial transactions. The Hindu love for the horrible and the grim found its modern expression, we were informed, on the streets of Calcutta, not far from the village of Sita, where 'secret plotters and killers vied with open assassins who opposed the will of the new-made saint Gandhi'. No one was spared as Katherine Mayo raised her accusing finger at the Indian nationalists who were alleged to have terrorized in the name of Gandhi's curse the inoffensive widow to put an end to her own tragic life![155]

In 'The Centipede' by Alice Perrin, the ayah's Indian cure for fever caused death but the ayah remained undaunted. The Indian mind, the imperial refrain underlined, was confident and arrogant even in its depressing superstitions and irrationality.[156] Commending the work of Mayo, Claud H. Hill, an eminent civil servant, argued that consciously or unconsciously the British in India had tacitly acquiesced in the policy of leaving intact the social custom of the country with the firm conviction that time, education and contact with Western civilization would generate the self-consciousness of the people. Katherine Mayo's *Mother India*, he wrote, tore apart the veil 'behind which we have all, perhaps too silently, been carrying on our day-to-day work; and I believe that the moment she has chosen for her revelation is a most happy one'.[157] Even a temperate Edward Thompson thought it necessary to applaud Mayo publicly for her remarkable insight on the Indian realities and for her daring expose of the flim-flam and prevarications of the Mahatma.[158]

The impact of Katherine Mayo was more than ephemeral. She rendered the racial arrogance of the exclusive clubs into a self-righteous assertion. A reviewer in the left wing journal the *New Statesman* acclaimed Katherine Mayo who, it was maintained, in her *Mother India* forced upon the British power-elite a 'series of interrogatives'. 'Ought we to leave India? But how can we?', the bewildered reviewer soliloquized, 'if we withdraw our army all the failed B.As. of the Nationalist agitation would have their throats cut within a week or so. If there were no British Tommies in Lucknow, Calcutta and Benaras to hold the ring for the rhetoric of the Babus they could not exist'.[159] There was a general agreement on the issue that there was no rational ground for the development of democracy in India and that there was little likelihood that one could discover any method by which a stable government could be established upon 'any other foundation than of British bayonets'. All their 'sub-human civilisation', 'repulsive personal habits', 'amazing egocentric mania' and 'unparalleled sexual degradation' were exposed by Katherine Mayo and in the process she reduced 'India's claims for Swaraj to sheer nonsense' and 'the will to grant it' in some quarters to 'almost a crime'.[160] An uncompromising animosity was thus craftily embroidered into a delicate pattern of pseudo-psychology much to the approval of Claud Hill and Edward Thompson alike: 'Bengal is the seat of bitterest political unrest—the producer of India's main crop of anarchists, bomb-throwers and assassins. Bengal is also among the most sexually exaggerated regions of India; and medical and police authorities in any country observe the link between that quality and "queer" criminal minds—the exhaustion of normal avenues of excitement creating a thirst and a search in the abnormal for gratification.'[161]

Katherine Mayo set the trend for a new branch of literature whose preoccupation was to stretch the morbidity of Hindu customs, superstitions and rituals to a point of absurdity and invest it with a unique spiritual inhumanity. W.A. Frazer's *Caste* was one of them.[162]The locale was Maharashtra where Scindia Holkar and Bhonsle had been plotting the overthrow of the British and the Chitpawan Brahmins had been praying to the black goddess for the destruction of the hated whites while a pathetic Peshwa helplessly looked on. Captain Barlow and Bootea, a local girl, had been in love and desired to go for a formal conjugal unity only to be foiled by the Hindu orthodoxy. Swami Sarasvati, 'a fine specimen of true Brahmin', tall, with a wide forehead and expressive eyes, a symbol of piety and abnegation, declared that the woman was already dead in the company of a white man and that if Captain Barlow wanted to take her to his people it would mean breeding hatred in the hearts of the Hindus and an open rebellion against the government. She was to ensure, he added, a place for herself on the *Kailash* which implied, as the Captain knew fairly well, a human sacrifice. To Barlow the compelling voice of the Brahmin signified the mad infatuation of a fanatic people prostrating before false gods, ugly idols and a depraved materialism. As the spiritual murder was conducted with all its ritualistic mumbo-jumbo, Captain Barlow, dressed as a Hindu, lay prone on his face sobbing and cursing himself for a sin that was not his. The scientific and Christian West, Frazer underwrote, was incompatible with a 'barbarous' and 'fanatic' Hinduism even if the West made the necessary adjustments and carried out effective surgery in its own value system in order to meet the East on its own terms.[163]

Kate of Kipling's *The Naulakha* had a lot of pluck and capacity for silent endeavour and was animated by an intense desire to help the Indian women out of their eternal subjection. She was, however, to discover before long that she had stepped into a land where it was always twilight—a labyrinth of passages, courtyards, stairs and hidden ways, all overflowing with veiled women who peered at her and laughed behind her back. It was impossible that she would ever know the smallest part of this 'vast warren'. The uncanny fear of an enigmatic India left behind a feeling of defeat, remorse and torture on her hyper-sensitive mind.[164]

A long stay in India, it was apprehended, would inevitably distort the perspective of even the best representative of a pure race. George Orwell puts it succinctly in his 'Shooting an Elephant': either as the stern teacher of a faceless crowd or as a sensitive Briton living up to the expectations of the primitive people, Englishmen were apt to imbibe in their distant outposts the savage instinct of the subjects. One wonders at the strange vintage of Orwell's much-trumpeted anti-imperialism: 'I am struck between my hatred of the empire I served and my rage against the evil-spirited little beasts who tried to make my job impossible. With one part of my mind I thought of the British Raj as an unbreakable tyranny. . . with another part I thought that the greatest joy in the world would be to drive a bayonet in a Buddhist priest's guts'.[165] Is it an overstatement by a patriotic Socialist converted by the inexorable logic of circumstances into a racist pamphleteer ? An ultra-nationalist, an intense admirer of British distinctiveness and virtues, Orwell sought to rediscover the English society from an imperial outpost. A member of the ruling class, he repudiated imperial inheritance and moved away towards an amorphous version of socialism. But he associated class with social snobbery and affiliated imperialism with the bad guys temporarily in charge of an honest and sturdy British family. Neither capitalism nor imperialism was comprehended by him as a system.[166] The baleful paradox is that although Orwell, like many others, was convinced that the British Empire was on its death-bed, he was equally confident that 'it is good deal better than the younger empires that are going to supplant it'.[167]

In 'The Rise of Ram Din' the Indian *khansama* was greedy for baksheesh. But, in due course, he acquired more wealth than he had ever desired. His power increased in direct proportion to the ascendancy of his master's cruelty and cowardice.[168] In Christine Weston's 'A Game of Helma' the condescending European adventurer of Aligarh, 'rude, sarcastic, brilliant and witty' in defeat and 'cool and lordly' in triumph could never reconcile himself to the reality that an Englishman could be defeated in a game of chess by a member of the subject race however highly placed he might be.[169]

Leonard Woolf, a favoured member of the Bloomsbury Group, posed the dilemma of the British in India and expressed it through a discourse between a Liberal and a Conservative Englishman both having extensive Indian experience.[170] The Liberal maintained that one could impose the values of Western civilization upon an Eastern people—not 'without a little disturbance' and the turbulence was a good sign embodying the spirit of 'an awakening among the people'. Such agitations, he cautioned nevertheless, should not be controlled by the extremists. The Conservative picked up the thread and exposed the shaky foundation of the former's logic. 'There's too much liberalism in the East, too much namby-pamby-ism. It is all right here, of course, but it's not suited to the East. They want a strong hand. After all they owe us something; we aren't going to take all the kicks and leave them all the half-pence. Rule'em, I say, rule'em, if you're going to rule'em. Look after'em of course; give'em schools, if they want education—schools, hospitals, roads and railways. Stamp out the plague, fever and famine. But let them know you are top dog. That's the way to run an Eastern country. I am a white man, you're black; I'll treat you well, give you courts and justice, but I'm the superior race, I'm master race'.[171] Both the Liberal and the Conservative agreed that 'all the ryots, vakils and students running up the ladder of European civilisation would not work the system'. Leonard Woolf, despite his pronounced sympathy for a liberal society in India, almost echoed Orwell: 'The result is—instead of getting hold of the East, it's the East which gets hold of you'.[172]

Invariably there was the familiar story of a tragic metamorphosis. In Ganpat's *The Speakers in Silence*,[173] the British medical doctor became a reluctant convert to the theory of evil spirit propounded dextrously both by a Sunni mulla, Badr Din and a Dogra Brahmin, Bakshi Ram. His faith in the existence of an utterly unknown power, 'fomenting revolution here and reaction there, nationalism in Egypt and internationalism in Berlin, stirring labour in Europe and capital in America, playing always on mob psychology as a musician might play on an instrument,' had been consolidated over the years. The doctor was aware that unconsciously he had been caught up by Badr Din's evil wind.[174] But this distortion, as Orwell seems to argue, was a natural phenomenon—a typical case of morbid self-torture in an alien land.[175] When the white man turned a tyrant, as Orwell put it, he was torn between his battered conscience and the reality of the Empire and the latter tilted the balance of his opinion in its favour. The white man destroyed his own freedom. 'He becomes a sort of hollow dummy, the conventionalised figure of a sahib. . . . He wears a mask and he grows to fit it'.[176] Orwell hid the contorted face of imperial Britain behind a synthetic moral fog. In this he was in the enviable company of the leading luminaries of the Empire who would have fought for the king and the Empire to the hilt if only to prove an essential point that distinguished the imperial sensibility: A white man must not be frightened in the presence of a subject race. He must assume the role of a stern imperial James Bond who, at times, might be encouraged to ruminate his exploits in the Empire with a special love for India.

Even Leo Myer's tetralogy, *The Near and the Far*[177] (composed during the high noon of Fascism in Europe) where the action is placed in the time of Akbar and the characters are made to illustrate certain illusions and delusions that beset the human mind and adjudicate the conflicting claims of Buddhism, Christianity, Hinduism and other creeds, betrays a similar prejudice despite the timeless quality of the work. According to the author, the only person drawn with any regard to historical truth is the Emperor. It is the portrayal of a mysterious and gigantic figure of the unlettered Mughal ruler who desired to be revered as God. The gradual evolution of Akbar's personality in the work is remarkably impressive. He whets the reader's ever-growing curiosity. But when the reader gets the full view of the Emperor he is disappointed by the sight of a royal buffoon. Mobarak—a character in this work, certainly inspired by Abul Fazl, was a mystic. He had envisioned the unification of temporal and spiritual powers. His mind had been dazzled by the splendours of Byzantine sacerdotalism at the height of its glory. He was authoritarian and his ideals constituted a rigid hierarchy. He saw in the caste system and in the privileged position of the Brahmins a machinery ready at hand and in the person of the emperor a man with prestige, power and ambition required to give a concrete shape to his fantasy. What was considered unique in the whole panorama was that so long as Akbar occupied the imperial throne he was a 'figure of Destiny brooding predestination' as 'millions of lesser creatures helplessly danced at his feet. . . .'[178] Perhaps, the central theme is Raja Amar's resolution to renounce his status and become a monk. Aloofness from humanity, a search for serenity in the bleakness of the mountains and the mysterious contentment of the lonely individual in the *Pool of Vishnu* typified in imperial sensibility the most attractive quality of eternal India, Myer, a near Communist, belonged, so far as the Indian perception was concerned, in the same lineage as Kipling and Forster.[179]

John Eyton added force and vigour to Kipling's image of India. Introducing his compilation of short stories, he wrote with remarkable candour: . . . If you would gather pictures of a land that never changes—Where Brahmans, though three thousand years have passed, are Brahmans still, From sunny Coromandel coast into the northern ranges—Then come as I would guide you, and see history from a hill.[180] Jackson, an incorrigible drifter, was John Eyton's replica of Kipling's Strickland. Despite his love for India and his identification with the life of her million mendicants, Jackson had disregarded hatred of the English and their ways that had become a common theme in the bazaar. But when a babu agitator, Gopi Nath, raised a frenzied crowd to destroy the club, the visible embodiment of the sircar bahadur, the dancing fakir led the mob towards the treasury away from the club. He fell as an isolated and nameless hero in the service of the Empire.[181] The Raj had, Eyton affirmed, a permanent place in the confidence, loyalty and support of India's common men. It was an invaluable asset of the Indian Empire and was typified by Tek Chand with his wooden leg, his distinguished service medal and the hands of the daughter of Perbhoo Diyal.[182] His loyalty was juxtaposed to the inhumanity of the babu contractor, Debi Dutta, to whom the old Dom was no more than an animal asking for nothing, hoping for nothing and accepting fate without a murmur.[183] Whether in *Expectancy, Jungle-born, The Dancing Fakir,* or *Diffidence* the gifted writer grafted onto his love for India and his sympathy for its folks an abiding faith in the righteousness of the British cause and its rational character, overshadowing the clamours of the noisy nationalists.[184]

To the imperialist ideologues, India was incorrigible. This race, it became axiomatic in imperial hypotheses, was miserably inept to emulate the scientific attitudes of the West. Set against the period of the transfer of power in 1947, Hallam Tennyson, a descendant of the poet, underlined in her *The Dark Goddess*[185] the hollowness of India's future promise and the futility of British experiments on the Indian mind: 'We copy your civilisation, you see', Robbi Das Gupta of Sen Street of Calcutta, an average educated Indian, confided to Joan Raydon, a dynamic young English woman who believed it her duty to bring notions of sanity and sanitation to the Indian masses, 'but we don't understand it. We pull your nice new machinery to pieces and leave the bits out in the fields to rot. We learn democracy and forget all our undemocratic practices. . . . Yes, Miss Joan, we turn India into a sewage farm. Not one nice hygienic English sewage farm where children can be sailing model yachts, but a stinking, crawling, gaping pit of horror. . . .'[186]

At times, there was an element of optimism which was reflected in official verdicts. It appeared to some that the energetic measures adopted by the Government would offer a brighter future to the fascinating country. It was promptly added, to introduce circumspection and doubt in the analysis, that the sufferings of the lowest classes in India were attributable to causes beyond the power of any government to prevent.[187] It was not reasonable to expect, J.D. Rees added with firm conviction in the righteousness of the British cause in India, that the cosmic, climatic, ethnic and economic conditions of Asia would undergo a radical change, because so huge a portion of her sacred soil had fallen under the rule of Britain. Besides, Indian concepts and values were unique and one should not attempt to apply European standards to a country where wholly different customs prevailed.[188]

There were also many who were upset by the fact that the country had been suffering from abject poverty despite British rule. They considered it a disgrace to the British Empire that there should be any large body of citizens who were continually hungry. It was conceded that the Indian gentlemen were equal in intelligence and administrative competence to the Englishmen and, therefore, seek, though somewhat impetuously, political independence. Arnold Lupton in his *Happy India*, a reasoned rebuttal of William Digby's *Prosperous British India*,[189] found the roots of India's poverty and misery in the apathy of its callous upper castes and their peculiar social attitudes. Lupton lambasted the Hindu social system and its self-centredness. The poor peasant, he lamented, lived in a mud house with a roof of stick and palm leaves, read no newspaper, went for no entertainment and 'survived contentedly until starvation lays him on his back'. Englishmen, Lupton bemoaned, could teach but if only the Indians would care to learn![190] Explaining the poverty of India, Eric Musaprat adopted the airs of a pragmatic philosopher: 'Eastern materialism was unbelievably worse than any other in the world. And in general, through this moral crime of extreme materialism they are poverty-stricken. When people live directly for their senses and material satisfactions, then there will always be great poverty in the society in which they exist.'[191]

Some celebrated members of the exalted civil services experienced, though not very often, an insidious feeling of self-torture as they recounted the social insecurity of Britons in India on the one hand and the life of gross humiliation led by educated Indians on the other. The balance sheet of British rule was, however, drawn up with a promising note. One of them announced: 'I am proud that our country should have been chosen by fate, nature, God or whatever you call it, to clear up the debris of the Mogul Empire and to unlock for India the treasures of Western thought. I think on the whole we were worthy of it'.[192] The date of this self-righteous exhilaration is not 1917 but 1943, when the memories of the movement of 1942 were still fresh. The author was neither a swashbuckling champion of the Raj nor a poet laureate of the Empire. He was the modest Penderel Moon known for his sympathies for a new India.

Dwelling on the position of India in the British educational system, the India League, in 1945, came to an unfaltering conclusion that the children of the British school system had been over the years taught on the assumption that since they lived in a country which had for centuries held a great empire under control, they were peculiarly fitted to rule. Although this did not manifest itself crudely in the same way as in the Nazi *Herrenvolk* teaching, it was almost as dangerous in the underlying acceptance without question of all the implications of such a position. The teacher's committee of the League noted that although the British children had been encouraged to appreciate and assess the contribution of countries other than Great Britain to world civilization, the curriculum was judiciously selective and misleading. The countries which were covered by the enquiry of the students fell into two categories: those which had contributed to the development of Christianity and to Western civilization in general and those which were fighting on the side of the allies in the Second World War including the U.S.A. and the U.S.S.R. Most serious gaps occurred in the case of Japan, China and the Islamic countries while India, the brightest gem in the British crown, witnessed a remarkable distortion. Thus while the caste system, child marriage and Sati as reprehensible institutions were heavily underlined, the absorptive capacity of Hinduism, the general attitude of tolerance, the role of Buddha, Ashoka, and Akbar, the development of a composite culture, the historic roles of the Sufi and the Bhakti movements were either overlooked or pushed into a twilight of hazy information. Even the resurgence of India in the nineteenth and twentieth centuries was glossed over and the name of Rabindranath Tagore did not figure in the school textbooks although the works of American writers like Longfellow and Whitman found adequate representation and the work of Christian missionaries in India was emphasized on a disproportionate scale. The civilizing mission of Britain in India continued to dominate the minds of both the teachers and the students. In contrast, India's contribution in the spheres of art, literature, science, and politics as also its nationalist movement remained a well-guarded secret from the average Briton.[193]

There was, of course, much that was fascinating and innocent in India that rendered her attraction all the more seductive. The Indians, it was believed, were accustomed to doing many things that no Englishman would have dreamt of doing.[194] That Dewan Sir Puran Dass KCIE had renounced positions, palace and power and taken up the begging-bowl and robes of a sanyasi was considered extraordinary.[195] India, it was stressed, had no demands, the Indians had simple habits and so long as there was a 'morsel to divide in India, neither priest nor beggar starves'. There was no dearth of this remarkable idealization of poverty which simplified the obligation of the rulers. It was noted with much fanfare that the life in poverty, as only the Indians could lead, was one that was worth living. Like many others, Puran Bhagat renounced life when he was still alive in search of the eternity beyond worldly fame, comforts and pleasures and amidst the filth of India's towns and rivers, along the dusty roads and in the unknown villages of the Himalayas. Why should not Gandhi, the Mahatma, it was sincerely felt by some, leave the murky Indian politics to the care of lesser men and follow the footprints of Puran Bhagat to the peace and harmony of the Himalayas?[196]

For the ideologues of the Raj, the human race was divided into two categories: that of the poor of the black and brown colonies and that of the rich which was restricted to a small white European stock. It was believed that in both these areas, men might attain salvation—but by different means. The road to freedom opened to the wretched colonies was conditioned by the nature of their subjugation to the white race. It was to traverse through a world of humility, patience and submission—a long and tedious journey to be undertaken with faith, conviction and cheerfulness. The Empire-builders, on the other hand, were to sanctify their superior ability, authority and honour by infinite mercy, oblivious of the fact that room for misunderstanding was spacious and the result of their munificence was sure to meet the 'ungratefulness of the conquered races'.[197] Each was equally God's creation and they were made for each other. This provided the essential natural balance, it was argued, in a world of unequal societies which were otherwise destined to confront each other. Thus the Indians ought to be forced, if necessary, to discern and acknowledge their cultural, social, religious and economic inferiority and trace their restrictive frontiers of life. The information industry of imperial scholarship was sustained to provide the basis of this supplicant and subordinate relationship. Once conscious of their status, as ordained by the law of creation, the lesser breeds should voluntarily opt for a prolonged period of apprenticeship. As Edmund W. Said has conceptualized, the idea of 'Orientalism' has come to fashion an academic tradition.[198] It has become a positive doctrine and created closely knit idioms. India figures predominantly in the whole process. By its very definition, the perception inherent in Orientalism is racist, imperialist and ethnocentric. It consists of a 'mobile army of metaphors, metonyms and anthropomorphisms'.[199] It is, in short, a sum of human relations, which have been enhanced, transposed and embellished poetically and rhetorically. After long use it seems obligatory to people. Thus truths have given way to illusions which saturated imperial perceptions. When Curzon declared that 'east is a University in which scholars never take a degree' he meant, among other things, Edmund W. Said aptly put it, that East in general and India in particular required European presence for ever and that the relationship between the two was destined to be static and not reciprocal. The white man's burden was thus placed even theoretically on force and it was to be buttressed by a constant exhibition of physical might. It was a sentiment, an attitude, a policy and a reality. The white man, as a consequence, was never to meet the East on equal terms. Even E.M. Forster admits it with the vexed feelings of a defeated Liberal. The self-complacent virtuosity of imperial culture betrayed both an artistic arrogance as well as an applause-seeking vanity. It was marked by fallacious limitations and 'slavish repetitions of old canons'.[200] It was far removed from human warmth and sentiments. It became more often than not a set of professionalized rhetorics. Ideology enlisted the arts in its service and presented a prolix unreality; and its hollow homily became imperial ideology objectified. It constituted a unique manifesto of imperial consciousness and as the 'content' got lost in the preponderance of 'form', realities were obscured by a remarkable lack of confidence.

3

Uncomfortable Claims : Untenable Positions

The overpowering atmosphere of a cantonment was ubiquitous in official India. This was, it was believed, but a natural product of the interaction between a rational Western mind and the lurid customs of a spooky land full of snakes, cholera, superstitions and babus. The civil lines, the cantonment, the sadr and, along with it, a lalbazaar provided the physical expression of an overbearing Raj on the outskirts of an Indian city.[1] Of course, there was the inevitable buffer zone of 'fat Indians' as a reliable cushion.[2] While the 'hill stations' were acclaimed as an English spring superimposed on an Indian summer[3] and the select clubs fashioned an odd world of make-believe,[4] New Delhi epitomized an imperial fantasia complete with its majestic furniture placed on an imposing acropolis overlooking an applauding agora.[5] Only a handful of Englishmen did not take delight in the official atmosphere of Simla or New Delhi. Writing in 1928, Walter Roper Lawrence recollected that it was on the whole a happy and a healthy life. He relished its simplicity and social *politesse*. 'Everyone knew', he wrote, 'what his neighbour's salary was. . . . The youngest civilian knew that he might one day become a Lieutenant-Governor, or a member of the Council, and our charming and courteous Seniors always treated us as though they recognised this possibility'. It was, he recalled nostalgically, a society of young people.[6]

Samuel Sadoc made no bones about the social and sexual exclusiveness of British India.[7] In fact, he carefully drew the lines of argument that were advanced frequently to underline the claims of superiority of the ruling minority in India. Most of the Indian girls, he wrote, 'who marry Europeans spring from the lowest class of Indian society'. Dr Cuthbert gave vent to the experience of his race in India as he vouched that these women were mostly recruited from such menials as ayahs. It is equally true, he wrote, that no white man 'worth his salt would marry an Indian'. 'I do not deny the fact that some Indian girls', he added, 'think it a great cause for pride to marry a white man, and some educated Indian girls commit this folly. But who are the white men who marry them ? Mostly Tommies and such like riff-raff. Even these find to their cost that they have committed an error, and run away, leaving their black wives behind them to repent at leisure'.[8]

There was a curious and piquant sense of unreality in the life of that India. It was a promiscuous throng of horse carriages, turbaned chiefs, military uniforms, elaborate ceremonials, frock-coats, *khidmutgars* and subsequently, an impressive flock of native elite. It was a spectacle of stunning aloofness, awe-inspiring marchpasts and conspicuous bungalows. Its life was distinguished by gloomy forebodings, forced subordination, infectious suspicions, mysterious affectations and an uneasy secrecy.[9] It did not care to be acquainted with the inhabitants of the country. It was more than satisfied with the familiar prototypes of its own creation and its deep-seated prejudices. Whether in his camp parked in a dense forest or in the circuit house of an inland country district or in the cosy compartment of a transport train or at Landikotal, a lonely sentry-box on the Empire's rim, or on a deck-chair in the cool veranda flanked by the stretches of green, the imperial attributes of an Englishman had to be scrupulously maintained.

It might seem anomalous to an observer that there should have been an ardent desire in the heart of every Englishman in India to go one better than one's neighbour—to have better horses, smarter carriages, a larger house, a more expensive suit—especially when in most cases their income was known to the last rupee.[10] Then there was social snobbery. Paul Scott suggests that even this deformity in the British character was a product of the Raj. Miss Edwina Crane could not help noticing that only when the Nisbett-Smith family reached Bombay that the Major's wife gradually withdrew and by the time they reached the husband's station in the Punjab, Miss Crane was being treated 'not exactly like a servant but like a poor relation with whom the family had somehow got saddled. . . .'[11] She stood in a position far superior to that of any native servant but at the lowest rungs of the ladder of their own self-contained society. This attitude, she thought, conflicted with the claims of white supremacy and white solidarity. But despite irrational rivalry and snobbery there was a common bond cemented by a deep emotional vacuum and a sense of acute physical insecurity. The Englishmen enjoyed their privileges in India, relished that the *burra missisahib's burraness*— in other words, the imperial haughtiness was their sure and absolute protection against all kinds of danger from outside the charmed circle of privileges, dreaded their status of nobody at home, and mourned their lost glory in their retirement. And, yet they were equally convinced that their own land was the best land; that the fat babu with his carefully oiled and parted hair could not be mentioned in the same breath as an Englishman and that their daffodils and primroses were sweeter than the heavy-scented blossoms of the East. As Lutyens put it 'India turned every Englishman—Tory, ultra Tory conservative '.[12]

Insularity bred innocence which, in its turn, gave birth to complacency and arrogance. India became, as a consequence, an unknown country to the English inhabitants of Calcutta, Bombay, Madras and elsewhere. What was unknown, natural conservatism always condemned. 'The social ideals changed', Spear added, 'from a desire to live like a Nawab to a desire to make each settlement and cantonment down to the smallest station a replica of an English model'.[13]

Thus despite the fact that at places the Indian 'muddle' confused the symmetry of the civil lines, the 'efficiency' of the civil lines was superimposed on the Indian bazaar by means of a partial surgery. But by and large, the British community in India lived its own life, ran its own shops and newspapers, entertained itself at exclusive halls and concerts, admired or criticized itself on Chowringhee Road and Connaught Circus, congratulated itself at the official receptions at the government houses and the viceregal palace, exalted itself as the Imperial Orchestra played *Rule Brittania* on the Mall at Simla or titilated itself down memory lane as a certain Mr Cunningham performed *Othello* at the Gaiety Theatre.[14] 'The Brahmins', F. Yeats-Brown put it bluntly, 'made a circle within which they cooked their food. So did we. We were a caste, pariahs to them, princes in our own estimation'.[15] The compulsions of imperialism negated all passions for democratic equality or Christian egalitarianism. Imperialism, by virtue of its very nature, was insular, racist and arrogant.

The Englishman in India , Kipling wrote, was invariably a clever man and his onerous duty drew the best out of him. Naturally, even the silliest woman 'could manage a clever man' while it needed a 'clever woman to manage a fool'.[16] Kipling painted the profile of this special breed warily. A young lad, leading a sheltered life, came to India where he was deprived of the support of his parents and had no one to fall back upon in times of crisis. India was a slack country where all men, it was maintained, worked with imperfect instruments.[17] Even the British administrators were overwrought by its damp climate, scorching sun and general lethargy. Decadence was endemic in India where 'the sullen sun strikes down full on the bosom of the tortured town' and the Empire seemed almost crumbling beneath its hands.[18]

Despite the fierce environment, there was no scarcity of daring adventure, passionate rapture and lyrical romaunt. It consisted in hard work and steadfast application. Strickland or 'Estreakin Sahib',[19] for example, held fast to his theory that an administrator in India should try to know all about the country and its people. In him Kipling sought to offer the stereotype of a perfect British administrator in India. He was the only European in the entire country who could pass for a Hindu or a Muslim. He was feared and respected, it was added, by the natives from Ghar Khatri to the Jumma Masjid. He was supposed to have the power of invisibility and also possessed extensive executive control over many devils. He was, said Kipling (having a field day with mysterious India), initiated into the *Sat Bahi* at Allahabad, he knew the *Lizzard song* of the Sansis and the *Halli Hukk* dance, 'a religious can-can of a startling kind'. He had mastered the language of the *Changers,* had taken a Yusufzai horse-thief alone near Attock and conducted service at the border mosque in the manner of the Sunni mulla.[20] In short, an English official in India was expected to grasp her diabolical philosophies, appreciate her fiendish social institutions and identify the nuances of her semi-savage rituals. Strickland, the idealized Englishman in India, was versatile, paternalistic, authoritarian and a missionary; he was endowed with the attributes of a stern imperial Apollo. He represented a determined white man destined to subjugate the odd forces of nature and extend the Rule of Law of a Christian power over a semi-civilized mankind although in the process he was rendered somewhat eccentric by the impact of the divine obligation having made some suitable adjustments with Hindu spiritualism.[21] The idealized Englishman not only knew India, he knew it better than the Indians. Strickland reappears again in 1962 as Rodney Savage, 'the great grandson of the Deliverer' in John Masters' *To the Coral Strand.*[22]

Kim, on the other hand, was the pragmatic hero of British India. He was closer than Strickland to the realities of life.[23] Like T.D. Forsyth he adored the seductive mysteries of the Himalayas; like Munro, Elphinstone or Metcalfe he loved the simple Indian folk; like Francis Younghusband he was attracted by Buddhist mysticism; like Lord Ripon he condescended to patronize even a Bengali babu for his efficiency. But despite his knowledge of and proximity to the Indian way of life his lineage roped him off and he stood apart from the rest of India. He refused to succumb to the 'negative' and 'non-material' allure of an undefinable India. He did not accept the power of nothingness.[24] The 'malignant chuckle' from the 'formless jaw' of 'eternal India' appeared to him both innocent and horrible. He continued to serve the Raj as a sturdy soldier of the Great Game in Asia.[25]

Strickland and Kim provided the two distinct imperial stereotypes. But a continental Empire produced men of considerable diversity. They varied in terms of the qualities of their characters. There was, for example, Mr Strutt of the *Chronicle of Dustypore*[26] who, like Sydenham Clark or Michael O'Dwyer, was dignified both in triumph and defeat. He concentrated in his person all the functions and attributes of his department. He was prompt, indefatigable, self-satisfied and lucky. There were Butler and Malcolm Hailey whose answers were unanswerable and whose reports were most effective and explanations most convincing.[27] There were W.W. Hunter, M.C.D.O'Donnell and William Gait whose figures were constantly quoted by people who wished to talk about India to a British audience and whose very names constituted a pillar of strength to the champions of British rule. Even the sorest enemies of Dunlop Smith, Maurice Hallett and Reginald Maxwell admitted that they possessed the art of 'putting it' to a degree of fearful and wonderful perfection.[28]

There were also small men like Cockshaw of *Dustypore*, who though superficial, hated deliberations and every form of uncertainty. But there were Reginald Craddock, Frank Sly, Montagu Butler, Henry Haig and R.F. Muddie who, like Blunt of Cunningham, were businesslike, straightforward and unconciliating.[29] They were somewhat different from their colleagues and had a fairly rough manner of saying what they thought justified. Carmichael was lymphatic, indolent and vain and could never be persuaded by Hardinge to appreciate that Calcutta was not the seat of a white colonial Government until the endless bombs of Bengali anarchists troubled him sufficiently to adopt an energetic policy. Malcolm Hailey and Keeling parked the pride of the civil services permanently on the Raisina Hills despite Lutyens and his architectural and aesthetic arguments. Irwin, who had a great sense of propriety, concealed the dissensions of his colleagues from the public eye and preserved the Government's dignity from ignominious collapse while a flamboyant Mountbatten[30] pocketed the credit for the transfer of power in sheer indifference to everyone both in England and India.[31]

The self-effacing task of the Raj, it was regretted by some, was vitiated by a lack of communication between the rulers and the ruled and the absence of a human touch, while some others complained that Mr Paget MP debased a national consensus on India. Major General Agate of *The Rains Came*[32] had been in India half of his life and was a perfect Kipling general both in appearance and temperament. It was 'on his own solid shoulders', he reminded his over-awed neighbours, that 'he carried the burden of all the dark races'. He could outshout all comers on the subject of the Realm. He remained smug in the belief that he was serving the British Empire in its grand tradition. But if Agate or Sydenham Clark, Reginald Craddock, Monty Butler, Michael O'Dwyer or Maurice Hallett were overtly imperialistic and self-righteous they were retained in their sensitive posts by a set of liberal secretaries of state to brace up the flagging nerves of a timorous Carmichael, to rejuvenate the failing spirits of a bomb-stricken Hardinge, to animate the infirm will-power of a tired Fleetwood Wilson, to terrify a suspect Ali Imam into submission, to keep a cautious Irwin on his toes or to ensure the hearty cooperation of Sir Jwala Prasad in endorsing the repression let loose by Marsh-Smith.[33]

There were subtle men like Harcourt Butler who could run equally well with the 'Congress hare' and 'the League hound' and could flirt with the Rajas of both Mahmudabad and Darbhanga with comfortable ease.[34] Besides, Simla was full of young men who collected diverse, useful information and cultivated an ornamental style of expression. They were regarded in official circles as the rising men of their generation. There was a sly David Monteath who interpreted Gandhi's tactics in July 1942 as 'strongly reminiscent of Hitler's in exaggerating or manufacturing grievances of Sudaten Germans and appealing to the world for moral support for the rectification of an alleged situation'.[35]

There was an orthodox Winston Churchill sneering at the 'naked fakir' and refusing to preside over the liquidation of the Empire, a crafty Linlithgow adept in the game of seductive political angling, a hardened Amery foxed by a 'diabolical' Gandhi, and a painter-turned-general, A.P. Wavell, muffled by his own inarticulation.[36] They all combined to produce a hoax of Cripps' Mission oblivious of the certainty of its failure.[37] Amery vouched for action and prompted a vacillating prime minister to pre-empt the threatened 'Congress anarchy' promptly:

> Twice armed is he that has his quarrel just,
> But thrice armed he who gets his blow fust.[38]

One would not like to suggest that this English caste in India was a monolithic combination without tension. There were men like Verrall of Orwell's *Burmese Days*[39] who managed to keep for themselves the only things they cared for: clothes and horses, found in the Indian army great freedom for polo, detested Burma because it was no country for a horseman, could manipulate transfers whenever they wanted and had no intention of mixing with all the petty *sahiblog* of the district, those 'nasty, poodle-faking, horseless riff-raff'. There were also men of the vintage of Flory—an angry, non-conformist young man, who had a sneaking sympathy with the Eurasians and professional Indians, politicals and non-politicals alike and who tried to take interest in the 'filthy, disgusting habits' of the natives. There were many others who in the face of a threatened mass-disobedience would call for the German methods of 'how to treat the niggers' and insist: '... And when you've arrested them, if you aren't sure of getting a conviction, shoot them, jolly well shoot them! Fake up an escape and shoot them.... Get somebody anyhow. Much better hang a wrong fellow than no fellow....'[40] There were also the burra memsahibs who matured rather early with accentuated, hardened manners, unleashing a reign of terror at home over a host of native servants. They gave charming little dinner-parties and knew how to put the wives of subordinate officials in their place. But once the station was beseiged by the natives they closed their ranks. Division, distrust and hostility withered away. The conspicuous feature of the life of cantonments and civil stations was a disciplined unity against an alleged native insubordination.[41] It was typified in 'the European Club, that remote, mysterious temple, that holy of holies, far harder of entry than Nirvana!'[42]

Edmund Candler, a vagabond in Asia, had been fascinated in his early youth by the elusive lights and shades and the intangible sense of the Himalayas. But the 'raw actuality' of India repelled him. It was once again a spectre of illusion, debasement and inscrutability that drove Candler away. Earlier he had felt disconcerted by the racial arrogance of the British in India but in his prime he learnt to accept racial prejudice as a natural phenomenon and found in the stubborn immobility of Hinduism its greatest strength. Candler, like many others, became aware of the incongruity of the presence of a reforming British administration in India and was conscious of the futility of the exercise. He sought to rediscover for himself a spiritual tranquility amidst the familiar, the ordinary and the known in England, undisturbed by the fakirs, sheikhs and lamas of India.[43]

During the first two decades of the twentieth century, a debate was conducted by the Round Table Group on the reorganization of the dependency of India. It was prompted by a desire to provide coherent shape to the conception of an imperial super-state which, according to the Group, was inherent in the loose fabric of the Empire. The members of this fraternity had come to the conclusion that the problems, connected with the demands of political obedience, ought to be resolved within the frame of the Empire.[44] This could be effected, they thought, by transforming the

Empire into an organic super-state representing the different segments. It would then be able to articulate through new and distinct organizations capable of performing the higher and essential imperial functions. In the first instance, the imperial Government was expected to concentrate on the problems of defence, foreign relations and negotiations of all matters affecting their common interests. Lionel Curtis, in particular, sought to infuse fresh vigour into the constitutional discussion both in England and India regarding the future pattern of Government in India.[45] He had successfully roped in administrators like James Meston and Williams Marris who worked hard to tilt the official mind towards the working papers of the Round Table. The Group had decided not to entertain the claims of black colonies. But India's demand for colonial Swaraj was far too pressing and popular to be casually ignored . The problem of India, as Marris, Meston, Chirol and Curtis realized, was no longer merely that of proper governance of the Indian people, it was also one of possible re-adjustment of the relations between India and the British Empire. It was held unanimously that India was not loyal to the Empire in any real sense of the term. She had an amazing devotion to the king, but that loyalty was dismissed as a purely religious sentiment. Empire meant, it was assumed, little to India. She had been in the past merely acquiescent and was somewhat indifferent to the future. What appeared more alarming was the fact that she was becoming self-conscious and the powers that had been stimulating her self-consciousness were the Asiatic ones like Japan and China.[46]

The cry of Indian politicians, it was noted with concern, was self-government. The Group noticed that there had been, of late, a tendency to repudiate the tacit assumption that the East was inferior to the West. Writers on religion, both Hindu and Muslim, it was observed, had been emphasizing the great spirituality of the Eastern religions; writers on morality had been denying the materialism of Eastern ethics; and commercial men had been extolling the rapid advancement of Japan.[47] There was a growing alarm in the official mind that there was a possibility of a social, moral and political resorgimento of the East. However illogical these sentiments might have been, they were powerful impulses in politics and Malcolm Hailey saw no reason to appease these political thinkers.[48] The members of the Round Table Group read in the exotic term Swaraj disturbing ramifications. 'If she is allowed', Buchan minced no words, 'to grow apart from the Empire, there is a real danger that she may set her face towards independence and separation. It is for us to bring her in touch with the Empire, to make her think impartially and realise that she is and must always be an integral part of the Empire and that by that connection her best interests will be served'.[49] It was indispensable for India, the Group maintained, to retain a firm imperial connection despite her inferior political status, race and civilization in the face of obvious opposition from the colonies.[50]

Everyone agreed on the point that the problem of integrating India within the framework of the proposed super-state was essential. But there were differences of opinion with regard to the definition of India's goal. James Meston seemed to feel, Chirol confided to Curtis, that the goal ought to be Indian self-government and Kerr was inclined to agree with that view.[51] The debate, however, concluded on the satisfactory note that where India was concerned, the art of circumspection was considered to be the supreme test of statesmanship. In the first place, one was advised to be careful about the use of the word 'self-government' in relation to India. Unlike India, the dominions were bound together by a common race, creed and civilization and common interests.[52] 'In my humble opinion', Chirol wrote, 'it is inconceivable that within any reasonable period of time, be it generations or centuries, India could occupy any position' as had been occupied by the dominions.[53] It was possible, the Group argued, that in the fullness of time, contact between the Eastern and the Western civilizations under the aegis of British rule might evolve a new civilization in India in which 'the thousand and one existing discords of race and creed and custom and traditions will merge into complete harmony. . . .'[54] But that harmony and equilibrium ought to be achieved within the Western civilization and not simply by developing emotional ties with it. It was not certain if India's goal of self-government would correspond even remotely to the ideas that had inspired the existing dominions. The Round Table conceived the possibility of a self-governing India in full control of the Indian administration through mainly British agencies.[55] It could be far more representative than it had been in the past of Indian sentiments and responsive to Indian interests having much greater independence than it had enjoyed. But the Group could not be persuaded to accept a self-governing India with an Indian executive responsible to an Indian Parliament as a member of the British Empire.[56] It was felt necessary that a new word should be coined to connote the measure of independence which a British Government of India would be permitted to achieve. There was complete unanimity about the inadvisability to refer to Indian self-government even as a remote possibility. They feared that despite carefully worded reservations and limitations, such an expression would merely stimulate vain aspirations and sow the seeds of disappointment.

The basis of the prescription of the Round Table was its well thought-out perception of Indian society. Chirol was the expert of the Round Table on the Indian society and her people. The fascinating feature of contemporary Indian society, Chirol maintained, was its remarkable diversity. It was possible, he acknowledged, that a discriminating observer might ignore the unifying bond of Indian society. But although the impact of the singularity of the forest was overwhelming, even a naïve onlooker would not overlook the significant diversity of individual trees that dominated the Indian scene. The novel Eastern atmosphere might grip a casual visitor who could be tempted to highlight the artificial unity created by Hinduism. But it was difficult for anyone not to take note of the fact that amidst the cross-currents of the time none was more striking than the growth of fissiparous tendencies accentuating the innumerable lines of division which divided Indian society.[57] The Round Table did not recognize the claim of the educated Indians, drawn almost entirely from a narrow circle of professional classes in the town, to speak on behalf of a vast agricultural population. It was alleged that this small westernized minority had hitherto been both careless and ignorant of the interests and aspirations of the rural population of India and its Western education tended to estrange them still further. The greatest lack of vision was exhibited by the British administrators, Chirol complained, when they failed to watch the drift of the educational system during the last decade of the nineteenth century.[58] The Government was not justified, he claimed, in accepting the Western educated classes as trustworthy and qualified representatives of the wishes and interests of India. The Round Table was unanimous in thinking that it would be a betrayal of trust 'for us to transfer to them the responsibilities' which 'we have assumed towards the vast masses that have remained inarticulate'.[59] The political ascendancy of this self-centred class of Western educated politicians, the Group alleged, synchronized with the elimination of social reforms and the substitution of purely political propaganda in the Congress movement. The result of the process had been quite extraordinary as the divide between the urban educated groups and the vastly preponderating rural and agricultural classes was formalized. The Group asserted that the Congress politicians had done virtually nothing to fight the evils inherent in the Hindu social system which were largely responsible for the poverty and backwardness of the masses. In short, the Group defended the officious demeanour of the British mofussil official who, unlike the Congress-wallahs, was 'in touch with the masses' and who was thus justified in not recognizing these 'upstarts'.[60]

On the basis of the analysis outlined above, it was relatively easy to conclude that the mainspring of the Indian agitation was the very human fretfulness of young India. Imperfectly educated on Western lines and having no adequate outlet, the educated Indian was hungry for loaves and fishes. He was morbidly sensitive to and impatient of the restraints which he attributed to mere racial prejudices. He was convinced that he had nothing more to learn from the West and that the intellectual superiority he possessed over the vast masses of his fellow countrymen justified his claim to be the sole interpreter of their needs and desires. It was a small minority which had so far assimilated Western ideas and had a firm belief in the potency of political institutions on the British model to raise their whole nation on to a higher plane than the Western civilization.[61] It caught on to the Western theory that it was far better for a country to be ill-governed by its own people than well-governed by aliens. It regarded self-government of India as a safeguard against a fundamental moral degradation and rejected the concept of sharing power with the British Government of India as a junior partner. Behind all these political gestures, the Group concluded, stood a spirit of fanatical hostility towards the whole agency of British rule. Chirol and his associates were vituperative against all classes of nationalists in India.[62] Not to speak of Gandhi, the National Congress and the extremists, they did not spare even the Moderates, the Constitutionalists and the Liberals. The indignation and antipathy of the Group was indicative of the virulent attitude of the Government of India towards nationalist India. The diagnosis was simple: all of them had been working at different levels for the destabilization of the Raj and thus supplementing each other with remarkable facility. Their purpose, Marris argued, was to create the driving power of so-called public opinion which, they knew, would carry with it many who in their hearts distrusted nationalist rhetoric. They had set up, he added, a standard of political demands which no Indian could decline to endorse without being exposed to the reproach that he was unpatriotic. The Moderates and the Liberals succeeded, it was feared, in securing to that standard the adhesion of nearly the whole body of politicians who claimed to be the chosen representatives of the Indian people. The dangerous feature of the movement launched by these moderate leaders was that they knew much better than their enthusiastic followers that no Government could possibly concede to their demands without betraying the interests of the Government, the Empire and the 'trust under which we rule India. . . .'[63] The primary object of the nationalists was to create an atmosphere, they concluded, which would produce the maximum disappointment and bitterness. The leaders knew that the administration was prepared to give half a loaf which could be accepted by the people with satisfaction, and therefore, when it was offered they 'were determined to foster the faith in the country that the people were entitled to the whole loaf and a denial by the Government could be used to foment further tension'. The administration distrusted their profession of loyalty to the Crown coupled with their accusations against the bureaucracy and thought it a cunning strategy to estrange the country from the British connection. The profession of loyalty was interpreted as a mask to hide the irrational vindictiveness of self-centred leadership determined to whip up an agitation for the establishment of vakil raj.[64]

The Round Table was supplemented by some devoted members of a Cambridge fraternity known as the Apostles. This group, known for intensity and inconsistency, sent over some scholars to India and many of them reached Aligarh. Theodore Beck, T.W. Arnold and Theodore Morison concentrated their energy on the growth and development of a Muslim Cambridge at Aligarh. Their task was noble and their sense of purpose was never in doubt. Together they worked hand in hand to develop the contours of the Islamic personality of a Muslim India, worked out its political terms of reference, delineated its frontiers and located its place in the Raj on the basis of complete loyalty to British rule and selfless service to the *quam*.[65] During their Cambridge days, the members of the fraternity had inherited in full measure the legacy of John Strachey and James Fitzjames Stephen whose outlook rejected human warmth between the ruler and the ruled. An unfaltering faith in a strong executive, a firm distrust of any form of paternalism, an inflexible dislike of the Indian educated classes, an open assertion of the doctrine of the hegemony of sword and the absolute primacy of law and order were the various aspects of that inheritance. There was no hypocrisy in their perception of the intention of British rule. Both Strachey and Stephen made no bones about their determination that all key executive posts in British India controlling political and military power would be commanded by Englishmen.[66] As a ruling race it was not the friendship of the ruled that was to be sought after. They required no friendly overtures from the natives. On the contrary, they believed in the unswerving obedience of the Indians and cultivated a calculated detachment from them. It was a matter of satisfaction if the sahib gave the Indians the impression of a hostile superman, so long as he was accepted by all as just and manly.[67]

The Oxbridge men in Aligarh were romantic and generous and were known for their ardent enthusiasm. Intensely practical, they shared a common belief in social intimacy and the power of ideas and looked to a common understanding of a set of moral concepts as an effective guide to social action. Social action, they believed, depended on kinship ties and political institutions were seen as an extension of family feelings. Simplistic in their formulation of the theories of society and history, these men were drawn by the seductive simplicity of the action-oriented life and programme of Syed Ahmed Khan. He was, they believed, to devote his life 'to restoring a people who once thronged the palaces and commanded the armies of the great Mughals'.[68] The decision of the Apostles was rewarded and before long they became the theoreticians of a separatist movement in India, the ideologues of a synthetic 'Muslim patriotism' and the darlings of the British administration. All of them were enrolled in the India Office's list of trained and trusted India hands. More than anybody else, these men collectively tried to give to the political aspirations of the decaying Muslim aristocracy, a historical dimension: 'The Muhammadans were, you know, for two centuries, the rulers of Upper India', one of them wrote to his friend,'. . . The British Empire involved new conditions of individual success. The most downtrodden of the Hindoos, the Bengalis eagerly embraced the opportunities offered to them by English education, while proud Muhammadans held aloof. . . . Under these circumstances what was wanted was a college which would give an English education, and at the same time teach the Muhammadan religion. . . . Accordingly our founder, Syed Ahmed Khan, set to work to mould the opinion of his countrymen'.[69]

Beck, Morison and the rest did not fail to endow British rule of India with Kiplingesque attributes. 'It is easy to find fault with the constitution, but we cannot fail to recognise that for a hundred years the Government did splendid work'. Morison wrote, 'The English administrators, military no less than civil, worked hard at the establishment of even-handed justice, the assessment of land revenue, the making of roads, railways and canals and the prevention of famine. This was administrative work of a high order, and it is to this administrative work that the prosperity of India is due'.[70] Like Maud Diver, Morison was eager to emphasize that the process of administration was not dramatic and that it had not been marked by brilliant episodes, but that it was a record of the honest, hard work of devoted civilians in the service of a country that had been distinguished by lawlessness and poverty. What was required in India, Morison stated in no unambiguous terms, was not a Swarajist elected legislative assembly but a strong executive capable of prompt and vigorous action especially because 'a gust of passion' might at any time sweep through the depressed castes and 'impel them to some wide Jacquerrie. . . .'[71] In contrast to the bitter antagonism towards the Bengali nationalists, the political line of Aligarh laid down by Beck, Morison and Ahmed envisaged a firm and friendly relationship between the Englishmen and the Indian Muslims. This was to be promoted through thought and action under the strict supervision and veto power of the head of the institution. There was no room in it for 'Bengali-type sedition' or any enthusiasm for representative institutions that would harm Muslim interests. The rules of the union club of the college maintained that 'no matter shall be discussed which raises the question of the permanence and stability of the British rule nor any subject which involves the necessity of speakers . . . taking up a disloyal and seditious attitude toward the British Government in its internal policy or external relations. . . ' Beck, Morison, Cox and the rest provided one of the important planks of imperialism with a theoretical model.[72]

In keeping with the general trend of official thought, imperial violence was given a sociological explanation. Dwelling on the Punjab disturbances and the Hunter Commission Report, Stanley Reed in a background paper to the editor of *The Times* emphasized the possible fall-out of a spontaneous subjective response in England to the act of commission and omission by General Dyer. Reed thought that it was his obligation as correspondent to educate men in authority on the urgency of a prudent and statesmanlike approach towards the 'unfortunate' episode. He wrote that there were certain broad issues connected with the maintenance of order in India 'which are not always appreciated, but which are nevertheless beyond dispute'.[73] These were that the Indian population, ordinarily law abiding and capable of being kept in order even by a fairly inefficient police, was apt to suddenly flame into extreme disorder that always became homicidal. That was the characteristic, ran the observation of this seasoned journalist, which distinguished the Indian people from all Western communities. This meant, he argued, that military and fire-arms had to be used in India for suppression of disorders 'which in England would be dealt with by the Police'.[74] While this was true of the whole of India, it was especially true of the Punjab. Reed ascribed the situation to the fact that there was a large martial population in the province, that the general population was loyal but not law abiding and that in every village there was a lawless element waiting to break into loot. The basis for Reed's call for compassion in favour of Dyer was buttressed by another significant note of caution:

> We who live in the great towns and administrative centres of India are always reasonably protected. But

> what of the small British communities, consisting of half a dozen men and women at the utmost, who are scattered over hundreds of upcountry stations? It is impossible to protect them and during disturbances the Government was overwhelmed with appeals for British military assistance which it could not satisfy. If disorder gains the upper hand, even momentarily, there is every reason to anticipate murder on a widespread scale.[75]

Like many others before and after him, Stanley Reed drew a graphic picture of the 'Great Fear' in India that was looming large over the alien race governing the country. In northern India, in particular, Englishmen and women always lived, it was reported faithfully at regular intervals, under the dark shadow of an uprising. Reed also maintained that it was difficult to convey to those who had no experience of India, the lightning speed at which race hatred boiled over. He argued that racial antagonism was always dormant in the country and even an innocent incident could be interpreted as a grave provocation for igniting it. These were the conditions which the administrators had to contend with. At times, situations could become explosive, conditioning the judgement of an officer in distress. In view of these considerations, Reed tried to assess the role of Dyer and came to the conclusion that his decision was the only choice open to him. '. . . If murder was being done', Reed wrote, 'I should fire strongly because it is the truest mercy in the long run'.[76] He conceded that Dyer had committed excesses and that there was no justification for acts designed not to punish or prevent but to humiliate. Reed, however, felt strongly that the Punjab disturbances and the measures to restore order were to be judged in the light of very special circumstances of war, the collapse of civil authority, the drought situation in 1918, the complete alienation of the educated classes and the tension arising out of the uncertain turn of events in a country accustomed to turbulence, violence and lawlessness.

All these arguments and many more were collated by the Round Table and the administrators during and after the World War and they became the imperial stereotypes in the decades that followed. Katherine Mayo summed up some of them in her *Mother India*; a number of civil servants recommended them in their memoirs written in retirement; official reports such as that of the Simon Commission put authoritative stamps on them; the Round Table Conference turned them into the talking points of British public opinion; administrators and viceroys explained their uncomfortable hard lines on these terms of reference; the British press picked up the threads of these arguments and wove their own reactionary patterns; delegate conferences were held in Britain to popularize the imperialist image of India and even a genuine liberal opinion was obliged to appreciate the so-called tragic dilemma of an over-worked and misunderstood civil service operating in an ungrateful and turbulent land.

Party positions on India were blurred during the 1930s when the children of the First World War turned into iconoclasts desiring to smash the tin gods of society and politics. Between the peace movements, economic theories, political conferences, anti-Fascist front and the Spanish Civil War and the almost unending debates of the thirties on the future of human society; amidst the unprecedented economic crisis when the hungry marchers were out in England and the impoverished unemployed had been reading the *Daily Worker* and clamouring for social justice; in face of the ascendancy of Fascism, regimentation and militarism, India was reduced to an uncomfortable and an unenviable drag of the rebellious decade. In fact in the wake of the intellectual radicalism of the period, the Indian question was treated by the Left as an important though not quite urgent matter whose settlement could be conveniently deferred for a more stable political occasion. Few had the time or the inclination to ponder over the proposition that the struggle against Fascism was not compatible with the existence and assertions of imperialism. The debased social system of the Hindus, the great historical divide between the two major communities and the numerous divisions of society constituted the intellectual nexus even of the Friends of India, and the Fellowship of Conciliation. Operating within the parameters defined by a well-synchronized propaganda, British public opinion, including that of its enlightened segments, diffused the real issues of the Indian question and drifted towards an animated discussion on the futility of India's self-determination, the absurdity of the severance of the British link, and the terms of so-called safeguards for the interests of the Empire, the princes and the minorities. Meanwhile imperialism got away with its inhuman ordinances, its broken pledges, its autocratic bureaucracy and its facile promise about the prospects and future of the Raj. 'A Low Dishonest Decade' came to an end when the Allies celebrated their victory and Britain was forced to adjust herself to a painfully lower international status. In his *The End of the Empire*, W.H. Auden, the rebel of the thirties, mourned the termination of the Raj and raised his accusing finger at the cold, calculated and callous piece of inhumanity that the British power enacted as it partitioned India.

But did he rise above the Raj stereotypes?

Unbiased at least he was when he arrived on his mission.
Having never set eyes on this land he was called to
  partition
Between two peoples fanatically at odds,
With their different diets and incompatible gods.
'Time', they had briefed him in London, 'is short'. It's
  too late
For mutual reconciliation or rational debate;
The only solution now lies in separation.
The Viceroy thinks, as you see from his letter,
That the less you are seen in his company the better.
So we've arranged to provide you with other accommo
  dation.
We can give four judges, two Moslem and two Hindu,
To consult with, but the final decision must rest with
  you.[77]

There was also E.M. Forster who like C.F. Andrews, Edward Thompson and Horace Alexander devoted himself to tracing the essential missing link that could have legitimized an intense symbiotic relationship between the two races and strengthened its nerve centre. It was to be symbolized in the personal friendship between Aziz and Fielding which, despite the author's unfailing efforts, remained largely an erratic outburst.[78] Horace Alexander shared in full measure the sensitivity of Andrews and Forster and desired to rescue the essential human aspects of Anglo-Indian relationship from an impending racial suicide. It could be cemented, he persisted, outside the bar libraries and the exclusive clubs and beyond the pale of unsubstantiated rumours.[79]

E.M. Forster would have recommended Rudyard Kipling's flamboyant evocation of the white man's burden but for the stirring political climate of India. Unlike Kipling, he lacked confidence. He had witnessed at his very doorstep the outbreak of a popular upsurge away from the regimented life of the North-West Frontier.[80] He was cognizant of a resurgent India and was sensitive to its diverse potentialities. Even a combative Valentine Chirol who would have otherwise smothered it, estranged as he had been by the democratic pretentions of the professional classes, counselled caution. But Maud Diver, insensate, self-righteous and as egocentric as ever, continued to underline the banal assertions of Kipling in an atmosphere of melancholy uncertainty of political India.[81]

Forster came to terms with India during his two visits in 1912–13 and 1921–22. His first visit coincided with the growing disillusionment of the

Muslims under the turbulent Young Turks swayed by an alleged conspiracy of the Cross against the Crescent while the second visit closely followed the Rowlatt Acts and the massacre at Amritsar and he watched the first all-India Gandhian movement that had pushed the Hindus and the Muslims towards each other against the 'satanist' state. Forster was himself associated with the secret Cambridge Conversazione Society and he had imbibed an abiding faith in the British imperial mission in India although his was a liberal mission couched in personal relationships. *The Passage to India* was initiated in the first phase but Forster postponed its completion for several years. The gap between his memories and his personal experience in the early twenties were a stumbling block. He was aware of the increasing lack of confidence in personal equations between the Indians on the one hand and the British on the other. Three of the Apostles who had helped Forster to mould his own perception of the British Empire were G.L. Dickinson, Robert Calverley Trevelyan and Gordon Hannington Luce who accompanied him during his first trip. Sarah Duncan reinforced the impact and Edmund Candler impressed the traditions of Kipling upon the mind of a receptive Forster.[82] His close association with Masood, a grandson of Sir Syed Ahmed Khan, enabled Forster to imbibe the perceptions of India as viewed by Aligarh's first generation ideologically fed by a volatile Theodore Morison. Aligarh and Masood provided Forster with a clear-cut perspective of the so-called mono-dimensional 'Muslim India' hostile to a chaotic Hinduism with its profusion of cruelty. The little State of Dewas, its strange Maharaja and his even stranger ideas, Kanya and Godbole, whose very names amused a snooty Morgan, offered him what he thought to be a satisfactory panorama of Hindu India. With characteristic self-confidence, Forster boasted that he had seen and grasped the three significant elements of Indian polity.[83] The paradox of the situation was that his was a shared vision of the official India. His childlike enthusiasm took him to areas ignored by the officials and the artist in him was repelled by some of the obnoxious elements of the 'alien race in action'. He paused for a while to amuse himself in the Hindu ceremonies of Gokul Ashtami and Dussehra; he noticed the impudent distortions in British behaviour in India; he squatted on the floor with the natives to eat Indian dishes with his unseasoned fingers. But despite outrageous philandering with the Indian institutions and customs, he scrupulously carried with him an official prism. He appreciated Masood's sincerity and spontaneity and yet marked the striking difference between the awkward habits of Masood and the polished demeanour of the English gentlemen of the public schools. He did not consider that Dewas was 'the oddest corner of the world outside *Alice in Wonderland* and insisted that it represented India.[84] He continued to believe that the intrusion of an English woman into the mysteries of India remained a permanent grudge that vitiated national relationships. When the American tourist in *The Hill of Devi* insisted that servants of various sorts would not travel on the footboard facing the chill wind to arrive at Jaipur with pneumonia, the boyish Forster was rapturous: 'Cheers for Democracy! He seemed absolutely English-upper class. Oxford manners—and had eventually moved in higher circles in Delhi dining with the Viceroy and the chiefs according to his own account'.[85]

In all fairness to E.M. Forster, one should admit that he sought to rise above the myths and stereotypes of Kipling and his imperial prescriptions. A Liberal by conviction, Forster tried to examine British rule with a modicum of scepticism. There were, however, some in-built inhibitions which clouded his vision despite himself. As Benita Parry puts it, almost all the historical, analytical, propagandist and fictional writings on India devised a way of presenting world history in such a way that British rule in India appeared a political imperative and a moral duty.[86] Forster does not affirm or reject the assertion. He is disturbed by the social exclusiveness of the rulers; he mocks at the limitations of officially sponsored purdah parties; he pleads for a constant human interaction between the ruler and the ruled; he is unusually sensitive to what he calls the infectious Oriental suspicion and believes that a fundamental chasm separated the Hindus and the Muslims. He makes an attempt to appreciate the nuances of Muslim aspirations and is puzzled by the mysteriousness of Hindu institutions. He fails to provide a consciousness of imperialism's historical dimensions...[88] This denotes the limitation of Liberalism which could not construct an integrated theory of human society and reflected its inability to produce a critique of imperialism. In this sense, *A Passage* represents the tragedy of liberal-humanism. Its impotence is laid bare by its inadequacy to transcend Kipling's stereotypes and its tragedy is manifested by its incompetence in constructing any tangible framework to comprehend a subject people of different cultural and social mores and attitudes.[89] G.K. Das underlines Forster's protest against the goodwill visit of the Prince of Wales:

> ...If the subordinate Englishmen in the county had also been *naïf* and genial, if the subalterns and tommies and European engineers and schoolmasters and policemen and magistrates had likewise taken their stand upon a common humanity instead of the pedestal of race—then

> the foundation of a democratic Empire might have been well and truly laid... Until the unimportant Englishmen had condescended to hold out their hands to the 'natives', it is a waste of money to display the affabilities of the House of Windsor.[90]

Forster misjudged the imperial situation owing to his faith in a myopic Liberalism and he misconstrued imperialism as a rational system distorted by individual failings and a pukka sahib tradition. Forster could not comprehend his problem; his critics by and large could not grasp Forster's Liberalism. Forster's humanism could not sustain even a purely personal relationship. The friendship between Fielding and Aziz finally disintegrated as both of them retired to their embittered communities. Aziz went back to his folk; Fielding drifted away to Ronny Heaslop. Imperial Britain could not be persuaded to accept a subject race as an equal and honourable friend.

Charles Andrews would have concurred with Forster but for the fact that he had also desired to initiate a singular synthesis between the new India and the old and consecrate the imperial mission with Christian piety. When necessary, he goaded a reluctant Mohandas Karamchand Gandhi to leave Smuts alone with his problems in South Africa and withdraw himself to his guru in India[91]; when required, he pressurized Rabindranath Tagore, albeit ineffectually, not to grace the materialistic Soviet Union with his spiritual presence[92]; when expedient, he advocated the abolition of the system of indentured labour and when considered indispensable, he urged a reluctant Government to make the necessary concessions to nationalist India in order to consolidate the wavering support of its moderate wing.[93]

In 1934 Robern Byron echoed Forster's uncomfortable claims and untenable positions with regard to the demands of imperial partnership as well as his general faith in England's civilizing mission. The Indian bazaar, he described, represented the chaotic variety and 'muddle' that was India. There were the tiny humped cows wandering at will, traders, sweetmeats, brassware, fakirs, sadhus, deformed babies, pugarees, dhotis, nose-rings, painted godmarks, the 'fantastic emaciation of one' and 'the astounding corpulence of another'.[94] Everything sounded echoes in the memory, Byron murmured, 'an echo from the nursery days and nursery literature'. He felt that he was more than a stranger in that world: 'For here was I in a position which I had never had, never conceived, nor wanted, a ruler among the ruled'.[95] The human sensitivity of Byron as that of Thompson and Forster drifted unhappily towards the ruling impulses of a white governing race amidst a prostrated brown people. It was unsure of itself placed as it was on an unsteady equilibrium of conflicting emotions.

Edward Thompson having acclaimed the fulfilment of the British goal in India gazed remorsefully at the decline of the Raj. He had sought to recapitulate the thoughts of his countrymen at Fort William and so many points of isolation in an unknown and hostile land. He had witnessed the pageantry and splendour of an arrogant Empire. It was as certain as Rome had been. He had forseen the last days of British rule as he helplessly watched a rising tide of opposition around the issue of the partition of Bengal. By 1931 he had been preparing himself to bid farewell to India. By then the 'childish' nationalism of 1905, Thompson sighed, had grown into a powerful political contender. 'Education was on sufferance, an imperious and reckless Nationalism ruled the stage', Thompson lamented, 'jerking his students back and forth like puppets'. British presence had become a waste of time in the 'flat monotony of the Indian existence'.[96]

Indian nationalism, Thompson thought, had been turned into an uncompromising dogma based on some obstinate abstractions deduced from Western experience and political thought. 'Point out to them that their Hindus and Mohammedans aren't agreeing', Thompson's Alden gibed after a life-long service in India, 'even while they're still in the stage of sheer fun, drawing up imaginary constitutions for an imaginary United Indian Nation. They all reply by quoting from the Durham Report before Canada got her self-government to show that they can't possibly be in a worse mess than Canada was then. . . .'[97] What both Alden and Findley shared in common with the general imperial perception was that the Indians would, if the British left, 'cut one another's throats'.[98]

The Indian mind, Thompson anticipated a growing historical literature, was fertile enough to spin out fictitious anecdotes. Thus, there was a fantastic crop of political rumours involving the magic and miracles of Gandhi, the marvels of Nehru, the humiliation suffered by viceroys and the surrender of the British Parliament.[99] But the focus of Thompson's political interest was concentrated on the iniquitous Dinabandhu Tarkachuramani. For Thompson, he represented a remarkable Indian consensus.[100] Full independence had become Tarkachuramani's preoccupation and he had no patience with Gandhi's methods. He was well-read and well-informed. He quoted Tennyson, Mill and from the history of Ireland with competence and felicity. He rose above his ancestral pride in race, caste and creed and had been seeking to 'link all India against us'.[101] He was obdurate in his stand and derided the talk of a peaceful partnership with the rest of the Empire.

The new India was beyond Thompson's comprehension though he could detect some of its conspicuous features. It was not, for example, overtly Hindu. It viewed non-violence as a private 'fad' of Gandhi and treated him with scant respect.[102] The unchanging India had become a 'Vesuvius' and even more mysterious.[103] 'You'll have special reasons for special watchfulness and special action as long as you stay in India'.[104] Paradoxically, Thompson was still keen to make the 'unbragging' India come face to face with the 'unbragging' England. He was convinced that so long as a 'non-violent humbug' confronted the 'look-what-we-have-done-for-India humbug' there could be no comfortable room for agreement.[105]

As had been the case with many others, Thompson could not quite figure out the impulses of the new India. Neither King George nor the Mahatma, he gave vent to his cynicism, ruled here. On the contrary, 'Past is king' and it was sitting pretty waiting for 'us to go'; and wondering 'how much longer we shall take or how many hints we need'.[106] Gandhi, a disturbed Thompson cogitated, was no longer guided by reason. Under pressure, the Mahatma, Thompson lamented, had been living almost invariably impelled by an unstable soul force. To Thompson, it meant spontaneous instincts, irrational passions and the promptings of an uncanny past.[107]

In a sense, Edward Thompson reflected what is somewhat indulgently stylized as the liberal dilemma. In the early thirties, Thompson had been closely watching the Indian political realities on behalf of the Rhodes Trustees with a view to locating the possible areas of cooperation between Indian and British writers while operating as a special correspondent for the *Manchester Guardian*. The outcome of his experience was *A Letter from India*.[108] This was a characteristic liberal tract centring around the problems emanating from the Irwin–Gandhi Pact. Viewed superficially, Thompson seemed remarkably objective. To him the arrest of Gandhi was both premature and a blunder while the Pact was vitiated by undesirable circumstances. A sense of self-righteousness saturated all his observations. Negotiations between the ruler and the ruled, he argued, were inevitable and had been delayed far too long. The economic and social outlook in India was worse than disquieting and might even render a 'revolution' and its 'attendant sufferings' almost inevitable.[109] A disturbed Thompson hastened to add that the need of the hour was for a more decided and a more reckless Government. The backdrop of the prescription was his firm conviction that no democracy or colourful imitation of democracy could ever handle the affairs of India. Authority, when exercised repressively, he expatiated, might postpone a crisis while aggravating the final explosion. Authority, when exercised constructively, had a chance of winning through.[110] If one did not pretend to negotiate one might as well be prepared for a system of police and military rule sitting over an alleged self-government which was, in its turn, destined to be a sure failure.

By then Thompson did not think it necessary to adopt a liberal posture. The Indian Government, Thompson wrote gleefully was not 'very wicked' as many supposed, 'but there is a good deal of evidence that they are sometimes half-witted' and often subjected to 'an unfair press'.[111] Commenting on the political upheaval of the North-West Frontier Province, Thompson defended the stern official measures. It was a 'storm centre' and 'an exceptional area of violence' demanding harsh treatment but requiring honest explanations as well. Shooting in the Hijli detention camp, he thundered, was justified, and reprisals in Chittagong were understandable. He recommended the reports of the Congress on both the incidents as honest and accurate even though they had been drawn up unwillingly. In both the episodes, Thompson argued, the Government had a case. He was for a frank assessment of the situation because suppression of facts merely led to exaggeration. Rumours might, he warned, push even 'moderate men', who recognized the necessity of keeping some sort of order and who were unwilling to make even an alien Government's task impossible, into opposition. He believed that it was fair to assert that the 'poor English community' of Calcutta had been 'so threatened and so murderously used' that it had been goaded into a policy of force; that the Congress was in communication with the terrorists; that the Bengal Congress was no exception to the general rule and that it had been playing a deceptive role; that Gandhi's diabolical spiritual references were designed to offer 'one meaning to a dull listener and another to an intelligent one' and that Hollywood's contribution to the low estimation in which Europe was held in India was immense.[112] About India's independent future, Thompson had been harping on the familiar stereotype. The temporary unification of India under British rule had been consolidated by political agitation and activity especially since the First World War. But it was breaking up, he prognosticated, as the Roman Empire had been broken up into the nations of Europe. Bengal, Bombay, Madras and Punjab, Thompson was convinced, were different countries, 'yearly growing into a wider disparateness.' Bengal was 'straightforward murderous'; the North-West Frontier Province was thoroughly unreliable with a steady subversive campaign; U.P. was overtly disloyal with the prospect of a peasant uprising—a green revolution—'dishonestly' formulated by the Congress having 'an excellent eye for places and countries where government is at a disadvantage'.[113] In the face of the precarious political situation and episodic violence and brutality, Thompson bragged, the world had never before seen such forbearance as has been exercised by Britain, herself 'an old and haughty nation nursed in arms', having both traditions of power and pride in authority.[114] Thompson commended the remarkable perseverance and tenacity of purpose of the Government and expressed, in no uncertain terms, three cheers for the British mission in India. He was conscious of the fact that the educated Indians resented the argument that Britain had a trust in India. He condescended to acknowledge that it was impolitic to use the term and Englishmen should be careful not to prattle it. But he was not oblivious of Britain's self-imposed obligations. '. . . The only thing worth striving for is to lessen human sufferings,' wrote the liberal observer, 'and an abrupt departure of the British from India. . . would cause very great suffering, though we should be the gainers in everything but self-respect'. If India, 'secures a peaceful passage to freedom', Thompson underlined the unprecedented British experiment, 'garlands will be due to us, no less than to India'.[115]

An admirer of Tagore, Thompson was iniquitous even in his assessment.[116] He was vituperative against the Mahatma. Gandhi, according to him, was both mysterious and mischievous, his strange ways hardly sensible. Gandhi revelled, Thompson continued, in his isolation, speaking in rambling expressions and inconsequential phrases and indulging in twisted and teasing ambiguity. Instead of 'a spiritual, a John the Baptist', Thompson found in Gandhi, especially in his dealing with Ambedkar, 'a Bania, in close alliance with other Banias (who claimed to be nothing more). . .' Charlie Andrews, Thompson added, agreed with him that a deep deterioration of the Satyagraha movement in India had set in. It was no longer as pure as it had been in South Africa.[117] Non-violence, Thompson claimed, had been reduced to 'undiluted nonsense'.[118] He scoffed at the 'infinite duplicity' of Gandhi and gave his final judgement on the Indian movement: '. . . If an incongruous alliance of bazaar women, ladies just emerged from purdah, and girls between six and ten years of age lie on the path by which students must come to their lectures—if a shopkeeper who wishes to supply British goods to people who wish to buy them is made socially miserable—you may call all this "non-violence", of course. But you must travel eight thousand miles west of India to find anyone except M. Rolland who agrees with you'.[119] Both he and Andrews, Thompson claimed, were convinced that the Mahatma had been at one stage capable of 'the highest form of truth'. But over the years, they reluctantly concluded, Gandhi had become elusive, evasive and even untruthful. This metamorphosis was so acute and so complete, Thompson complained, that the official view of a Gandhi juggling and quibbling, having no intention to cooperate, acquired credibility and extensive acceptance. He was 'as cunning', an official quipped, 'as a cartload of monkeys'.[120] Thompson added that Gandhi was always a 'provincial', a Gujarati who ought to be taught the difference between politics and administration and should be encouraged to cultivate a sense of proportion and be forced to acknowledge the fact that Gujarat was not the whole of India. In the east, Bengal did not represent the National Congress. Sharp racial antagonism, a powerful gunman's tradition and official repression had rendered her hysterical with a grim future.[121] In the north-west, Khan Abdul Gaffar Khan with 'his crudity, vanity and ignorance' was incapable of appreciating the remarkable constitutional experiment in an Eastern country which was being watched across the border all the way from Kabul to Bokhara. 'If that constitution is a success', Thompson, in 1931–32, seemed infinitely innocent of the trends of Indian history, 'even very moderately a success, nothing contiguous to it will be left unchanged' while the Red Shirts would remain only a 'vexing interlude'. 'Well, thank God, we had a chief-commissioner who was the right sort, a soldier and not a political, a chap who stands no nonsense from anyone, whether A.G.K. or Delhi or those damned Swarajists!'[122] The sahib doctrine, shaken elsewhere in India, Thompson seemed pretty satisfied, stood 'erect and strong' in the Frontier Province with the approval of the army. Thompson's liberal consciousness had long been submerged in the irresistible flood of an autocratic backlash of a self- righteous imperialism. He had never doubted that General Dyer's action had saved the Punjab from a revolt and its attendant horrors although he did not also doubt that it did irreparable damage to the Raj. But he was now able to resolve the dilemma. He was convinced that General Dyer had never been 'anti-Indian' or a 'man of natural cruelty'. Dyer 'never knew that there was no way out' of the Jallianwalla Park and when the crowd did not disperse, he expected a massive counter attack. Miles Irving, the deputy commissioner at Amritsar in 1919, it was alleged, was aware of the situation but he forgot to tell this to the Hunter's Commission and a proud Dyer decided 'to wear the martyr's mask' thereby terribly messing up his own case. 'Dyer persuaded himself and us', wrote Thompson confidently, 'that he went to Jalianwala determined on a deliberate massacre. It is simply not true. He went to do the job of an officer called in to suppress disorder with which the civil authorities could not cope. The rest happened as I have said'.[123]

By 1933, Thompson and many others had discarded even the thin veneer of liberalism that had enveloped their attitude towards India. His assessment of Indian developments had become mono-dimensional. The nationalist stage, he argued, had come to be dominated by men of the vintage of Sasadhar Tarkachuramani, a strange amalgam of superstitions, transcendentalism, mental exaltation and intellectual obscurity together with European ideas thrown in as an incompatible ingredient. Aurobindo Ghosh, who lived on the same street, appalled Thompson.[124] In a sense, Indian nationalism exhibited the shifty mentality of an impulsive, spoilt child. Thompson condescended to assign some responsibility to the stern aloofness, chill efficiency and morbid arrogance of the officialdom for the estrangement of the Congress. But such an alienation, it was resolutely upheld, was inevitable as the Congress refused to accept a reality: the Indians were not yet proficient in self-government.[125] Increasingly, this prophet of human understanding became an arrogant spokesman of ultra-Tory imperialism: 'Every Indian matter should be brought on the plane of scientific and rigid scrutiny—Indian history, literature, philosophy, Indian civilisation in every branch and details, should be shaken by the throat'.[126] However absurd the metaphor might sound and however tenuous an association might be traced between the proposed exercise and the demands for self-government, Thompson in his wisdom thought it imperative to stress them. As a patronizing cover he sought to fan the dying flames of a deceptive liberalism: 'The angry ghost of nationalism and imperialism must be exorcised from a region where they have stalked so long'.[127]

Reflecting on Indian realities from the same perspective, Thompson, in October 1936, felt somewhat rattled by Congress' decision not to touch the constitutional reforms. Eager to formulate his own opinion as a 'pure liberal', he tried to draw out searching commitments from Jawaharlal Nehru on several issues. In particular, the liberal in him felt cheated by the statement of Nehru that the Congress would not touch the constitution despite the assurances of the viceroy and the secretary of state. He could not visualize any substantial gain for India if the constitution was thus wrecked by non-participation. He was at a loss to understand why the Congress always tended to ignore the most stable force of Indian society—the princes. Nehru was asked point blank if a 'genuine independence within the Empire', as enjoyed by the dominions, would satisfy the nationalists and if a Balkanised India would be cheerfully entertained by him.[128] Fearing the prospect of concentration of authority in a few hands, Thompson enquired about Nehru's opinion on the political future of India, then being developed away from all democratic norms. This was necessitated, Thompson thought, by the spurt of religious ascendancy, communal animosities, social and religious disabilities of the outcastes and the inability of an independent India to reshape its army then representing preponderantly, the Punjabi element with U.P. contributing to it as a 'bad second'.[129] Persuading Nehru to cooperate with the Government he urged this undisputed leader of the Indian masses, having a firm command both on his feelings and speech and gifted with a cultivated Western sensibility, to enlarge his perspective, extend his vision and to recognize the realities that lay beyond immediate perceptions. As sceptical as ever of Gandhi, Thompson lambasted that unless the Mahatma discovered some new message, 'he runs the risk, from now on, of being merely a powerful Ganapati. . . .'[130] This, he thought, was written on the wall as the Civil Disobedience movement, having nearly succeeded, petered out. The new Ganapati would be able to rouse the *ganas* but with 'no objective to direct them'.[131] He would turn out, Thompson sneered, to be merely a conservative intriguer. Surrounded by liberal Indian politicians, Thompson framed the outline of his arguments. 'The facts of fact today seem to me', Thompson pleaded, '(1) that the forces who govern have a far greater superiority than ever before, over those who are governed and (2) that the standard of ruthlessness has risen immeasurably'.[132] In view of this immense hardening of forces, Edward Thompson implored, 'Your tactics seemed to me bad. . . .' Rebuffed for his immaturity and reprimanded for the silly company he kept, Thompson decided to write his final testament to his enraged friend, Nehru.

Edward Thompson was about to leave India for good 'after 36 years wasted in trying to help forward what seemed to me truth and decency'.[133] Dejected and awfully sad, Thompson concluded that 'any Englishman who troubled himself about India is a fool. This is the judgement of Indians also, and no doubt they are right'.[134] He had become bitter as his complaisant gestures were spurned by nationalist India and noted with surprise that only foreigners 'whom your countrymen approve of and will accept as allies' were those who saw 'everything Indian through the haze of rose coloured ecstasy'.[135] If the Indians could not perceive the utter ineffectiveness of those 'idolators', Thompson felt helpless, 'I must conclude—it must be because they are really effective, in some fashion hidden from my sight'. He thought the 'great army of sentimentalists' and 'uncritical enthusiasts' have made India look like a 'silly nightmare wearing a fool's cap. . . .'[136] It was a pity, Thompson exclaimed, that Nehru would not be able to prevent being increasingly 'surrounded by a circus, such as beset Mahatmaji!' 'It is your fate. And it is abominable bad luck, because you cannot help sometimes seeing what has happened!' He was sorry to see an intelligent man like Nehru being forced to do 'puja' to the new mandir of Bharatmata in a land where 'utter mumbo-jumbo triumphs'.[137] It was time for both of them to part company as Nehru, it seemed to Thompson, was determined to break his heart 'on the folly of your own people'. India, like Aurobindo Ghosh, remained incomprehensible. He was mystified to observe that while the educated Indians were eager to struggle uncompromisingly for political independence, they were prepared to fight unscrupulously to keep the distorted social realities intact. In Shastri, Ambedkar, Sapru and the Modern Review Group, he found, unlike Nehru, a set of realists, rationalists and even patriots. Thompson did not think it expedient to contest Nehru's opinion on them. But he found in Nehru's camp more dangerous elements 'who have as much patriotism as that of a hyena' and presaged that the time would come when Nehru would admit this. Even Nehru, 'so magnanimous' in his *Autobiography* had become, Thompson complained, frivolously contentious and had been 'consistently ungenerous to my people' throughout *Glimpses of History*.[138] He assured Nehru that he was not carrying back with him any anti-Indian feeling or malice. But all the same he refused to become an eulogist of the deplorable social and political realities in India. He had failed to impress upon a westernized 'Panditjea', that even the so-called 'unreasonableness of Englishmen' had a rational basis. Sixteen years earlier he had thought it entirely justified on ethical grounds to go for non-cooperation and was sure of its success if carried through. But its long half-hearted continuance merely strengthened the Muslim League and vested interests. He had never thought Gandhi wrong until the Round Table Conference when the Mahatma 'became both arrogant and irrelevant'. Having come to the Conference, the Mahatma was not justified in refusing to recognize the other Indians many of whom 'had paid a price for their opinions' and were engaged in a common endeavour and hope.[139] Thompson's seasoned opinion was that the Congress as an organization did not make any substantial progress since the anti-partition days and Gandhi had no longer the power to do anything other than rousing specious and destructive passions.

As for the profession of socialism by the Congress Left, Thompson was categorical. Socialism was, in the context of Indian poverty, fairly tempting, though viewed with a long-term perspective, a bad tactic. Thompson believed that with the firm opposition of the Muslims and the princes as a constant irritant, it was foolish to release the forces of 'priestcraft and superstition' as the vanguard of the Congress party and to indulge in language that would be contradicted by practice.[140] 'You are going to defeat yourselves,' Thompson warned. 'The reaction is going to be terrible and damaging'. Imploring Nehru to accept office in order to prevent the growing consolidation of conservative forces in India with the British Tories, Thompson added: 'You will make the National Movement an almost solely Hindu movement as (I am sorry, but) it now is.'[141] Thompson summarily dismissed Sunderland's *India in Bondage* as an unreliable book, but he did not stop for a moment to point out its inaccuracies. He fell foul of Sunderland because of his suggestion that the Hindu-Muslim ill-feeling was often due to sinister official influence.[142] In a number of articles in the *Spectator*, Thompson made a significant contribution to the imperialistic cant by his thesis that England did not exploit India simply because India was not rich in natural resources. He conceded generously that in South Africa Gandhi was 'overwhelmingly in the right', but, he complained, in India he was not, because, among other things, Gandhi did not 'find time to visit my own country'. Thompson was appalled by Gandhi's views on the cow, caste and Lancashire. His soft heart bled at the injustice Gandhi did to Indian women by asking them to spin. In fact it became apparent that although the author of *Atonement* and *The Other Side of the Medal* was also the author of *The Reconstruction of India* and the letters in *The Times*, it was a different personality and a different mind. The former could be seen by the sickbed of Indian students in London while the latter was to be seen only in official parties and dinners in West End.[143]

Thompson and his friends could never comprehend that the strength of the Congress organization could not be measured by the pronouncements of some odd individuals consisting of a bunch of illustrious obscures and sheer nitwits but by the forces of the larger masses. In that test, Nehru emphasized, 'our strength is far greater today than it has ever been'. Nehru was amazed that although much was made of the poverty of India, Thompson's prescriptions had no reference to either poverty or unemployment. Thompson talked of democracy in most exciting terms and regretted its failure in Europe and yet he was inclined not to appreciate the value of 'the only democratic organisation' in India in 1937 and derided it as a 'handful of people at the top imposing their will on others'.[144] Referring to Thompson's theoretical formulation, Nehru invited him to appreciate that even the Congress had the right to make mistakes. But both in triumphs and defeats, Indian politics was increasingly being shaped by mass urges. The human material available in India, notwithstanding its shortcomings, was to form the base of the nationalist movement. One could not build illusory castles and empty dreams. Nehru made a national consensus admirably clear. The idea of a commonwealth of independent states could not be realized under the British Empire even if that Empire dropped its imperialist characteristics and emerged as a truer commonwealth. 'I do not think' he added, 'that it is possible for an Empire like this ever to shed its imperialism without liquidating old structure and building afresh on a new basis. So far India is concerned, it is almost impossible for it to become a really true member of a free British commonwealth.'[145]

F.E. Penny had presaged Thompson as early as 1909 and in doing so added a firm foundation to the imperial assessment of Indian nationalism.[146] Dharma Govinda, the well-dressed figure, was the nationalist leader who had a special capacity for attracting a young audience. Many of them were mere boys who lacked experience but were eager to enter the difficult field of politics with the rashness of youth. 'They were panting to promulgate doctrines of practical consequence of which they knew nothing and cared nothing. They mistook the enthusiasm of prejudice for noble devotion'. They professed to be acting for the benefit of the country, whereas they were inflated with a desire for notoriety. They were, Penny noted, 'actuated with an insane wish to rouse emotion in the multitude and stir dangerous passions not easy to allay'.[147] None had, he added, any sense of responsibility or a real devotion to the precepts of brotherhood and equality. No one had foregone caste prejudices or set aside religious or racial antipathy. Education had left these raw, 'rudderless youths', Penny analysed, without discipline, since the rod had been abolished by a benevolent government from their schools, without religion, since John Stuart Mill's and Herbert Spencer's books, along with those of their successors, had been placed unreservedly in their hands and without occupation, since they had all sought to improve their condition and had failed to attain that particular object of their ambition. The Congress, Penny concluded, merely reflected the ambiguity and incongruity of this lopsided development of Indian humanity given to empty slogans of Swaraj and Swadeshi.[148]

The situation was viewed almost in the same vein in 1935 by Lord Lothian, a well-known socialist in his correspondence with Jawaharlal Nehru.[149] Reminding Nehru that 'we are in the midst of one of the most creative epochs in human history' resplendent with 'the ideals represented by the word socialism', Lothian exhorted that 'Britain is shedding the old imperialism and is actively concerned with trying to find the way to prevent the anarchy involved in universal national self-determination from ending in fresh wars or in a new deluge of imperialism'. He held forth optimistically that Britain would also shortly embark on the practical problem of reconciling socialism with the liberal tradition of individual liberty and initiative. In this context, he maintained, that as power passed into the hands of the political classes in India and as education and the press increased their influence, religion, race and language would assume increasing political importance and power, and 'will become fissiparous in effect'. He asserted, like many of his compatriots, that religion was still the most powerful influence with the masses in India as it had been in Europe. If the constitutional road was rejected in India, he was certain that she would inevitably follow the example of Europe. To start with, he asserted, religious wars would become endemic especially when they were stimulated for political purposes and India would not emerge as united but divided into a number of dictatorial states separated by race and language and armed to the teeth against one another 'both militarily and economically with their internal development consequently paralysed, or she will once more fall under the control of some external Imperialist power as is happening in China'.[150]

C.F. Andrews, E.M. Forster, Edward Thompson, Horace Alexander and Robert Byron tried to resolve the contradictions of imperialism by weaving a sense of obligation into the system. 'To see a great race given scope for the exercise of its greatest strength, to see it conduct the art of government on a scale and with a perfection accomplished by no previous race, is to achieve that sublime pleasure in the works of man, which, ordinarily, is conferred only by the great artists. This I saw in India'.[151] With regard to the future of Indo-British relationship, Robert Byron was seriously concerned; but he merely reiterated the views of Andrews and Forster when he pleaded for a delicate balance of human relationships.

The Western man's assumption of racial superiority, Byron argued, had rendered him odious to the East. And the only means which the East devised of resisting this assumption were either to swallow the materialism whole and undigested, or else, take a little of it and rebel against him forcibly. Japan tried the first course and was about to lose her soul; China opted for the second and relapsed into chaos.[152] 'India remains', he felt, 'holding in her precarious balance, the residue of hope.' The problem, as he saw it, was to regulate the contact between the East and the West.[153] The Englishmen were to strike a balance between the masses attached to land and religion, the princes firmly entrenched in an advantageous position and having 'little real sympathy for social and political ideas which pass in our time for progress', and the westernized intelligentsia who provided 'the political motive power to the country'.[154] Jane Roy in her *Fascinating India* preferred to opt for this remarkably liberal prescription. She thought that the real culprit was the cumulative misunderstanding between the well-meaning ruling race and the polite and civil Indians.[155] The ignorance of Western manners often unwillingly caused offence to the Western observers. Jane Roy concluded that the cause for misrepresentation ought to be sought in the existing system of education which turned out 'infamous Gods of all Gods but masters of none!' In common with many Indian experts, Roy held that if the British Government spent money on sanitation, provided wells and other improvements instead of 'millions of expenditure on education of a wrong sort' a very satisfactory reward would have awaited them in India.[156] 'We have attempted', Jane Roy lamented, 'to westernise an Eastern people rather than revive and purify them to build on what was already there. Less western and more simple may well be our motto.'[157] She was convinced that a great deal of unrest in the country was largely due to a mutual misunderstanding that could have been remedied at the outset.[158] This purblind demeanour with regard to a possible accommodation of diverse interests provided the uneasy undercurrent of *Zakaullah of Dilli*, *A Passage to India* and *Farewell to India*.[159]

This India of Strickland, Kim, Agate, Forster, Penderel Moon, Puran Bhagat and Gunga Din was also shared by jungles, tigers, babus and sepoys. Besides, the 'borderland area' where the 'last drop of White blood ends and the full tide of Black sets in' was inhabited by the so-called Anglo-Indians. They looked down upon 'the natives as only a man with seven-eighth native blood in his veins can do'. Michele D'Cruze was one of them who, in his telegraph office at Tibasu, had a lonely existence. But when the Hindus and the Muslims 'raised an aimless sort of Donnybrook', the Indian police officer, 'obeying his race instincts', recognized the diluted drop of British blood in Michele and pleaded with him to rise to the occasion as the sole representative of the white race.[160]

In India the white man was always the ruler and the native was always the ruled. It could not have been the other way around.[161] To put it in other words, the Englishman was painted as virile, bold, energetic and masculine, while the natives were presented, with the exception of some Pathan tribesmen of the frontier, as effeminate, weak, cowardly and lethargic. Masculine Christianity was firmly established as the governing principle of imperialism and this perception continued almost unabated. One hears its echo in the taped reminiscences of Mountbatten as printed by his literary spokesman. Jawaharlal Nehru, it has been emphasized, was no more than an impetuous political innocent who had to learn much from

Lord Mountbatten on the virtues of the ruling class. Vallabhbhai Patel appears as a mewing pussy cat cut to size by Mountbatten's aristocratic temper. The ever-smiling Gandhi appeared as inscrutable as Kipling's India[162] and, at times as inflamed and impetuous as a dangerous Trotskyite. Of the earlier generation, Percival Spear has left behind no better and perhaps a more quaint gallery of pen-portraits.[163]

The most sympathetic spokesman of Anglo-India was E.M. Forster. But even he did not discern in India any coherent element or an intelligible core. It was, he thought, 'a vague jumble of rajas, babus and elephants...' It was, wrote Forster, in an attempt to locate a meeting point beyond superficial human differences and tragedies, 'country, fields, then hills, jungles, hills and more fields. . .' without any romance and without any Pan-Indian entity. It was a muddle, a grand chaos.[164] It was inscrutable—an undefinable continent of the most outrageous contradictions. Forster could not step out of Kipling's paradigm that it was impossible to 'plumb the Oriental mind', and even if one did it was not 'worth the toil'.[165] That perception was restated by Flora Annie Steel. She found India stagnant, featureless, a dead sea, a mere waste of water without form or void. It was unchanging and unchangeable. Like Mrs Moore of *A Passage to India* she could only visualize and grasp India as a collection of mosques, temples, factories, hovels, offices, palaces and mansions—all enveloped in a blue mist. 'India was as multitudinous as the sands of the Sea'.[166] Eric Musprat in his *Journey Home* experienced a feeling of relief as he boarded his ship at Madras: 'All my dreams were going to come true. At last this land of India was going to be left behind me. I was surely the happiest man on that ship as she ploughed out of the harbour this morning. I had muddled my way back on to my own path and all the sadhus and gurus of India were welcome to theirs. The houses of Madras and the land of India died away in the hot blur behind me'.[167] But a 'muddle' was not an adequate definition. It was an escapist's fear of reality. It exposed the subjective narrowness of the viewer and conceptual shallowness of his perception. It signified a remarkable lack of comprehension.[168]

Rudyard Kipling's aphorism, 'half-devil and half-child', the Mowgli, bred in the jungle with Sher Khan, Baloo and Hathi, was a representative imperial stereotype of an average Indian. He is Kipling's Gunga Din, Jim Corbett's Kunwar Singh and his loyal friends, the poor of India.[169] Flora Annie Steel's Deen Mahomed, 'the guardian of the Church of St John in-the-wilderness',[170] Margaret and Percival Spear's chowkidar and the head mali, April Swayne-Thomas' dhobi.[171] In India he was here, there and everywhere. He was, in imperial perception, either a *khidmutgar* or an unknown peasant or an impoverished artisan.

The *khidmutgar* seemed to have a natural aptitude, F.A. Aitken concluded with a patronizing relish, for detecting or even inventing the master's wants and supplied them before the master was aware of them.[172] They included the Indian 'boy' with a fantastic area of domestic concern under his command; the syce with his implements, *jhule* and *booroos* and his concept of *agadee, peecharee* and *curraree;* the *bootlair* sahib with his preference for 'indirect to direct taxation' and his established claims 'to go to the market'; the *hamd,* the duster and the dhobi with their passions 'for destruction'; the ayah hanging like 'a black cloud over and around the infant mind'; the durzi in close contact with the dhobi; the mali with his *khurpi* as the 'necessary machinery by which our exile life is made to be the graceful thing it often is'; the silent *bhisti* never asking for a raise in his pay, the *hajam,* the barber with an inherited natural instinct for shaving and for circulating that lively interest in one another's well-being which characterizes the little station and the *chaprasis* 'the outward expression of our authority and the metre gauge of our importance' endowed with both official obligations and private duties 'including that of escorting the coming generation of government servants in their little perambulators'.[173]

Together with the 'miscellaneous-wallahs' these men with their splendid 'capacity for obedience' probably taught, Aitken wrote, the English once again 'how to govern which is one of the forgotten arts in the West'. The *khidmutgar* obeyed orders without question, did not quarrel with fellow servants and tried not to squander wages in the bazaar.[174] Caught between a bitter hatred for the feringhee and the Hindus, Flora Annie Steel's Deen Mahomed would not hesitate to risk his life while saving the life of a brown-haired baby of a small British colony adjoining the church.[175] By and large the *khidmutgar* was obedient and servile. Dr Westlake of Flora Annie Steel had felt astounded when he found that his patient, Raheem, prayed for him with a radiant smile. 'I never expected', the doctor exclaimed, 'to hear a man thank me rapturously for cutting off both his feet!'[176] The *khidmutgar* was an innocent and inconspicuous creature endowed with a set of superstitious imperatives. He could not believe, for example, that anything was ever done without a purpose and without some promise of return. Moonaswami, the mali, had never been able to comprehend his mistress' love for flowers. He was convinced that she had some secret purpose in her mind. The proud butler had assured him that the blossoms were needed purely and simply for the adornment of the visiting room. But this was not an adequate explanation for the swarthy mali. Deep within his heart he believed that the memsahib used them for propitiating an arcane demon and performing a puja that would extract valuable information. How else would she know, he questioned, how to make the flowers grow with the wonderful powder she sprinkled on their roots?[177] The *khidmutgar* was, however, also a calculating animal and like Ram Din, the *khansama*, he could even display remarkable inhumanity for the sake of a few rupees[178] or like the chowkidar of a dak bungalow, a laughing cavalier with 'a perpetual hilarious demeanour', he was always keen for a baksheesh and had to be dismissed as a jungly-wallah.[179]

The Indian peasant, on the other hand, was but a human replica of his own ox. Both of them would not even raise their heads to see if the Pindaris, the revolutionaries, the '*paltan*' or the Swadeshi-wallahs moved across the countryside like a storm. He was, as Lockwood Kipling detected and Meston, Marris and Craddock confirmed, the foundation of the Raj as he toiled hard to feed his fellowmen.[180] His meagre income on the fragmented patches of land, his complete subordination to the law of karma and his life-long ideal revealed in the folklore of Puran Bhagat[181] were his sole possessions. Much to the happiness of administrators he did not even go for food riots in times of scarcity. Malcolm Lyall Darling argued that the Punjab villages needed less to be reconstructed than to be reconditioned. He underlined that it was to the village that one ought to look for its regeneration and to the peasant that one ought to go to ascertain its needs and desires. It was the peasants, Darling urged, that one must inspire, plan and lead. 'The townsmen might be quicker, clever, smarter, richer', he insisted, 'but the peasant has one advantage which overweighs all these'. He had the unconscious depth of character of all who lived and laboured in the open air 'the constant fellowship with the great companions—with the earth and sky and the fire of the sky'.[182] Claud H. Hill found Kipling's description of the voiceless millions in India as sound as ever. To expect that the non-vocal millions would rise and help the British in their dilemma was a vacuous claim and an idle dream.[183] Meston, Craddock, Pentland, Butler, Darling, Hallett and Irwin were conscious of it. All of them were hesitant, circumspect and suspicious. But they continued to hope against hope and pray for the Raj, for British absolutism felt secure in the poverty and fatalism of the Indian peasantry. British India was impregnable, safe and exalted in the company of peasants, artisans, sepoys, servants, orthodox Brahmins steeped in mythology, Sanskrit learning and a 'fabulous kind of history'[184] and the ulema with their remarkable instinctive sense of authority and love for official patronage. 'Those who visit India for pleasure or profit never come in contact with the real Indian—the Indians whose loyalty and devotion alone', wrote Jim Corbett, a hunter, a storyteller and a Christian gentleman, 'made it possible for a handful of men to administer, for close on two hundred years, a vast subcontinent with its teeming millions. To impartial historians I will leave the task of recording whether or not that administration was beneficial to those to whom I have introduced you, the poor of my India'.[185]

Out of the melting pot of *khidmutgars* and the fatalist peasantry, the English evolved another significant stereotype, the martial races of India. They formed the foundation of the proverbial Indian loyalty and forged the security system of the Raj. As opposed to the 'soft' and somewhat 'urbanized' upper castes of India, it was sketched with remarkable competence, the martial races showed the traits of endurance, valour and izzat.[186] They included a variety of people from the Pathan tribesmen of the frontier to the forest men of Assam.

Edmund Candler in *The Sepoy* catalogued some of the traits of these men on the basis of his long association with the Indian army.[187] Of all these races, it was universally recognized, the Gurkhas were distinguished by a boyish cheerfulness. The Gurkha laughed, it was added, like Atkins, even when the shells missed him, describing both a small skirmish and a big battle indifferently as shikar. His visual image was his mental range; soldiering was his ritual. He shunned hatred and fanaticism and suppressed his personality religiously with a tardy smile. He did not intrigue or brood. He was exclusive and churlish but not indifferent or disrespectful. He was shy and mechanically smart and loved his officer not because he was a sahib but because he was his sahib and the officer had to prove that he was his first.

The Sikhs formed another 'race'. It was claimed that the 'Indian Army kept Sikhism alive'. War, Candler philosophized, was a conserver of the Khalsa, peace a dissolvent. It was a '*quam*' with no bigotry in faith. Without the incentive to honour and an 'open door' to military services for the Sikhs, it was maintained, the ineradicable instincts of the Hindus would have reasserted themselves. The British Government thought that it was its primary responsibility to insulate the Sikh youths from the irresistible lure of nationalism. The ideal Sikh soldier was stubborn, tenacious, patient, devoted, courageous and independent of spirit and he was tempered by the 'noble traditions' of the Khalsa. He was at peace with his cosmos, respected his officer and received no injury to his self-esteem. At times he might feel wronged and his pride could run riot. 'The brooding or intriguing Sikh', the imperial prescription warned, 'is a nuisance and a danger'.[188]

Next to the Sikhs, the P.M. or Punjabi Mussulman made up a substantial part of the army. He came from varied stock but he fell 'easily, unlike a Hindu, into disciplinary ways'. Although he was conspicuous by the absence of a distinctiveness, he was 'every bit as good as the best' in gallantry, endurance, coolness and dependability.[189] The English officers invariably hailed him as a cheery soul with modest ambitions and for having a 'wholesome contempt of the civilian ways' of the Hindus. In him, 'you find the pick of Islam in the Indian Army'. He was not a man of wonders, it was argued, but the sahib found comfort in his obscurity.[190]

The Pathan, Candler voiced a universal assessment, was genuinely more of a democrat than the Sikh and more careless and happy-go-lucky than the Punjabi Mussulman. He was a bit of an adventurer and restless by nature. He was a gambler and a sportsman and had a good deal of *joie de vivre*. By all counts he had 'more in common with the Englishman than any other sepoy' despite 'his savage code of conduct'.[191] The Dogra was considered shy, reserved, sensitive about his private affairs and a bit fussy about his personal appearance. He did not have the Pathan's devil-may-care attitude or the 'pleasing swagger' of the Sikh. But he was intensely proud, conservative and aristocratic. He showed the highest qualities of endurance and courage under the most trying circumstances and also intense affection for his sahib in equal proportion to that of the Gurkha for his officer.[192]

The Maratha, a less conspicuous type, was the 'Cinderella' of the Indian army in Mesopotamia. Though he looked dreamy and pensive, he could fight and had grit. Dark skinned and with irregular features, he had all 'the virtues and limitations' of an agriculturist. He was slow in thought and unsophisticated but invariably endowed with strong affections, firm endurance and a spontaneous bravery. The Maratha, the imperial character roll recorded, was ready for anything that was going on. The Jats who composed the backbone of Punjab had a certain solidity about them. Neither seduced by Islam nor attracted by the Khalsa these 'descendants of the Scythians' possessed a strong fibre. It took 'earthquakes and volcanoes to turn a regiment of these hard-bitten men', wrote Candler, 'out of a position they have been given to hold'. Seemingly unacquainted with fear, initiative and enterprise alike and not troubled by nerves and imagination, Candler added, every 'knock hardens him' and renders him increasingly 'unconcerned of defeat'.[193]

The Garhwali had the 'cheerfulness and simplicity of the Gurkhas and the same love of a scrap for its own sake... and the same inability to grow up'.[194] The officers were delighted to find that 'they are always children' who saw red in a fight and go for anything in front of them regardless of the consequences. The Khattak, impulsive, mercurial, easily excited and seldom dispirited felt strongly that he ought to return home from war as an acknowledged bahadur if only for the attendant social prestige. The Hazara of Mongol origin was, on the other hand, quite different from the rest. He was perhaps 'the nearest approach to the Europeans you will find in the Indian Army'. In his sense of humour, quick temper, rough and tumble wrestling, ragging and practical jokes, Candler jibed, the Hazara was not so very far removed from the Islanders of the West.

There were also the Mers, lacking in initiative but never failing in emulation, the Ranghars of eastern Punjab, a class of born horsemen and horsemasters and the Meenas who had a strong Rajput blood-myth whose training into a fighting force represented the 'domestication of a wild creature'. The Jharwas of Assam were lazy and hard to train, but were considered as ' first class men at any jungle work'. The Drabi and his mules provided the 'last work of scientific transport'. The Santhals constituted the principal labour corps with expressions on 'their faces endorsing everything Rousseau said about primitive content'. 'Evolution has spared them', Candler indulged himself, 'they have even escaped the unkindness of war.'[195] The myth of martial race rested on the simple formulation: where the soil did not leave enough to go round, one would get a good recruit. 'If you want recruits don't go to an irrigated district. Water demoralises them'.[196] The children of poverty and labour followed better than they could lead.

In search of a second line of defence, the British administration turned to the faded aristocracy with its husk culture. There were the Awadh talukdars, trained in Colvin School and addicted to 'poetry and perfume'[197] and the Rajput Rajas, the picturesque survival from the age of chivalry.[198] They were appreciated as skilled sportsmen, endowed with a code of conduct based on the values of the British public school. There was no lack of curiosity about their mythological genealogy and no dearth of attempts to eulogize the achievements of the reforming rulers and their modern and efficient dewans.[199] Thus, Udaipur was hailed as the shrine of chivalry and romance; Jodhpur was recommended as the warrior state and Sir Pratap Singh as the noblest Rajput of them all; Bikaner was honoured as the desert conjured into a garden by its soldier-statesman, Sir Ganga Singh; Gwalior was applauded as the Gibraltar of the desert; Baroda was acclaimed as the state of India's philosopher prince; Hyderabad was exalted as the Prussian princedom; Bhopal was cited with reverence in white papers as the begums governed from behind the purdah with vigour; Patiala and Kapurthala evoked unquestioning confidence; while Kashmir, the diadem of India, sparked off lyrical verses from viceroys and civil servants alike. Finally, there was the legendary Ranji of Nawanagar who played for England to the stunning delight of an indulgent British audience.[200] Whether as a resident or a private tutor, the young Englishman had turned the half-savage boys of princely India (like the young prince of Louis Broomfield's *Ranchipur*) into instruments of change and they were moulded and sharpened into men and rulers.[201] Mayo, Lytton, Theodore Morison, Valentine Chirol, Lionel Curtis, Curzon, Hardinge, Maud Diver and Irwin agreed on one point: Royal India remained, with its legendary genealogy and inflated achievements, the strongest and the most stable element in the land. It was the loyal India. It mattered mighty little if the princes were not enthusiastic about vote and ballot paper. They were perturbed by the ascendancy of an upstart democracy. The best of them, it was reminded, were well-versed in the theory and practice of good government.

India, Maud Diver expatiated, was a land of peasantry and the power they wielded was expressed through one of her oldest institutions, the panchayat, that 'builds itself as a pyramid, from the smallest village up to the Maharaja, whose aristocratic rule is thus seen to rest on a democratic basis'.[202] In modern democracies, wrote an expert of the Round Table, the personal factor was still as great as ever. 'Much more is this the case in India, which is still at heart conservative and aristocratic'.[203] In these native states, there was a larger field in which India could experiment and progress on its own lines. They were, it was affirmed, 'a barometer of progress of India'.[204] Forster's *Hill of Devi* nursed these sentiments although the author was far too sensitive not to mask his position with liberal formulations thereby offering some positive points to his enthusiastic literary critics.

If the choice was confined between a benevolent autocracy and a corrupt democracy, everyone enjoined, the decision was automatic and unambiguous. It was invariably for the 'perpetual ally against a common enemy', the babu.[205] The princes responded warmly to those gestures. 'The princes of India', one of them confided to Katherine Mayo, 'made no treaty with the Government that included Bengali babus. We shall never deal with this new lot of Jacks-in-office. . .'[206] Pat came the strokes from the patronizing master and by the time of Irwin's viceroyalty they were encouraged to demand from their exalted Chamber of Princes a dominant voice in the Round Table Conference.

The comical creation of Western education in India, popularized by administrators and ideologues, globe-trotting tourists and sensitive writers, journalists and pamphleteers, Conservatives and Liberals alike was the odd droll, the babu, 'a potential rival'. Ramanand of Flora Annie Steel was one of them. He had read Herbert Spencer and Stuart Mill. He was perhaps needlessly lavish in vague expressions such as the individual rights of man, etc. but then he, in common with his kind, had only lately become acquainted with the political ideas of the West although he had not as yet learned the exact connotation of these terms—'this being an art which needs centuries of national and individual struggle for its attainment'.[207] No man, Aldous Huxley discerned, loved another who threatened to deprive him of his privileges and powers.

The babu was a distinct imperial prototype. He was often spelt and pronounced with an infinite number of 'os' seeking to impress his close affinity with baboons.[208] Edward Thompson who, like all Englishmen, must have mispronounced all Indian proper nouns, made fun of the Indian schoolteacher's English pronunciation without embarrassment when he talked endlessly about the 'dishipline' of the 'ischool' being 'bhery bad'. In Flora Annie Steel's Ramanand's hallucination and Casserly's Chunnerburty's 'idiomatic' English, the Hindu 'mumbo-jumbo' becomes irksome. Invariably, the pen-portrait of the babu became unfalteringly malevolent.[209]

Sydney Low's characterization of the Bengali babu is perhaps a modest summary of British perception.[210] To the resident of Calcutta, the typical Bengali babu was 'the man of the clerkly, semi-educated class'. He had, Sydney Low vouched, nearly the best brains in India. He had the readiest tongue and a prodigious memory and his fertility in talk was inexhaustible. 'He is something of an Irishman, something of an Italian, something of a Jew: if one can conceive of an Irishman who would run away from a fight instead of running into it, an Italian without a sense of beauty and a Jew who would not risk five pounds on the chance of making five hundred'. He was very clever but his cleverness did not lead far on the road of achievement. He had no initiative, no enterprise, no mutual confidence. He was timid and lacked confidence and courage. He was not picturesque like the 'wild man of the north-west frontier'. He had no 'swagger of the militant brotherhood of the Punjab'. In appearance he was by no means attractive; he was dark, short and corpulent and yet, if properly supervised, he rendered useful service, being adaptable and intelligent. Strangely enough, he played football barefoot and might 'make a good match with Thomas Atkins in his thickest ammunition boots'.[211] Paradoxically, this odd creature became the object of supreme hatred and a source of unpredictable danger. The Bengali babu had his natural allies in the shy but determined Chitpawan Brahmins in Maharashtra, the extrovert and militant Aryans of the Punjab, the graceful and subtle Nairs and the persistent and meticulous Tamil Brahmins of the South.[212] Like a 'googly' or 'chinaman', in the game of cricket, these were the deceptive social elements representing the unpredictable exhortation of an inscrutable India.

But all these professional middle classes were not seditionists and it was more than apparent that the British were thinking of manipulating this vacillating stratum to labour for and propagate British virtues, values and duties. They searched for characters like Nilkamal Ghoshal 'the toady who pocketed insult and humiliation for the sake of a few kind words from a Lieutenant-Governor and a worthless *Rai-Bahadurship*; but he pretended not to care'.[213] His own brother turned over to extreme hatred for the West but Nilkamal remained loyal. Although he lent his sympathetic ears to the nationalist rhetoric in his advanced years he kept aloof from politics and upheld his faith in England that was wise, fearless and generous. His son was also an Oxford man and was the collector of Vishnugram. His ties with the alien Government were, however, less firm than his father's. He cultivated closer relations with the Brahmo Samaj but 'the Samaj had moved far from its older enthusiasm'. It had become anti-Christian and its unitarianism got linked up with Vedanta doctrine and it had moved closer to the nationalists. In the new generations of this professional class, Thompson found in 1937, there was less enthusiasm. On the contrary, there was an element of unbalanced depression, a mixture of nervousness, assurance and doubt. It appeared to Thompson that the two English codes of ethics were in conflict in this strange predicament of the Bhadraloks—between the commitment of duty and obligations and the demands of being 'propah'. It was possible for the Empire to absorb hesitant loyalty and organized doubts. The sceptic Indians would, despite moral reluctance, continue to serve the Raj efficiently and their service would provide the necessary legitimacy to the Government by providing a sort of habitual obedience. An Indian would never be accepted as an Englishman despite his immaculate British training and sensibility; but some of them had to be humoured for the maintenance of the Raj depended for its existence on a vast army of loyal citizens with different levels of diffidence, doubt and opposition. If some of them imitated the English to a point of near perfection they became a subject of sneering ridicule in the clubs; if some others presented a spectacle of crude aping, they would provide the mess and the clubs with unmitigated amusement. In both these capacities these 'collaborating' Indians would be the basis of its rule in India demanding careful social management. Thompson would continue to believe that despite the atmosphere of hatred and bitterness both the rulers and the ruled had over the years learned to appreciate each other's merits. The Raj, according to this synthetic logic, was therefore not founded on simple brute force and an adjustment was still possible within the Empire.

Vernon George, in 1942, dedicated *The Crown of Asia* to Rudyard Kipling in gratitude and admiration.[214] India was central to his concept of the Empire and it was threatened by a combination of annoying forces that included a Japanese invasion, an internal nationalist *émeute* and the criminal apathy of British public opinion at home towards India and its strategic and commanding positions. India, the Devil's playground, was a conquered land.[215] It was considered, by the small English community in India, almost sacrilege if Mary an English girl, continued to encourage Prince Izat Khan, an Indian aristocrat, despite his British public school manners. 'They are imitative blighters', E.W. Savi made British attitude unambiguous, 'and English public schools do a lot to lay on veneer and polish. When they are multi-millionaires they managed to pay for the best, and culture is acquired if the opportunities are to hand'. No one wants to deny 'that the Indians are a brainy lot, but the fact remains that they are racially unfit—a case of East is East and West is West'.[216] As a crowd, the Indians could be almost formidable and therefore nearly uncontrollable. But as individuals, the imperial character roll proclaimed, the Indian invariably exhibited, in relation to the overlord, a strange creepy subservience. The Indian, Charles Monoly observed, added a cubit to the stature of his dignity when he found a master. This was, he added, the most significant national characteristic. 'And for that reason I have come to doubt the capacity of India as a whole for independence'.[217]

Forster's babu, Godbole, is not funny.[218] He is farcical. He has some dated bookish knowledge but he inspires no respect. As a teacher, he is remarkably insipid and cannot be trusted with any responsible assignment. Forster doubts if he represents any substantial opinion in the country. He, however, makes no bones about the tacit assertion that Godbole reflects the aspirations of a new middle class with half-baked education.[219] Flora Annie Steel's Govind Sahai, a Kayastha, with his pale intelligent face is a bookworm and has a passion for examinations. Full of mysterious thoughts, he is verbose, confused and a pronounced failure in life, unconcerned with the hazards of accepting realities.[220]

If the portrayals of Professor Godbole or Govind Sahai irritate the reader, Girish De of the *Head of the District* betrays a definite political prejudice of the Englishman in India.[221] He is presented as a Bengali of the

Bengalis, crammed with code and case laws. But he is more than an object of innocent satire. He represents the aspirations of the educated Indian gentlemen then competing successfully for government appointments. Kipling hated him and all those mischievous do-gooders who appointed him. This man, it is pointed out, is unfit to rule. Yardley-Orde,[222] probably an idealized Sundeman, ought to be appreciated for his superficial knowledge of India and her customs but the Bengali, Girish De is mocked at for his equally shallow references to Oxford, 'Home', bumb-suppers, cricket matches, hunting runs etc. Yardley-Orde's exhortations in rude, half completed, rough and commanding Urdu sentences were revered divinely. In sharp contrast, Girish De's 'effeminate utterance' of three innocent words, *hamara hukum hai* sparked off a spontaneous uprising. Yardley-Orde had the tenacity to know India; he had the determination to enforce obedience; he had the devotion of an imperial missionary commissioned by destiny in a savage land to make life a wee bit happier for many who were placed under his charge. Girish De, M.A., in contrast, though fairly successful in his lower Bengal district by creating a family preserve through bribery and patronage could not, despite favourable circumstances, rise above the rank of a 'despised babu', without character, without leadership, without a sense of mission and without the necessary pluck and grit. He was unfit as a natural leader of Pathan tribesmen who could easily be tamed by a young lad, Wee Willie Winkie, with British blood throbbing in his lionized heart.[223] This was not the inadequacy of an individual. It was, Kipling almost echoed a general consensus, the insufficiency of the race that inhabited the country.

It is quite natural that in the face of rising nationalism and its increasing militancy, all political differences in Britain melted away. The Conservatives, the Liberals and even the Radical Socialists lost their ideological specificities in relation to India. Kipling's banal assertion and uneven subtleties formed a permanent backdrop of British sensibility and it inspired the ascendancy of an insensate Maud Diver. Charles F. Andrew's ordeal of love was confined to a futile search for a new equilibrium of relationship between India and Britain. The Pyrrhic adventures of Curzon and the magnificent flamboyance of the Delhi Durbars were muffled by a stolid Minto, though his successors recognized the need for cautious steps and circumspection. A combative Valentine Chirol learned the lessons of adjustment. E.M. Forster relentlessly pursued the battered threads of personal relationship from a mysterious cave.

Even as late as 1946 the place did not change. 'Outside the carriage door', Forster majestically announced, 'India unrolls as before—monotonous, enigmatic, and at moments, sinister'. Poverty and malnutrition, he argued, still persisted. He was as ever unconcerned with the responsibilities of the rulers. He was, as ever, superficial. 'Rats ran about the labour camps at Bombay. One saw the chimneys', a rattled Forster discovered to his amazement, 'of the cotton mills at Ahmedabad but you see its mosques too'.[224] The factories in Calcutta, a bewildered Forster exclaimed, were tucked away amongst banyans and palms. 'And this unchangelessness in her', Forster continued to relate his experience with remarkable innocence, 'is called by some observers "the real India". I don't myself like the phrase "the real India". I suspect it'.[225] An administrator in Harcourt Butler, viceroys in Irwin, Linlithgow or Wavell, an architect in Lutyens and a visionary in Lionel Curtis agreed with the more extrovert exponents of imperialism that the history of India was a crowded annal of frequent foreign invasions and conquests, ruthless exploitations, inhuman practices and a childish extravaganza of impulsive lines, ugly forms and a morbid obsession with superficial veneers.[226] It was all 'tommy rot'.[227]

As the principal object of the State was reduced to the enforcement of law and order, there was neither the requirement nor the inclination for innovative ideas. The administration needed down-to-earth men. It was feasible, however, that it could have been saddled from time to time with men like McGoggin, 'clever—brilliantly clever' who could have worked inadvertently the wrong way.[228] It was reasonable to conjecture that the ideas of Comte, Spencer and Mill had 'fermented' his mind and he had come to India with a 'rarefied religion over and above his work'.[229] But such ideas based on 'soulless atheism' and 'concern for humanity' it was widely believed, were the product of an industrial and urbanized world and they could not be applied to the Indian realities. 'In India', Kipling wrote, 'where you really see humanity—raw, brown, naked humanity—with nothing between it and the blazing sky, and only the used-up, overhauled earth underfoot, the notion somehow dies away, and most folk come back to simpler theories'.[230] The administrators in India were unanimous in their endorsement of Kipling. There was no room in India, it was presumed, for a Wedderburn, a Cotton, a Robertson, an Andrews or any other inane do-gooder. Only a fool would have 'tried to hustle the East'.[231] There was no reason why a British administrator should have wasted his time in abstract theories and sought to prove an inconsequential point. The tenure of his assignment was short; the conditions of his service fairly severe; physical facilities limited; climate hostile and human environment both uncertain and, in some ways, awful. The stratified society of Simla, despite some of its comical aspects and artificial air, was eminently suitable for prompt and pre-emptive actions without any references to theories once the long-term purpose of the rule was grasped and popularized.[232] India appeared far too heterogenous and her problems too variegated to be compassed by a 'travelled idiot' of the Parliament or a well-meaning Wedderburn who sneered at the so-called misgovernment of India, or a Horace Alexander who endeavoured to discover an articulate lobby outside the exclusive clubs, or an Andrews who would have loved to clothe imperialism with Christian virtues. The sheer simplicity of the flow of instructions from the top to the bottom was admirably adapted to the requirements of a harsh land marked by the absence of personal contact between the ruler and the ruled. The Benthamite 'utilitarianism', the Liberal compromise of T.H. Green, the sensitive *petit bourgeois* complexes of the Fabians, the self-defeating logic of Liberalism of Gladstone, Montagu, Edward Thompson, Horace Alexander and the more extrovert opportunism of Ramsay MacDonald and the Labour ideologues were considered irrelevant prescriptions and relegated as fanciful conceptions in relation to the Indian situation.

4

Haughty Arrogance: Recurrent Adjustments

The absolutism of the Raj, it was presumed, was tempered and anointed by a moral obligation to civilization and history. The 'Deputy is above the Assistant, the Commissioner above the Deputy', Kipling stated categorically without any fuss, 'the Lieutenant-Governor above the Commissioner and the Viceroy above the four, under the orders of the Secretary of State, who is responsible to the Empress'.[1] This uncomplicated lineal progression of responsibility was sanctified by the dialectics of the system. Kipling would have liked to lead his readers to the inevitable conclusion that the Emperor was under the Maker. On this point there was a hush hush agreement. No one was prepared to opt for a rational explanation. The business of the young officer was to obey orders and follow the notings in the files instead of 'devastating the club with isms'. Men did not get 'beany in India', Kipling assured his avid readers, 'the climate and the work are against playing with words'.[2]

Work was essentially prosaic: there was no opportunity for the intrusion of outlandish poetry into it. Besides, it was felt inexpedient to meddle with the high policy of the State, especially when well-placed officials had been appointed to work it out.[3] Evidently, it was a well-ordered society. The members of the civil services were placed in their respective earthly stations by Providence and in the fulfilment of the tasks assigned to them they were to attain their salvation. There was no scope for deviation from this rule: *Pax Britannica* was complete in itself. It was amoral. Whether as an indigo planter establishing a complicated system of serfdom based on brute force in Bengal,[4] or as an opium magnate operating between Malwa and Ghazipur on the one hand and Hong Kong and Shanghai on the other defending boastfully the item of trade and its cultivation in the name of Christian morality[5], or as a tea colonizer of

Assam advocating unbridled acquisition of land and services by the Europeans with a devious system of repatriation of profit to dear old grey England simply by virtue of state power, the members of the 'Overseas Club' transcended petty moral scruples.[6] In the name of the rule of law, the bandobast of the Raj nurtured various exploitative systems for the benefit of the collaborating native groups.[7]

Under this centralized system, the viceroy and the secretary of state invariably drew popular attention each claiming a final say on every matter of first class importance. The tug of war between London and Simla for precedence in policy-making kept the official world spellbound. Considerations of experience, wisdom, statesmanship and judgement were interpreted as mere euphemisms for an inevitable clash of personalities. As a consequence, the inflated image of the private secretary of the viceroy emerged unchallenged. And if the private secretary was ambitious and the viceroy not frightfully alert, there was the possibility of the ascendancy of a Dunlop Smith or a John Finnil Wonder, who sought to 'draw matters which were entirely outside his province into his own hands'.[8] In such a contingency, there was the appearance of a more intriguing prospect of 'too much of Wonder' and 'too little of Viceroy'.[9]

With all the objectives of the British rule clearly defined, 'expediency' rather than 'a blue print' was adopted as the general rule. It was argued that there could not be any fixed policy when one had to deal with a country which was too vast for anyone to appreciate definitely and too complex and infinitely particularized even for a 'worthy oriental gentleman' to discern. The situation suggested two specific alternatives: 'A Policy is the blackmail levied on the fool, by the Unforeseen. I am not the former, and I do not believe in the latter. . . . Perhaps this is the Viceroy's way of saying, "Lie Low"'.[10]

Second, although there was neither the East nor the West, nor border, breed or birth, especially when two strong men happened to stand face to face irrespective of differences in the colour of their skin etc.,[11] one conspicuous consideration was to remain unalterable. The general principle of social communion was boldly asserted despite romantic sentiments to the contrary: 'A man should, whatever happens, keep to his own caste, race and breed. Let White go to the White and Black to the Black'. If anyone wilfully stepped beyond 'these safe limits of decent everyday society he paid dearly for it'.[12] E.M. Forster delineated carefully the frontiers of this imperial exclusiveness: 'Intercourse, yes. Courtesy, by all means. Intimacy, never, never. The whole weight of my authority is against it. . . .'[13] Edwin Charles Benthal who in 1940 spent hours with

Ghanshyam Das Birla discussing the nuances of Indian politics and deciphering the intricacies of Gandhi's mind refused to have tea with his host as he had no time for it. In any case, he was far too eager not to compromise his position as he did not as yet know Birla's political stand.[14]

*

The principal pillar of the Raj was the Indian Civil Service. The sporadic outburst of the 'Hindu bomb-cult', the success of Abdul Hamid's pan-Islamic propaganda, the desperate adventures of an extremely 'reckless element among the Sikhs' and the unity of an ever-pressing movement of a saint-politician, Gandhi, for three decades, chilled the zeal and numbed the enthusiasm of even the most ardent advocates of the Raj.[15] The British power-elite became increasingly claustrophobic. It could not afford to turn a blind eye to the indifferent handling of the ICS, the most dependable battlement in India. As glaring evidence of British failure to uphold the cause of imperialism, the ICS had raised its finger early in 1913 on the partition of Bengal in 1905 and the attendant agitation. It had been announced loudly that the partition was essentially an administrative measure necessitated by the inability of a single government to show efficient care for a mass of humanity inhabiting Bengal.[16] The touch of Curzon's genius, it was believed, was stamped out by a pedestrian compromise worked out by a mediocrity frightened as it was by the immensity of the task of Britain in India. Minto's clumsy treatment of Fuller ignited much fire and fury.[17] But Chelmsford's action against Michael O'Dwyer was considered nothing short of a disaster. The safety of India largely depended, it was asserted, on that frontier province of Punjab. From that province the bulk of the Indian army was recruited and in the years of the First World War it was the theatre of a widespread conspiracy. Austen Chamberlain voiced a substantial opinion when he claimed that Chelmsford's public rebuke had been conducted with a view to playing to the public gallery and it was destructive to the dignity of the British power: 'Scold your officials if you must or will, but in private. Don't lecture them and apologise for them in public, and beg of their angry and factious critics that they may be excused and let go like naughty children. That way danger lies elsewhere, and above all in India.'[18]

British public opinion was convinced that the provocation had been most disquieting in Punjab and it was indispensable to warn the 'talking gentry' that they were 'not everything nor the most important thing in India', to enjoin 'the actions of some of them are an ill support for their great pretensions' and to exhort that 'O.D. by his position and services was just the man to do it'.[19] An excited Chamberlain was incensed as he found that there was in Montagu's statement in Parliament not a word of sympathy for Dwyer and no sign of appreciation of his difficulties.[20] Montagu, he complained, was stirred to a passionate display of British anti-racial feelings. A frenzied public opinion found in a malicious Chamberlain a faithful spokesman. To many, the massacre at Amritsar was more than a question of the lives of a few hundred semi-savage Indians or a case of an indiscreet use of authority. It was widely believed that the actions had become imperative and its open denunciation in public was merely an impetuous call for rebellion. 'We are heading straight for another "Ilbert Bill" agitation by Englishmen on the one side', Chamberlain exclaimed in distress, 'with great risk of another Ireland on the other'.[21]

The determination of the Indian Civil Service to hold India at all costs remained inflexible over the years. The British Empire in India was essentially based on force and, if necessary, it had to be sustained by force. 'Never forget that unless the outward and visible sign of Our Authority is always before a native he is as incapable as a child of understanding what authority means, and where is the danger of disobeying it'.[22] The Civil Services valued the dynamics of the system. They were inclined to expostulate the policy of going too far in conciliating Indian interests. A widespread feeling against the insistence of the home Government to ghostwrite the policies of the Indian administration persisted despite frequent official disclaimers. It was feared that the situation might lead to an unhappy confrontation between the two Governments and the untimely demise of the Empire.

On the eve of the mission of Stafford Cripps, Linlithgow the viceroy, maintained the position of a Government in distress. In his official despatch he upheld without any ambiguity that force was the basis of British power in India: India and Burma had no natural association with the Empire, from which they were alienated by race, history and religion, and for which neither of them had any natural affection, and both were in the Empire because they were conquered countries which had been brought there by force, kept there by British control, and because hitherto it had suited them to remain under British protection. 'I suspect that the moment they think that we may lose the war or take a bad knock, their leaders would be much more concerned to make terms with the victors at our expense than to fight for the ideals to which so much lip-service is given. . .'[23] This frank admission of the reality of the situation might have disturbed some romantic idealists of the imperial idea. Clement Attlee, for example, was disconcerted by the 'astonishing statement' of the viceroy which sounded to him 'more like an extract from the anti-imperialist propaganda speech'.[24] The sentimentalists believed in the value of 'gestures' towards the National Congress which would cover up the apparent 'ugliness' of crude domination by a cloak of pious sentiments about liberty and democracy. They would not deny the importance of force in imperial history but they would insist that 'it was not the whole truth'. The whole of India was not, Attlee wrote, the fruits of conquest. Large parts of it, he added, had come under British rule to escape from tyranny and anarchy. The history of at least one-hundred-and-fifty years had forged close links between India and the United Kingdom.[25] Attlee, who represented the Labour Party and reflected the views of a substantial section of British professional intellectuals, defended and applauded the great achievements of British rule because of its alleged moral victories. Educated Indians, Attlee proudly added, accepted the British principles of justice and liberty. 'We are condemned by Indians not only by the measure', Attlee asserted his imperial conviction, 'of Indian ethical conceptions but by our own, which we have taught them to accept'.[26] This exercise in deception was fashioned to create a degree of optimism in a society whose rulers had been planning various repressive organs of state power. Ideology became the servant for false consciousness, empty phrases and hypocrisy. It was decadence in the name of greater efficiency and order.

Geoffrey Tyson, a journalist of immense Indian experience, agreed as late as 1932, with Lytton the Governor of Bengal, on two basic imperial protocols. They maintained that British trade interests were seriously threatened by the existing trend of Congress politics and that no safeguard which had to be imposed on a reluctant Indian population and which depended for its operation on the reserve power of the Governor-General or the provincial governors could prove to be sufficiently effective.[27] Besides, they argued that the essential factor was to ensure that constitutional problems could only be discussed between parties of equal status. This could never happen so long as negotiations were conducted between Great Britain and India for in the existing conditions the two parties did not enjoy the same status. On the contrary, they emphasized, such negotiations should be conducted between organized groups and interests.

By then, the groups had increased rapidly in number. There were the Hindus, the Muslims, the Scheduled Castes, the maharajas and the like. Tyson in 1932 and Benthal in 1940 opined that even British financial interests in India were to be assigned a significant role in the political process.[28] If the young office assistant, Tyson expressed a familiar imperial consideration, 'bears the correct impress of the British public school (better still if he be a Varsityman and an athlete as well) he is the right stuff' and in the course of time he would get the necessary reorientation.[29] Unless the British non-official regulated his outlook to the fluid conditions of the country in which he worked, Tyson cautioned, 'he will be rapidly reduced from the position of leadership in commerce and industry which he now occupies to the status of a cold-weather peddler'.[30]

There were some who would have liked to step forward and accommodate, to some extent, 'realistic' Indian aspirations. It was held that, immediately following the Revolt of 1857, the essential requirements of high policy had compelled the Government to retain in the hands of Englishmen, positions of responsibility and control. But in the subsequent generation the number of Indians employed in high office had increased. Even a conservative British official noted with amazement the remarkable natural intelligence of some Indians as they overwhelmed their English competitors. In view of the progress of education during the preceding decades, they would have made the necessary adjustment in their earlier assumption regarding the prospect of Indian nationalism and the future of British rule in India.[31]

Yet supreme circumspection, both the officials as well as the Simon Commission warned, ought to be the watchword in dealing with the appointment of Indians in the civil services and in proposing expansions in the Indian legislative councils. The number of Indians in the ICS, instead of being determined by the result of a London examination, it was advanced, might be settled definitely and appointment would be made in India according to the Government's requirements.[32] Similarly, although it was acknowledged that the legislative councils needed a modicum of expansion it was thought premature to double their membership. The non-official element on the councils, it was felt, should be adequate to secure a respectful consideration of its views but not strong enough to outvote the Government or even to harass the departments.[33]

Proposals for reform were invariably accompanied by a lively official debate on the vital safeguards. The consensus emanating from the official discussion was carefully formulated and it formed the backdrop of official pronouncements. The officials emphasized as a cardinal rule that all declarations ought to be made by the Governor-General on behalf of the Government of India rather than by the viceroy as the mouthpiece of the king. This strategy was stressed in order to retain adequate flexibility so that the proposed reforms could, if necessary, be brought under further modification. The administrators also hoped that the Government of India would not print 'self-government' with capital letters in any official statement.[34] Besides, the civil servant urged the hazards of refashioning the upper storey of a building, the very foundation of which had to be relaid. They were aware that it would be preposterous to expect contentment if the Indians were told to play about for years with constitutional puzzles, panchayats and local bodies. Since the Indian political opinion had come to believe that it was entitled to a larger scope in a bigger arena, the civil servants advised caution. The Government must wait, Meston cautioned, watch the situation, hark back, if possible, and then advance slowly and patiently unimpaired by the compulsions of a theory or a dogma.[35] As an immediate measure, the administrators urged that it was desirable to admit trained Indian public servants into the executive council.[36] It was, Marris thought, a sound, safe and a slow line of advance. 'Only the presence in the Executive of a strong element of trained Indians, versed in our ideas, cognizant of the difficulties of our administration, and habituated by official service to look at questions impartially can ultimately help to secure our ideals of government against the attack of emotional and impatient amateurs'.[37] The problem was to minimize violent conflict, to prevent the growth of the concept of the executive's responsibility to the elected legislature and to ensure that the real responsibility was never transferred to the Indians. Marris voiced the united opinion of the civil servants and the approval of the home Government when he wrote :

> Between us and the best of them is, let us admit it, an honest difference of views about government. The best hope of minimising the difference, and so of securing an eventful equilibrium which shall content India, while making it still possible for Englishmen to give their services to India, seems to me to lie in enlisting capable and practical Indians on our side.[38]

The civil services never accepted any move for reform. It continued to haunt them that the step taken by Morley-Minto constituted an uncomfortable plunge with the possibility of unpredictable ramifications. They noted with dismay that subsequently 'substantial' legislative powers were handed over to the Indians in some form or the other while maintaining an official direction that the civil services 'must die in the last ditch for our financial and executive control'.[39] Some of the officials were far too sedulous not to question that 'gracious conception'. But all of them, with marginal exception, entertained a profound disbelief in the practicality of the policy. They were concerned about the possibility of 'foolish, perverse and factious law making.[40] But they were even more disturbed by the fact that the tactical advantage thus accorded to the Indian politicians in the legislature would turn them into better fighters and would render the use of veto more difficult. This would, they feared, lead to the utter paralysis of the Government. Every now and then, the civil servants argued, the executive, in the course of ordinary humdrum administration, would find himself confronting some vested interests or jarring Indian sensibility. The result of the clash would be reflected in the temper of the legislation and bit by bit, the civil servants feared, the governmental measures would be emasculated or killed. Notifications, ordinances or veto would not be able to supplement ordinary legislation without creating powerful causes for popular reaction. A claustrophobic administration felt that it would become completely immobile and would be left with little option. The bureaucracy, as a result, would merely shrug its shoulders, hope for the best and settle down to work out an unworkable law. But soon the 'narcotic word of compromise' would be uttered and an impotent Government would rush for the illusive relief held out to it, failing which it would inaugurate a regime of ruthless terror to sustain itself. It was feared that the last choice would be between turning the clock back at the price of something like a revolution or taking another leap forward and still hoping blindly on the best.[41] The politicians in India, it was assumed, would never be keen on the welfare of the people. The proposed reforms, it was maintained, might have worked in Transvaal but that remedy would not work in India because 'you are going to maintain British ideals of government without Indian executive control and there was no hope of a rapid growth of restraining responsibility of the legislature in the absence of the prospect of having to take on the job in turn.[42]

In view of the ascendancy of nationalist politicians in the legislatures, the administration called upon chiefs, landowners and soldiers to redress the balance, like an old world redressing the balance of the new. It was argued time and again that since the British began associating Indian opinion with the administration 'we have failed to provide for representation of influential, aristocratic and conservative parties in the country'. Recognizing that aristocratic influences were still a vital force in the Indian social sphere, some experts declared that it had been a grave error to overlook the need for securing representation of conservative and orthodox opinion in the councils of the country and that it was necessary to remedy the defect.[43] At a later stage, the nervy administrators went one step forward. It was not possible and judicious, they argued, to collect the representatives of various shades of public opinion in one chamber. Even if the elective system was so devised as to ensure proportionate representation of the minorities, there would be little doubt that the landed interest would feel unhappy and unstable in an elected body. The very elective process, it was maintained, had been designed to favour an extrovert and opportunistic element in the society and it would hopelessly handicap the candidature of those who stood on the basis of 'dignity and wealth'. No one could therefore look forward with confidence to a balance of power by which a British executive could be durably maintained in legislative ascendancy by an alliance with country against town, zamindars against vakils or Muslims against Hindus.[44]

There was a general feeling that the whole process of reform in India contained a fundamental fallacy. The maintenance of the supremacy of British rule was incompatible with any 'form of self-determination' and it was neither wise nor necessary to talk about this so-called long-term strategy. If the legislature continued to increase its power, the administrators argued, it would develop sharp contradictions with the alien executive and, in India, race feelings and national sentiments would convert that opposition to a ferocious assault. The process of reform had been initiated with a view to increasing 'the element of influence' of the elected members and denying the content of power to the Indian politicians.[45] In actual practice, the process was being reversed and before the Government became responsible to an irresponsible legislature, the administrators had determined to unite and stand against the pusillanimous attitude of the timorous politicians at home than be dragged by the clamorous pleaders of India. Supremacy of British rule had been the inflexible governing principle of British imperialism. In actual practice it meant the sovereignty of the British Parliament and the electorate behind it and treating the Government of India as a subordinate government even though it might be encouraged to toy with an elected legislature. It was therefore necessary for the *Nineteenth Century*, the *Quarterly Review*, the *Round Table*, the *Asiatic Review* and *The Times*, to name a few, to stress the Hindu-Muslim controversy, the marginal impact of the political gestures of the Congress and the blessings of internal peace inherent in *Pax Britannica*.[46]

A correspondent from India captured the mood of an average Briton when he taunted that there was neither a stable political force in India nor any inclination on the part of any political faction to understand the importance of the substance and content of political power and its attendant social responsibility as opposed to empty forms and daily rhetoric.[47] It was easy to say, the experts maintained, that the United

Kingdom was under an obligation to give India freedom. But there could be no freedom, they averred, if there was no one willing to assume the responsibility of protecting and maintaining it. If freedom could be neither protected nor maintained, nor law and order guaranteed, the ideologues contended, the substance would be thrown away for a mere shadow. India would become, instead of an example of a self-governing country, 'a plague spot and a running sore—a standing invitation to every warlike and acquisitive power in Asia'.[48] Castigating the character of the National Congress, the chief platform of nationalist India, Hugh Molson wrote, much to the satisfaction of his extensive readership: It was, in fact 'a sort of Grand Fascist Council. Like that prototype, the Congress Working Committee is totalitarian; it claims to represent the minorities in the face of their denials; it claims to be more democratic than parliamentary institutions which it seeks to manipulate; it claims to be the organ of national regeneration, and it is in fact a political caucus'. Britain could never hand over power to such a conclave, he asserted, and the Congress was fully aware of that resolve.

As late as 1943, the *Nineteenth Century* was at pains to prove that although the live issue in Indian politics had been self-determination, neither democracy nor nationalism was covered by Indian tradition.[49] Even at that critical moment of the Second World War, it was added, the tendency of Indian life and politics was to split rather than to coalesce and to agitate for a transient political gesture than to form a 'United State of India'. The *Nineteenth Century* would have liked its readers to believe that the moderate Indian politicians picked up the stock democratic phrases without reflecting whether they were appropriate to India or not while the extremist elements, searching for an anti-government idea, seized upon the more subversive concept of nationalism.[50] It emphasized that Indian nationalism was an opposition strategem and for all intents and purposes it was opposed to the concept of democracy. In the absence of the essential foundation of an independent modern State, the journal prognosticated with an air of profundity, that a democratic and nationalistic India would witness following the War, 'a period of stagnation, malaise, ineffectuality, in which it would become increasingly apparent that no proposal, no party, no political doctrine had any possibility of permanence'.

There was another dimension to this political propaganda. It was asserted that there were two Indias and a glance at the Indian map would underline the importance of the yellow patches as an unbroken line from the Chinese and the Russian borders in the north to Cape Comorin in the south and from the Iranian frontier to the Bay of Bengal. In contrast to the pink background, these patches denoted five-hundred-and-sixty-two States covering one-third of the surface of the sub-continent. Emphasizing the weight and value of these States the *Nineteenth Century* called for a pragmatic attitude towards the princes. It highlighted the quasi-feudal relations of the princes with the British crown, their loyalty and their readiness to play the role of long tradition and inheritance, their willingness to improve the standards of their administration as typified in the case of Baroda, Gwalior, Bikaner, Jaipur, Mysore, Travancore, Cochin, Kashmir and Hyderabad and the uncertainty of the Congress utopia as expressed by the Mahatma and the Pandit. If the Government were to capitulate before the demands of the demagogues,[51] the *Quarterly Review* argued, operating among an uneducated people to whom politics was a mystery, it would lead to a political oligarchy on the lines of the Kuo min tang in China under the leadership of a dictator, Gandhi or Nehru.[52] The *Asiatic Review* could not quite comprehend why the Government should have allowed the Congress to create a disturbance in the political nursery of India.[53] It was a pity, they thought, that so much effort had been made to pacify a 'petulant' Gandhi and an 'obstinate' Congress party for such actions created a very adverse impression on the 'other communities' and 'loyal elements' in India. Verney Lovett, Harry Haig and Malcolm Hailey had stressed the importance of giving an official impetus to the formation of a moderate opinion sufficiently strong to form a central party composed of landowners and commercial interests and to back the Indian Liberal Party. Over the years, it had been witnessed that such a combination could not provide the necessary cohesion and courage. But in 1943, it was felt that there were concrete reasons to kindle hope and make a fresh start.[54]

Indeed it was difficult for the imperialists to comprehend a situation when the defence of India would cease to be dictated by the demands of British global strategy and when India would not dance to the tune of well-orchestrated imperial calculations. In any case, it was not acceptable for the imperialists to reconcile themselves to an independent military policy in India devised and enforced by an Indian cabinet with the approval of a nationalist assembly and to be carried out by an army manned and commanded by Indian personnel. The demand for defence control, which had become, since 1920, a prominent item in the nationalist cause-list, was viewed as a fundamental dent in the imperial power and no one—not even the Liberals, the Quakers and the Socialists—could afford to weaken this most significant bastion of imperial authority. It was argued, in opposition to the demand, that the military policy of British India had not been seriously challenged prior to the First World War by political India. The demand for military control, it was added, was essentially the military perspective of the new intelligentsia entirely drawn from the Hindu middle class.[55] It was suspected that unless these nationalists could control the army, the strength of the Muslims in its ranks would make it difficult for a Government, based on a Hindu majority, to hold its own. The imperialists argued that the speedy Indianization of the officer cadre was the first step undertaken by the nationalists to ensure a permanent Hindu domination. The political aspirations of Hindu India were, to some extent, met by the establishment of a military academy. But India found herself relentlessly disturbed by the demand for military autonomy. Treaty obligations for the protection of the princes, concern for the security of the minorities and the 'Untouchables', problems of internal security, the defence of the turbulent North-West Frontier against the evil designs of the Bolsheviks and the strategic position of India on the map were some of the reasons advocated to deny military independence to India.[56] The imperial logic was remarkably intricate. The imperialists applauded Muslim realism for its insistence on Muslim predominance in the army as an effective bulwark against Hindu supremacy. On the other hand, they hailed the shrewd observation of the Mahasabha who mistrusted the ultra-montanism of the Muslims, apprehended a Muslim military revival in Asia and sought British military protection against a possible Muslim deluge. In 1943 the imperial prescription was clear: it advocated that both the communities should accept the principle of British military partnership as the pre-condition of their political emancipation.[57]

The material benefits conferred upon India as a whole along with her cultural growth and intellectual resurgence under the sensitive care of the imperial Government, it was added, won for the alien power in India the active cooperation of various classes and communities, the passive acquiescence of many others and the generous and habitual obedience of a vast majority of its agricultural rural people. It was held out to an applauding audience in Britain that even those whose consent was no longer considered as unconditional knew far too well what would happen if the British hold on India was suddenly relaxed. It was vaunted with a sense of gratification that very few amongst those Indians who professed the bitterest resentment against British rule would deny that its withdrawal would be immediately followed by a welter of anarchy. It was believed that although the vast and intricate administrative and economic machinery could be managed by the available trained Indians, it was very unlikely that the 'intellectual elements which have attained the highest development in contact with Western civilisation under the British Raj would prevail against the more elemental forces' which the British alone held in restraint. The imperial braggadoccio was remarkable in self-righteousness and a generous flight of imagination. Nothing would remain of the India built by the Raj once its paternal hands were withdrawn; nothing of the machinery reared so patiently over the years by the self-effacing administrators could be maintained by the native genius unguided by the British mind; very little of the mighty structure of peace and progress built by generations of civil servants in India would be able to withstand the deluge that would be released by the vacuum created by the decline of the Raj. India was still to learn the habitual obedience to law. Very few of the active ideologues would have concurred with the view that India was competent to imbibe that habit of spontaneous obedience to the rule of law.[58]

It was necessary, the officials continued, to stop for a while and assess the situation carefully. The educated few who made their way to the councils should not be invested with the strength to obstruct any legislation to which they might be disinclined. It was conceded that the right of interpellation could be granted within limits as a means of bringing 'genuine' grievances to notice. But it was readily added that to extend that right so as to cover supplementary questions would be rash and unwise because it would enable a skilful questioner to put the authorities not merely into the witness box but in the pillory. As a consequence, the State might emerge from a fierce battle of words much maligned and bruised adversely affecting the mystique of the Raj.[59]

The country, it was held in the 1930s, was still in an embryonic stage of nationhood if the particular features of 'Indian unrest' could be called as such. It was, everybody urged, singularly unsuited to democracy especially in view of the sharp antagonism of its interests, its caste system, its indifference to public progress and its general illiteracy.[60] The appointment of Indians to the executive council of the viceroy, it was maintained, was a dangerous precedence although a judicious selection of personnel might be desirable to demonstrate that race was no bar to high office. This could nurse a fading sentiment if only for its favourable political impact. But all these innovations, should be thought of as British experiments in a colonial administration independent of political agitation and nationalist propaganda.[61] There was a determined official demand that sedition must lower its crest and the Government must receive its due obedience. Otherwise, it was repeated, concessions would give the appearance of weakness and surrender to brute force.[62]

The primacy of the viceroy and the secretary of state, it was resolutely upheld, irrespective of the Indian sentiments concerning self-government, had to be retained. An Indian self-government within the Empire on par with the white dominions was dismissed as a contradiction in terms.[63] It would merely mean 'a government in opposition'.[64] Even if encouragement was extended to Indian industries, by a policy of selective preference, no one was prepared to back India in a policy of selfish isolation disregarding her imperial obligations.[65] It was affirmed that the Government should not be allowed to become immobile. The function of the Government was to take decisions and to rule. This was called the 'root idea' of administration and it was not to be disturbed by novel ideas of a representative government and a parliamentary system especially in India where such political institutions were grafted with scarce chance of success under a hostile social milieu and a despotic historical heritage.[66]

H. Blair's *1957* presented a well-constructed tale of rebellion and retribution in India charged with a tremendous sense of suspense that inebriated the custodians of the Raj.[67] It was more than a convincing story of adventure: it was a political pamphlet underlying an enduring faith in the moral strength of the rulers in the hour of crisis. *Governor Hardy,* Blair's companion volume, projected the situation of 1931 in Bengal.[68] The governor was a supercilious and blundering master of the province faced with the relics of a democratic experiment in the East. By then there was a firm recognition by the Government about the futility of planting parliamentary institutions on the despotic soil of India. The Congress movements had turned exclusively Hindu, and the Muslim antagonism to Hindu pretentions had driven them into the arms of the British. For the governor, the chronic evils of Bengal called for immediate attention. With remarkable administrative simplicity, Hardy catalogued them in order of priority: rising unemployment and distress among the Bhadraloks, the innumerable lawyers to whom there was no outlet except sedition and agitation, the exploitation by the whole race of money-lenders and absentee landlords and, finally, the infamous dowry system. Hardy dismissed the claims of the middle class that they were animated by patriotic motives. 'The child that plays with fire burns itself. So any misguided individual or group which sets itself deliberately to nullify the honest efforts of the Government', Hardy warned, 'will be brought rigorously to book. There has been too much peltering with sedition during the past few years. There is going to be none today'. Hardy was satisfied that the commerial magnates of Calcutta were wonderfully loyal, that there was no official incentive to racial segregation and that anyone could walk straight to the burra sahib. He denoted the central place that India occupied in the British Empire and appreciated the cardinal role played by the princes and the

Muslims that lubricated the whole system in support of the Raj. The Congress, Hardy concluded, was certainly the bad egg in the Indian basket: it was 'Hindoo', it was led by 'briefless lawyers' and 'frustrated journalists'; it was malevolent and mischievous; it was hostile to the interests of the minorities. He carefully took note of the fact that the revolutionary movement was being led by an old man with an austere but beautiful face and with 'eyes burning with the sombre fire of a fanatic'. It was suspected that the nationalists might have established close links with the Bolsheviks. Governor Hardy could not afford to toy with them and his indiscretion, he knew, would be overlooked by an indulgent parliament preoccupied with war and economic hardships and practically unable to contain its man-on-the-spot dealing with a tough situation at the nerve centre of the Empire.

India was Britain's chief concern despite the abundance of babus and a good deal of dysentry and cholera. No one cared any longer for a sophisticated argument for retaining that central outpost. 'To hell with justification,' Rodney Savage of John Masters cried out. 'I was in love with India, and she'd have the hell of a job getting rid of me'.[69] Administration in that strange country demanded remarkable circumspection and a firm will to defend the errors of judgement or serious acts of commission. Even the mistakes of the Government acquired a sort of moral dignity that was not to be spoken of in 'an off-hand or irreverential manner'.[70] It might make mistakes but, as Cunningham defended, it was not prudent to assent that they were so.[71] All outside critics were resented as impertinent malefactors of the Raj and all these men were put down with a contemptuous decisiveness. The ICS was always alert to shield its interests and ensure that nothing substantial was given away and all flippant initiatives were blocked off or held back.

Some of the civil servants were struck by the failure of Montagu in his *Diary* to see the 'elemental India'. The Indian secretary, it was complained, delighted in the society of the 'sophisticated urban population' in the company of 'politicians, sedition-mongers, fanatics, Viceroys, Governors, members of Council and Secretaries, of some merchants and many lawyers'.[72] Al Carthill sought to correct the perspective of Montagu by going into the problem of real India. His backdrop was Madampur district, his first independent charge. It was typical of changeless India.[73] The new institutions of popular consultations had over the time brought about certain cosmetic changes. Despite a whole generation of self-government, he argued, the people showed small signs of activity and that democratic child, though thirty years old, was groping for guidance. The institution of elections had added another opportunity for exhibiting caste loyalty. In view of a sympathetic public opinion at home, the Indian unrest had adopted a specific form of agitation bearing two faces. Towards the British people and its representatives, the Government, it turned the political face eg, a demand for Home Rule while towards the Indian masses a religious face calling for the expulsion of the Christians.

Even the temporizing policy of Irwin, who combined shrewd compromises, firmness and illusory promises, was not appreciated by the civil servants. The state of Europe had been deteriorating in the 1930s and the politicians in Britain were perturbed by the progress of events in India where the attitude of Irwin seemed disconcerting.[74] It appeared as if he had been toying with treason. The civilians were upset to find that a Round Table Conference had been convened somewhat impetuously. They were piqued to discover that conservative elements of the Conference had been carried away by the logic of popular movements. They were especially irked with the royal princes for not providing a firm conservative rampart and for joining with the forces of revolution.[75] The princes had expressed, it was complained, their displeasure with the claim of the British crown to paramountcy. There was a general apprehension shared by all, who had any concern with India, that the Government had been forced by circumstances to build a travesty of a democracy. Some others argued that the Government had been guided in the whole process by a conscious design of gradual devolution of authority. They were nettled to note that the members of the professional middle classes had over the years been moulded into a seasoned opposition in the councils.[76] During the prolonged gloomy evening of the Raj many in their pensive moments must have pondered over their inability to assist the growth of a reliable Indian electorate or a dependable Indian constituency.[77] There was in some an element of bewildering helplessness as well as a decisive contempt for the educated Indians wrapped up in a strange seductive attachment towards the 'eternal India'. India fascinated them as well as repelled them, like yoga, like Benaras.[78] Others continued to flatter themselves by a singularly strange make-believe: 'By a bit of judicious buying of sorts we might keep the Raj going for another century.'[79]

If and when logic failed, the last refuge of the imperialist was always there to help him out. British interests were identified with the welfare of the people of India and the well-being and interests of the inarticulate masses were to be defined, collated, sifted and assessed by British administrators then becoming increasingly intolerant of the crisp English accent of the Congress-wallahs. Their prescription for Indian unrest even as late as the Cripps Mission in 1942 was neat and limpid: limited freedom, certain franchises, a few legislative influences and some executive authority; but no attempt was made to graft British liberal institutions onto the Indian society which was to be given a constitutional framework that would aggravate its inherent traditional hostilities. 'I'm out here personally because I need a job. I cannot tell you why England is here or whether she ought to be here. It's beyond me.... Is it fair that an Englishman should occupy one when Indians are available? . . .'[80] Forster was aware that there was only one answer to a conversation of this type in the exclusive clubs and that was: England held India for her good. Forster's Fielding was to voice it: the zeal for honesty had eaten him up. But Craddock, Claud Hill and Harry Haig were more forthright. Years later (and much after the imperial sunset), John Masters made his endorsement of British imperial pride patently clear: 'I thought India was ugly, beautiful, smelly, predictable and as material as the West. It was inhabited not by Yogis and Saints but by people—knaves, giants, dwarfs and plain people—of various shades of brown'.[81]

In India the introduction of parliamentary institutions was not a concession intended to absorb those on the outside within the system, but a laboured exercise to fashion and revamp existing institutions of control. The whole process was based on an intense search for traditional conflicts and an astute shuffling of allies and supporters. Representatives of landed property and nominees of substantial commercial interests, backed by religious orthodoxy and conservative princes, provided a firm and stable base for an effective political operation. 'There never was any splendid loyalty,' Butler had spelled out candidly the genesis of the Muslim League; 'Mohsin-ul-Mulk and others came to see me at Lucknow to take my advice. They were quite frank. They could not hold their young men and feared their joining the Hindus which meant ultimate absorption of the Mahomedans. It was purely in their own interests that they formed the Muslim League'.[82] In 1913 Hardinge recommended the Muslims of Bengal to Carmichael as 'your future folk'.[83] Again in 1915, Butler reprimanded a wavering Nizam of Mahmudabad and forewarned him against a continual vacillation which might invite severe retribution. When the Young Turks of the League proved to be plucky and unyielding and the Aligarh movement moved away on to a war path demanding liberation from official control, the imperial policy swerved adequately and offered to patronize a rival Islamia college movement.[84] Besides, it gave a gentle push to the Benaras movement, patted both the Raja of Darbhanga and Malaviya to get on with their job in right earnest and encouraged them to trap both Jaipur and Kashmir in the Hindu nest.[85]

The policy was marked by remarkable flexibility. If the Malaviya party had to be encouraged to stir up the Hindus, the Amanists of Lucknow were prodded to turn the Municipal Board into an arena for communal strife. If the Swarajist elements had to be shunned in Punjab, Chaudhuri Chotu Ram was to be appointed in preference to Narendra Nath of the amenable Hindu Sabha because of his earlier connection with the Swarajists. If fifteen uncompromising opponents were to be elected from the rural areas of Bengal, the electoral constituencies were carefully manipulated in order to ensure that only one returned from the Dacca division and a small but influential aristocracy of Dacca, Mymensingh and the Raja of Murshidabad could be encouraged to resist the tide of nationalism by sending seven loyalists and a minister. In the midst of *arati-namaz,* Dussera-Tazia, *shank-azan* and cow-pig controversies, tensions, riots and religious polarization, British policy thrived while secular politics were blurred by the ascendancy of issues based on obscurantism and whipped-up public emotions.[86]

It is true that realities were more complex and tortuous than the generalizations of historians. The trend was, however, consistent and it remained undisturbed despite significant detours. The Indian body-polity was touched with meticulous care so that by the time the Congress set out on the road to Dandi, the beneficiaries of the Raj surged forward to hedge and protect it and by the time the Round Table Conference took place, reaction closed its ranks and took bold steps to defend its interests in the eventuality of the decline of the Empire.

As the Second World War progressed and Cripps failed to find a solution, the die-hards in the British cabinet realized that the Indian Liberal and Moderate groups would not be able to obviate the pressure of the Congress. British attitude adopted a simple policy of *ad hoc* measures. One of the cardinal features of the policy was prompt and vigorous action against any public unrest. Heavens would not fall, it was argued in 1942, if Gandhi was arrested in time.[87] Hallett convinced his chief in New Delhi that possibly the mistake in the past had been delay over taking action. In 1930, he argued, Gandhi had been given two months' grace and in the meanwhile the movement has grown widespread and that was the risk one could no longer take.[88] The officials believed that a mass movement would be 'a bit of a nuisance' but the situation should be resolutely faced with equanimity and confidence and should be expressed in the Government's ability to deal with it.[89] Another feature was a firm resolution not to deal with the National Congress as the 'favoured child' in any official overture.

That body, it was believed, had become the most bitter opponent of British imperialism and yet Stafford Cripps, Hallett observed, made it clear to all parties that unless the Congress and the British Government could come to terms, it was useless to negotiate with anyone else.[90] This attitude, the governor believed, had demoralized those who would have liked to move constitutionally to independence without severing British connections. The British policy, the seasoned administrator held, had pushed these middle-of-the-road people to the Congress camp. Hallett was sore about the effect of the policy on the loyal Muslim League. There was a definite feeling in the League that Congress obstruction had led to their being given a place of supreme importance and that 'the wisest plan is to follow more or less in their footsteps'.[91]

There were other serious factors to reckon with. The Revd J. Mackenzie with long years of close association with the student community in Bombay wrote confidentially that there was a new disturbing feature in the Indian situation. The deep springs of discontent which were largely economic in nature had been over the years exploited to the full by the political leaders. But until the end of the First World War it appeared to the parson that there had been a general agreement that British connections had been largely beneficial to India. But a belief had been inculcated subsequently that it had been always, and in almost every way, harmful. The nationalist campaign had become widespread and had acquired credibility. McKenzie was irked to find that the Congress had successfully belittled every advance that had been made towards self-government. It had used every means to create distrust in the motives and intentions of the Government[92] and had taught the younger generation that the political progress of India had been the fruit of its struggle with the hostile British Government. It had diverted peoples' attention from social evils and led them to believe that all difficulties including communal dissensions had been 'brought into being by a Machiavellian ruling power'.[93] A flustered administration had come to the conclusion that they would never get a party with men like Jwala Prasad Srivastava to put up a really effective opposition to the Congress.

Yet there was no lack of political manipulation. It was still believed that a number of Indian politicians had been frankly critical of the ability of the different Indian communities and parties to come together to frame an agreed constitution or even on a generous interpretation of the word 'agreed'. Apart from the depressed classes and the Muslims, the viceroy was informed with satisfaction about the Brahmin-non-Brahmin conflict in Madras, the internal tensions in Assam, the dormant demands for the creation of Andhra Pradesh and Tamil Nadu, the re-partition of Bengal and the re-absorption of Assam. Though all these movements were neither sincere nor important, the official report noted that they were nevertheless substantial areas for official intervention much to the discomfiture of the Congress. It was believed that the movement for Pakistan was slowly securing adherants even in the South.[94] The officials detected that although the Communists were bitterly anti-imperialist, they were also equally anti-Congress. They wondered if it was not possible to encourage men like M.N. Roy to go against the Congress? It was seriously considered if 'we cannot make more use of the spirited anti-Congress articles which Roy produces in his paper *Independent India*'.[95] With regard to the growing American pressure on the British Government regarding a 'fair-deal' to India, there was a general consensus. It was essential to avoid adopting an apologetic attitude and prevent the United States from having a say in matters where she had no tangible experience and for which she had no responsibility. Taking into account the long standing misunderstandings, jealousies and prejudices in the USA against Britain it was believed that the USA might relapse into her periodical isolationist posture. Even an electoral change might render any definite policy completely out of tune with its new shape of things.[96] The British Government was still not inclined to see the reality. An ostrich-like policy appeared to her tired statesmen as the best road to salvation.

Under the strain of sedition, mass movement and war, the Government was being brutalized. The uncertainties of the possible turn of events had stupified the administration and shaken its self-indulgent complacency. It became bewildered and desperate. As the Mahatma undertook a fast unto death in British custody to prove the purity of his intentions in 1942–43, the British power elite cloistered itself in an artificial world of make-believe, losing all human feelings. Officials, governors, the viceroy and the secretary of state seriously debated whether the Mahatma, 'the Hindoo Gunga Din in his loin cloth' should not be allowed to breathe his last in the Agha Khan Palace.[97] It would redeem, it was suggested with a modicum of relief, the disturbed Raj from the mischievous potentialities of an uncanny 'half-naked' figure. In this glorification of self-love there was not even an iota of warmth, tolerance, and respect for human beings different from oneself. It was an image in which harshness, cruelty and ruthlessness predominated. If the decline in the Raj's self-confidence was perceptible and its isolation from the people complete, its dehumanization and decadence were absolute.

The 1930s were a decade of commitments. Even the Conservatives felt the anguish of the period. A deep introspection, a thorough reassessment of the society and a concerted struggle for a better world distinguished the period. India figured in the contemporary controversies as she stepped into British political debates. The Labour Parties and the Communist Party had developed definite views on the problems of India; various pacifist movements sought to connect the continued imperial rule in India with their 'No More War' demand; despite 'Mond-Turnerism' and other reformist influences, the Labour movement as a whole found time to turn to the Indian problems with uneasy embarrassment and muffled protests; intellectuals lined up behind Gandhi, the Congress and the India League. An element of dreary isolation however characterized the Indian question amidst restive British politics. The threat of war had goaded a whole generation to resist the recurrence of violence on a large-scale; the rise of Fascism and militarism pushed that sensitive and creative age ideologically on to a war path; Spain became the symbol of the militant era. India stood somewhat uncomfortably at the bottom of the political agenda of the defiant era. The Round Table Conferences of the early thirties were symptomatic of India's paradoxical position in British Liberal opinion and it underlined the intense imperial consciousness of Britain and her inflexible pride with regard to the Raj.[98]

It may be noticed that once the economic crisis engulfed Britain, the ardent supporters of India's cause were tempted to consider the Indian question as a matter of peripheral importance. Some opted for the view that even an advocacy of the Indian case during that crisis should be condemned and dismissed as an open exhibition of a small mind at once prejudiced and ignorant and given to misrepresentation of facts. The first session of the Round Table Conference was convened when the Labour Party, though in minority, was in power. The Party had voted in favour of dominion status for India and could have, if it wanted, turned its victory at the poll into a mandate for its professed programme despite its delicate numerical strength in Parliament. The session of the Conference without Gandhi and without the representative of the Congress was marred by a visible shift in the Party's priorities and before long it became a prisoner of its own vexatious political ambiguity. The Labour Party could not transcend the ruling impulses of imperial Britain so carefully nursed over the centuries by her history, politics and sociology. In fact the party strove hard to discover a paternalistic hood to camouflage imperialist affiliation and attachments. Its right wing leadership could afford to cosset its left wing fringe. The wayward boys might chirp and chafe but they would be unable, it was firmly believed, to dislodge an entrenched leadership.

Imperialism thrived as the frontier of Labour politics crept into the borderland of a conservative England. Differences of objectives and strategies were reduced to a petty wrangling over a set of 'rational' and 'credible' manoeuvres.[99]

The changing perspective of the Round Table procedure offered an interesting study. The original idea had been that Indian representatives should meet the Government for a discussion in a free conference out of which the basis of the proposals for the Parliament would arise. Before the Conference actually met the original idea was modified and it became a meeting of British and Indian statesmen at which the whole question of India was under review. The prime minister's speech at the Federal Committee and the whole conduct of the second Round Table Conference was a contradiction of the idea of a free conference for reaching a settlement on the Indian question.[100] Though Ramsay MacDonald repeated the phraseology of the Labour declaration, its meaning had been altered. To a discerning observer the very fact that the prime minister did not think it necessary to go beyond the declaration of the first Conference was itself a retreat. The 'working committee' appointed by the Conference soon converted itself into 'consultative committee' and the British side was represented on it by the viceroy and not by any impartial British statesman. As a result, the view of the Indian civil services, whom the viceroy really represented, was adopted whole scale. Since the 'consultative committee' was to work in coordination with a parallel committee of the India Office under the direction of Lord Sankey the 'free and frank conference' between the British and Indian statesmen as visualized at the inception of the proposal became, willy nilly, a departmental enquiry by the officials in India and at the Whitehall with the final voice resting with London. Assessing the Conference from the Indian point of view, V.K.Krishna Menon complained that the second session under MacDonald, 'then prisoner of the Tory batallion that engulfs him' had taken some definite retrograde steps. The speeches of Ramsay MacDonald and Samuel Hoare in the house had provided ample evidence to justify that allegation. It was evident that both of them accepted certain aspects of Churchillian doctrine and assured the die-hards that the amendment suggested by the spokesman of the Conservative Party was unnecessary since the Government's policy would not commit the country to any of those steps which Churchill feared.[101] The progress registered in the Irwin-Gandhi settlement in the adoption of the phrase, 'safeguard in the interest of India', which had been the 'pivotal conception of the Round Table statesmanship', was abandoned altogether. Both the prime minister and the secretary of state reassured the Conservative Party on the nature of the safeguards and reaffirmed the ultimate responsibility of the British Parliament for India. The secretary of state did not share his chief's natural inclination towards evasion and ambiguity and stated bluntly:

> Until India is in a position to defend herself, our commands over the army must be clear and widespread and our control over the foreign affairs must be reserved. Secondly, our relations with the Princes must be retained by the Crown. Financial stability must be effectively safeguarded and so also ultimately must be internal security. Minorities must be protected and there must be no unfair economic and commercial discrimination against the British trades and rights of the Services recruited by the Secretary of State must be safeguarded.[102]

The speech of the secretary of state, as Krishna Menon quipped, 'merely reduced responsibility to farce'.[103]

The backward step of the MacDonald administration was confirmed in another way. In 1929, the viceroy, with the authority of the Labour Government, had affirmed that dominion status was implicit in the Montagu declaration of 1917 which spoke of progressive realization of a responsible Government and this came to be known as the Irwin–Benn declaration. This declaration was designed to allay the suspicions in India owing to the attitude adopted by Lord Reading's Government which had made a subtle distinction between 'responsible government' and 'dominion status'. It had also been rendered necessary by the efforts of the Simon Commission to avoid the term dominion status. Evidently, MacDonald had retracted from the Irwin–Benn declaration and had taken up the Simon–Reading position. Under this revised stand, India would not be on the same level with the other dominions and the Government affirmed that it did not contemplate equality of status between the dominions and India.[104]

The third direction in which the MacDonald position constituted a move backwards was in relation to the nature of the conclusions of the Conference. The declarations of the previous Conference were tentative and provisional in nature and the proposed safeguards had been open to discussion. Following the Conference it was officially portended that the safeguards were to be such as were agreed on at the Conference. But the Conference had not been conducted as a voting conference and the Government, reticent on this issue, desired to close it amidst an air of mystifying ambiguity. The strategy of the Government was to highlight the communal question and a protracted discussion on the subject vitiated the atmosphere so much so that unanimity on any other issue became impossible.[105]

The whole operation of the Government coincided with a much-publicized press campaign against India. The tenor of the attack on India was provided by the Conservative members of Parliament. In his maiden speech in the House of Commons, Colonel A.W. Goodman, the member for North Islington, adopted an authoritative posture on Indian affairs. His was the most representative position faithfully reflecting the attitudes of civil servants ruminating on India in retirement and consciously influencing a large body of opinion throughout the country. In turn, this influential segment of public opinion conditioned the India policy of the Conservative Party and affected the official perspective irrespective of party positions. Reporting the speech of the MP at length, the *Islington Gazette* asserted that Goodman had something more than a slight acquaintance with the Indian problem having spent nearly twenty years in the service of that dependency.[106] Goodman argued that it was difficult to conceal the fact that 'we have gone a long way towards self-government' and that the British Government had definitely committed to such an extent that it was no longer possible to go back. He, however, underlined that the pledge of the 1919 Act was conditional and no great change should be contemplated until these conditions were fully satisfied. The qualifications were expressed, Goodman emphasized, in clear and unambiguous terms such as 'gradual', 'progressive', 'successive stages' and development 'as an integral part of the British Empire' and these basic conditions could not be overlooked. Goodman was convinced that the suspicion of the Hindus by the Muslims and of the Muslims by the Hindus was so deeply rooted that it would be generations before either would have any confidence in the other. Apart from acute caste differences and antagonisms, Goodman reminded, there were sixty million untouchables in Hindu society not entitled to any rights of humanity. Even the minorities, he affirmed, would not agree among themselves. Goodman added that before one could consider any settlement of the Indian problems, two vital considerations would have to be resolved. In the first place, it was unthinkable, he thought, that the House should hand over the full control of business, finance, external affairs, army and law and order to the National Congress representing not more than five per cent of the Indian people. In the second place, before the House could agree to any Constitution, it was to be ascertained that it had the support of all the important sections of the Indian people, that it was acceptable to all creeds and classes and that in actual practice it would work. India was not as yet prepared for a fresh dose of self-government and Goodman recommended that this frank assessment was to be communicated to the Indians in plain words. 'History teaches us', Goodman pontificated as he played to the national gallery, 'that it is folly to limit the aspirations of a nation for self-government, but it is folly also for people to aspire to great heights which they are unfitted to occupy, and the responsibility of those, who give power where realisation of the duties which accompany it is lacking, must be a very heavy one'.[107]

As the press continued to publicize the Anglo-Indian and Tory views recommending coercion of an impatient and disobedient India, there was a remarkable paucity of a determined British opinion demanding justice for India. Enlightened opinion began to doubt its own conviction in the face of official and non-official propaganda. It became equivocal and began to mistrust the applicability of Liberal democracy in India. Laurence Housman lamented the 'apathy and indifference' of public opinion in Britain and almost foreglimpsed the inevitability of the Irish road in India. He found it arduous to find a dozen influential Liberal names to sign a protest letter. C.P. Scott, he thought, could have got them together but he had just died.[108] There were others, but they were, Housman complained, 'full of goodwill—but their convictions don't go far enough in the direction of India's freedom really and help much'. He had come round to recognize that nothing was going to help any more to bring about a peaceful solution. He had no doubts that there would be outrages on both sides but most Englishmen would regard the affronts of the terrorists as damning the case of Indian freedom while the violence of the Government they would either refuse to believe or would regard as a 'regrettable necessity'.[109] Like many others, Housman was convinced that freedom would ultimately come to India but he was sorry that the pace had been forced by renewed conflict either on civil disobedience or on other more violent lines. The situation had been precipitated by the National Government inhibited by inherited political prejudices, immobilized by an unstable political arithmetic of a coalition and brutalized by its own self-righteous demeanour. F.A. Wenyon, an earnest supporter of the Labour Party over the years, was rattled by the fact that the news that was being broadcast by wireless and then put in most of the papers concerning India was censored and carefully edited and had been designed to give the impression that the policy of the Government in India would eventually succeed.[110] Like many other Labour sympathizers of India, Wenyon would maintain that it might still be possible to retain India within the Empire by granting her a measure of self-government. Evidently, self-government, as conceived by them, was a political adjustment short of independence. 'What the government is now doing in India', Wenyon wrote in distress, 'must be increasing the number of those who will say that only absolute independence would do'. Wenyon abhorred that painful reality. The real culprits, he thought, were the Tory advisors in India and in the India Office.[111] He wondered if the *Daily Herald* could be induced to come out more boldly for India and grumbled if the journals sympathetic towards the Labour Party were properly informed or adequately briefed.

In 1933, Lansbury was still resting on his self-satisfying ambiguity.[112] He was forthright in his assessment that the Government had convinced itself that it was right and that its policy would overcome Indian resistance. The Government, he complained, scoffed at any attempt at restoring friendliness and cooperation and dismissed all such suggestions as unnecessary interference by irresponsible sentimentalists. Lansbury was equivocal about the position to be adopted by his own Party. He was inclined to the view that a substantial section of the Indian opinion would probably agree to work out a Constitution framed on the Round Table proposals with minor adjustments. As an 'International Socialist' he would have welcomed any settlement 'in which more nations can cooperate as free partners' and wished that the Congress could propose a Constitution in which some connections with Britain were incorporated.[113] The Labour Party was still wavering about the content of permissible self-determination for India. The Party seemed to believe that imperialism, a system of domination and exploitation, could be dissolved by friendly gestures and constitutional gimmicks into a free partnership. The dynamics of the system stood beyond the comprehension of most of the Labour leaders. The Empire had become so intricately woven into the psyche of the British people that it was very painful to watch it liquidated, dismembered or even weakened.

The paradoxical position in which the Labour Party found itself was reflected in the suggestions given to the Mahatma on the eve of his departure from England in 1931 by a number of intellectuals noted for their Liberal views.[114] Evelyn Wrench, who was typical of the Liberal Conservatives of the day, brought to the notice of the Mahatma that there had been a sea change in public opinion in Britain. Rothermere and Churchill did not in any way, he argued, represent any substantial section of the British public and the Moderates had been in control. Wrench considered that the statement at the conclusion of the Conference by Ramsay MacDonald was responsive and far better than what it could have been. He was convinced that the steps taken at the Conference had been in the right direction. He felt that the Tory majority had been under pressure from within and proposed that if the Indian movement showed restraint for three years the onus would be on Britain. It might be better for Gandhi to stop for a moment and try to appreciate the genuine problems of the Government. A politician of Gandhi's eminence should have no difficulty in assessing the practical difficulties of British politics. Wrench believed that Samuel Hoare was honest and frank but he was also hard and rigid. Hoare shared, Wrench argued, the limitations of the average British administration and had full faith in the positive blessings of British rule. He had no confidence in the ability of the Indians and affirmed the necessity of periodical exhibition of force for ruling a hostile alien race. The redeeming feature was that Hoare firmly voiced the real feelings of other members of the Government.[115]

Kingsley Martin, known for his left wing affiliations, thought that in the declaration MacDonald was able to defeat Samuel Hoare and divide the Conservatives and he insisted that the whole constitutional exercise could not be pooh-poohed as an eye-wash. Martin pleaded that Gandhi might as well do everything that he could to put off the adoption of extreme steps so as to offer his sympathizers in England a chance and himself a better opportunity. Martin was categorical that the situation in Bengal, despite the ordinances, was not as bad as had been made out to be.[116] H.N. Brailsford's arguments were based on the premise that although the situation had been adverse and public opinion not favourable towards Gandhi, the British prime minister did not think it necessary to betray him. Brailsford thought that what Gandhi was able to get from the three political parties was more than what he could have got from the Labour Party a year earlier. He considered that the whole question of martial law ought to be dealt with as a matter for bargaining. Ramsay had been under pressure. Although MacDonald was able to maintain his position on constitutional questions, he would legitimately expect Gandhi to appreciate his problems and forego his position as a necessary quid pro quo. 'It is MacDonald's sacrifice', Brailsford emphasized, 'in order that he may save the rest of the cargo'. Brailsford would be happy, he said, if Gandhi would agree to make the reciprocal gesture.[117]

Picking up the thread from Brailsford, Harold Laski, the most sensitive and erudite intellectual of the Labour Party, maintained that it was characteristic of anybody who was keen to get through his programme to give way on one point in order to gain another. It was in this context, he thought, that Gandhi might as well wait for a while and go slow in order to strengthen the hands of MacDonald. He did not think it quite fair to assert that the whole cabinet was united behind the ordinance and repression for there were many who had reservations against a strong rule but were restrained by the compulsions of collective responsibility. He requested Gandhi to consider the situation from the point of view of those who would love to assist the Indian struggle in Britain. Harold Laski effectively argued his case for cooperation. The prime minister, Laski maintained, had achieved two points by postponing the hour of decision. In the first place, MacDonald had made the strategic position of Gandhi more arduous in British public opinion and secondly, he had rendered the position of Gandhi's sympathizers in England still more onerous to support any immediate and impetuous reaction on the part of Gandhi. Laski was keen to impress that having opted out of the terms of reference of Churchill, MacDonald had caused much confusion for Gandhi. Laski argued that Gandhi would be logically entitled to ask the prime minister for full proof of his good faith. Gandhi might, Laski prompted, ask MacDonald for the satisfaction of various demands in order to normalize the situation in Bengal and also see to it that the Congress got its due share in the development of the envisaged policy.[118] He considered that the problems of 'safeguards' were matters which could neither be compartmentalized nor be treated by the Government alone and felt that there should be a mutually agreed satisfactory line of action to be undertaken jointly by the Government and the Congress. Laski appealed to the Mahatma to declare that he was prepared to participate in the future course of the Round Table Conference, that he would call for civil disobedience only as a last resort and display his eagerness to come to a settlement negotiated across the table. Such an attitude, Laski emphasized, would make things easy, win for Gandhi the goodwill of the British people and thereby help 'our task which we can embark with a good heart'.[119] What Laski overlooked in his enthusiasm to ensure Gandhi's cooperation and retain the so-called Round Table spirit was the Mahatma's predicament. As a circumspect leader of a movement against imperialism, Gandhi had and would have used his weapon of civil disobedience only as a last resort and his remarkable flexibility, indicated by the Delhi Pact, was well-known to MacDonald, his cabinet, Harold Laski and all other participants in the informal discussion. Laski was aware of the fact that what Gandhi had been fighting for was a meaningful negotiation conducted on equal terms and a settlement of the Indian question by mutual adjustments without being dictated by the cabinet operating on the promptings of the reactionary civil services. Evidently Laski and some others were inclined to see a sort of an 'independent India' but they dithered to watch and endorse a permanent political and emotional termination of the Raj and its imperial nexus. They were prepared to turn a blind eye to the determination of the Indian administration and the British financial interests in India to reverse the process of reconciliation and the logic of the home Government to stand by the man-on-the spot.

Thus as the door was slammed by the viceroy on the face of Gandhi, Laski found himself in a quandary. In an article entitled 'India at the Crossroads', he tried hard to strike a balance between the two contradictory pulls on his intelligence and conviction.[120] The second Round Table Conference, he wrote, might not have been an outstanding success but all the same, he added, it 'cannot yet be pronounced a striking failure'. Examining the area of darkness in Indo-British relations he maintained there were some definite gains and it would be folly to minimize their importance. Applauding the fact that a government, dominated by the Conservatives, had been able to secure the approval of 'immediate responsible government', Laski claimed somewhat over optimistically that die-hardism was dead as a practical philosophy.[121] Even the tepid advance suggested by the Simon Commission, Laski wrote, had been a part of dead history. He believed that only a total breakdown of goodwill would revert the situation to the pre-Irwin days. An optimistic Laski concluded that the real essence of the Indian problem hinged upon psychological considerations.

Laski and his associates were impressed by the influence exercised over the Round Table by Tej Bahadur Sapru, Srinivas Sastri and Jayakar. The India they envisaged, Laski wrote, 'would have its freedom in most things that matter profoundly at once; over the army, finance, and the princes, control would be postponed for some such statutory period as ten years'.[122] But unfortunately, Laski commented disconcertedly, although they were able and respected leaders, they had little or no following among the political classes of India, least of all among the younger men. They might have succeeded in the days of Reading but the temper of Indian nationalism had become so intense that the compromises their realism suggested, appeared to a political India an insult to her status. There was little relation between what they thought and what Gandhi and his followers were prepared to accept.[123]

Laski claimed that although Gandhi charmed everyone at the Conference by his genuine saintliness, skill and humour, his position had been determined by two major considerations, 'neither of which the British government was prepared to accept'.[124] Laski complained that Gandhi denied the claim of any other Indian member of the Conference to speak on behalf of India and asserted for the National Congress the sole right to state India's case. Laski was also critical of Gandhi's decision 'to regard the difficulties by which the British Government felt itself confronted as anything more than a smoke-screen behind which, under the name of safeguards, the shadow of self-government could be conceded while its substance withheld'.[125] Laski was unhappy that Gandhi had refused to consider that the army should be a matter whose problems were settled by the legislature and that the peculiar place of British capital in India 'made the problem of financial security no more than a real one'.[126] From Gandhi's angle of vision the Conference was' a stage in the evolution to the effective independence upon which the National Congress has set his heart'.[127] Gandhi insisted on this attitude, Laski accused, 'even in the face of the difficulties to which the minorities problem gave rise'.[128] For Gandhi, Laski was sure, it was a trial of strength rather than an effort at compromise. It is striking that Laski in the same article condemned the attempt made by the Government to play up the Hindu-Muslim difficulties unfavourably to the nationalist claims, criticized MacDonald for being indecisive, for his endorsement of the suspension of the ordinary forces of law and the imposition of a strong rule by drastic ordinances instead and for allowing the atmosphere of goodwill which Irwin had sought to evolve disappear, as it were, overnight.[129] Apprehensive of the fact that repression was the sure road to rebellion and that it would align both the Moderates and the Extremists against the Government, Laski gave a call for a reorientation of British policy. In particular, he urged that the Government must return to the Round Table position and do its utmost to revive and continue the spirit of conciliation and convince Gandhi and his associates that they should not sacrifice the substance for the shadow. Laski was sincere but somewhat naïve when he pleaded that 'America, Ireland and India, all prove the essential lesson that what holds a great empire together is its generosity of spirit and not its physical power. That was what Lord Irwin saw. It is upon that, again, that Mr MacDonald must insist to Lord Wellingdon'.[130] While giving a handsome tribute to the remarkable achievements of British rule in India he also acknowledged the ascendancy of Indian nationalism with considerable popular support. Laski made it clear that minor concessions would only stimulate the nationalistic aspirations and repression would merely increase its intensity. Since Britain would not be able to reconquer India, Laski voiced the universal opinion of the British Left, 'wisdom demands that she should seek the formulae of cooperation'.[131] To act otherwise would involve India in a tragedy, poison

British politics and 'deprive Great Britain of the energy she needs to play her part in rebuilding the foundation of Western civilisation'.[132] A 'real' self-government within the British Empire was the prescription of the Labour Left. This was offered against the background of an analysis of the poverty and social backwardness of the Indian society which required regeneration as if this had been the object of British mission in India interrupted by the forces of an irrational nationalism which, in its turn, called for circumspection and judicious handling. In an eloquent passage Laski expressed that mission in the political terminology of the twentieth century much to the satisfaction of the British Left that encompassed a wide political spectrum extending from the Liberal Conservatives to the intellectually influential Marxian Socialists:

> The Indian mind is today so obsessed by the problem of Nationalism that every other issue is set in its perspective. Yet the problem of Nationalism is in fact of quite secondary importance from ultimate angle. The big Indian problem is poverty. Reorganisation of the agrarian system, the development of the Indian industry, a comprehensive effort to deal with the problems of health and education, these with such social problems as child marriage and the depressed classes, ought to be the real material of public discussion. No Indian politician can be persuaded to face them seriously until responsible Government is in being. Until then he will pursue the ostrich policy of attributing all evils to foreign domination. There will be a continuation of listless inertia in the face of momentous social difficulties which is the curse of India. Rhetoric will occupy the place of thinking; denunciation will comfort those who ought to be busy with constructive effort. Enthusiasm will be concentrated on the shadow, instead of the substance and large problems. The lines of division in Indian opinion will be utterly unreal because they will not be set by the material with which it is urgent to cope. India is the outstanding proof of the fact that only in self-government can the means of social regeneration be found. Deprived of that, India lacks that sense of responsibility which is the condition of social progress.[133]

What the learned political scientist decided to overlook was that 'self-government within the Empire' with effective military, financial and legislative safeguards in the hands of the imperial Government and the ultimate right to veto retained in the viceregal authority was a negation of freedom and justice, that imperial pride could not have been dissolved by humanitarian invocations and that the social salvation of India and her rapid economic emancipation had never been on the cards of imperialism.[134]

There were many who might have applauded Laski for his courage and conviction. But his was a call for humanizing imperialism; it was not a decisive voice against it. It was a renewed effort to reorganize imperialism in the light of the experiences of the history of the twentieth century. It was not an open acknowledgement of Indian nationalism as a progressive force in history but a reluctant adjustment with that force for tactical reasons within the orbit of the Empire so that Britain could play its historic role in rebuilding European civilization. Laski maintained that under the Labour Government it had appeared as though through the combined efforts of Irwin, Wedgwood Benn and John Sankey, a real partnership between England and India would have been evolved on the basis of responsible Government. The new policy of the coalition ministry consisted in part to divide and rule and in part to crush by force the yearnings of a people for freedom. This policy had been tried, he wrote, by Britain in Ireland, by Russia in Poland and by Austria in Italy though the end of such a policy had always been disastrous to the people which attempted it. Invoking the tradition of freedom and justice, Laski warned that Samuel Hoare had been consciously committing the British people to methods and policies which denied that very tradition. The dilemma of the Labour Party was aptly described by the Mahatma when he was asked if that Party's attitude offered any sign of encouragement and if India could bank on the goodwill of the Party which was then under a temporary cloud.[135] Mahatma Gandhi frankly admitted that although he trusted in the good intentions of the Labour Party he doubted its ability 'to translate the intentions into action'. The Labour Party, he added, had not yet obtained that status in society to make itself heard effectively. Members of both the Labour and Liberal parties had said in effect, 'Take what you can get today, but do not expect us to be of much use to you'.[136] Gandhi had come to believe that statement literally. He was convinced that the electorate would not allow the Labour Party its own way so far as India was concerned. The Party, Gandhi asserted before the leading socialists of the day, was yet to be trusted by the English people.[137] 'Either you get the thing you want', General Smuts had told Gandhi, 'or you must fight'. Gandhi must have disturbed the Liberal and Labour intellectuals on that cold December evening in 1931 at the house of Horrabin when he said plainly in reference to Smuts' words: 'It is the only way, it won't come through argument. I do not know a single instance when freedom has come through argument'.[138]

*

Between the extrovert publicists of the Raj and the lunatic fringe of the British Left, there were many who found it difficult to make up their minds. In a sense they were caught up between the reality of an arrogant Empire and a much publicized British inheritance of individual freedom and democracy. On the one hand, there were the irresistible compulsions to defend the interests of an imperial commonwealth; on the other, there were Christian inhibitions 'to rob Peter to pay Paul'. Forster sought to humanize imperialism and soften its harsh realities; Thompson was embittered by India's resilience, her truculent nationalism and Gandhi's uncompromising adherence to it; Orwell was frightened by the enigmatic embrace of imperial psychology sapping the noble inheritance of a free and adventurous people; the Socialist ideologues underlined India's economic disparity and backwardness, her social system and communal disunity and conveniently walked over into the courtyard of a pretentious imperialism. Out of the army of Liberal sentimentalists one saw the emergence of a definite body of humanists seeking reconciliation between estranged peoples, antagonistic emotions and contradictory political positions separated by closed doors and unfortunate misunderstandings. The basis of the endeavour of the Fellowship of Conciliation was their belief in the unity of mankind and their faith in negotiated settlement through the process of an unhindered dialogue.[139]

The prolonged tension between Britain and India had been a burden on the minds of the Friends for many years. India was not new to the Friends and over the years they had been working there in the missionary services. They believed that the chronic friction between Britain and India, a country of nearly four hundred million inhabitants, an ancient civilization and the birthplace of some of the world's great religions was one of the main political tragedies of the modern world. During the Civil Disobedience movement and the imprisonment of political 'offenders' in 1929, 1932 and 1936, visiting Friends went to India with the support of the 'Meetings of Sufferings' and tried to build a bridge over the chasm of distrust. They tried to learn the truth about things, establish friendship with Indian people and national leaders and consolidate the bond of personal relations. The idea was to break down some of the barriers that had often prevented contact between Indian national leaders and British officials. Despite opposition of the die-hards in Britain and the hostility of the Extremists in India the Friends felt that it was not a lost cause. A quiet, steady and determined progress of India towards a greater measure of political freedom, Horace Alexander thought, had been the significant feature of the post-First World War situation. And from the Indian side there was, the Friends cheerfully noted, a responsible response to the fraternal gestures of British statesmen. This trend was vital in view of the ominous attitudes of the Ultra-Conservatives in Britain, the irrational behaviour of the harassed administrators in an alien country and the impatient adventures of the angry young men of India.[140]

The Friends sought to strengthen the moderates of all faiths in India, made them sit together, denied all possibilities of giving offence to one another, worked out a mode of understanding between them, opened all closed doors, softened the blows of unsympathetic official action and made both sides appreciate the problems and difficulties of each other. They sought to draw the empathy from as many as possible and welcomed all those who would have acknowledged the merit of reconciliation in a strife-torn world. They had Conservatives, Liberals, Labourites, administrators, clergymen as well as missionaries in their extensive contacts in Britain. At the Indian end, there were Mahatma Gandhi, Madan Mohan Malaviya, Tej Bahadur Sapru, Srinivas Shastri, Amrit Kaur, Jamnalal Bajaj, G.D. Birla and many others. Contact with Krishna Menon, Minoo Masani and Jawaharlal Nehru was maintained to feel the pulse of some of the radical young men.[141] The uneasy conscience of the British nation provided imperialism with a suitable instrument to manipulate divergent emotions and keep a channel of communication open between the 'progressive' Indian opinion and the British ruling impulses.

The attitude of the Indian Conciliation Group, formalized in 1929 with Carl Heath as the chairman and Agatha Harrison as the secretary, carried on a relentless campaign for transforming domination into partnership. Some of their gestures modulated the harshness of official action and responses, some endeavours opened the doors slammed shut by official over-action, some attempts at reconciliation assisted the moderating influence in India to consolidate itself while some others sought to find a way out of the political impasse. Strictly from the imperial point of view, the whole process of reconciliation maintained a line of communication between the ruler and the spokesmen of the ruled. It was a responsive and sensitive endeavour performed silently and remaining largely unacknowledged. The Group had undertaken to improve Indo-British relations with full faith in the unique historical experience in India which would develop, they thought, into a happy and harmonious commonwealth of nations and would lead to a real and meaningful exchange of ideas and understanding between the East and the West.[142]

So far as India was concerned, these missionaries of goodwill were convinced that the freedom-loving tradition of Britain still held good. They believed that the real culprit responsible for the strained relationship was a judicious admixture of racial arrogance coupled with a lack of imagination. It was myopic, they asserted, to assume that the British Government and statesmen 'understood India's mind better than her own sons and daughters can do'.[143] As a result, even though the British statesmen had been interested in assessing India's advice, suggestions and criticisms, the British authorities had been somewhat reckless and arbitrary all the way through. A most formidable army of diverse personalities had been gathered at the Round Table. But Horace Alexander thought that there was a remarkable inability in the effort to touch the heart of real India or even to enlist the support of Gandhi, the secret of India's friendship and cooperation.[144] Contesting the position of Nehru with regard to the interplay of historical forces, Alexander maintained that Nehru was one of those who believed that economic pressures counted for everything and the actions of the individuals—whether viceroy, governors or secretaries of state or well-meaning Friends of India—for nothing. The Quakers had an absolute faith in their belief that the spirit of God working in the hearts of men had a greater power than any economic process. The purpose of reconciliation was to discover for 'ourselves' the 'facts' devoid of subjective emotions. It was basically, as he saw it, a great educational process.[145] The members of the fellowship insisted that the discussions with the Indian national leaders should not be broken off till an agreement had been reached. 'We must think and act' he wrote, 'in the light of the fact that India belonged to the Indian people'.[146] Here was a great task and when 'a heart-agreement' was reached with India the whole world would be inspired to hope that the age of imperial and race domination was beginning to pass away.[147] In this noble social and religious undertaking Alexander urged that the prophetic insight of Gandhi ought to be fused with the political common sense of the British. The art of living in India must be linked to the practical aid in the science of social welfare. Both the East and the West would thus help each other to 'a renewed vitality in which moral obligation springs from an organised political action'. They had opted to work between the groups and their mutual distrust as individuals and to see if, even at the risk of a futile effort, closed doors could be opened, passionate hatred neutralized or warring factions made to sit together.[148]

The Conciliation Group of India came to life owing to the efforts of Andrews and the blessings of Gandhi. In 1929 the turn of events had disturbed the peace of mind of many Friends. 'These are extremely critical times in India', Andrews informed the American Friends Service Committee in Philadelphia in December 1929, 'much more so than nine or ten months ago'.[149] If things went well in the following few months, he believed, then one might witness the remarkable event of 'the East and the West growing near to each other on higher grounds'[150] in an open defiance of Kipling and his sort. There were however serious apprehensions. Andrews, for one, thought that the forces against peace had been very powerful and it was likely that they might overcome the forces of good for a time. The Friends had great faith in Irwin as the viceroy of India and felt that his was the best selection that could have been made. Irwin was, Andrews recommended, 'an idealist in theory, but conservative in practice'.[151] The Group was troubled by the fact that in the previous winter, impatience had taken over the reigns and young India had resolved that if Swaraj was not granted by December 1929 they would begin passive resistance. Andrews was somewhat assured by the tactical move of Gandhi who, while considering the great unity behind the declaration, had offered to lead the resistance. There was also a positive response from the side of the Government. The confirmation of Irwin's viceroyalty and the official declaration in favour of granting dominion status or Swaraj following the Round Table Conference had raised hopes for the resolution of conflicts although Andrews was not slow to detect that the Delhi declaration of the nationalists had gone a little too far beyond the scope of official statement.[152]

The Friends were convinced that the viceroy had been trying to meet Gandhi half-way and if it denoted a change of heart in Britain, they were sure that Gandhi would wait and respond. The Group saw in the whole struggle between India and Great Britain a much larger question concerning the relation between the East and the West. Reviewing the situation in Britain, Andrews had concluded that MacDonald was an idealist and the Labour Party had been solidly behind him on the Indian question. He was also supported by Stanley Baldwin and his bloc of Conservative Party. Against this combination stood Churchill and Birkenhead who objected to the whole attitude and the so-called 'wild policy' of the Labour Government. Unfortunately, Lloyd George had lost his idealism and had been carrying a number of Liberals along with him towards Birkenhead and the uncertainty of the situation had been aggravated by the fact that the Labour Government was based on a minority vote. The result of the efforts would depend on the groups voting together against a Conservative combination.[153]

The British Government desired Congress cooperation and a harassed Wedgwood Benn, the secretary of state, implored Alexander to exhort himself: 'I can only say that I trust that the spirit in which the Prime Minister referred to the possibility of clemency with regard to persons now in jail in connection with the Civil Disobedience Movement, will find an echo in the hearts of the adherents of Congress and make it possible to give further consideration to the question of a gesture such as you suggest.'[154] The Conciliation Group was hopeful that the door would not be shut and the Gandhi-Irwin Pact would not end as a truce but would lead to an East-West reconciliation. Andrews responded; so did Polak and Alexander. But the men-on-the-spot had other ideas. The Government of India was determined not to show an olive-branch. Alexander was curtly informed that the administration of a colonial dependency was not a game of pious reconciliation and noble gestures, and that the practical experience of the administration merely proved that an attempt to be responsive in the existing political atmosphere was beset with extraordinary difficulties. There could be no question of a compromise in the matter of power and prestige. Imperialism had its own logic—there were certain fundamental positions on which there was little scope for reconciliation.[155] At every level of political dialogue, its supremacy and paramountcy had to be jealously guarded.

The members of the fraternity were not unaware that their effort might result in a trivial exercise and that the arrogance of the Raj, though mellowed at a certain given point of time under the pressure of political exigencies, would reassert itself if asked to offer tangible conciliations towards Indian nationalism. In 1929, MacDonald had asked Andrews pointedly to 'take the PM's side in the struggle that was going on between the Labour Government and Gandhi'. Andrews had hesitated; it had appeared to him that Gandhi had been 'on the whole right' and Great Britain wrong.[156] Gandhi's case had been morally unimpeachable. But since the Gandhi-Irwin Pact, Andrews' heart had been with the Labour Government in its endeavours to fulfil its own side of the Pact and Andrews decided 'to play the game with MacDonald' although he was equally sympathetic with 'Gandhi in his magnificent struggle to fulfil his side of the Pact in the face of tremendous difficulties'.[157] Overwhelmed by the political developments, Andrews wrote to MacDonald as an old friend and offered to work for him. Andrews was aware of the difficulties that MacDonald would face in trying to trust Gandhi implicitly without ever having seen him. On the basis of his own experience of twenty years, Andrews assured the prime minister that Gandhi was essentially a truthful person even in the smallest details and if MacDonald were to deal with him, it would be necessary for him to share that belief with Andrews. He was also aware that such implicit faith might cause some difficulties for MacDonald but nothing could be done without that faith which was shared even by Gandhi's political opponents in India.[158] 'On no other basis except this confidence', wrote Andrews, 'in Gandhi's honesty and sincerity can the situation in India, as I see it today, come to a right settlement'.[159] Andrews recommended that Madan Mohan Malaviya, a reliable politician enjoyin is confidence, be invited to the Conference. Andrews asserted that although Malaviya was an orthodox Hindu and did not enjoy the sympathy of the Muslim community at all, he was 'supremely desirous of peace' and would help Gandhi to come to reasonable terms.[160] His suggestion was quite simple and categorical: 'If these two men can actually be present in London and put their signatures to what is generally agreed upon by the body of the Conference, there is real chance of a permanent peace in India when the Conference dissolves.'[161] Andrews felt that two things had to be settled initially in order to expedite the settlement of the Indian issue. On the Lancashire problem, Andrews assured MacDonald that he was willing 'to do anything possible' to convince Gandhi and Malaviya that they should realize the extreme distress in Lancashire resulting from civil disobedience so that 'if not a settlement, at least some hope of settlement should be arrived at beforehand. . . .'[162] Andrews was convinced that some such understanding could be reached with regard to the second important problem, i.e. the Hindu-Muslim equation by bringing both the Nawab of Bhopal and Ansari into confidence. Andrews was already in correspondence with Gandhi. On the Lancashire issue the case was prepared by an experienced professor who was to explain to Gandhi the nature of the economic distress of the people. On the question of the Hindu-Muslim accord, Andrews was convinced that only one-fifth of the issue was ticklish and a suitable and timely intervention on the part of MacDonald would settle the problem once and for all.[163]

Polak and Andrews took charge of Gandhi while in England. Constant briefings and a frequent exchange of views between the three enabled Andrews, Alexander and Polak to form their opinion of the Mahatma's mind and to gauge the possible trend of his thoughts. Long sessions at

Friend's House with missionaries and the Friends of India threw light on some other issues.[164] Irwin, Ramsay MacDonald, his son Malcolm and Samuel Hoare among others got the feedback of these impressions in ample measure.[165] Gandhi had blessed the India League under the secretaryship of an indefatigable Krishna Menon who had been pushing its objectives towards Purna Swaraj. Andrews, Polak and Alexander sought to turn Gandhi away from that 'extremist organization' to the spiritual eclecticism of the Friends of India. Gandhi was thoroughly exposed to the moderate wing of British politics with regard to India and before he left England, the Friends got the impression that Gandhi was fully cognizant of the battle that was being waged by a reasonable Samuel Hoare against the Churchillian reactionaries and that the Mahatma was inclined to a respectable cooperation with the Government.[166] In any case Gandhi, they concluded, would use his influence in favour of peace and not of civil disobedience provided adequate conciliatory measures were offered.[167]

On 4 December 1931 having passed the gist of Alexander's letter on 'something of what is in Gandhi's mind' to Ramsay before he met the Mahatma, Malcolm found himself in a cheerful frame of mind. It was to be communicated to the Mahatma, he wrote, that in the Statement of Policy, Ramsay had 'gained a great point in getting the Conservative Party committed to this'.[168] Of course, there were many difficulties ahead and Ramsay understood the Mahatma's uncertainties even about the Statement of Policy. Malcolm, however, hoped that Gandhi would realize that 'on this side we are working under difficult conditions, and that he will be able to do a great deal to help us'.[169] Gandhi was also to be assured that things would, henceforth, move rapidly, and 'both public and parliamentary opinion here would be enormously impressed if Congress could see its way to cooperate in its work lying immediately ahead'.[170] By 10 December, Malcolm was to report optimistically that 'the P.M. and Sam Hoare' had assured the Mahatma of their sincerity to get something really satisfactory done and had also thanked Alexander for having stated frankly Gandhi's chief misgivings.[171] Things, however, swerved dramatically in the opposite direction. The imperial mind, however, assessed the situation according to its own priorities. The Government of India did not accept that Gandhi had any significant influence on the Congress Working Committee. Both Ramsay MacDonald and Samuel Hoare concurred with the man-on-the-spot and the door was slammed shut with a bang. By 18 December, Irwin, the political proponent of reconciliation, was feeling uneasy.[172] He was inclined to consider that Gandhi had swung a good deal in the wrong direction. He could not, for example, reconcile Gandhi's reported Italian interview with his letter to Irwin a week earlier affirming that the way for reconciliation was still open. Irwin viewed the Bengal situation as tragic but he could not possibly find it in his conscience to condemn the Government of India for taking whatever preventive measures they had. As the notorious Ordinance Rule was inaugurated in full swing, Irwin wrote authoritatively to a wavering and disconcerted Alexander: 'I feel also bound to conclude that with the knowledge of the very different temper actuating the Working Committee, the Viceroy had no very strong ground, from his point of view, for hoping that any conversation would secure peace at that stage.'[173]

With the arrest of Gandhi on 4 January 1932, the Conciliation Group became more active than ever before in the cause of promoting understanding. It had become indispensable in mobilizing 'the Xtian forces' for the Indian cause. The parliamentary debates on India filled the Group with misery. 'More than ever I feel,' wrote Agatha Harrison, 'that I must try to push open the doors'.[174] Foot, Burneys and Polak were in close contact; Carl Heath was to go to India to make preparations for the Round Table Conference.[175] Andrews, it was believed, would be indispensable in England and would be able to do far more at home than in India picking up 'the many threads he was weaving'. When he had been in Britain in preparation for Gandhi's visit, Harrison had resolved to hand over to him 'all the threads we have in hand'.[176] It was believed that the establishment in England would have to listen to him for they would not be able to dismiss his long experience in India. Both Bajaj and Birla concurred with them.[177] The Friends were not pleased to watch the proud and uncompromising defence by Samuel Hoare of the Government of India and were afflicted by a sense of frustration in the Christian forces with the reversal of the policy of reconciliation. Letters from missionaries about the Indian situation had been pouring in. Meetings were held to highlight the morbid deadlock in India and to focus on the urgency for a breakthrough.[178] Spellbound by the 'forceful' exposition of the cause by an 'inspired' Alexander in one of these meetings, Agatha Harrison recognized the truth of Gandhi's judgement when cut adrift from the Mahatma's guidance and inspiration, she had asked him whom she should work with. 'With Horace Alexander' had been Gandhi's answer.[179] Pleading for a more active assistance she implored Alexander: 'You saw something of the threads I am trying to weave; I should be glad if you will criticise freely and make any suggestion, for being a freelancer, while it has its advantages, has drawbacks.'[180]

The threads were many, the pattern of the scheme was intricate and the efforts were enormous. Hoare had to be challenged and his attitude had to be softened. When Graham wrote in the *Manchester Guardian* on Gandhi, Eric Hayman was commissioned to write a reply on the basis of the report prepared by Harrison and Alexander while William Crozier was contacted with a request to make an editorial comment.[181] William Paton was put in charge of soothing feelings in India. Meanwhile the India League decided to send a team to prepare an on-the-spot study of the realities in India and Harrison joined hands with the League to raise money,[182] declining however, to take the responsibility of the League in Menon's absence.[183] It was an active body of publicists who were given to a vigorous propaganda for the Indian Swaraj. The Conciliation Group could assist and act in cooperation with it on issues but it was neither feasible nor desirable to be identified with it. In the context of the League, Agatha was candid: 'It takes all my time to explain that they are not Bolshevists, and to get the interests and vital contacts of men like Polak etc. linked up with them. . . .' The background history of all this, Harrison quipped, 'will never be written—perhaps it is as well!'[184]

Round the corner in London's Whitehall, Agatha was happy that the Group during its long conversation with Sankey was able 'to disturb him' and she reported that Sankey 'showed very plainly that he was very troubled' by the affairs in India but he would like to wait until the return of the committees.[185] It was pointed out to him that the Indian National Congress, the 'chief group in India', had no part in the findings and that 'Gandhi and his group' would have to be treated well to achieve any chance of success. Agatha Harrison, optimistic as ever, thought that they had made a powerful dent in the heart of the establishment and Andrews was left to pick up the threads.[186] Among the intellectuals it was suggested that Laski was the person 'that we should tie very tightly' for he touched 'circles that some of the rest of us do not'.[187] When Sapru wrote to Polak about the position of the Moderate opinion, Polak passed it on to Harrison who went over to Sydney Welton for an expert opinion and within hours it was at the offices of all the London papers with a special plea to some of the editors for publicity. Then there was Nagen Ganguli getting into places like the Empire Society and needing a pep talk because he had spoken against the British and when Cornalia was 'given to tongue again' Agatha saw to it that she was to be covered by someone else who would put a counterpoint of view.[188] Irwin, not happy with the treatment at the hands of the India Office, had to be nursed, Malcolm MacDonald, a useful contact at the prime minister's breakfast table, had to be kept in good humour, [189] Kamlani, Krishna's rival, had to be maintained on friendly relations and

Menon had to be restrained.[190] It was also decided that Polak ought to meet Menon on a friendly footing and, if necessary, pat him on the back,[191] and if required, Polak should also be seen in the front row in the India League's meetings even if he did not share the platform.[192] Further, the press had to be carefully treated and a press lunch could be organized as an occasional interlude where Walter Layton, Lord Allen, J.A. Spender, Kinsley Martin, H.M. Smith, E. Wrench and the editors of the *Christian World* and the *Star* could be invited.[193]

As Gandhi decided to go on a fast over the question of communal award in September 1932, Andrews cabled Gandhi to delay his fast until he arrived in India. On the basis of the opinion of Andrews, the Group suggested that in order to meet the difficulty, a non-communal basis of voting in the 'special areas' of the depressed classes could be tried out. Both the secretary of state and the prime minister were nice to the Group's delegation and Agatha Harrison began to appreciate that there was a real problem in that if the Government gave way to one group they would have the others clamouring. All this while, Birla and Polak were in active communication.[194] Lothian and Irwin were pressurized to release Gandhi which would, it was insisted, enable the achievement of a satisfactory solution for the problem of the depressed classes.[195] Accordingly, at a meeting at Chatham House, Carl Heath and Alexander strongly supported the demand for Gandhi's release. Irwin, unable to take a prominent part, agreed to be present at the meeting adding 'great strategic importance' to the gathering. P.Hartog put the case before the audience on behalf of the Group. 'By case,' Agatha Harrison explained in no uncertain terms, 'I mean to present the expressed feelings of moderate men in India about the estrangement of moderate men towards the present policy'.[196] This could be covered, if necessary, by quoting the debate in the Legislative Assembly, the Madras Council, the Bombay Council, the Welfare of India League and the National Liberal Federation.[197] The position would be strengthened, Agatha added, if the statement of Samuel Hoare in the parliamentary debate was cited. Andrews was chided for describing Gandhi in close circles as 'pathological' which could mean 'unbalanced',[198] while Polak was despatched to Geneva to meet Privat and Rolland to tell them of the existence and purpose of the Group and their willingness to cooperate.[199] Irwin and Sankey were brought closer to the Group as they were found more sympathetic and sensitive to the spiritual significance of Gandhi than anybody else.[200]

When, in the summer of 1933, the Indian leaders of moderate vintage arrived in London, the Group kept up its close contact with 'Sapru–Joshi and Co.', and when accosted with a hostile 'savage' state of mind in the Indian hotel, the Group activated itself in order to diffuse the critical situation.[201] To the Group it was a problem of crisis-management and the crisis was diagnosed mainly as a psychological one. Few seemed to understand, Agatha wrote to Alexander, the psychology of these men, who had been busy and important people, and had been listening day after day to the most humiliating things about their fitness to govern themselves.[202] There was an increasing ascendancy of the die-hards, Agatha reported, in the India Office despite her effort to counter that evil and the Indians, she felt, were once again mismanaged. The papers had been vituperative against India in general and the Indian delegation in particular; there had been an excessive concentration of interest on an alleged split amongst them and a considerable fuss about the Economic Conference. The knowledge that the White Papers might be whittled down and the fact that people who 'should be talking with them have no time to sit down quietly with them' had resulted in a serious temper.[203] It was a pity, Agatha thought, that Lothian, Irwin, Samuel and others had been ignorant of the feelings of the delegates, that they did not have time to sit down with 'Sapru and Co.' and talk to them 'as man to man'.[204] The atmosphere in the hotel, as a result, was full 'of depression, suspicion and poison'. Someone had to watch the situation behind the scenes, sense the feelings and bring the people together for that was the missing link. In order to salvage the situation, Polak was made to dispatch letters to Lothian, Irwin and Reading urging them to take proper steps in view of the grave situation. Coatman from the London School of Economics, himself adept in the art of 'sensing', was pushed to meet Hoare and arrangements were made to have Sapru, Jayakar and others feel at home and the hosts to explore exactly what they were feeling.[205]

As Gandhi busied himself with his Harijan work, the Conciliation Group grew eager in anticipation. It was concluded that the most practical thing was to get the Harijan Paper as widely circulated as possible for people to see what was being done by the reformers themselves. It was believed that with the knowledge of this social evil and the efforts of Gandhi to eradicate it, people would be able to defend the Mahatma's actions and if they were impeded the Group would raise its voice.[206]

It was, however, becoming somewhat difficult to sustain interest in India unless an agreed basis of the work was chalked out. Polak had prepared, with the consent of the Group, a short draft on the leading points of the White Paper that ought to be modified in order to satisfy the Moderate opinion. This was largely 'the Sapru–Jayakar–Shastri and Co.'

and it was quite likely, Agatha thought, that this could be a good basis for an agreement that could be put before the Muslims with the views of the Congress enclosed in the preamble.[207] It appeared to some others that this was an opportunity to act and some of the important delegates could be encouraged to issue a joint statement urging the Government to take advantage of the truce.[208] This was considered important because the White Paper could pale into insignificance before long as the situation could alter overnight 'either by the death of Gandhi or by the fact that he survives, and at the end of his fast realises that no move has taken place as a result of his gesture. He will, I imagine, call on C.D. again and go to prison . . .'[209] As hours would go by, the situation would harden, wrote Agatha Harrison, and much discussion would go on whether Gandhi had been playing a game in precipitating a crisis. Harrison was convinced that there was an opening and the Group ought to take advantage of it immediately which could help to break through the stalemate. By mid-1934, the Group began to waver and felt uneasy at the prospect of being dubbed as 'Gandhi, Gandhi and Gandhi' although it was also keen that the 'untouchable' attitude towards Gandhi and the Congress should not be continued any longer and that some means must be discovered of bridging the gulf. Polak was not happy with the new stance of the Group and was gradually drifting away.[210] Unlike C.F. Andrews, Agatha and Horace had concluded that they should broaden the base of the work[211] and were desirous of opening the door wide for anyone who would like to come. The secretary of state, the ex-viceroys, the governors of provinces, the Servants of India Society, and a host of others were to be roped in effectively.[212] While Sapru and his Co would be the favoured group in India, Gandhi, still the revered one, would be subjected to the objective scrutiny of Horace and Agatha.

In 1934, both Agatha Harrison and Horace Alexander had been intrigued by Nehru's letter to his daughter. Both had watched with surprise the strange ways in which the children of modern India were expected to learn history. The Friends were intrigued by Nehru's concept and theory of history and his historical values. Nehru's history, they thought, was fairly different from their own concept of history for it did not include any idea 'of the world beyond'—beyond the struggles, tensions and conflicts—and of 'all its wonders'.[213] They were annoyed to note that in 1936, Nehru's programme in England was drawn up largely by Menon who was exclusively in charge of it and were unhappy with Menon's attempt to project Jawaharlal Nehru as the acknowledged leader of the Indian independence movement. Responding to the move positively, they thought that the presence of Horace Alexander in the meeting of

27 January 1936 might 'bring this meeting on to an entirely different level'.[214] But it was pointed out to Menon that it was of imperative urgency that what 'may be termed the "middle of the road opinion" comes into close contact with Nehru so that the force of this opinion gets communicated to him. I reminded him of the fact that the tremendous force of opinion against the Hoare-Laval Pact was a result of the ordinary man and woman in the street—taking a hand—not just the left wing opinion. And if he did not get into touch with this section—we shall lose out'.[215] They were also chagrined to see Nehru entertaining 'the so-called Indian Progressive Writers here' and by the fact that some of them like one Mr Anand 'have evidently impressed him'.[216] It was increasingly apparent to Agatha and Horace that the path of conciliation was hard and thorny, that the ways of the Lord were inscrutable and that it was judicious to await events. The idea was to push open all the tightly closed doors. The Group had already developed the distinct advantage of having decisive contacts with a wide range of people so that it acquired, Harrison believed, an outreach that other groups did not have.[217] Increasingly they moved more towards the direct inclinations of the Government.[218] Amery and Horace Alexander agreed in 1941 that Gandhi unfortunately mixed up pacificism as a principle with the political refusal by Congress to participate in the War when there was, they thought, no connection between the two things. The viceroy, it also agreed, was quite willing to let Gandhi exercise the same freedom to voice genuine pacifist convictions as was admitted in Britain. Alexander and Amery also agreed that mere pacific convictions were incompatible with maintaining the unity of the Congress as a political organization and Gandhi was invariably bound by the rules of the Congress politics.[219] A friend in Edward Thompson was already convinced that Gandhi and his noble principles had been reduced to a collection of *ad hoc* measures based on sheer opportunism but in 1941 they realized the difficulty of a general release of civil disobedience prisoners and that the resolution of this vexing situation was largely 'dependent upon Mr Gandhi and his followers'.[220] By November 1941, Alexander also agreed with Amery that there was no scope for any move for reconciliation through a constitutional step.[221] The mission of Stafford Cripps was doomed to fail. It was, however, felt that the impression left by Cripps in India was much too deep and no thinking Indian henceforth would like to equate British, German and Japanese imperialisms. Besides, it was discussed with satisfaction that Cripps was responsible for bringing an element of realism to Indian politics. In particular, he had been able to focus on the issue of the Muslim minority in the Indian political vocabu-

lary. Both Gandhi and Rajagopalachari acknowledged the existence of this political force which çould no longer be ignored as fictitious.[222] And as the August declaration came to be known, the Friends condemned it with vigour. The Quit India resolution was not acceptable to anyone. The Bengal famine had been used by the Congress, it was alleged, for a political end and Gandhi and Mahadev Desai were not completely innocent of the reprehensible political use of human suffering. By 1944, however, it was no longer possible to ignore the eventual destiny of India. The Friends got a new recruit in Wavell and initiated their new scheme of 'an Indian Kindergarten, on the South African model and fearing that Amery might appropriate the idea, they insisted that Wavell ought to pick a group of people of good sorts who would be acceptable to the Liberal Indians.[223]

The attempt to organize an 'Indian Kindergarten' in 1944 and to give a fresh lease to life to the imperial idea in India betrayed a melancholic frustration on the part of the Group that had outlived its objective and yet was unable to reconcile itself to that reality. Some form of self-government for India was within sight and after 1942 it was no longer certain if the political rebirth of India would be compatible with an imperial sacred thread. Both Horace Alexander and Agatha Harrison like many others who had been congregating at the Friends House, were somewhat perturbed by the prospect of a self-governing India resurrecting itself outside the Empire and the Commonwealth. Politics of India had been passing away to men of radical vintage and their ideological position often smacked of Bolshevik materialism. Gandhi's loneliness was quite visible to the Friends especially in a world of men in a hurry.[224] There was a feeling of estrangement between the Friends and Jawahárlal Nehru[225]; N.M. Joshi was moving towards the Left and had lost all his earlier faith in the British sense of justice and fairplay[226] and was awaiting without enthusiasm a fresh concoction from Westminster's constitutional cellar. The dependable Tej Bahadur Sapru and the energetic Hridaynath Kunzru had been totally alienated and were given to the rhetorics of the Congress Socialist Party.[227] The situation was gloomy indeed as an 'impetuous' Jawaharlal Nehru with a programme of total cessation of the viceroy's veto had been moving steadily as the undisputed national leader on the road to state power.[228] Yet the Friends could not sit still to helplessly watch history moving ahead of them.

Horace G. Alexander, having returned from India where he had spent a year with the Friends Ambulance Unit, led, on 9 March 1944, a private discussion meeting at the Royal Institute of International Affairs in the presence of a galaxy of British power elite with an interest in India.[229] Since he had visited India first in 1927 as a friend of C.F. Andrews and had come to know the Mahatma and was accepted by him 'more or less as one of his household', Alexander had the opportunity of acquainting himself with a number of Indians. Over the years they considered him 'safe' from their point of view and talked to him as if he was one of their intimate colleagues. In the closely guarded secrecy of the meeting at Chatham House, he went about examining the impulses behind these men and women of India, their conflicting motives and tendencies 'behind the mask which almost all public men wear when they make public statements'.[230] Surveying the political situation in India, Alexander was convinced that serious efforts should be made in Britain to help Rajagopalachari in his attempt to build a united India and an India that would feel itself a part of the world struggle.[231] Rajaji was 'the most English Indian'; had the 'Englishman's sense of humour' and politics for him was never an obsession. He was patient, persistent and prepared to back any agreement that was to be made with Jinnah and would try to make the Congress back it. Cripps, Rajaji confided to Alexander, must come again to complete his unfinished work and for this he was prepared to stir up the whole country on behalf of the Mission. Alternatively, he was prepared to come to England to be an unofficial ambassador of goodwill and to interpret India to England. Rajaji's unquestionable optimism was magnificent. In spite of a rebuff, he still believed in Jinnah and liked him and in spite of his breach with the Congress, he was still devoted to Gandhi. His admirable pamphlet, 'The Way Out', was an exciting tract showing the way to permanent reconciliation. A Muslim League leader of Bengal, Alexander said, had told him that Jinnah's opposition mentality had got the better of him and that he had lost his chance and recommended Rajagopalachari, a Brahmin from South India, as India's first national premier. In Madras, the Indian Christians, earlier critical of Rajagopalachari, had altered their stance and felt that as the premier he would protect the rights of the minorities. Vijayalakshmi Pandit, 'one of the best Congress ministers in the U.P. ministry of 1937–9', was most anxious, Alexander claimed, to help in finding a way out of the impasse if it could be achieved while remaining loyal to the Congress and was eager to come to terms with Rajagopalachari.[232] Rajaji enjoyed the respect and affection of Gandhi who looked upon him as belonging to the Congress Party despite his independent line. Rajagopalachari, in turn, though dubbed by Jawaharlal Nehru 'as very Right Wing for a number of years', had never become a critic of the Congress.[233]

Of the others, Jinnah was presented as being in a better frame of mind than he had ever been. He desired Pakistan intensely but was interested in becoming India's friend on'the basis of sovereign equality'.[234] B.R. Ambedkar, an old associate of the Friends, was an embittered and lonely man, fighting a forlorn battle on all fronts at once and 'nursing an impossible political ambition'. Jayakar, Sapru, Kunzru and others were sceptical of every British promise, but Horace Alexander constantly marvelled 'at the charm and sweetness of their manner even though they are most wrought up over their country's political grievances'.[235]

For some more reasonable people he looked to Bengal which had been singularly lacking since the days of C.R. Das in all-India political figures.Fazlul Haq, an agreeable and colourful personality, struck Alexander by his ability to extricate himself from awkward predicaments in a frank and sincere tone. His successor, Nazimuddin was marked by his grasp of administrative details. Another political from Bengal was H.L. Suhrawardi, a man of much energy and ambition, quite willing to take a very violent communal line and, who, paradoxically, was fairly friendly with Kiron Shanker Roy of the orthodox Congress Party. Of the Hindu figures, Alexander was quite unable to appreciate B.C. Roy and the grounds for his claim to fame.[236] A clever and popular doctor, he was the chairman of most committees in Calcutta who managed to remain out of jail. N.R. Sarkar, a man of obvious ability, was as elusive as Roy but too independent to follow a party line. Both of them did not have the calibre of first class leaders. In fact after Rajagopalachari, Alexander vouched, Syama Prasad Mookerjee was the ablest man in Indian politics. Still in his forties, Mookerjee impressed Alexander with his great energy and political realism. It appeared to Horace that Syama Prasad entered the Hindu Sabha because it would be the surer way to eminence for he had no anti-Muslim prejudice and was not at all like Moonje and Savarkar.[237] In other words, Alexander concluded that expediency and political calculation would always form a part of his politics and he wished India had rather more of this kind of political realism. He was the only man who consciously watched how near he could sail to the wind. He and Jinnah would be the sure choice of Rajagopalachari in a national government when it was undertaken. Alexander was delighted to find that the new viceroy, Wavell, had spent an hour with Rajagopalachari who was considered the key man in Indian politics and hoped that before long Wavell would feel it possible to suggest to Rajagopalachari to make an impression on Gandhi and that would be a good beginning.[238]

Thus recommending an open support for the candidature of Rajagopalachari, Alexander found it necessary to place it in contrast to that of Nehru. Alexander had known Nehru over the years but the Friends were not very close to him. He himself was not as sympathetic to Nehru's outlook as he was to Gandhi's[239] but he agreed that Nehru had more of a world outlook than Gandhi and was more realistic than him in world affairs. He, therefore, saw the importance of India in refusing to take a line that would embarrass China and Russia. He had struggled against the resolution of 1942 but all the same he genuinely believed that the British Government in India was fundamentally inefficient and that a real national government would do a much better job than the British Government. Alexander found that 'there was a doctrinaire side of Nehru's mind' and he 'lived much in a world of certain words, such as imperialism'.[240] He believed that the British Government was by nature imperialist and therefore inefficient and did not believe that there could be any cooperation with a viceroy who, however good, was a part of the imperialist system. Gandhi did not take that view and although he was mainly responsible for the Quit India Resolution, he 'was an easier man at bottom to bring into cooperation than Nehru,' who would 'not be satisfied with anything less than the complete handing over of the government'.[241] And as the final act of the Raj was concluding, the Fellowship of Conciliation was still in its old moorings. There was an unending search for issues ripe for personal intervention, there was the same intensity to open the doors, there was that sincere but shallow sympathy for India and its problems and institutions, there was the same desire to retain the political connections with India in the honour of humanity and history, there was the echo of the assertion that India was still to form a nation and that a military connection with Britain and the supremacy of the viceregal veto were indispensable conditions for her political reorganization and that there was the same good old proclivity to pass over the system and instead appreciate gestures and motions.

The attempts at reconciliation continued nevertheless. Both the governments of India and Britain could afford to depend on the Group as an effective channel of communication with the nationalist India especially when a particular move was contemplated. It represented areas in British politics where the enlightened Conservative opinion, restrained and reserved Labour views, tepid Liberal opinion and vague humanitarian and ethical attitudes of organized Church and of the right wing sections of the Christian Socialists could comfortably co-exist. This was the plane where imperialism in distress could always retreat for support from every segment of British public opinion. Some would welcome it as a necessary and tactical withdrawal; some, as the essential *sine qua non* of Indian cooperation, some others with the fanciful thought of the emergence of a happy commonwealth and others would welcome it as a brake, albeit temporarily, on an unbridled aggression of imperialism. The Friends had extensive contacts which cut across party lines; they could move around with ease between diverse organized opinions, sense the pulse of men and groups and could always depend on their own extensive experience and their 'feelings in the bones'. In terms of Indian sympathy they were at home with Gandhi and his gentle ways and enthusiastic with the Moderates and Liberals like Sapru, Shastri, Kunzru, Birla, and subsequently, Vijayalakshmi Pandit, Rajagopalachari and Amrit Kaur. They were sceptical of Nehru's radical opinions, his concept of history, his reluctance to meet men in authority, his firm faith in Menon and his outspoken views on international situations.[242]

In sheer desperation, the concept of a united India had been dropped by the Cripps Mission. It was time to watch a pattern emerging out of the favoured policy towards the minorities. Churchill continued to correspond with Jinnah secretly while Salisbury, Altrincham, Croft, Cherwell and Rankeillour guarded a shady avenue between the House of Lords and the Muslim League.[243] A simple withdrawal from India was considered impossible. A partition, with British supervision if necessary, was desirable, while transfer of India to a 'Hindu Raj' was neither acceptable to the League nor under the active consideration of the imperial high policy. Clement Attlee stood by his pronouncement that there would be no weakness and no betrayal. British strategic consensus on India, though modified over the years, was still to be governed by the age-old sensibility despite tactical differences between the last three viceroys.

It was universally acknowledged that Englishmen had committed a number of blunders and, after all, to err was human. But the most cruel mistake that Britain had made, J.H. Muirhead propounded with all sincerity, was that in 'setting about the education of these people we have taken no trouble to understand the people we are educating'.[244] Deep-rooted customs, superstitions and ancient faiths were overlooked and an attempt was made to replace them either by the worn-out views of orthodox European sects or by a superficial acquaintance with European sciences.[245]

Two questions were posed by the author: were these natives fit for education and did they have the capacity to make that education worth their while? It is doubtful if the queries could have been answered either categorically or in the affirmative. Muirhead and the British officials in India agreed in their assessment that the progress of education had created a pressing problem. It had directly caused the formation of a perceptive and captious public opinion.[246] Government control had proved ineffective.[247]

Values of 'public school', it was noted with concern, had acquired a strange caste flavour[248] and elite institutions had produced dangerous anarchists.[249] 'You hear of the Unchanging East, but what strikes me', a jittery Chamberlain wrote, 'is the rate at which India is moving at least on the surface where the current for the last ten or fifteen years has gone with ever-increasing velocity. No doubt that below deep still waters of ignorance, custom, prejudice and conservatism persist, but this only makes the problem more difficult, for how is one to meet the legitimate (as far as they are legitimate) aspirations and ambitions of a small but increasingly united and increasingly influential educated class, who look to the institutions of Western democracy for their model. . . when in fact the materials for democracy do not exist.'[250] In India the attempt to make *la carriere enverte aux talents* proved to be inadequate. It was a universal conclusion that one could not make an idol of the clever schoolboy and the sole test of merit and promotion should not be the passing of examinations. 'I prefer to look for character', Melony put it bluntly, 'that is for character as the Indians understand it'.[251]

The predicament was sought to be explained away by confuting the extravagant claims of higher education. All such pretensions were firmly quelled. From Fleetwood Wilson to Sydenham Clark, from Ramsay Muir to Harcourt Butler, from Aldous Huxley to Percival Spear, Englishmen with even a tenuous Indian connection, dwelt at length on the farcical tragedy of Indian education, its malformed universities producing a swarm of graduates, its 'crammed' degrees in the humanities, its wooden syllabuses and its unimaginative examination system.[252] Asked what they taught at the mission school where she had been educated, Muirhead got a simple answer from the native girl: 'everything'. They learnt everything, a dejected Muirhead moaned, but it amounted to nothing.[253] In fact the principal ground on which British antipathy towards Indian demands was pitched was the universal assertion that education meant mighty little to the Indians. The eternal India of superstitions survived even a determined Christian education. Lipeth of Kipling ..s well as Allah Ditta of F.F. Sherwood of the Cambridge Mission of Delhi had been purified and refined by Christianity.[254] If Lipeth's people hated her because she had, they complained, become a white woman and washed herself daily, Allah Ditta was snatched away from the padre sahib, the rational Christian society, and, perhaps, from his faith in Jesus by a fanatic crowd of maulvis backed by emotional blackmail indulged in by a selfish mother. Evidently, it should have taken a good deal of Christianity, Kipling snuffled, to wipe out the uncivilized instinct of the Eastern people of giving vent to their personal feelings. A frustrated Lipeth took to her people 'savagely as the servant of the Tarka Devi' while a sentimental Allah Ditta returned to his *millat* never to reappear before Father Crowford again.

The 'guardians' were not devoid of sympathy for these lesser breeds. But they were convinced that the peoples of the unchanging East deserved special care which was often not compatible with the Western values of individualism and rationalism. Sherwood's Lindsay Sahib had to turn to the questionable magical rituals of the fraudulent maulvi to recover his pair of gold cuff links from his *massalchi,* once the third degree of the police station had failed to move the culprit to give up his resistance.[255] Christianity remained merely an uncertain doctrine for Nathu Chamar in his encounter with a privileged society of high caste landowners led by Jiwan Singh.[256] Thus Muirhead, like Milner before him and the *Round Table* after him, concurred with the feelings of the high caste leper, Sita Ram, in his loneliness forsaken by all his dear and near ones.[257] They all felt that imperialism must turn out its best form in every department if it had to leave its impact. The Indian questions could not be resolved either by an increased participation of Indians in the administration or by an extension of franchise and the dissemination of European knowledge to them. On the contrary, the children of the Raj ought to be assisted in harnessing the elemental forces of nature for their own material interests. 'If the British empire is destined to endure', the *Round Table* declared, 'it will be only as the guardian of the moral welfare of the peoples. Faith in this mission alone can justify the efforts to further its considerations'.[258]

As Indian nationalism maintained its momentum, retained a sustained growth and developed its various expressions, the official mind straddled for a while, reviewed the situation and called for a fresh endeavour. The young Indians, it concluded, were exposed to a variety of seditious influences from an unbridled press oblivious of its responsibilities and an uncontrolled school system. Harcourt Butler's advocacy of regional universities taking their colour from local traditions and emotions and drawing their students from particular linguistic and cultural groups had become the accepted official policy. The Government's decision to improve the tone of society was cushioned by its conviction that an efficient system of education must stimulate sound moral training. This could only be secured, it was believed, by religious instructions which, while maintaining the principle of religious neutrality, would provide a specific value system and exercise close supervision of the development of young minds. The University of Calcutta was the first to be pruned.[259] Its jurisdiction was circumscribed, official command over its proceedings tightened and its vice-chancellor disciplined. The Sadler Commission recommended a deglamorized Calcutta. It offered, instead, the prospect of manageable residential universities and confirmed afresh the commendable role of Christian institutions (despite tough competition from government colleges) in building the character of the students and moulding their unruly minds. The training of a set of loyal elite-groups patterned after the British public schools, distinguished by an overwhelming college bond and an exclusive community feeling, and rendered conspicuous by integrating dining-halls and attractive playgrounds was the essence of the policy ostensibly presented as a desperate quest for excellence.[260]

Victor Dane expressed much the same feeling of despondency. 'One of our greatest mistakes in the East has been', Dane wrote in his *Naked Ascetic*, 'to try to educate the East according to Western standards. To attempt such a thing is quite absurd. What we should have done was to have given them what we could of our mechanical progress, and let them develop in their own culture, which is suitable to their psychology.'[261] Candler's Sri Ram was glowing with the spiritual pride of his race. But he was in a fix to appreciate the failure of the Hindus over the centuries and to account for their material and scientific backwardness. He had mastered the English language which had become his passion, but his mind remained, Candler stressed, static, broadening very little over the years. 'His moral code', Candler wrote, 'was drawn from certain vague formulas which had little to do with the experiences of his daily life and the textbooks in college'. Worst still, he could hardly be goaded to develop a liking for cricket, football or any of the games which would have brought him into genial relationship with the 'healthier-minded of his companions'. He had convinced himself that history was going to repeat itself. The English were the asuras who had 'ravaged the Motherland', but fortunately a new breed of dragon-slayers had been born who were predestined to 'rid her of the evil'. Against the names of Rama, Arjuna and Bhima, Candler sneered, 'were inscribed the names of modern martyrs like Tilak, Kanhyalal and Khudiram Bose'. One must abstain from and resist, Candler's Sri Ram vowed, the English rule, English piecegoods and English everything except, 'ideas and idioms of the itinerant Labour Member and his political catchwords'.[263]

Candler was eager to dispel the official fallacy that the Samajists and the seditionists in Punjab were synonymous. The Samaj stood, he argued, for reform which 'we cannot but admire, though it is our business to see that it does not threaten the stability of the British rule'. Recommending the famous institution of Kangri as 'the product of the soil', 'bound up with the traditions of the people' and identified warmly with the ideals of the Government, the Gurukul, he hoped, could become the best educational institution in the country. Candler made his position limpid: if there were no English schools and colleges, but only Gurukuls in the country, possibly there would be no Sri Ram. The reader should remember that Gandeshwar Skene College was responsible for Sri Ram. The anarchists 'got at' Gandeshwar in the book, just as they 'got at' or tried to 'get at' the Gurukul, whose honourable aim was attainment of independence, not by bombs or Browning automatic pistols, but by strengthening the character. Sri Ram was not worthy of the Gurukul: he could not attain its character.[264] The assassination of an Englishman, Candler pontificated with an air of righteousness, did not bring the Raj to its end. It was far too firm, stable and durable for Sri Ram and the conspirators. Awaiting his last day in prison Sri Ram became, in keeping with the distinct traits of his race, a pathetic victim of an unbridled fear of death while his politics grew brown and died much before his own death. Even a revolutionary India remained, Candler vaunted, childish, pusillanimous, debased and superstitious.[265]

Some observers felt that Western education left a lopsided impact on the Indians. The two cousins of Penny's *A Love Tangle*, typified this paradoxical and perplexing aspect for despite their strong family ties, the difference in their bearing and manner was wide. One was reserved and restrained showing 'unmistakable signs of Western polish'[266] while the other was the prosperous, self-satisfied product of the modern system of education in India. The latter's ancestral religion had been atrophied by rationalism and nothing had been substituted for it. His traditional courtesy had been replaced by a certain aggressive self-assertion and his inherited dignity had been lost in a swagger. There could not have been a greater contrast than was apparent between the two men.[267]

The dilemma in which Britain found herself in India was sought to be explained away by denying its very existence. As a civilization, it was resolutely upheld, it lacked coherence. As a nation, it was underlined time and again by all who had any stake in the Raj, that it did not exist. As a society, it was centrifugal. As India, it was an artificial imperial creation which was still to acquire an organic unity. The unfortunate phrase 'unity in diversity' was an unhappy expression, and administrators, publicists and writers found considerable difficulty in overcoming its implications. The country was a vast land mass inhabited by races, linguistic groups, caste and sub-caste particularisms, regional loyalties, ritualistic rivalries, Brahminical orthodoxy, a sensitive-to-touch consciousness and an intricate hierarchy of racial purity. Self-government, majority rule, legal and political equality had become some of the inconvenient legacies of nineteenth century Liberalism, especially when Englishmen in India found themselves being egged on by some bizarre countrymen and their Indian admirers to apply these esoteric principles of European politics to the bizarre Indian realities. The rise of organized labour in Europe and the prospect of its paralyzing grip on the industries were viewed as a new onslaught on the stable societies the world over. The new phenomenon hardened the attitudes of the imperialists who were petrified even by the remote possibility of the Indian nationalists discovering a militant ally in the industrial labour of India or elsewhere.

That the British Empire was a permanent political structure and India constituted an organic part of that Empire formed the inner core of the imperial consensus. Despite doses of self-government, it was implied in that assertion that India was to remain a British dependency and that the relationship was to be accepted in the natural order of things. Liberal spokesmen of imperialism and its constitutional pedants sought to soften the hard position. India would develop into a self-governing dominion, they tried to persuade an attentive congregation, through a process of constitutional evolution. Both these political positions, however, were dismissed by all those who worked incessantly to humanize the much-applauded imperial obligation which to them, seemed a superficial and shortsighted view based on half-truths. In a world whose moral foundations had been undermined, the prophets of reconciliation underlined the unique relationship between India and Britain and emphasized the need to dissolve domination into a fraternal partnership within the Empire. These three segments of imperial perception converged and modulated each other as required by the fast moving panorama of the Indian political scene. Compulsions of the turbulent 1930s and the violent 1940s, brought them visibly closer. The result was striking and often one was presented with apparently paradoxical situations because of the inherent unity of the imperial perspectives. Thus it was remarkable that although less eloquent and vivacious than Curzon, both Morley and Montagu had proved to be more persuasive than their more illustrious adversary. They had achieved (what Curzon could not have contemplated) amazing success in rounding up a rousing support for their concern for India from the very heart of India's nationalist world. Subsequently, C.F. Andrews, the 'Dinabandhu', carved out a niche for himself in the history of modern India; E.M. Forster sparked off a legend of a delicate human relationship between the ruler and the ruled; Lord Irwin offered to many the prospect of a political reconciliation; Edward Thompson adored Tagore the poet, jeered and abused Gandhi and established an enigmatic rapport with Jawaharlal Nehru, the acknowledged leader of militant Indian nationalism; Louis Mountbatten left behind for many, bonds of affection and friendship. And they all served the Empire.

5

In Retrospect

Over the century, the information industry of the Raj had been stimulated to fashion and foster an opprobrious perception of India. Administrators, politicians and specialists had been earnest in highlighting the heterogeneous realities of the country, its peoples, its religions, castes and customs, its languages and the diversity of its natural surroundings. Over the years the civil servants had claimed complete moral and unimpaired ascendancy for the Raj. An overwhelming majority of the Indian people had been committed, it was added, to an uninterrupted continuity of British rule. It was stated that the so-called problems of self-determination had been contrived and manipulated by a clamorous minority unconcerned with the interests of the inarticulate masses. The intent of the administrators, writers, intellectuals and missionaries had been to locate and scrutinize the unseemly Hindu practices and to demolish their implicit social hegemony. In the process, the observers thought, they would be able to confirm the intellectual superiority and the righteous authority of Western civilization and buttress the ideological edifice of imperialism.

Some of the observers noted that since the nineteenth century, Indian society had been witnessing a remarkable internal review, reform and resurgence.[1] The rigid social system, that had grown around the laws of karma, was being questioned and its commandments being denied undisputed sway. A spirit of service had been grafted on to the fatalistic concepts of Hinduism. However tardy and slow the process might have been, these innovative developments had made significant inroads into the amoral perceptions of Hinduism. Yet even as late as 1935, these social and intellectual ferments in India were dismissed by Western critics as cosmetic changes calculated to infuse fresh vigour into the Vedantic pantheism and to stabilize the extraordinary inertia of Hindu society. The most enlightened observers, for example, explained away the intellectual stir in India as peripheral ripples resulting from the reflex actions of an arid social system and its insensate consciousness in the face of an extrovert and rational civilization. This insidious viewpoint constituted the matrix of the imperial sensibility and stood as a self-imposed limitation obfuscating all objective investigations. As a result, deliberate distortions and fragmented realities became the essence of the invidious imperial perceptions.[2]

During the second half of the nineteenth century, India was not insulated from the external world. As recognized omphalos of the Empire, the Raj had been integrated into the world capitalism. It was no longer possible to identify the exclusive external impact on the Indian developments without any reference to the remarkable internal impulses. If the Lindsay Commission disregarded the symptoms of Indian regeneration,[3] there were some who desired to view the historical proceedings in India more pragmatically. Depressed by the futility of Christian endeavours in India, they regretted the inefficacy of the missionaries who had been operating *en rapport* with the imperial forces and saw the urgency to enliven the prospects of the Christian movement in India. Viewed from this vantage point they presumed that there would be no harm in according the religions and institutions of India a sympathetic treatment. Stanley Jones was one of those few liberal missionaries who felt uneasy by the sterile world of Indian Christianity.[4] He gave a call for a rational analysis of Indian society with a view to incorporating the best elements of Indian traditions into the perspective of the Christian movement, thinking it unnecessary to concentrate on the darker side of Indian society which would merely arouse the derision and contempt of the West towards the East. Along with some others he strove hard to assemble the basic terms of reference for a firm and lasting 'Indian road' for Christianity. Over-emphasis on the seamy side of Indian life, he held, had caused much disservice to the Christian movement in India. The whole exercise, he argued, had been conceived to inspire a sense of pity and repugnance in the minds of the readers. The consequence of such a reckless endeavour, he cautioned, could be counter-productive and even disastrous. It was feasible, he argued, that an Eastern traveller in the West might be tempted to etch an unfavourable portrayal of the Western world by carefully selecting uncomfortable facts according to his own convenience. Stanley Jones did not question the image of India as depicted by Western observers. He was, however, uncertain if the presentation had been discreet and judicious. He emphasized the vital failure of Western observers to acknowledge the changes in Indian society and to view it in its integrated totality and like many others, thought that it would be rational to evaluate the attempts made by the Indians to combat their social evils. He believed that the racial lines were so drawn that it would be realistic to leave India to put her own house in order and not to pressurize her to do so under compulsion. Jones pinned his hopes on the expectation that the foundation of the Christian mission in India could thus be laid deeper in the mind of new India.[5]

Although the demands of expediency had sparked off the patronizing gestures of the pragmatic Christian missionaries, one cannot pass over the interesting areas of Stanley Jones' prescription. He discerned in the contemporary intellectual excitement in India and in traditional Hindu thought, a few fascinating features which constituted the core of the Indian heritage. To him India was a land of 'mummied forms and customs of Hinduism', but felt that it could nevertheless boast of 'her five living seeds'. These were the concepts that the ultimate reality was spirit, that there was a sense of unity running through things, that there was in it a passion for freedom, that there was a justice in the heart of the universe and that there was 'a tremendous cost of religious life'.[6] These seeds, it was also believed, could easily be disentangled from the enervating influence of the laws of karma. Stanley Jones counselled that the world would not do much good to itself by losing these five ideas which had been embedded in Indian life and thought. Given the necessary nourishment they might sprout forth morning-glories and help integrate the 'compartmentalised and tentative' thoughts and actions of the West.[7] The pragmatic liberalism of Stanley Jones and others was repudiated and tossed away by the ego-centric and high-spirited imperialism. The perceptions of an eclectic Christianity were never incorporated within the canvas of an arrogant imperial sensibility.

European attitudes towards the non-European societies were largely conditioned by a significant Euro-centric consciousness. For all intents and purposes Europe was presented, in sharp contrast to the non-European world, as the centre of the universe. The rest of the cosmos was never regarded as anything but a solid mass of inert barbarism. Thus the West declared with perfect equanimity that the Orient constituted an area where the element of change had never occurred in history without the inspiration and intervention from without. It was but natural, therefore, that the West announced, much to the amusement of its attentive audience, that the East did not have any history save some dynastic changes and had no historical movement. It was static and frozen within its rigid moral codes, its inflexible social customs and its cold and uninspiring religious laws.[8] This Euro-centric law of historical development imposed by its very logic a sacred obligation to the Western civilization to expand towards the non-Western peoples even without their overt approval and despite their active opposition and passive resistance. The West has been credited as the recipient of Greek virtues like philosophy, individualism and democracy.[9] In sharp contrast, the Middle East, it was presumed, had been 'ossified by the particularism and exclusiveness of Judaism on the one hand and by the lethargy of fallen Islam on the other'.[10] The 'Oriental ease and repose', it had been added, were the characteristic features of Indian culture distinguished by self-sufficient village communities dominated by the State as the ultimate landlord and the absence of any change in a self-perpetuating social structure.[11] This particular perception gave the West its birthright to engineer desired developments in the East and to delineate the contours of imperial sensibility.

The most influential philosopher who offered an integrated social frame for the articulation of imperial perception was G.W.F. Hegel. His analysis of the independence and dependence of social consciousness provided the blue-print of imperial psychology and left a permanent imprint on European thought. The self-assured and the domineering self-consciousness, according to the German philosopher, existed only in being acknowledged. Life, in this compelling philosophy, was the natural setting of consciousness and was essential for pure self-consciousness. For the survival and perpetuation of independent self-consciousness, the pure consciousness existed as two opposed shapes of consciousness. One was the independent consciousness whose essential nature was 'to be for itself' and the other was dependent consciousness which lived and toiled for the other. Hegel called the former the lord and the other the bondsman. He maintained that the subjugation of the bondsman to the lord was a natural order of things and its recognition led to the liberation of the individual. It was almost axiomatic that the action of the lord was represented as pure and essential and that of the bondsman as impure and not essential.[12] Hegel's conceptualization formed the parameters of imperial consciousness.

Servitude was the essence of that relationship. It was the core reality to be experienced by the lord. The experience of servitude of the bondsman was the supreme test of the success of the lord. For the bondsman, disinterested service to the lord, Hegel emphasized, would keep his ephemeral desires, a self-destructive phenomenon, in check. It would ensure a terrifying fear in the heart of the bondsman. This would spark off the beginning of true wisdom and thus, the bondsman's self-realization would be formed and shaped. Absolute fear, ceaseless service and 'formative activity' were considered as the essential conditions for the liberation of the bondsman who was to experience 'absolute fear' of the 'absolute independent self-consciousness'. It would constitute the bondsman's 'rediscovery of himself by himself' as he was urged to be aware of the confusion in his own mind resulting from the 'dizziness of a perpetually self-engendered disorder' and to submit before the truth as deduced by the lord from a universal 'absolute dialectical unrest'. The whole process of the evolution of self-consciousness would be helped, Hegel asserted, by the punitive, constraining and rewarding instruments in the possession of the lord. Hegel's *Phenomenology of Spirit*, published in 1807 was prescribed as an essential classic for the perusal of gentlemen during their formative years. The dialectics between 'Lordship and Bondsman', as a result, left an indelible mark on the imperial mind. It was approved without any shred of doubt as the most authentic confirmation of imperialism as a legitimate phase in the evolution of Western civilization and the salvation of mankind. Domination, dependence, service, loyalty and fear became the significant signposts of imperialism. These sentiments conditioned the colonial mind of the nineteenth and twentieth centuries when imperialism ran amok in the name of Western civilization in alien lands overturning the polity and culture of the 'heathen' and 'impure' bondsmen.[13]

James Mill was appalled by the 'hideous' state of society in India which, he thought, was much inferior to that which had been acquired by Europe in the darkest feudal age. His *History of British India* was primarily an attempt to assess the position held by Indian society in relation to the achievements of human civilization.[14] The 'Utilitarians' were keen to overthrow the hold of the flimsy faith that had endorsed a sentimental adoration of the immobile despotism of the East.[15] At the root of the 'disgustingly ugly' Indian social institutions—'that barbaric conglomeration'—Mill found primitive social formations, a vast despotic polity and religious tyranny and in this, he was supported by many others.[16] There was a distinct line of continuity running through Hegel, Macaulay, James and John Stuart Mill, James Fitzjames Stephen, John Strachey, Gladstone, Morley and the more extrovert exponents of imperialism.[17] Contempt for Indian society and polity, over-emphasis on efficient government, ruthless suppression of native insubordination, cold and callous opposition to native leadership, insistence on law as regulated force and on the requirement in India of a despotic government with power, authority and will to enforce stern laws were some of the prescriptions of the so-called investigative modalities of the Raj.[18] They formed the permanent backdrop of imperial endeavours and constituted the core culture of imperialism. Everyone in India who mattered agreed even as late as 1942 with James Mill and Fitzjames Stephen that despotism, power and authority were the integrated ingredients of administration. Together, they constituted the soul of the Raj.[19] A warm heart and a lively imagination unaffected by superficial sentimentalism were recommended to administrators in enforcing stern laws undaunted by ephemeral public opinion. The Empire was the embodiment of peace, it was claimed by the Empire-builders and confirmed by historians following the demise of the Raj, established by firm hands 'from Adam's Bridge to Peshawar' beyond the shattered walls of Delhi and over the fort of Lahore.

The vision of the Roman Empire did not merely inspire the Raj.[20] It was universally claimed that the Raj was the inheritor of the political and cultural legacy of Rome. This was characterized by snobbery, ruthlessness and intolerance which were given the nomenclature of patriotism, loyalty and fortitude. Economic benefits were dressed in idealist garb, mercenary motives in a moral crusade and romance and adventure camouflaged political and military aggression.[21] Closely associated with this was the adoration of character instead of merit.

As a substitute to Greek and Roman theatre, the American films arrived —early Christian films complete with gladiators and lions, those of Tarzan and the Apes, the 'westerns' with trigger-happy cowboys chasing the feathered Indian, followed by the urbanized 'westerns' where cars replaced horses and 'cops' replaced cowboys.[22] The impact was remarkable because the attempt had been to reduce the quantum of wisdom and wit to the minimum. Superimposed on this was the idea of 'the chosen people' operating on the doctrines of Christianity. God was supposed to back only the Christians. Christianity was offered as synonymous with science which was called service and service was the other name for sharpshooting guns. Cruelty was necessary, the imperial ideologues emphasized, for the 'savage wars of peace'.[23] The cult of the Raj was a racial congregation and it was hypocritical to think that it could be humanized by 'purdah parties' or the patronizing admission of the '*Rais* ' and the notables among the natives into its charmed circle.

Eric Stokes, an eminent historian of imperial sensibility, distinguished the spirit of the Raj from the various types of imperialism in the world. In contrast to the experiments in South Africa, Malaya, Egypt and Nigeria, he found a unique demeanour in British India. There was in India, he thought, an unflinching sense of duty towards the fallen people. Stokes emphasized, as the proud chronicler of the glories of the Empire, that the evangelical spirit of the Raj did not allow itself to be misled by any concern to buy support or earn cheap popularity. The Raj, Stokes proclaimed, cared not for flattery, odium or abuse. Stephen and Strachey had been, he added, its spokesmen; Kipling was its poet and Curzon gave the fullest expression to the imperial idea in India.[24] One would refrain from commenting on Stokes' transparent imperial eloquence.

Small wonder, then, that the prospect of the independence of India was viewed from Britain as a signal for the retreat of the Empire from its traditional fortresses in Africa and Asia. The strain and stress of War, the growing influence and hegemony of Indian nationalism, the declining strength of British elements in the services, the increasing insubordination in the armed forces and the persistent implorations of international public opinion in favour of the Indian cause had rendered withdrawal from India almost unavoidable. The Raj had passed its prime. Its liquidation was indeed a painful thought.[25] Agatha Harrison and Horace Alexander, the sedate members of the Friends' fraternity, were discomposed by the ramifications of a possible severance of India from the Empire.[26] They were concerned about its debilitating impact on Western civilization. Imperial Britain was shaken up by the eerie uncertainties of her future as she witnessed imperialism being forced to pull out of Java and Indo-China. Indian independence, it was apprehended by many cutting across party and ideological affiliations, would release a gusty wind of change. The political map of Asia and Africa, as a consequence, would witness an unprecedented whirlpool. A topsy-turvy world of strange political units with stranger nomenclatures clouded the vision of the statesmen who found it difficult to anticipate the nature of the surprise in store for them. Some continued to believe that it was necessary for the good of humanity to restrain the forces of nationalism in India with an ever increasing garrison to keep it down.[27] Others maintained that it should be possible to get out of India warily without snapping off the imperial umbilical cord.[28]. Imperial impulses were sufficiently strong, but the appeal of Indian nationalism in a brave new world was more compelling. Caught up in a strategic cul-de-sac the Raj was neither graceful nor generous during its dying hours.

Labour record in the Government was not very different from the Conservatives. British and Indian troops had been employed in assisting in the restoration of French rule in Indo-China and to prop up the antiquity of Dutch rule in Java in order to protect the dividends of those who sat quietly at Amsterdam. The feeble equivocations of a hesitant Wavell against a concerted move to restore imperialism in South East Asia in view of its adverse reaction in India were overwhelmed by the swagger of an overbearing Mountbatten.[29] The decision to hold the trials of the Indian National Army soldiers and the attitudes towards the Royal Indian Navy ratings were remarkable as they betrayed the continuity of imperial arrogance under the Labour Government. There was still a marked absence of a real will, Harold Laski contended, to help in making a free India in the full sense of the term. There was too much exploitation of a 'partly real and partly unreal' communal difference in India which was 'partly made and partly exploited by ourselves. . . .'[30] Attlee's pronouncements and Wavell's attitudes confirmed that the British Government was still committed to the viceregal veto, the defence portfolio, the native states, the rights of various minorities and the retention of the British connection with India in some form. The Cabinet Mission Plan held out the prospect of a fragmented India. It was envisioned that the departure of imperial authority would be followed by the spectacle of a congeries of States with different levels of tensions and affiliations dividing and binding them. The chaotic constitutional situation, it was believed, would be nursed by misleading official interpretations, carefully formulated ambiguities and sporadic official affirmations of the rights of the native States. The resulting tensions would be stimulated by the phrase, 'lapse of paramountcy'.[31] No amount of glamour and disquietening self-confidence of Mountbatten and the peppery style of his biographers could obscure the fact that the last viceroy was not God's gracious gift to India at the most perilous moment of her political transition.[32]

Armed with wide discretionary powers, Mountbatten was engrossed in negotiations as late as March 1947 to carve out a united Bengal independent of the rest of the country, failing which to make a free port of Calcutta as an interim measure and, if possible to turn it into a joint conclave of Pakistan and India.[33] In May 1947, Mountbatten, still protected by freedom of action and uninhibited by any domestic despatch, produced a document designed to create a Balkanized India.[34] Even at the time of its departure, the Raj offered no special opportunity to elicit the gratitude of the Indian people. The administration continued to exhibit its zealous partiality towards British personnel during the brutal period of human crisis in India in 1947. The insouciant attitude of the viceroy towards the failure of the Punjab Government to maintain even a semblance of law and order and his endorsement of the audacious reply of the governor of Punjab to the charges of inefficiency and connivance with communal forces are instructive. E.M. Jenkins, in his memorandum contesting the charges of administrative failure and mischief, sought to counter-charge the critics for having missed the significance of what had been happening in Punjab.[35] 'We are faced not with an ordinary exhibition of communal and political violence', Jenkins reported with sardonic relish, 'but with a struggle between communities for power which we are shortly to abandon. Normal standards cannot be applied to this communal war of succession. . . .' Jenkins claimed that the two nations fought one another in the streets, markets, fields and the villages. He shared the equanimity of British officers in asserting that changes of such magnitude were bound to produce massive civil disorder. It was largely owing to the steadiness and impartiality of the British officials, the governor puffed, that Punjab had got through 'as well as it has done'.[36] All the king's horses and all the king's men, Jenkins gibed, could not have prevented or contained the inevitable carnage. A posture of self-righteousness was adopted by the Raj as it prepared itself to leave the shores of India and gleefully watch its freed 'bondsmen' taking rapid steps on the road to violent self-destruction.

Public opinion in Britain was reminded that it had been predicted over the years that much bloodshed would follow the independence of India. It had been presumed that the political unity of the country had been an artificial creation and that it would be unable to withstand the strain of British military withdrawal. Mountbatten recollected the plight of the nervy ministry who thought it desirable to beg the Governor-General to assume full power once again on the morrow of freedom and assist the restoration of law and order![37] In fact some of the civil servants and politicians had persuaded themselves to believe that the nationalists would never graduate in the school of administration and the British would be welcomed back once again. It was more than wishful thinking. There was in it a strange admixture of nostalgia, guilt, adventure and imperial pride. John Masters like many others, continued to mourn the death of the Raj. Masters blamed the ineffective and flaccid bearing of the British politicians of the post-War days for the sacrifice of India at the altar of Hindu-Muslim rivalry.[38] Rodney Savage, Masters' prototype of Kipling's Strickland, could not quite reconcile himself to the immature attitude of the British rulers of India in throwing away the Empire in just half-an-hour—one that had taken the blood and sweat of a whole century.[39] Nostalgic about the lost jewel and the far pavilions, imperial perception was somewhat bewildered. The greatest significance of British endeavour in the East, the post-independence observers maintained in unison, had been the unifying and civilizing years of power and influence. The unity of the subcontinent, it was maintained by many, had been the source of legitimate pride for more than a century.[40] Lady Manners of Scott's *The Jewel in the Crown* lamented that the glorious tradition was drowned in the blood bath of 1947. It appeared to some of her generation that India's independence had not been achieved for the sake of the expansion of human freedom but was worked out by a few self-seeking British politicians in order to comfort their narrow political game in the context of British parliamentary life.[41] Instead of continuing the tradition of governing and shaping the future of the semi-savage people, they carped, the self-centred politicians walked out of India quite unconcerned with the noble inheritance.[42] Pride in the Empire was dissolved into collective shame for failing to uphold tradition.

Discerning observers, however, had taken note of the erosion of the Raj since 1940 and the arrival of a Swadeshi rule to replace it. The ostentatious imperial demonstration of Kipling had been mellowed by a more composed appreciation of the magnificent achievements of the British in India and it was entwined with a sense of futility that was inherent in that experiment. The Raj had become at once the embodiment of British pride as well as a poignant memory of a futile but noble liberal dilemma of an exiled race in action. Christine Watson in 1944 was remorseful as she felt an increasing distance being imposed on the glories of the Raj by an advancing nationalism. She was visibly unsettled by the prospect of India becoming 'a no-man's land of dreams'.[43] Eric Cathcart of Jon Godden's *Peacock* had been in the Indian army following the footsteps of his father, grandfather and great-grandfather. At the close of the Second World War, Eric Cathcart was to realize that the British Empire of India was about to fall. Worst still, he was fully aware of the fact that he was a misfit both in England and in India. Overtaken by the two worlds, a lonely Eric found himself helplessly alienated from both and salvaged his tortuous predicament by terminating his own life.[44] Jon Godden thus underlined the utterly unrewarding and thankless task undertaken by the 'secular missionaries' of the civilized West. Masters' Rodney Savage and the small European community in Marapore in Paul Scott's *The Alien Sky* were equally vexed and ruffled by the loss of power, privileges and status in India on the eve of its independence.[45] They were upset by the uneasy fact that they would be unable to sustain their Indian standard of living in Britain. They were piqued by the signs of visible insubordination from the natives, the duplicity of wily Indian politicians and the prospect of public humiliation. Rodney Savage had decided to stay put in India as he was convinced that the inept Indians would be forced to accord him the honour due to him, content in his illusory world of make-believe. But the small community in Scott's *The Alien Sky* was disgruntled as they busied themselves in preparing to leave for Nairobi in a desperate bid to recreate the lost realities of imperial India in a favourable colonial atmosphere.

In the wake of a remarkable nostalgia for the Raj, an orchestrated endeavour was being made to reassert the intricacies of the white man's burden. Since the withdrawal of imperialism from India was neither a voluntary undertaking nor a generous abandonment it was all the more necessary to perpetuate the myths of the European mission with all its nuances. The image of a hardened burra sahib with a desperate desire to create an atmosphere of all-pervading domination around him and the artificial countenance of the burra memsahib in a discomforting tropical atmosphere and in the company of innumerable *khidmutgars* became initially the objects of wry humour. But behind the reaction of derision, helplessness and, in some cases, even a genuine sense of shame, there has been a powerful backlash of pride for it is the story of the good old days in India—the memory of immense power and social snobbery, the bitterness of military retreat and the after thoughts of the unhappy severance of the Indian connection. The accumulated pride and prejudices of the Raj have been presented in various forms. We are reminded of the efforts and achievements of the British soldiers, missionaries, administrators, planters and educators operating in a land marked by civilized existence along the British *kacheries*, *thanas* and civil lines and amidst a people known for their mysterious religions and repulsive social systems and in an age when antibiotics were unknown and modern communications not easily available. Racial superiority had been typified in the exclusive existence of a small ruling community confronting the immensities and fears of India. The 'fears' of India were popularized as the ever menacing possibility of sexual outrages by Indians on lonely English ladies.The compulsions of ruling an alien race, the impact of an inhospitable climate, the resistance of primitive social forces and the incompatibility of the scientific and Christian ethics with the native institutions were projected in order to weave an intricate pattern of synthetic imperial logic. Kipling continued to produce the modules of this literary architecture. The prototypes and stereotypes created by him and his apostles still continue to serve the literary effulgence recreated in memory of the Raj.[46]

One of the constant refrains of imperial nostalgia has been the firm conviction that the Englishmen would be welcomed back in India by the inarticulate rural masses if they were given the opportunity by a genuine electoral choice. It was presumed that although the work of the British in India had been well done, it was still unfinished. There was, nevertheless, a firm decision to get reconciled to the political accord to quit. The retreating Empire concluded with an air of despondency that it was time to go and leave the rest to the articulate classes of India. Philip Woodruff, who did not disguise, along with many others like Paul Scott, British animosity towards the Congress nationalists, spelt out the philosophy of imperial retreat. Christopher of Woodruff's *The Wild Sweet Witch* had been aware that the great task in India was still incomplete and that the natives desired the British to stay on as long as possible in order to fulfill their mission in the country.[47] But it appeared to Christopher morally wrong to take refuge behind that request and say that 'we must stay because they want'. Every people, he argued, must express itself through its vocal classes. The American opinion, he recalled, had expressed itself through the farmers of the Mid-West during the American War of Independence. It was true, he affirmed, that the vocal classes in India were miserably out of touch with the peasants but that was 'just because we are here'.[48] The earlier generation who had spent the best part of their lives in India might carry on with their duties towards India, but the younger generation, it was believed, would find all the good that had been done to India would be invalidated if they were to resist any longer and linger on. Christopher shared the common view that things would change in India adversely once the British left their imperial charge. New values would emerge and it was feared that frustrations would be the keynote in the ordinary district administration. 'You have to acquiesce in much that you hate', Christopher cautioned, 'and can't achieve a thing you want'. It was the time to go where one belonged and settle down, 'make home for the children, and drive our roots deep into the soil'.[49] Despite the claim of the fulfilment of the British mission in India, there was an undercurrent of melancholic despondency about the incompatibility of the two civilizations, the inevitability of political withdrawal and the glorious uncertainty of British achievements in India. The supple and emotional Indians and the cold and aloof English, it was resolutely upheld by some, had been engaged for about two centuries in a tragic experiment to work out a happy human rapport. Dennis Gray Stoll emphasized the absence of a warm heart in British breasts[50]; Rumer Godden underlined the remarkable lack of comprehension of each other's motives and intentions[51]; Philip Woodruff lamented the absence of communication between the 'politicals' and 'guardians' on the one hand and the Indians on the other[52]; Mary Margaret Kaye conjectured that probably the imperial Government had been in a hurry to impose Western values and British institutions on to an unwilling and unprepared people[53]; A.T.W. Simeons assumed that the Indian leadership of an independent India would not be able to cope with the complex realities of the Raj.[54] These feelings of doubt, diffidence and futility were based on the assumption that the fundamental chasm between the two communities could not be bridged. The incompatibility of the two races was placed beyond the comprehension and control of human endeavour. India was the black narcissus[55]—too mysterious and too overpowering for the West which tended to lose its distinct rational character in her company. Woodruff continued to talk of the lack of coherence in India, the inevitability of the political ascendancy of Hinduism following British withdrawal, the irrationality of expecting the minorities to reconcile themselves to a Hindu India and the total inability of the Indians to organize their own house.[56]

In fact many veered helplessly between Kipling and Forster with unsteady steps. They were conscious of the fact that the British had played out their role in India with doubtful wisdom and debatable success. Like Miss Edwina Crane of Scott's *The Jewel in the Crown* they considered themselves as the relics of the past—as the remnants of a futile endeavour to bring about a reconciliation between two races having unequal social status and uneven political standings. The liberal tradition of E.M. Forster served as the guiding pole-star for the new generation of writers. That legacy was idiosyncratic, pessimistic and, very often, self-destructive. It was contradictory although to many its very contradictions rendered it so very attractive. It was aware of the crisis in the imperial system and conscious of the inconsistency of the imperial pretentions in India. It was uncomfortable with the incompatibility of imperialism in India with the professed creative impulses of Liberalism in Britain. It called for a drastic change in imperial attitudes without initiating even a modest revision in the system. There was an element of pessimism of Oswald Sprengler in Forster's liberal worldview. There was also a dread of being 'abstract' and a stern refusal to theorize. Evidently the Liberals, including Forster, were compelled to opt for a certain amount of evasiveness and a wilful refusal to say systematically what they desired and meant. They were caught between two polarized philosophical positions. Oswald Sprengler's *Decline of the West* had challenged the belief in progress and popularized the image of fragmentation and decline. However, the vision of human vitality and a creative faith in the success of culture against anarchy continued to linger on amidst the gloomy laments of a general cultural pessimism. 'Sprengler plus resistance' summed up accurately the ideological root of the whole Liberal political and social enterprise. Iain Wright found in it a passionate crusading zeal together with a haunting conviction that all efforts were in vain and the disease was incurable.[57] The Liberals felt in relation to British India the same inadequacy as had been felt by Forster's native princes with regard to the British Constitution. The princes had ruled personally and despite their impeccable training in the

Chief's colleges they could not quite comprehend, Forster reported, how the king-emperor, their overlord, was not as powerful as themselves.[58] Being used to extensive powers derived under a feudal system, the rulers misunderstood, Forster wrote, the nuances of constitutional monarchy while the 'measured constitutionalism' of the king-emperor was explained away as extraordinary difficulties of an abnormal imperial structure. They hoped optimistically that a 'turn of the wheel will shake them off'.[59] Similarly, the Liberals could not grasp the singularly dominant position enjoyed by the Englishmen in India. That domination was complete, extrovert, snooty and visible. The fundamental arrogant position of the British in India had rendered any meaningful interaction between the rulers and the ruled quite impossible against the backdrop of hatred and suspicion. All attempts towards this direction were destined to be nothing more than sporadic emotional outbursts. Even Forster had come to the conclusion that human relationships outside the exclusive clubs would be a fleeting exercise: all the forces of nature were turned against it and they declared in unison: No, not as yet! No, not as yet![60]

Liberal perception, when articulated in constitutional terms, offered a more muddled spectrum. It believed that probably in the course of an inevitable constitutional struggle between the nationalists and the imperial Parliament, a sort of a dominion status would be worked out and British democracy would rejoice in itself adding another constitutional feather to its cap.[61] This evolutionary theory ignored the racial and imperial barriers and took the spirit of racial amity for granted. It ignored politics and economics and relied exclusively on human sentiments and emotions. It was oblivious to the trends and problems of modern Indian history and helplessly looked forward to the enactment of British experience by the Indian nationalists on the banks of the Ganga and the Godavari.[62] For Miss Crane, for example, it had been a life-long dream despite the 'atmosphere of blindness and deafness'. Miss Crane faithfully reflected the author's perception when she thought that racial bitterness was excerbated since 1 May 1942 when 'Mr Gandhi demanded that the British should leave India—leave her, he said, to God or to anarchy—which meant leaving her to the Japanese'.[63] But for this 'irresponsible' act, Miss Crane believed that by 1944 an Indian cabinet would have been in control in Delhi, Lord Linlithgow would have been the Governor-General of a virtually independent dominion and 'all the things that she had hoped and prayed for to happen in India would have happened. . . .' Living in this world of illusion, Crane also blamed the sun-baked civil servants in India and pliable politicians at home in not acting on the lines of a promise of self-government as a perfect gesture of equality, friendship and love reflecting a relationship of thoughtfulness, kindness, peace and wisdom. That promise remained unfulfilled: '. . . For years we have been promising and for years finding means of putting the fulfilment of this promise off until promise stopped looking like promise and started looking like a sinister prevarication . . . .'[64] To Miss Crane and many other Liberals the noble experiment of English Radicals and Liberals in India had been frustrated both by the mendacity of British politicians as well as by the mischievous double talk and deceptive 'non-violence' of Gandhi.

Indeed, over a period of time, ideological specificities in relation to India were submerged in the vortex of the imperial tangle. As a result, even the most sympathetic observers appeared to be remote from the main forces of life that stirred India, and their reactions, therefore, appeared strangely unrelated to the environment over which they had complete administrative and political control.[65] Kipling's banal assertions and uneven subtleties formed a permanent backdrop of British sensibility. The Raj had centred around the average Englishman. It was celebrated in the biscuit tins, chronicled in the cigarette cards, reflected in the music halls, 'that very stuff of social history'[66]; advertised in cinema, radio and the press, researched in the imperial institutes, popularized by imperial societies. In fact the world of *banderlogs* and *fuzzy-wuzzy* settled down in British consciousness as layers of sediment. It is but natural that even after independence British perceptions of India has been standing, like the wounded feelings of Mrs Layton of *The Tower of Silence*,[67] as the self-appointed guardian of the 'golden age' of the Raj in full knowledge of the fact that it could never be brought back again. It is far too keen to trace the elements of glory and honour in the annals of British India. But it is somewhat diffident and unmindful in locating the ingredients of horror and ugliness that upheld and embellished British imperialism in India as elsewhere. It is far too eager to overlook the fact that although imperialism and humanism were historical realities, they were not parallel phenomena. It is keen to turn a blind eye to the fact that while imperialism had been a continuous process in British India, humanism might have been just an occasional and sporadic intruder. In any case , British memory has been scrupulous and careful and in the process of selecting the facts of the Raj it is prone to drop its sense of judgement. Writing the epilogue to the Empire, Jon Stallworthy urged: ' . . . If you condemn their violence in a violent age—Speak of their courage'.[68] Noel Coward, a perplexed onlooker of an altered political perspective in India, wondered if independent India was to keep intact the pukka sahib tradition.[69] But few think it prudent to stop for a while to recognize the realities beyond the ephemeral Raj syndrome. India has continued to haunt the British sensibility down to the days of Mountbatten, nay till date, as the sought-for playing field of the chivalrous knight-errants of the Empire 'that spread its wings wider than Rome'.[70] It was power, autocracy and social Darwinism. It was glamour, snobbery and the basis of imperial economy. It was a certain indicator of imperial might. It was the principal signpost of Britain's sun-lit empire where 'boxwallah, missionary, clerk, lancer, planter' carried 'maxims or gospels to lighten a dark continent'.[71] The Raj was the cult of Christian military heroes. It was the principal instrument to direct the class-consciousness of the labouring men in Britain into the controlled decorum of imperialism and help extensive diffusion of its core culture.[72] It was the barometer of British imperial sensibility.

Notes and References

Chapter I

The Omphalos of the Empire

1. A set of selected volumes might be cited in this context: Monica Campbell-Martin, *Out in the Midday Sun,* London, 1948; Ursula Graham Bower, *Naga Path,* London, 1952; *The Hidden Land*, London, 1955; Jessie Duncan, *Golden Interlude,* London, 1955; Hilton Brown, *The Sahib,* London, 1958; Philip Napier, *Raj in Sunset,* Devon, 1960; John Beams, *Memoirs of a Bengal Civilian,* London, 1961; J.K. Stanford, *Ladies in the Sun: The Memsahib's India, 1760–1860,* London, 1967; Frank Richards, *Old Soldier Sahib,* London, 1965; Philip Woodruff, *The Men Who Ruled in India,* vol. i, *The Founders,* London, 1953 and vol. ii, *The Guardians,* London, 1963; Mollie Panter-Downes, *Ooty Preserved: A Victorian Hill Station*, London, 1963; Michael Edwardes, *Bound to Exile*, London, 1969; A.P. Thornton, *For the File on Empire*, London, 1968; Mark Bence-Jones, *Palaces of the Raj,* London, 1973; Pat Barr and Ray Desmond, *Simla: A Hill Station in British India,* London, 1973; Geoffrey Moorehouse, *Calcutta,* London, 1971; Charles Allen, ed., *Plain Tales from the Raj,* London, 1975; Larry Collins and Dominique Lapierre, *Freedom at Midnight,* Delhi, 1976; Theon Wilkinson, *Two Monsoons,* London, 1976; Janet Pott, *Old Bungalows in Bangalore,* London, 1977; Charles Allen and Sharda Dwivedi, *Lives of the Indian Princes,* London, 1984; Charles Allen, *A Scrapbook of British India, 1877–1947,* London, 1977; Percival and Margaret Spear, *India Remembered,* Delhi, 1981; Kenneth Ballhatchet, *Race, Sex and Class under the Raj,* Oxford, 1980; M.E. Yapp, *Strategies of British India, Britain and Afghanistan, 1798–1850,* London, 1980; Robert Grant Irwin, *Indian Summer: Lutyens, Baker and Imperial Delhi,* Yale, 1981; Jan Morris with Simon Winchestor, *Stones of the Empire: The Buildings of the Raj,* Oxford, 1982; James Morris, *Pax Britannica: The Climax of the Empire*, London, 1968; and *Heaven's Command: An Imperial Progress,* London, 1973; and *Farewell the Trumpets: An Imperial Retreat,* London, 1978; Michael Satow and Ray Desmond, *Railways of the Raj,* London, 1980; April Swayne-Thomas, *Indian Summer: A Memsahib in India and Sind,* Delhi, 1981; Evelyn Battye, *Costumes and Characters of the Raj,* Delhi, 1982; Andre Singer, *Lord of the Khyber,* London, 1984; Raymond K. Renford, *The Non-Official British in India to 1920,* Delhi, 1987; Taya Zinkin, *French Memsahib,* London, 1989.
2. There is no end to this Raj nostalgia. The ever-growing library on the glories and grandeurs of the Raj goes a long way to dispel the academic

prejudice that affirms that there existed in Britain a remarkable innocence about and a notable indifference to the India Empire and that the Raj, therefore, never stirred the imagination of the British nation in any significant way. (cf. Henry Pelling, 'British Labour and British Imperialism', *Popular Politics and Society in Late Victorian Britain*, London, 1979, pp. 82–100 and James Morris, 'The Popularisation of Imperial History', *Journal of Imperial and Commonwealth History*, 1973, vol. i, pp. 113–118. India made no appeal, Reginald Craddock wrote, 'to people who have not been there'. Reginald Craddock, *The Dilemma in India*, London, 1923, p. 16. A conspicuous feature of the Raj sentimentality is the attempt to churn the myths, legends and stereotypes of the imperial culture and, if possible, to present them in liberal idioms. And, of course, there is no dearth of pathos. J.K. Stanford, for example, concluded his monograph on the memsahibs in exile labouring under the glare of a tropical sun with a melancholy note, 'And even Mr Hunter could never have imagined a moment when he and his like would be sent packing willy-nilly; when India he hoped to rule would be one with Nineveh; when a Vicereine would be photographed, for all the world to see, putting an affectionate arm on the shoulder of one of the Hindu politicians who had brought it about'. J.K. Standford, *Ladies Under the Sun*, op. cit.

3. Charles Allen, *Plain Tales from the Raj*, op. cit., p. 23
4. James Morris, *The Pax Britannica* (trilogy), op. cit., is the most readable and comprehensive survey of the different nuances of British imperial psychology and culture. Together these volumes constitute at once an exultant commemoration, a delicate oration and nostalgic requiem of the Empire. For the contours of cultural consciousnes, see an interesting discussion with regard to the forms and contents of cultural formations in Maurice Keen, *Culture*, Yale, 1984.
5. James Morris, *Farewell the Trumpets*, op. cit., pp. 48–49.
6. For an instructive work on the impact of imperialism on British public opinion between 1880 and 1960 see the illuminating study of John MacKenzie, *Propaganda and Empire: The Manipulation of British Public Opinion, 1880–1960*, Manchester, 1984. MacKenzie has examined diverse material including packing boxes, postcards, music-halls, cinemas, boy's stories, schoolbooks, exhibitions and parades to show how imperial messages were conveyed methodically to the British people for a century. Army and Navy, in imperial propaganda, became a shield for both the mother country and the subject people. Boys' brigades and scouts were expected to stiffen the backbone of the youth who were inspired to expand and defend the Empire. The imperial idea was firm and resilient, surviving the demise of the Empire itself.
7. Quoted in MacKenzie, *Propaganda of the Empire*, ibid., p. 108.
8. For the significance of the music-halls in imperial history, see J.A.

Hobson, *The Psychology of Jingoism,* London, 1907; Charles Carrington, *Rudyard Kipling,* London, 1970, pp. 415–16; H.M. Hyndman, *Further Reminiscences,* London, 1912; Lawrence Senelic, 'Politics as Entertainment', *Victorian Studies,* 1975, pp. 150–180.

9. James Morris, *Farewell the Trumpets,* op. cit., p. 49.
10. Rudyard Kipling, 'An English School', *Land Sea Tales (For Scouts and Guides),* London, 1951 (edn.), pp. 253–274. Behind the show of melodrama, spectacle, adventure and make-believe, a concerted programme had been launched to disseminate racial prejudices, imperial mission, militarism, royal pageantry and the doctrine of the survival of the fittest. Patriotism and racial arrogance became the key components of the imperial ethos and served as the vital counter-weight to the class consciousness of the British working class.
11. James Morris, *Farewell the Trumpets,* op. cit., p. 49.
12. G.A. Henty wrote umpteen volumes on India and on imperial themes. See, for example, *At the Point of the Bayonets: A Tale of Mahratta War,* 1902; *Colonel Thorndyke's Secret,* 1898; *On the Irrawady: A Story of the First Burmese War,* 1897; *Through the Sikh War: A Tale of the Conquest of the Punjab,* 1894; *With Clive in India,* 1884: *With the Allies in Pekin,* 1904: *Through Three Campaigns: A Story of Chitral, the Tirah and Ashanti,* 1905; *With Kitchener in Soudan,* 1906; *The Dash for Khartoum,* 1903, and *With Wolfe in Canada,* 1909—all published in London.
13. On British perception of the African world see, Christine Bolt, *Victorian Attitude Towards Race,* London, 1971. For the influence of Rider Haggard, see Mark Girouard, *The Return to Camelot: Chivalry and the English Gentleman,* London, 1981, pp. 262, 265, 269; and Osbert Sitwell, *Scarlet Tree,* London, 1944, p. 24; also Patrick Howarth, *Play up and Play the Game,* London, 1973, p. 112–13.
14. Newbolt's imperial consciousness may be studied in Henry Newbolt, *The World as on My Time,* London, 1932, esp. pp. 198–214; and Margaret Newbolt, ed., *The Later Life and Letters of Henry Newbolt,* London, 1944, p. 7.
15. See Henty's images of India, in Mark Naidis, 'G.A. Henty's Idea of India', *Victorian Studies,* 1964, pp. 49–58; and J.O.Springhall, 'The Rise and Fall of Henty's Empire', *Times Literary Supplement,* 30 October 1968.
16. G.A. Henty, *The Tiger of Mysore,* London, 1904.
17. In *The Tiger of Mysore,* ibid., Blackie and Sons, the publishers, advertised a set of thirty volumes of Henty's historical tales with a cryptic note that 'no boy needs to have any story of Henty's recommended to him and parents who do not know and buy him for their boys should be ashamed of themselves . . . .' For the nature and intensity of imperial propaganda in juvenile literature, see Patrick A. Duncan, 'Boys Literature and the Idea of Empire, 1970–1974', *Victorian Studies,* 1978 and MacKenzie,

Propaganda of the Empire, op. cit., pp. 199–227.

18. Norman J. Davidson, *Pennell of the Afghan Frontier*, London, 1927.
19. Jesse Page, *Judson, The Hero of Burma*, 1926; Edward Gilliat, *Heroes of Modern India*, 1924; Canon E.C. Dowson, *Missionary Heroines in India*, 1921; Edward Gilliat, *Heroes of Modern Crusade*, 1927; *Heroes of the Indian Mutiny*, 1926—all published in London were only a few of the hundreds of titles brought out by the publishers Seeley, Service & Co. in its 'Missionary Library for Boys and Girls', its 'Library of Adventures' and 'Heroes of the World Library'. Written with enthusiasm these volumes were recommended as inspiring works without a single dull page.
20. Amy Carmichael, *Raj, Brigand Chief*, London, 1927.
21. Rudyard Kipling, *Captain Courageous*, London, 1961 (edn.).
22. Osbert Sitwell, *The Scarlet Tree*, op. cit., p. 24.
23. ibid.
24. Patrick Howarth, *Play up and Play the Game*, op. cit., pp. 78–82; also see Rudyard Kipling, 'An English School', op. cit., pp. 253–274.
25. Charles Dilke, *Greater Britain*, London, 1868; also see John R. Seeley, *The also see Expansion of England*, London, 1883.
26. ibid., p. 306; also see, Peter Burrough, 'John R. Seeley and the British Imperial History', *Journal of Imperial and Commonwealth History*, 1972–1973, pp. 191–211; also see, G.A. Rein, *Sir John Robert Seeley; A Study of a Historian*, ed. and trans., John L. Herkless, Dover, 1983.
27. Martin J. Wiener, *English Culture and the Decline of the Industrial Spirit, 1850–1980*, London, 1981, pp. 32–33.
28. ibid., pp. 30–31 and 119–21.
29. J.H. Robb, *The Primrose League, 1883–1903*, New York, 1942; Samuel Berbard, *Imperialism and Social Reform*, London, 1960.
30. Winifred Baumgart, *Imperialism: Theories and Realities of British and French Colonial Expansion, 1880–1914*, Oxford, 1982, p. 40; also see F.H. Hinsley, *Power and Pursuit of Peace*, Cambridge, 1967, p. 143.
31. Quoted in C.E. Carrington, *The British Overseas*, London, 1950, p. 681.
32. Sarah Gertrude Millin, *Rhodes*, London, 1970; Richard Faber, *Vision and The Need: Late Victorian Imperialist Aims*, London, 1966; Walter Nimocks, *Milner's Youngmen*, London, 1960.
33. Quoted in James Morris, *Heaven's Command: An Imperial Progress*, op. cit., pp. 522 and 526; for Rhodes, see Millin, *Rhodes*, op. cit.; for Parkin, Denison and Grant, see the highly readable and sensitive work of Carl Berger, *The Sense of Power: Studies in Ideas of Canadian Imperialism 1867–1914*, Toronto, 1970.
34. For the virtues which were given an imperial dimension in the stories of Kipling, see *Life's Handicap*, London, 1952; *Wee Willie Winkie*, London, 1951; and *Captain Courageous*, op. cit. Also see, Maud Diver, *The Unsung*, London, 1945; and *Desmond's Daughter*, London, 1924; Flora

Annie Steel, *On The Face of the Waters*, London, 1896; and *Prince Errant*, London, 1912; Alice Perrin, *Rough Passages*, London, 1926; Hamish Blair, *Governor Hardy*, London, 1931; F. Yeats-Brown, *Dogs of War*, London, 1934.

35. Roger Louis, *Imperialism*, New York, 1976, pp. 6–7.
36. Suhash Chakravarty, *From Khyber to Oxus: A Study in Imperial Expansion*, Delhi, 1976, pp. 233–34.
37. See R.J. Halliday, 'Social Darwinism: A Definition', *Victorian Studies*, June 1911, esp. pp. 389–99.
38. Quoted in Random House Historical Pamphlet, *Social Darwinism: Law of Nature of Justification of Repression ?*, London, 1967, p. 53; also see Karl Pearson, *National Life from the Standpoint of Science*, Cambridge , 1907, pp. 16, 21–25 and 46–54.
39. Austen Chamberlain, *Politics From Inside*, London, 1936, pp. 567, 609 618–619 and 643.
40. ibid., pp. 567 and 609.
41. For Curzon's concept of imperialism see 'The True Imperialism', *Nineteenth Century*, January 1908, pp. 151–65.
42. ibid.
43. ibid.
44. Lytton to Salisbury, 17 April 1977, Papers of first Earl of Lytton, India Office Library, London—which hereafter are referred to as the Lytton Papers in this section.
45. B.R. Cunningham, *Chronicle of Dustypore*, London, 1901, p. 89.
46. For an interesting account of her career in India, see Flora Annie Steel, *The Garden of Fidelity* (an autobiographical work), London, 1930; Mabel Webster, 'Biographical Introduction'(to Flora Annie Steel), *Indian Scene: Collected Stories*, London, 1933.
47. Flora Annie Steel, *On The Face Of the Waters*, op. cit., p. 481.
48. Cunningham, *Chronicle*, op. cit., p. 90; also see W.W. Hunter, 'Rulers of India Series', Clarendon Press of India, Historical Retrospects (more than forty titles).
49. Lytton to Rawlinson, 20 July 1977, the Lytton Papers.
50. See Chakravarty, *From Khyber to Oxus*, op. cit., pp. 18–19.
51. Lytton to James Fitzjames Stephen, 1 June 1877, Papers of James Fitzjames Stephen at the University Library, Cambridge—which hereafter are referred to as the Stephen Papers in this section.
52. Curzon, 'The True Imperialism', *Nineteenth Century*, op. cit., pp. 154–155.
53. Rudyard Kipling, 'The Head of the District', *Life's Handicap*, op. cit., pp. 117.
54. Rudyard Kipling, the bard of the Raj, made repeated references to law in his works. Law, according to him, was the essence of Creation.

Development of law was a human privilege and was the motive-power of civilization. It was the sure sign of the superiority of the white man's world, the supreme justification of British imperialism and the core idea of the rituals and pageantry of the Raj. No amount of casuistry of scholars can obscure the assertive aggression of Kipling's imperial idea. For some metaphysical interpretations of Kipling's law, see C.E. Carrington, *The Life of Rudyard Kipling*, New York, 1955, pp. 206–08; Eliot L. Gilbert, *The Good Kipling: Studies in Short Stories*, Manchester, 1972, pp. 14–49; Alan Sanison, 'The Artist and the Empire', in Andrew Rutherford, ed., *Kipling's Mind and Art*, London, 1965, pp. 146–67.

55. Rudyard Kipling, 'How Fear Came', *The Second Jungle Book*, London, 1981, p. 19.
56. Rudyard Kipling, 'The Law of the Jungle', ibid., pp. 21–23.
57. Rudyard Kipling, *Kim*, London, 1967, p. 79. For Kipling's perception of the British mission in India see his, 'The Bridge Builders', *The Day's Work*, 1950, pp. 1–47; 'At the End of the Passage', pp. 183–212; 'The Mark of the Beast', pp. 240–59; 'Namgay Doola', pp. 278–93; 'Georgie Porgie', pp. 278–93—all in *Life's Handicap*. op. cit. Emphasizing the sacrifices of the British soldiers of fortune in India, many thought it prudent to share the feelings of Alfred Lyall:

    What far reaching Nemesis steered him
    From his home by the cool of the sea?
    When he left the far country that raised him,
    When he left her, his mother, for thee,
    That restless, disconsolate worker,
    Who strains now in vain at the nets,
    O sultry and solemn Noverea!
    O Land of Regrets!

    As quoted in Frederick Sykes, *From Many Angles, An Autobiography*, London, 1942, p. 38.

58. Rudyard Kipling, 'The Overland Mail', *A Kipling Anthology, Verse*, London, 1922, pp. 6–7.
59. Rudyard Kipling, 'The Head of the District', *Life's Handicap*, op. cit.
60. Rudyard Kipling, 'Namgay Doola', op. cit.
61. Rudyard Kipling, 'The Head of the District', *Life's Handicap*, op. cit.
62. ibid.
63. Rudyard Kipling, 'The Song of the English', *Rudyard Kipling's Verse-Inclusive Edition, 1885–1918*, New York, 1922; also see its romantic use in Irwin, *Indian Summer*, op. cit.; and as the recital of the British mission in Baron Jean Pellence, *Diamond and Dust: India Through French Eyes*, Stuart Gilbert, trans., London, 1936, p. 108.
64. Curzon, 'The True Imperialism', *Nineteenth Century*, op. cit., pp. 151–52.
65. ibid., p. 52.
66. Edmund Candler, *The Mantle of the East*, London, 1910, pp. 93–94; also

see Edmund Candler, *The Unveiling of Lhasa*, London, 1905. On 'The Great Game' in Asia see Rudyard Kipling, *Kim*, op. cit.; and among many others, Alexander MacDonald, *Through the Heart of Tibet*, London, 1910; and 'Ganpat', *High Snow*, London, 1918. (Ganpat was the sobriquet the paltan had bestowed on Captain M.L.A. Gompertz when he had been posted to an Indian infantry regiment.)

67. For the impact of the Boer War on the political and social life of England, see Mark Girouard, *The Return to Camelot*, op . cit., pp. 173–77, 251–52 and 282–86. The war spawned a large number of imperial propaganda societies. See MacKenzie, *Propaganda of the Empire*, op. cit., pp. 143–72.
68. A. Conan Doyle, *The Great Boer War*, London, 1904; and Thomas Pakenham, *The Boer War*, London, 1979, pp. 267–69.
69. Rudyard Kipling, 'Following British Failure Exposed by the Boer War', (date unknown), in Kenneth Baker, ed., *The Faber Book of English History in Verse*, London, 1988, p. 363.
70. Curzon, *Subjects of the Day*, London, 1915, pp. 5 and 44.
71. Thomas Pakenham, *The Boer War*, op. cit., p. 266.
72. Alfred Austin, 'The Jameson Raid', in Kenneth Baker, ed., *The Faber Book of English History in Verse*, op. cit., pp. 359–61.
73. Rudyard Kipling, 'The English Flag', *A Kipling Anthology, Verse*, op. cit., p. 91.
74. Rudyard Kipling viewed America's conquest of the Philippine Islands in much the same way as Theodore Roosevelt and put his thoughts into the poem which furnished the imperialist world with a ponderous claim and an attractive slogan. The poem is worth studying closely for it presents the duties that imperialism required of its followers in an eloquent phrase, 'The White Man's Burden'. It is the basis of Kipling's so-called 'liberal' imperialism. See the text in *Rudyard Kipling: Selected Verse*, op. cit., pp. 128–29.
75. Rudyard Kipling, 'Recessional', ibid., pp. 130–31.
76. Kipling saw in the developments in Japan a curious assortment of diverse elements, including a dreaming court, a divine king, childlike attachments to mechanical toys, sickening feudal values and oriental eccentricities overlaid with top-hats and frock-coats. The Japanese system, a vexed Kipling sniggered, was irresponsible, incoherent, and, above all, cheaply mysterious. It was stultified by intrigues and counter-intrigues, chequered with futile reforms begun on European lines and light-heartedly thrown aside. The imperial mind was apprehensive of Japan's industrial and military potentialities, cf. Rudyard Kipling, 'Our Overseas Men', *Letters of Travel, 1892–1913*, London, 1920, pp. 47–58. Valentine Chirol, an expert in imperial strategy, also viewed the Japanese experiments with serious misgivings, see Valentine Chirol, *The Reawakening of the Orient and Other Addresses*, Yale, 1925.

77. Bampfylde Fuller, 'The Foundations of Indian Loyalty', *Nineteenth Century*, August 1909, pp. 193–94; also see Valentine Chirol, 'The Far East',— an address delivered in the Raleigh Club, Oxford, 7 June 1914, Papers of the Round Table Group at the Bodleian Library, Oxford—which hereafter are referred to as the R.T.G. Papers in this section.
78. Bampfylde Fuller, 'The Foundations of Indian Loyalty', *Nineteenth Century*, ibid., p. 194.
79. Mayo to Andrew Buchanan, 20 September 1969, Papers of the sixth Earl of Mayo at the Cambridge University Library—which hereafter are referred to as the Mayo Papers in this section.
80. Lytton to Cranbrook, 3 July 1977, the Lytton Papers. For a detailed discussion on the contradictions between the global perspectives of the Indian and the foreign offices on the one hand and that of the Indian Government under Lord Lytton on the other, see S. Chakravarty, *From Khyber to Oxus: A Study in Imperial Expansion,* op. cit., pp. 249–59. While the home government was guided by the fear of the emergence of a militarized and industrialized Germany as a natural enemy of Britain, Lytton urged for an alliance with Persia and Turkey and worked for a united front of the Muslim powers in Asia along with the Indian Empire against Russia—then moving steadily towards India.
81. Curzon, *Problems of the Far East,* London, 1896, p. 8. For Curzon's appreciation of the central position occupied by India in the Empire, see Ronaldsay, *Life of Lord Curzon,* vol. ii, London, 1928; Lovat Fraser, *India Under Curzon and After,* London, 1911; S. Gopal, *British Policy in India, 1858–1905,* Cambridge, 1965, pp. 222–98.
82. Curzon, *Problems of the Far East,* ibid., p. 9.
83. ibid., p. 9.
84. Quoted in Valentine Chirol, *Fifty Years of Changing World,* London, 1927, pp. 299–300; also see Robin James Moore, *Liberalism and Indian Politics 1872–1922*, London, 1966, pp. 75–78.
85. Valentine Chirol, 'Memorandum on India', encl. in Chirol to Curtis, 3 June 1917, the R.T.G. Papers.
86. Curzon, 'The True Imperialism', *Nineteenth Century,* op. cit., p. 157.
87. Valentine Chirol, 'Memorandum on India', encl. in Chirol to Curtis, 3 June 1917, the R.T.G. Papers.
88. ibid.
89. ibid.
90. Quoted extensively in the letter of R.K. Das to Gokhale, 30 November 1914, Papers of Gopal Krishna Gokhale, National Archives of India—which hereafter are referred to as the Gokhale Papers in this section.
91. Culled from *The Times Annual Number, 1929*, London, 1929.
92. G.N. Molesworth, *Curfew on Olympus,* Bombay, 1965, p.v.
93. See three documents: Linlithgow to Amery, 21 January 1942, pp. 44–50;

'The Indian Political Situation, Memorandum by the Secretary of State of India', 28 January 1942, pp. 81–90; and 'The Indian Political Situation, Memorandum by the Lord Privy Seal', 2 February 1942, pp. 110–12— all in N. Mansergh and E.W.R. Lumly, ed., *The Transfer of Power,* vol. i, London, 1970.

94. 'The Indian Political Situation, Memorandum by the Lord Privy Seal', ibid.
95. Linlithgow to Amery, 21 January 1942, ibid.
96. 'Typescript paper issued by the Information Office', July 1940, Papers of Edwin C. Benthall at the Centre for South-Asian Studies, Cambridge— which hereafter are referred to as the Edwin Papers in this section. Edwin Benthall with his long family connection with India was a representative figure of British financial and industrial interests in the country. As a member of the viceroy's executive council during the Second World War, he was influential in the processes of policy formulation. His extensive reports on the attitudes and inclination of the leaders of the nationalist movement are illuminating in appreciating perceptions of India's 'real' demands and aspirations. I would like to thank Dr Shachi Chakravarty for this interesting reference.
97. Alexander Inglis to the Editor, *The Times,* London, 8 May 1940; and same to same 13 June 1940. Alexander Inglis, the Indian correspondent, wrote regularly to the Editor, *The Times,* London, on the developments of the Indian political situation. He enjoyed fairly intimate relationship with the viceroy, Linlithgow, and the confidential background papers of Inglis formed the basis of the policy of that influential journal. Some of them are kept in the archives of *The Times,* London— these hereafter are referred to as the Alexander Inglis Papers in this section.
98. See F.J.D. Lugard, *The Rise of Our East African Empire,* London, 1893, pp. 9–11; and *The Dual Mandate,* London, 1922, dealing with the duties of the European powers in tropical Africa. For the career of Lugard and the development of British power in Nigeria, see Margery Penham, *Lugard, the Years of Authority, 1898–1945,* London, 1960.
99. 'Note by the Viceroy on the Future Settlement of Turkey in Asia and Arabia' encl. in Crewe to Hardinge, 19 March 1915; 'Future Settlement of Turkey', Political Department, India Office, 16 February 1915; 'Memo by Kitchener on Mesopotamia', 16 March 1915—all in the Papers of Hardinge of Penshurst in the University library at Cambridge—which are hereafter referred to as the Hardinge Papers in this section.
100. Andre Maurois, *Cecil Rhodes,* London, 1953, offers a lively account of the vision of this romantic imperial proconsul and may be supplemented by Lionel Curtis' *With Milner in South Africa,* London, 1915. Readers are invited to appreciate the echo of Henty in the title of Curtis' volume.
101. cf. Suhash Chakravarty, *Anatomy of the Raj,* Delhi, 1983, pp. 28–29 and 232–34.

102. ibid., p. 28–29.
103. T.D. Forsyth, 'A Memorandum on Trade with Central Asia', Calcutta, 1870, the Mayo Papers; T.D. Forsyth, *The Report of a Mission to Yarkand,* Calcutta, 1875; 'Memo on Frontier of India', by the Viceroy, 4 September 1976, Papers of Third Marquis of Salisbury, at the Christ Church College, Oxford— which are hereafter referred to as the Salisbury Papers in the section.
104. cf. David Gillard, *The Struggle for India 1828–1914, A Study in British and Russian Imperialism,* London, 1977, pp. 26–27.
105. Jean Stengers, 'King Leopold and the Anglo-French Rivalry, 1882–1884', in Posser Gifford and Roger Louis, eds., *Britain and Germany in Africa: Imperial Rivalry and Colonial Rule,* New Haven, 1967.
106. ibid.
107. See A.S. Kanya-Forstner, *The Conquest of Western Sudan: A Study in French Military Imperialism,* Cambridge, 1969.
108. In fact within a short span of five years, the diplomatic and military atmosphere of Africa had been dramatically altered and if England had taken little initiative in the scramble for Africa, her statesmen decided not to look on carelessly for ever. They joined the race with Britain's well-known and unimpaired killer's instinct. The changed perspective of Africa and the determination of the colonial office not to lag behind is illustrated by the cryptic comment of Salisbury in 1905: 'When I left the Foreign Office in 1880, nobody thought about Africa. When I returned to it in 1885, the nations of Europe were quarrelling with each other as to the various portions of Africa which could be obtained'. Roger Louis, ed., *Imperialism,* op. cit., p. 27.
109. For the Indian factor in the ideological formulations of German and French imperial expansions, cf. P.M. Kennedy, *The Rise of Anglo-German Antagonism* 1906–1914, London, 1980; Fritz Fischer, *War of Illusion: German Politics from 1911 to 1914,* London, 1975; Agnes Murphy, *The Ideology of French Imperialism, 1871–1881,* Washington D.C., 1948.
110. Osbert Sitwell, *The Scarlet Tree,* op. cit., p. 117.
111. cf. Mark Girouard, *The Return to Camelot,* op. cit., pp. 224–25.
112. The Round Table movement was a loose association of small groups in England in association with similar groups in the dominions and had come into existence between 1908–09. Promoted by Alfred Milner and Lionel Curtis, the movement was devoted to examination, through discussions and the periodical, the *Round Table,* of imperial question. Since the group in England concentrated primarily on constitutional problems, it studied the demands of Indian nationalism and dwelt at length on the structures of the societies in India and their traditional loyalties, as well as the feasibility of developing a nation state out of the complex Indian realities. These and such issues were put across through thought-provoking papers which were

called 'eggs' and were presented and discussed in their meetings known as 'moots' and the report of their deliberations referred to as 'omelettes' were published in their journal.

For interesting insights into the Cambridge group, see A.S. and E.S. Sidgwick, *Henry Sidgwick,* London, 1905; Walter Raleigh, *Laughter From a Cloud,* London, 1923; and David Lelyveld, *Aligarh First Generation,* Princeton, 1978. Since the Round Table Group has been inadequately studied and the Indian Papers indifferently examined, the present author in *Anatomy of the Raj,* op. cit., has taken account of the group's extensive interests in India. For an interesting article on the group's movement in Canada, see James Eayrs, 'The Round Table Movement in Canada, 1909–1920', in Carl Berger, ed., *Imperial Relations in the Age of Laurier,* Toronto, 1969.

113. On the significant difference of the white colonies and India in imperial perceptions and policies see 'Memorandum by the Viceroy upon the questions likely to arise in India at the end of the War' (Confidential), October 1915, along with the opinions of the various governors and members of viceroy's executive council in the Hardinge Papers. For the ascendancy of illiberal traditions in authoritarian rule see Konard H. Jaransch, *Students, Society and Politics in Imperial Germany: The Rise of Academic Illiberalism,* Princeton, 1982.

114. MacKenzie, *Propaganda and Empire,* op. cit., pp. 168–70.

115. On the late Victorian suspicions of commercial society, attachment to country houses and nostalgia for rural life see Martin Weiner, *English Society and the Decline of the Industrial Spirit,* op. cit., pp. 30, 50, 64–66; and for the Gothic revival, see pp. 29, 64–65 and 67 of this work.

116. On British embarrassment with regard to industrialization, see Martin Weiner, ibid., pp. 25, 157; for characteristic criticisms of industrial values by Charles Dickens see pp. 31, 33–35 and 39–40 in the same volume. The dominant social thought of the period was a strange amalgam of Mathew Arnold, John Ruskin, Charles Dickens and the liberal thoughts of John Stuart Mill.

117. Even Herbert Spencer, the apostle of progress, felt the psychic cost of American devotion to material advance, but by the turn of the century such sentiments had become cliches of educated opinion. An Arnoldian Liberal of the following generation, G. Lowes Dickenson, developed unquestioning faith in the conviction that the future of the world 'lies with America'. Martin Wiener, *English Society and the Decline of the Industrial Spirit,* ibid., pp. 88–89.

118. Rudyard Kipling, 'The Secret of the Machines', *Rudyard Kipling: Selected Verse,* 1977, pp. 285–86.

119. 'We have another function such as the Roman had. The sections of men on this globe are unequally gifted. Some are strong and can govern

themselves; some are weak and are prey of foreign invaders and internal anarchy; and freedom which all desire, is only obtainable by weak nations when they are subject to the rule of others who are at once powerful and just. This was the duty that fell to the Latin race two thousand years ago. In these modern times it has fallen to ours. . . .' J.A. Froude, *The English in the West Indies,* London, 1885, p. 188.

120. Rudyard Kipling, 'A British—Roman Song', *A Kipling Anthology , Verse,* op. cit., p. 79. Frederick Sykes recalled the lines of Newbolt and the spirit of Rome as he recounted the adventures of the Englishmen in the East :

    O Strength divine of Roman days.
    O Spirit of the faith,
    Go with our sons in all their ways.

    As quoted in Frederick Sykes, *From Many Angles,* op. cit., p. 15.

121. Herbert Baker, *Cecil Rhodes,* London, 1934, pp. 10–20; James McDonald, *Rhodes, A Heritage,* London, 1943, p. 20.
122. Frank Aydelotte, *The American Rhodes Scholarships,* Princeton, 1946, pp. 3–6, 20–23 and 112–21.
123. Bithia Mac Croker, *Diana Barrington, A Romance of Central India,* London, 1888, vol. iii, p. 63.
124. Mark Girouard, *The Return to Camelot,* op. cit., p. 233.
125. ibid.
126. O. Douglas, *Oliva in India,* London, 1922 (edn.).
127. Rudyard Kipling, 'An English School', op. cit., esp. pp. 253, 258 and 263.
128. Quoted in ibid., p. 274.
129. Henry Newbolt, 'Vitai Lampada', Kenneth Baker, ed., *English History in Verse,* op. cit., pp. 350–51.
130. Robert Baden Powell, *Scouting for Boys,* London, 1908. This work is primarily a compendium of the codes of behaviour of the new chivalrous knights of the Empire.
131. Rudyard Kipling, 'Preface', *Land and Sea Tales,* op. cit.
132. cf. Gloden Dallas and Douglas Gill, *The Human Army: Mutinies in the British Army in World War,* London, 1967.
133. Curzon, 'The True Imperialism', *Nineteenth Century,* op. cit., p. 156.
134. ibid.
135. Rudyard Kipling, 'Winning the Victoria Cross', *Land and Sea Tales,* op. cit.
136. Maud Diver, *Desmond's Daughter,* op. cit., p. 29.
137. ibid., p. 49.
138. Maud Diver, *The Hero of Herat, A Frontier Biography of Romantic Form,* op. cit., p. 441.
139. Maud Diver, *Desmond's Daughter,* op. cit., pp. 40–43. In 1927, Valentine Chirol expressed this ennobling influence of imperialism thus, 'We had gone to India with no purpose of seeking dominion, but circumstances had

forced dominion upon us. With dominion had come the recognition of the great responsibilities which it involved, and having imposed upon India our own rule of law we imposed upon the agencies through which we thus exercise dominion—a self-denying ordinance for ourselves, for India a pledge of justice'. Valentine Chirol, *Fifty years in a Changing World,* op. cit., pp. 299–300.

140. The spirit of the Empire was actualized in British perception in the person of General Gordon whose image has been immortalized as a martyred Christian soldier leading the valiant defence of Khartoum against the invading forces of the Mahdi in 1885. Gordon was then already a national hero for his exploits in China especially against the Taiping rebels as the Commander of irregulars composed of ragamuffins for eighteen months in 1863–64. For his role in China he was widely spoken of as 'Chinese' Gordon. For an illuminating political biography of this imperial proconsul see Anthony Nutting, *Gordon,* London, 1966.

These were the new knights charged with imperial creed and they found a respectable place in the imagination of generations of students in the class-rooms and playing fields of Britain. For their devil-may-care audacity, see Flora Annie Steel, *On the Face of the Waters,* op. cit., esp. ch. 3, 'On the Ridge', pp. 103–18.

The imperial legends were inscribed in British consciousness with indelible ink. Kipling wrote ballads of the proconsuls, who created 'a new world towards the day' (The Pro-Consuls), of the soldiers who though 'subtle, strong and stubborn' gave their lives to a 'lost cause, and knew the gift was vain', (General Joubert) and of the generals and captains who 'clean, simple, valiant, well-believed/Flawless in faith and fame,/Whom neither care not honour moved/An hair's-breadth from his aim', *A Kipling Anthology,* op. cit., pp. 150–51.

141. Maud Diver, *The Unsung,* op. cit., p. 284.

142. Henley is quoted in Mark Girouard, *The Return to Camelot,* op. cit., p. 222. Tennyson was a household name in every educated Victorian family. For his lines about the Crimean War, see *Maud* III, VI , while his 'The Charge of the Light Brigade' might be seen in Baker, *English History in Verse,* op. cit., pp. 334–336. Also see Harold Littledate, *Essays on Lord Tennyson's Idylls of the King,* esp. 'The Arthurian Legends', pp. 1–13, London, 1912.

143. Quoted in Mark Girouard, *The Return to Camelot,* op. cit., p. 323.

144. Rudyard Kipling, 'The Gipsy Trail' and 'The Exiles' Line', *A Kipling Anthology,* op. cit., p. 57.

145. See Theon Wilkinson, *Two Monsoons,* op. cit.

146. Rudyard Kipling, 'Cholera Camp (Infantry in India)', *A Kipling Anthology,* op. cit., p. 6.

147. Charles Allen, *Scrapbook,* op. cit., p. 131.

148. Wilkinson, *Two Monsoons,* op. cit., p. 123.

149. Rudyard Kipling, 'The English Flag', as quoted in Theon Wilkinson, *Two Monsoons,* ibid., p. 4.
150. Henry Bruce, 'In Memorium to Thomas Goddard', June 1919 in Henry Bruce, *The Bride of Shiva,* London, 1921, p. 5.
151. Ethil W. Savi, *Dog in the Manger,* London, 1919.
152. Rudyard Kipling, 'Baa Baa Black Sheep', *Wee Willie Winkie,* op. cit., pp. 273–312.
153. Sara Jeannette Duncan, 'A Mother in India', in Saros Cowasjee, ed., *Stories From the Raj,* London, 1982, pp. 74–118.
154. J. Charles Monoly, *Antony Vanroy,* London, 1931, p. 77; also see Rudyard Kipling, 'Arithmetic on the Frontier', *A Kipling Anthology,* op. cit., p. 5. The civilizing mission of Britain was extensive and memories were many: 'With every shift of every wind/The homesick memories come/From every quarter of mankind/Where I have made a home.' Kipling, *A Kipling Anthology,* ibid., p. 3.
155. Kipling, 'The Head of the District', *Life's Handicap,* op. cit.
156. Urging the stay-at-home people to look after these soldiers of the Empire, Kipling urged: 'When you've shouted 'Rule Britannia,'/When you've sung 'God save the queen,'/When you've finished killing Kruger with your mouth/Will you kindly drop a shilling in my little tambourine/For a gentleman in Kharkhi ordered South.' *A Kipling Anthology,* op. cit., p. 103.
157. E.W. Savi, *A Forlorn Hope,* London, 1916, esp. pp. 10–12 and 357.
158. ibid., pp. 80–83. Silent, persistent and patient service became, in official and non-official pronouncements on the Raj, the slogans of British rule in India: 'The secret of the Raj lies in just service as this. Work planned out in some solitary bungalow, carried out in obscruity and never "mentioned in despatches"—a forest saved, a desert turned rice-fields, a road driven ten leagues further into the wilds—will save a million people from famine when the man who made the plan is a forgotten old retired civil servant. . . .' Basil Mathew, *The Secret of the Raj,* London, Missionary Society, London, n.d.
159. Victor Dane, *Naked Ascetic,* London, 1933. Victor Dane represented the core culture of imperialism. He lacked the subtle nuances of a paternalistic Kipling but continued to enjoy a good readership in view of the sharp political tensions between India and Britain.
160. Alice Perrin, 'For India', *Rough Passages,* London, 1936, pp. 151 and 169.
161. E.W. Savi, *The Glamourous East,* London, 1936, p. 21.
162. See, E.W. Savi, *The Glamourous East,* ibid.; *A Man's Man,* London, 1926; *The Way Thereof,* London, 1930; *God-Forsaken,* London, 1927; *The Devils Playground,* London, 1946; Alice Perrin, *The Anglo-Indians,* London, 1912; *Rough Passages,* London, 1926; *Idolatry,* London, 1909.

    Piqued by Kipling's random assertion about the lower tone of social morality of the English women in India, Maud Diver pleaded for a sympathetic understanding of the memsahib on the ground that she was very much a victim of adverse Indian circumstances, an insidious tendency to fatalism, the uncertainty of life and the excitement caused by the lightness, brightness and irresponsibility of the Anglo-Indian life. The life of the memsahib, Maud Diver underlined, was that of a wife, a mother, a hostess and a housekeeper—all in exile. Maud Diver appreciated the role of the memsahib in a tone that was undoubtedly proud, snobbish, self-congratulatory and sentimental. Pat Barr sought to add to this, the vigorous confidence of the Empire builders. (Pat Barr, *The Memsahibs, The Women of Victorian India,* London, 1976, pp. 196—202.) Years later, Margaret MacMillan concluded her dissertation on the memsahibs on the lines of Maud Diver: 'Today they tend to be remembered as dim, comic figures or as vicious harridans who poisoned relations between the Indians and the British. Neither memory does them justice. They were living women, with worries, happiness, and sorrows like anyone else. Their world has gone with its insular little community and its glory reflected from the Raj. They probably would not have worried much about how posterity regards them. They had a duty to do and they did it to the best of their abilities. Most of all, they simply got on with living'. Margaret MacMillan, *Women of the Raj,* London, 1988, p. 236.

163. E.W. Savi, *The Glamourous East,* op. cit., p. 280.
164. ibid., p. 284.
165. F.E. Penny, *Patric,* London, 1934.
166. ibid.
167. Rudyard Kipling, 'The Mark of the Beast', *Life's Handicap,* op. cit., p. 240.
168. Rudyard Kipling, 'Arithmetic of the Frontier', *A Kipling Anthology, Verse,* op. cit., p. 5.
169. Rudyard Kipling, 'A Tale of Two Cities', *Rudyard Kipling: Selected Verse,* op. cit., pp. 26–28.
170. ibid.
171. Rudyard Kipling, 'An Old Song', *A Kipling Anthology, Verse,* op. cit., pp. 7–8.
172. Rudyard Kipling, 'A Tale of Two Cities', *Selected Verse,* op. cit., p. 28.
173. Humphrey Trevelyan, *The India We Left,* London, 1972, p. 177.
174. Rudyard Kipling, 'A Tale of Two Cities', *Selected Verse,* op. cit.
175. Iris Butler, *Viceroy's Wife: Letters of Alice, Countess of Reading from India 1921–25*, London, 1969, p. 15.
176. Maurice Dekobra, *Perfumed Tigers: Adventures in the Land of Maharajahs,* London, 1931, p. 54; also see Maud Diver, 'The Khyber as it Was', *The Unsung*, op. cit., pp. 93–123; George Macmunn, *The Romance of the Indian Frontier,* London, 1936.
177. See Charles Carrington, *The Complete Barrack-Room Ballads of Rudyard*

Kipling, London, 1973, pp. 2–6 and 9–13. And yet the ill-paid Tommy felt helpless as the ungrateful Empire ignored him. He held the Raj and the Empire together, but despite honourable record, his social status was never envious notwithstanding Kipling's spirited literary gestures: 'For it's Tomay this an' Tommy that, an' Chuckin out the brute/But it's Savior of 'is country' when the guns/begin to shoot; /An' its Tommy this, an' Tommy that an' anything you/please; An'/Tommy ain't a bloomin' fool-you bet that Tommy sees!' *A Kipling Anthology, Verse* op. cit., p. 121.

178. Rudyard Kipling, 'Gunga Din', *Rudyard Kipling: Selected Verse,* op. cit., pp. 166–68.

179. Rudyard Kipling, 'The Ballad of the East and West', ibid., pp. 99–103.

180. Rudyard Kipling, *Kim,* London, 1895.

181. There has been, over the years, a consistent attempt to absolve Kipling from the opprobrious elements of the Raj. The whole exercise had been initiated by H.G. Wells through his *The New Machiavelli,* London, 1911. Some of the defenders of Kipling's faith are: C.E. Carrington, *Rudyard Kipling: His Life and Work,* London, 1940; T.S. Eliot, 'An Essay on Rudyard Kipling', *A Choice of Kipling's Verse made by T.S. Eliot,* London, 1941; Eliot L. Gilbert, *The Good Kipling: Studies in the Short Stories,* Manchester, 1972; George Orwell, 'Rudyard Kipling', *Decline of the English Murder and Other Essays,* London, 1957 (edn.); N. Annan 'Kipling's Place in the History of Ideas', *Victorian Studies,* vol. iii, 1959. Politically the primary concern of Eliot in his essay was to restate that although Kipling dwelt upon the 'glory of the Empire', he was not unaware of the faults of the British rule. He believed, Eliot added, that the British had a greater aptitude for ruling other people, but he could not thus be charged for holding 'a doctrine of race superiority'. T.S. Eliot, as usual, was brilliant in his exposition, but he displayed an inadequate acquaintance with the concepts of 'responsibility', 'obligations' and 'commitment' associated with the theory of liberal imperialism. It is also somewhat superficial, to equate Kipling's imperialism, as suggested by George Orwell, with the common habit of chewing candy-sweet by adults well into their prime. There are others who sought to explain away Kipling's imperialism and play down his political commitments. Thus Bonamy Dobree side-tracked the issue of Kipling's politics; Nirad C. Chaudhuri devoted himself to establish that politics was merely an irrelevant intruder in Kipling's writings; Shamsul Islam would have liked his readers to appreciate the central theme of Kipling which, according to him, was not concerned with power, privileges and responsibilities of a small arrogant power elite in a colonial world. See Bonamy Dobree, *Rudyard Kipling: Realist and Fabulist,* London, 1967, pp. 81–84; Nirad C. Chaudhuri, 'The Finest Story About India in English', *Ecounter,* vol. viii, no. 4, 1957, p. 48; Shamsul Islam, *Chronicle of the Raj,* London, 1979, p. 106. Beyond these purely sentimental interpretations, a new line of

approach has been initiated which does not deny Kipling his politics, but seeks to place Kipling's imperialism 'in prespective'. A significant attempt of this justificatory attempt is D.C.R. A. Goonetilleke, *Images of the Raj,* London, 1988. Goonetilleke asserts that the term imperialism is universally considered at present as 'pejorative', but it was not so in the 1890s. This is again a sentimental approach. The present author holds that imperialism is a distinct phase in modern history and agrees with Goonetilleke that the period of the Raj coincided with the high noon of imperialism. One, however, fails to see the logic of the assertion that Kipling was a liberal with a strong commitment for imperial responsibilities. The 'racial fear' in Kipling, his reaction to the nightmarish experiences of the white men amidst an alien people with incomprehensible beliefs and unpredicatable responses, his emphasis on the burden of the white man in the East and the responsibilities of imperialism to a conquered country, his noble appreciation of the character of Gunga Din and genuine efforts to comprehend the nuances and immensities of India's life, his association with the idea of an organic empire embracing a large section of humanity as a part of a world-wide movement, and his contempt for democratic interference in imperial affairs combined to develop in him the greatest minstrel of the Raj. For Eric Stokes, Kipling was 'the magician of the Grand Trunk Road' (Eric Stokes, *Times Literary Supplement,* 23 December 1977, p. 1499). One would like to add a footnote to explain that the Trunk Road symbolized the Raj. The magician, then, becomes more rational and comprehensible. Kipling was at once an interpreter and an ideologue of the Raj. One would do well to read once more the assessment of Kipling by R.C. Ensor in *England 1870–1914,* London, 1936, pp. 331–33.

182. Rudyard Kipling, 'Mandalay', *A Kipling Anthology,* op. cit., p. 26.
183. Curzon, 'The True Imperialism', *Nineteenth Century,* op. cit., p.163.
184. Curzon, *A Recent Journey to Afghanistan,* London, 1896; *Frontiers,* London, 1907; *Russia in Central Asia,* vol. i and vol . ii, London, 1889–90; *The Pamir and the Source of the Oxus,* London, 1898.
185. R.H. Davies, *Report on the Trade and Resources of the North-Western Frontier of British India,* (two volumes with maps) Lahore, 1926. Also J.S. Lumley 'Report on the Tea Trade of Russia', *Parliamentary Papers* no. 6, LXX,C. 3896, 1867.
186. J.S. Lumley, 'Report on the Trade and Manufacture of Cotton in Russia', *Parliamentary Papers,* LIV,C. 477, 1865.
187. See, for example, T.C. Montgomerie, 'Report of the Mirza's Exploration from Kabul of Kashgar', *Journal of the Royal Geographical Society,* (*J.R.G.S.*), 1971; and 'A Havildar's Journey through Chitral and Faizabad in 1868', *J.R.G.S.,* 1872; E.D. Morgan, 'Pundit Manpul's Report on Badakshan', *J.R.G.S.,* 1872; and 'Faiz Baksh's Journey via Badakshan and Wakhan to Yarkand', *J.R.G.S,* 1872.

188. Lytton to Salisbury, 30 November 1976, the Salisbury Papers. Also see, M. Cowling, 'Lytton, the Cabinet, and the Russian, August to November 1878', *English Historical Journal* , 1961.
189. cf. V.G. Kiernan, 'Kashgar and the Politics of Central Asia', *Cambridge Historical Journal* 1953–55.
190. T.D. Forsyth, *Report of a Mission to Yarkand,* Calcutta, 1875.
191. E.D. Morgan, 'The Old Channels of the Lower Oxus', *J.R.G.S.*, 1878.
192. Lytton to Stephen, 30 July 1877, the Stephen Papers.
193. Edmund Candler, *Unveiling of Lhasa,* op. cit.
194. See Premen Addy, *Tibet in the Imperial Chessboard,* Calcutta, 1984, pp. 59–223.
195. See S. Gopal, *British Policy in India,* Cambridge, 1965, p. 240.
196. In this context one may like to recapitulate some of the formulations of Ronald E. Robinson and John A. Gallagher on imperialism and imperial expansion. Their celebrated article, 'The Imperialism of Free Trade', and its sharply distilled incarnation in a chapter in the *New Cambridge Modern History,* Cambridge, 1962 and *Africa and the Victorian: The Official Mind of Imperialism,* Cambridge, 1960—seek to offer a unified theory of imperialism. As Roger Louis worked out the essence of this challenging historiographical perspective in a debate on Robinson-Gallagher model, there were some basic positions in the thesis and some important but subsidiary propositions. It has been asserted that the urge to imperialism in Europe was merely one factor governing the timing and scope of imperialist activity abroad, that the process was governed as much if not more by non-European politics and economics as by European, that the highest common factor in the calculations of the powers seeking the partition of Africa was the search for strategic security in the world. What compelled them to expand, however, were not strategic interests as such but crisis in Egyptian and South African politics. These local complications demanded that imperial interests must be ensured by territorial expansion. The thesis also emphasized the importance of diplomacy and intrigues in expansive impulses and made a significant distinction between the 'motives' and 'causes'. While motives included strategic considerations including personal, commercial and philanthrophic concerns, the causes, it was believed, ought to be sought in local impulses. It has been asserted that to protect the existing Empire in the East including India, the British were compelled to occupy strategic areas and carve out new spheres of influence, thereby extending their military line of communication from the Cape to Cairo and to Singapore. See Roger Louis, *Imperialism,* op. cit.
197. M.E. Yapp, *Strategies of British India, Britain and Afghanistan,* op. cit.
198. See, 'Introduction', Roger Louis, *Imperialism,* op. cit., pp. 2–52.
199. G. Barrachlough, *An Introduction to Contemporary History,* London, 1964, pp. 51–55.

200 Curzon, 'The True Imperialism', *Nineteenth Century*, op. cit., p. 161; cf. V.G. Kiernan, 'Farewell to Empire', *The Socialist Register, 1964*, London, 1964, pp. 259–79.

201. Roger Louis, *Imperialism*, op. cit., p. 24. Economic imperialism, it has been argued with a good deal of force, was not a mythical beast after all. It was, on the contrary, a real live creature with desire, and teeth. There was a close cooperation between government, business circles and centres of propaganda. Together, they provided not only a reality of the Empire but also an ideology consisting of humanitarian idealism, megalomaniac arrogance and Social Darwinism. An advertisement of 1887 displaying British soldiers declaring that Pears Soap was the best before the gaping Africans illustrated the point that imperialism was not merely instrumental in bringing order to the noisy masses thus earning private thanks of the people of India as elsewhere. It exhibited the fact that it had a firm economic link. Instead of reviewing the debate on new imperialism, it might be instructive to state the essential positions of some of the recent publications. Broadly speaking these could be assessed under three distinct moulds: those that are indifferent to the part played by economic considerations, those that deprecate and repudiate all such evidence and those that minimize their importance and dismiss them as events of little consequence. The statement that the metropolitan dog was being wagged by its colonial tail or the proposition that Europe was pulled into imperialism by the magnetic force of the periphery or the assertion that a profound pathological change was imparted by the lonely men-on-the-spot on the dangerous imperial frontiers leading to disequilibrium of forces or the theory that sudden disruptions of international politics by unpredictable circumstances leading to expansive impulses are far from being satisfactory explanations. An element of unreal speculative exercise looms large on these sophisticated historical endeavours. It is difficult to deny that the breechloader revolution, the machine guns, the steam-boat and steam-ships, the opening of the Suez Canal, the expansion of railroads, the development of road transport, the dumdum bullets and the discovery of malaria quinine lowered the cost, in both financial and human terms, of penetrating, conquering and exploiting new territories. The question of the priority of politics and economics with regard to imperialism is a falsely stated alternative. Economic circles no longer desired to see the continuation of their state as a night-watchman and began to look up on the state as the powerful and welcome partner. The entrepreneurial functions of the state were valued and attempts were made to enter into business with the state. The imperialist state reciprocated and cooperated with the economy then placed at its disposal for political use. Both the state and economy achieved a wide range of united perception, shared a common course of action and acted with determination. See the interesting volumes: Daniel R. Headrick, *The Tool of Europe: Technology and European Imperialism in Nineteeth Century*, Oxford, 1981; Heine Gollitzer, *Europe*

in the Age of Imperialism 1880–1914*, London, 1969. Also see Robinson and Gallagher, *Africa and the Victorian,* op. cit.

202. Curzon, 'The True Imperialism', op. cit, *Nineteenth Century*, p. 161.
203. Salisbury to Lytton, 7 July 1976, the Salisbury Papers; also see G.J. Alder, *British India's Northern Frontier*, London, 1962, p.19.
204. Premen Addy, *Tibet in the Imperial Chessboard,* op. cit., pp. 21–39.
205. Chakravarty, *Anatomy of the Raj,* op. cit., pp. 177–79.
206. Herbert Haynes, *Clevely Sahib: A Tale of Khyber Pass*, London, 1917, p. 413.
207. Curzon, 'The True Imperialism', *Nineteenth Century,* op. cit., p.152; cf. Lord Beveridge, *India Called Them,* London, 1947, pp. 347–48. Contemporary British political observers accepted two distinct stereotypes of British politics primarily because of their definitional clarity. It was believed that on the whole the Tory party was primarily the party of the Empire for they were viewed as the upholders of tradition, pride and commitments to the expansion of British law and freedom. They were described as the Big Englanders. The Liberals, on the contrary, were viewed as the champions of trade, industry, personal liberty and the consolidation of existing imperial gains, and hence, against unbridled expansion. They were characterized as the little Englanders. See A.P. Thornton, *The Imperial Idea and its Enemy*, London, 1966; R.L. Greeves, *Persia and the Defence of India, 1884–1892,* London, 1959; and A.L. Kennedy, *Salisbury: Portrait of a Statesman,* London, 1957. For a late nineteenth century statement on the theme, see H.C. Rawlinson, *England and Russia in Central Asia,* London, 1875.
208. Rudyard Kipling, 'The Riddle of Empire', *Letters of Travels, 1892–1912*, op. cit., p. 278.
209. An Onlooker, 'Lord Curzon—An Impression and A Forecast', *Fortnightly Review* 1901, vol. 70, pp. 700–08.
210. ibid., p. 701
211. ibid.
212. 'India under Morley', *Quarterly Review*, 1911, vol. 214, pp. 204–16; also see An Onlooker, 'Lord Curzon—An Impression'etc., *Fortnightly Review,* op. cit.; and John Morley, *Indian Speeches 1907–09*, London, 1909.
213. 'Political Crime in India', *Round Table,* February 1913.
214. Bampfylde Fuller, 'The Foundations of Indian Loyalty', *Nineteenth Century,* August 1909, p. 181.
215. 'India Under Hardinge', *Quarterly Review*, 1919, vol. 226, pp. 99–115.
216. ibid.
217. Bampfylde Fuller, 'The Foundations of Indian Loyalty', *Nineteenth Century,* op. cit., pp. 182–83.
218. Maud Diver, *Far To Seek: A Romance of England and India,* London, 1921.
219. Bampfylde Fuller, 'The Foundations of Indian Loyalty', *Nineteenth Century,* op, cit., p.182; cf. Linlithgow to Zetland, 30 December 1937, the

Linlithgow Papers.

220. Bampfylde Fuller, 'The Foundations of Indian Loyalty', *Nineteenth Century,* ibid., pp. 182–85. This is a constant refrain by Rudyard Kipling, Maud Diver, Flora Annie Steel, Sara Jeannette Duncan, Alice Perrin, E.W. Savi, F.E. Penny, Victor Dane, 'Ganpat', John Masters and almost all those who wrote on and about India.

221. Rudyard Kipling, 'Kitchener's School', *A Kipling Anthology: Verse,* op. cit., pp. 100–01.

222. Bampfylde Fuller, 'The Foundations of Indian Loyalty', *Nineteenth Century,* op. cit., p. 182.

223. ibid.

224. ibid.

225. Valentine Chirol, 'Constitutional Reform in India', *Quarterly Review,* July 1919.

226. E. Bruce Mitford, 'Causes and Effect in India', *Fortnightly Review,* vol. 112–1919, pp. 129–38.

227. Al Carthill, *Madampur,* London, 1931, p. 47.

228. F. Yeats-Brown, *Dogs of War*! London, 1934, p. 31–32 and 51–54.

229. Curzon, 'The True Imperialism', *Nineteenth Century,* op. cit., p. 152.

230. Bampfylde Fuller, 'The Foundations of Indian Loyalty', *Nineteenth Century,* op. cit ., pp. 181–94.

231. For a discussion on the impact of Edmund Burke on Morley, see Stanley A. Wolpert, *Morley in India, 1906–1910,* California, 1961, pp. 15–20.

232. cf. for a sympathetic treatment of the Liberal policy towards India see, M.N. Das, *India under Morley and Minto,* London, 1964, pp. 54–79.

233. For Lytton's claim that the British Indian Empire was the greatest Muslim Empire commanding imperial interests from Constantinople to Hongkong, see Lytton to Stephen, 29 September 1976, the Stephen Papers; Curzon's vision in *Problems of the Far East,* London, 1896, pp. 8–11; Valentine Chirol's analysis of the position of India in the imperial map in *Fifty Years in a Changing World,* op. cit., pp. 299–310. The hangover of the imperial illusion has been very heavy, see for example, John Masters, *Bhowani Junction,* London, 1954; *Bugles and A Tiger, A Personal Adventure,* London, 1971; *To the Coral Strand*, London, 1962.

234. Bampfylde Fuller, 'The Foundations of Indian Loyalty', *Nineteenth Century,* op. cit., p.194.

235. cf. Al Carthill, *The Lost Dominion,* London, 1924, pp. 276–78; Valentine Chirol, *India,* London, 1926; Ameer Ali, 'Some Racial Characteristics of Northern India and Bengal', *Nineteenth Century,* November 1907, pp. 699–715; Kenneth Jones, *Arya Dharma,* Delhi, 1976.

236. Morley to Minto, 16 August 1908, the Morley Papers.

237. 'History records nothing that can approach the British achievement in India: and the world will never see the like again'. This is Lord Sydenham of Coombe quoted by Maud Diver in *The Unsung,* op. cit., p. A 2. Imperial perceptions of India continued to stick to some stereotypes, contrived

images and inflexible political positions throughout the period of study. They correspond to the views articulated in the present essay. There were some marginal tactical adjustments over the years but there was a persistent imperial consensus about India. One would like to maintain that the 'transfer of power' in 1947 was not the culmination of a gradual devolution of authority. Viewed from the vantage point of world history, that political transformation was revolutionary causing much discomfort in Britain. Coming closely following the Second World War, the replacement of the Union Jack by the Tricolour on the Red Fort was a momentous event and it signalled the end of the Raj with international ramifications so far as the fate of the United Kingdom as a first rate power was concerned. For the stereotyped British perceptions of India one may refer to the following: J.H. Muirhead, 'What Imperialism Means', *Fortnightly Review,* August 1900; An Onlooker, 'Lord Curzon—An Impression and A Forecast', *Fortnightly Review,* June 1901; J.D. Rees, 'Indian Conditions and Indian Critics', *Fortnightly Review,* September 1902; Ameer Ali, 'Some Racial Characteristics of the Northern India and Bengal', *Nineteenth Century,* November 1907; G.W. Forrest, 'The State of India', *Fortnightly Review,* March 1907; Anon, 'The Unrest in India', *Quarterly Review,* June 1908; Bampfylde Fuller, 'India Revisited', *Nineteenth Century,* September 1912; Bampfylde Fuller, 'The Vision Splendid of Indian Youth', *Nineteenth Century,* July 1980; J.D. Rees, 'The Proposed Reforms in India', *Nineteenth Century,* September 1909; A.H.L. Fraser, 'The Press Law in India', *Nineteenth Century,* February 1910; Anon, 'India Under Lord Morley', *Quarterly Review,* March 1911; A.H.L. Fraser, 'The Changes in India', *Nineteenth Century,* January 1912; S.M. Mitra, 'Analysis of Indian Unrest', *Fortnightly Review* , March 1911; H.T. Prinsep, 'The High Court in India', *Nineteenth Century,* September 1912; E. Bruce Mitford, 'Cause and Effect in India', *Fortnightly Review,* September 1919; Anon, 'India Under Lord Hardinge', *Quarterly Review,* June 1916; 'The Changing Scene in India', *Nineteenth Century,* May 1940; Valentine Chirol, 'Constitutional Reform in India', *Quarterly Review,* August 1919; Verney Lovett, 'Indian Politics, 1940–41', *Quarterly Review,* September 1941; W.P. Barton, 'The World War and the Problems of the Defence of India', *Quarterly Review,* January 1942; Lionel Haworth, 'United India', *Nineteenth Century,* November 1942; Mulk Raj Anand,'The Situation in India', *Fortnightly Review,* June 1942; A Correspondent from India, 'Indian Problem', *Fortnightly Review,* June 1942; W.P. Barton, 'The Viceroy's Council and Indian Politics', *Fortnightly Review,* August, 1942.

Chapter II

Through the Imperial Looking Glass

1. Rudyard Kipling's prescription meant authority, commitment, discretion, determination and common sense. These virtues were affirmed as indispensable qualities of the Empire-builders. cf. Rudyard Kipling, *Letters of Travels,* op. cit.; *Plain Tales from the Hill,* London, 1920 (edn.); *Life's Handicap,* London, 1920 (edn.); and *Day's Work,* op. cit.
2. Eric Stokes, *The English Utilitarians and India,* Oxford, 1959; also see Valentine Chirol, *India,* London, 1926, pp. 238–40
3. Rudyard Kipling, 'Georgie Porgie', *Life's Handicap,* London, 1952 (edn.), p. 381; also cf. Philip Woodruff, *Men Who Ruled India,* vol. i and ii, op. cit.
4. Rudyard Kipling, 'Georgie Porgie', op. cit. 'Considering what the lives and actions of most of our so-called Indian heroes really were, the circumstances in which our Indian empire were formed, it is no doubt better for individual reputations and even for the fame of our country that the waves of obscurity and forgetfulness should continue to engulf much of our eastern annals. . . . The history of our Indian empire is pre-eminently that of the actions of ordinary men in extraordinary circumstances'. (Henry Beveridge in 'Warren Hastings in Lower Bengal', *Calcutta Review,* October 1877). This is how Lord Beveridge saw the origin and consolidation of British power in India. War, treachery and deception, Beveridge was to agree with Lord Curzon as late as 1947, were the necessary ingredients for the foundation of an empire which meant, in terms of the expansion of human freedom, the onward movement of civilization. This he underlined, when he quoted from the *Calcutta Review,* October 1884, the following sentence: 'Ceasars' unprovoked agression upon Britain led the civilisation of the country, and Clive and Hastings' spoilation had resulted in British India'. See Lord Beveridge, *India Called Them,* London, 1947, p. 348.
5. Ramsay MacDonald, Valentine Chirol and Ronaldshay, members of the Royal Commission on public services in India, closed their ranks despite political differences against the Indian demands articulated by the fellow Indian members of the Commission. Chirol to Hardinge, 19 January 1913, the Hardinge Papers; also see, Chakravarty, *Anatomy of the Raj,* op. cit., pp. 79–80 and 111–22; Valentine Chirol, *India,* 1926, pp. 238–40.
6. Amery to MacKenzie King, 17 March 1942, *T.O.P.,* vol. i, pp. 435–36.
7. George Schuster and Guy Wint, *India and Democracy,* London, 1945 (edn.), p.74.
8. Penderel Moon, *Strangers in India,* London, 1956, p. 199.
9. Rudyard Kipling, 'Naboth', *Life's Handicap,* op.cit., pp. 394–408. For the difficult and unrewarded job of administering a country where one could not focus one's attention on anything and life seemed unbearable under the

blazing sun, amidst a pulverized brown humanity and operating within a haze of dust, see Rudyard Kipling, 'At the End of the Passage', pp. 183–212; 'The Mark of the Beast', pp. 240–59; 'The Return of Imray', pp. 260–69—all in *Life's Handicap,* op.cit; 'Wee Willie Winkie: An Officer and a Gentleman', pp. 257–72; 'The Education of Otis Yeere', pp. 3–35; 'My Own Ghost Story', pp. 158–69; 'The Drums of the Fre and Aft', pp. 329–74—all in *Wee Willie Winkie and Other Stories,* London, 1951 (edn.); and 'The Bridge Builders', pp. 1–47 and 'The Tomb of his Ancestors', pp. 102–47—both in *The Day's Work,* op.cit.

10. Rudyard Kipling, 'The Tomb of his Ancestors', *The Day's Work,* op.cit., p. 103.
11. Rudyard Kipling, 'The Riddle of the Empire', *Letters of Travels,* op.cit., p. 278.
12. Maud Diver, *Hero of Herat,* op.cit., p. 216–17.
13. Rudyard Kipling, 'The Riddle of the Empire', *Letters of Travels,* op.cit., p. 279.
14. James Morris, *Farewell the Trumpets,* op.cit., pp. 34–35.
15. Lytton to Roberts, 18 October 1879, the Lytton Papers.
16. ibid.
17. S.B. Chaudhary, *Civil Rebellion in the Indian Mutinies,* Calcutta, 1957; P.C. Joshi, ed., *1857: A Symposium,* Delhi, 1957.
18. Flora Annie Steel, *On the Face of the Waters,* op.cit., pp. 9–11.
19. ibid., p.106.
20. E.M. Hull, *The Sons of the Sheik,* London,1920, esp. pp. 167–71.
21. Rudyard Kipling, 'The Riddle of the Empire', *Letters of Travels,* op. cit., p. 279.
22. ibid.
23. ibid., p. 281. Empire-building, Kipling emphasized, was not comprehensible to people who had not taken active part in the process. Kipling was unhappy with the assertion of innocent intellectuals and wide-mouthed Liberals who had been insisting that the British oppressed the people of India. He was disturbed by their pious counsels and disintegrated catchwords. Kipling was especially sore with the fact that these self-centred intellectuals had taken special care to work out good living conditions for themselves quite oblivious of the personal risks undertaken by the Empire-builders and unmindful of their deep sense of responsibility towards posterity. Kipling would have liked to dismiss the accusations and contentious innuendoes of the Liberal sentimentalists and intellectuals as frivolous in view of the serious commitments in India. Years later, he recollected with a sense of amusement that the Liberals had been praying over the years for the happy days: 'When the Rudyards cease from Kipling / And the Haggards Ride no more.' Rudyard Kipling, *Something of Myself,* London, 1951 (edn.), pp. 90–93.
24. Maud Diver, *Desmond's Daughter,* London,1924, p. 564–66.

25. Percival Christopher Wren, *In Wild Maratha Battle*, London,1917.
26. Rudyard Kipling, 'A Serpent of the Old Nile', *Letters of Travels*, op.cit., London, 1920 (edn.), pp. 232–33.
27. ibid.
28. The arguments of this section are based on a 'Memorandum' drawn by the third Marquis of Salisbury, encl. Salisbury to Richard Temple, 20 September 1878, the Salisbury Papers.
29. ibid.
30. Rudyard Kipling, 'Some Earthquakes', *Letters of Travels*, op.cit., p. 69.
31. Rudyard Kipling, 'Our Overseas Men', *Letters of Travels*, ibid., pp. 57–58.
32. ibid., p. 56.
33. cf. Stanley Reed to the Editor, *The Times*, London, 20 February 1920, following the action of General Dyer at Jallianwalla.
34. Rudyard Kipling, 'A Serpent of the Old Nile', *Letters of Travels*, op.cit., p. 233.
35. Rudyard Kipling, 'The Incarnation of Krishna Mulvancy', *Life's Handicap*, op.cit., p. 3; also see, 'The Edge of the East', *Letters of Travels*, op.cit., pp. 34 and 39.
36. Rudyard Kipling, 'A Return to the East', *Letters of Travels*, op.cit., pp. 222–23.
37. 'The Incarnation of Krishna Mulvancy', *Life's Handicap*, op.cit., pp.1–37; also see, Charles Carrington, *The Complete Barrack Room Ballads*, op.cit. It is remarkable how war and empire were presented for the rootless 'Tommy' in working class language and how the Raj made a powerful dent into the metropolitan underclass. This part of Kipling had paradoxically a profound impact on Bertold Brecht in *Mother Courage* and *Three-Penny Opera*. See Martin Esslin, *Brecht: A Choice of Evils*, London, 1980, pp. 35, 100, 102 and 258.
38. Maud Diver, *Desmond's Daughter*, ibid., p.49.
39. ibid., p. 50.
40. 'The Unrest in India', *Quarterly Review*, 1908, pp. 208–19.
41. Aldous Huxley, *Jesting Pilate: The Diary of a Journey*, London, 1930 (edn.), p. 4.
42. ibid., p. 5.
43. Robert Byron, *An Essay on India*, London, 1931, p. 15.
44. ibid.
45. Rudyard Kipling, 'Our Overseas Men', *Letters of Travels*, op.cit., p. 51.
46. Rudyard Kipling, 'A Return to the East', *Letters of Travels*, ibid., p. 223.
47. Rudyard Kipling, 'In Springtime', *A Kipling Anthology*, op.cit., p. 9.
48. Rudyard Kipling, 'Our Overseas Men', *Letters of Travels*, op.cit., p. 51.
49. ibid., p. 52.
50. See for example, Stephen to Lytton, 17 February 1979, the Lytton Papers; also see Maud Diver, *The Unsung, A Record of British Soldiers in India*, London, 1945.

51. Maud Diver, *The Unsung*, ibid., p. 284.
52. Maud Diver, 'The Grand Trunk Road and Some Early Railways', ibid., pp.15–26.
53. Maud Diver, 'The Khyber Railway', ibid., pp.124–46.
54. 'The Periyar Project: A Diversion on a Grand Scale', ibid., p.176.
55. Flora Annie Steel, 'In the Permanent Way', *In the Permanent Way and Other Stories,* London, 1898.
56. Maud Diver, *The Unsung,* op. cit., p. 284. Maud Diver's enthusiasm for the unsung heroes of the Raj was unbounded. Hailing their unrewarded work she invoked Walt Whitman:

    Pioneers, O Pioneers!
    Not the cushion and the slipper,
    Not for us the tame enjoyment;
    We take up the task eternal, and the burden and the lesson—
    Pioneer, O Pioneer!

57. Rudyard Kipling, 'At the end of the Passage', *Life's Handicap,* op.cit., pp. 183, 184, 193 and 194.
58. Rudyard Kipling, 'Our Overseas Men', op.cit., p. 57.
59. Flora Annie Steel, *King-Errant,* London, 1928, pp. 272–75.
60. ibid., p. 273. For generations after generations, Kipling had stressed, English went over to India as 'dolphins follow in line across the open sea' for the sake of love and to teach the elementary notions of civilized life; also see Maud Diver, *The Unsung,* op. cit.; Rudyard Kipling, 'The Tomb of his Ancestors', *The Day's Work,* op.cit., p. 102.
61. Flora Annie Steel, *King-Errant,* op.cit., p. 273.
62. Lionel Trilling, 'Kipling', *The Liberal Imagination,* New York, 1950, p.195.
63. Rudyard Kipling, 'The Bridge Builders', *The Day's Work,* op. cit., pp. 1–47. For the role of an author in ideological formulations, see Ernst Fischer, *The Necessity of Art—A Marxist Approach,* 1963, pp. 10–16; G. Lukaes, *Writer and Critic,* London, 1970, pp. 59–69 and Edward Said, *Orientalism,* London, 1978, pp. 1–6, 41–48, and 91–96.
64. '. . . the only serious enemy to the Empire', Kipling wrote, 'within and/or without, is that very Democracy which depends on the Empire for its proper comforts, and in whose behalf these things are urged'. Kipling, 'A Conclusion', *Letters of Travels,* op.cit., p. 205. This constitutes the refrain of the section of his *Letters of Travels,* entitled 'Letters to the Family', pp. 119–205.
65. Rudyard Kipling, 'The Bridge Builders', *The Day's Work,* op. cit.
66. Rudyard Kipling, 'In the House of Suddhoo', *Plain Tales from the Hills,* London, 1920 (edn.), pp. 144–54.
67. George Orwell, 'Shooting the Elephant', *Inside the Whale and Other Essays,* London, 1957, p. 95: 'And suddenly I realise that I should have to

shoot the elephant after all. The people expected it of me and I had got to do it. I could feel their two thousand wills pressing me forward, irresistibly. And it was this moment as I stood there with the rifle in my hands, that I first grasped the hollowness, the futility of the whiteman's dominion in the East. Here I was, the whiteman with his gun standing in front of the unarmed native crowd—seemingly the leading actor of the piece; but in reality I was only an absurd puppet pushed to and fro by the will of those yellow, faced behind'.

68. Rudyard Kipling, 'The Children of the Zodiac', *Many Inventions,* London, 1952 (edn.), pp. 363–85.
69. Rudyard Kipling, 'The Riddle of the Empire', *Letters of Travels,* op.cit., p. 284
70. W.W. Hunter, review of Rudyard Kipling's *Departmental Ditties,* quoted in R. Lancelyn Green, *Kipling: The Critical Heritage,* London, 1971, p. 40.
71. Ronald Wingate, *Not in the Limelight,* London, 1969, p. 82.
72. Edwin Harward, 'Kipling, Myth and Traditions', *Nineteenth Century,* 1939, p. 199.
73. G.M. Molesworth, *Curfew on Olympus,* Bombay, 1965, p. 3.
74. Edwin Candler, *Youth and the East: An Unconventional Autobiography,* London, 1924.
75. Claud Hill, *India-Stepmother,* London, 1929, p. 256; and Evan Maconochie, *Life in the I.C.S.,* London,1926, p. 39.
76. Leonard Woolf, *Growing, 1904–1911,* London,1961, p. 46.
77. A.P. Wavell, *Other Men's Flowers: An Anthology of Poetry,* London, 1944, p. 15.
78. A. Aronson, *Rabindranath Through Western Eyes,* Allahabad, 1943, p. 4.
79. *Globe,* Toronto, 16 June 1914, quoted in ibid., pp. 4–5.
80. For Western reponses to Tagore, see ibid., pp. 18–24.
81. *Liverpool Post,* 20 July 1927, quoted in ibid., p. 18.
82. *Queen,* London, 21 May 1921, quoted in ibid., p. 19.
83. ibid., p. 111.
84. See A. Aronson's informative analysis of Tagore's reception in the West by critics and interpreters, esp. see 'The Test of Sensibility', ibid., pp. 91–124.
85. Rudyard Kipling, 'In the House of Suddhoo', *Plain Tales From the Hills,* op.cit., p. 144.
86. 'India: Old Ways and New', *Round Table,* October 1912, pp. 52–80, esp. pp. 55–57. 'But if the skill of her military commanders and the courage and perserverance of her troops, both British and Indian, have played their part in laying the foundations of a new and happier India, and have since secured to her peace within her borders and immunity from invasions from without, it is the success of her administrators, both military and civil, in bringing so vast a territory, inhabited by so many and such diverse races, under a just and orderly administration that history will regard it as the outstanding

achievement of her work in Asia. For it is by the labours of her administrators, her judges, her educationalists, her sanitarians, and her engineers that the contrast between India of today and the India of two centuries ago has been effected. And what a remarkable contrast that is!' *India: Special Number of the Times, February 1930,* London, 1930, p. 5. This remarkable achievement, it was argued, was possible by the district officer whose 'chief fascination of life and work lies in his infinite variety of scene among which his lot is cast'. The principal representative of the sirkar bahadur in the district was a solitary figure devoted exclusively to the concern of the people in his charge. See this interesting account of the functions, responsibilities and commitments of the district officer in his majestic loneliness in R.G. Gordon, *The District Officer,* ibid., pp. 49–51; also see ibid., pp. 118–24. On the inflated self-image of the civil service, see for example, Thomas White, *A Good Day's Work,* Edinburgh, 1909, pp. 45–46; 'Civilian', *The Civilian's South India,* London, 1921, pp. 14 and 45; A.A. Irvine, *Land of No Regrets,* London, 1938, pp. 24 and 91; Claud Hill, *India-Stepmother,* op.cit., p. 21, 70–71; Guy Fleetwood Wilson, *Letters to Nobody, 1908–1913,* London, 1921, p.195. It was affirmed by all without any exception that modern India owed its very existence to the services of the paternalistic civil services.

87. 'India: Old Ways and New', *Round Table,* op.cit., p. 80.
88. Arthur Mayhew, *Christianity and the Government of India, An Examination of the Christian forces at work in the administration of India and of the Mutual Relations between the British Government and Christian Missions 1600–1920,* London, n.d., see esp. ch. ix, 'Bishops, Chaplains and Governor General in India', pp. 112–25.
89. ibid., p. 123.
90. ibid., ch. x, 'Advance on Christian Lines: Bentinck and Dalhousie'. pp. 126–37.
91. Nora E. Karn, 'The Bhaktani', *The Believer and Other Stories,* Delhi, 1941, pp. 8–13.
92. 'The Bhangi', ibid., pp. 20–26.
93. 'The Mystic', ibid., pp. 27–34.
94. 'The Old Sadni', ibid., pp. 35–44.
95. Maurice Dekobra, *Perfumed Tigers: Adventures in the Land of the Maharajahs,* London, 1931 (English edn.), pp. 234–38.
96. Peter Muir, *This is India,* New York, 1943, p. 225.
97. Aldous Huxley, *Jesting Pilate,* op.cit., pp. 55–56.
98. Valentine Chirol, 'Memorandum on India', 28 August 1917, the R.T.G. Papers.
99. Lockwood Kipling, *Beast and Man in India,* London, 1892, p. 9; for Hindu 'cruelty' see Rumer Godden, 'Mercy, Pity, Feace and Love', *Indian Dust,* London, 1989, pp. 141–58.
100. Valentine Chirol, 'Memorandum on India', 28 August 1917, the R.T.G.

Papers.

101. Walter Roper Lawrence, *The India We Served,* London, 1928, p. 164. For caste, see L. Dumon, *Homo Hierarchicus,* London, 1972 and M.N. Srinivas, *Social Change in Modern India,* California, 1970.
102. Edmund Candler, *The Mantle of the East,* London, 1910, p. 130.
103. E.W. Savi, *God Forsaken,* London, 1929.
104. Flora Annie Steel, *Indian Scene: Collected Short Stories,* London, 1933, p. 137; also see Rumer Godden, 'Possession', *Indian Dust,* op.cit., pp. 9–24.
105. William Robinson, *By Temple Shrine and Lotus Pool,* London, 1910, p. 52; also see M.L. Christlieb, *Uphill Steps in India,* London, 1930; W.A. Allison, *The Sadhus,* Calcutta, 1935; F. Yeats-Brown, *Bengal Lancer,* London, 1930; Richard Welfle, *The Ruined Temple,* Chicago, 1935; G. W. Briggs, *The Chamars,* Calcutta, 1920.
106. Lockwood Kipling, *Beast and Man in India,* op.cit., p. 5.
107. C.F. Bechhofer, *The Brahmin's Treasure,* London, 1923.
108. ibid. All British commentators were eager to maintain that India could never move forward to her destiny so long as she sat at the feet of a philosophy which declared that the world was an illusion, that life was essentially evil, that man was irredeemably chained to the results of his sins and must free himself through an eternity of reincarnations, so long as the Indian continued to worship a blood-thirsty Kali or a gross elephant-headed god or the demon-mother in a 'brick sprinkled with goat's blood' and so long as he continued to catch his ideals from Krishna, with his life story of sensual amours. The goal of India, it was maintained, could not be reached by throwing aside the British rule that had brought to her an internal peace. Basil Mathew, *The Secret of India,* London, n.d., pp. 126–27; Al Carthill, *The Lost Dominion,* op.cit., pp. 174–75; Aldous Huxley, *Jesting Pilate,* op.cit., pp. 158–59; Penderel Moon, *Strangers in India,* op.cit., p. 198.
109. Sarah Tytler, *In the Fort,* London, 1886, pp. 166, 183 and 276.
110. S.M. Edwardes, *Crime in India,* London, 1921, p. 158.
111. ibid.
112. William Robinson, *By Temple Shrine and Lotus Pool,* op.cit., p .66. The ideologues were convinced that India would be destroyed if she opted for democracy. 'Thus to the great barriers of distances and diversities of race, climate, language and mentality, which are really the work of nature and physical environment, by which under a Mendelian law, widely divergent racial characteristics have become fixed and well-neigh immutable, have been super-added and the man-made barriers of religious antagonisms and social partitions, maintained as in no other country on earth by rigid endogamy, by cash fines and severe religious penances. . . . And one wonders what shall replace this remarkable system of caste that has grown up in the course of thirty or more centuries. . . The fortress of caste cannot be taken by external assault. Its wall will only crumble when the garrison

within ceases to repair them. The only real discipline that India has maintained is the discipline of caste. If you really could create genuine democracy in India it would destroy caste. If it destroyed caste it would destroy Hinduism and if it destroyed Hinduism it would destroy India, at least the India that has existed for so many thousand of years. . . Far, far better that they should remain good Hindus than become rampant aetheists! And the theorist thinks that ballot box will solve this problem too!' Reginald Craddock, *The Dilemma in India,* op.cit., pp. 25–26; also see Penderel Moon, *Strangers in India,* pp. 149 and 197–98.

113. G.W. Briggs, *The Chamars,* London, 1920; also see 'The Outlook', ch. ix, pp. 224–47.
114. Henry Whitehead, *The Village Gods of South India,* London, 1921, pp. 154–58.
115. ibid., p. 152; also see A.G. Hogg, *Karma and Redemption,* Madras, 1909, pp. 41–66.
116. Richard A. Welfle, *The Ruined Temple,* op.cit., p.135.
117. ibid.
118. ibid., p. 136. Also see Aldous Huxley, *Jesting Pilate,* op.cit., p. 52.
119. See Edmund Candler, 'Kashi', pp. 1–30; 'Mount Abu', pp. 140–80—both in *The Mantle of the East,* London, 1911.
120. Candler, ibid., p. 150. 'Dilwarra attracts you with its cold complacent beauty outside, and repels you with its elaborate, perfect hideousness within. Achilgar, perched in the clouds, is wrapt in brooding mystery. It is a ghoulish place. The moss-grown rocks are pregnant with history and legend, spiritual and secular. The rocks leer at you with wry faces, conscious of all that has gone on. . . . Decrepit banyan trees lean on them for support. Hanuman, Bhairon and Ganesh conspire for evil in the crevices of their roots. . . . The Jain artists had defeated me. I blushed for the West. I was almost persuaded to be a little Englander'. Edmund Candler, *The Mantle of the East,* op.cit., pp. 163–64; also see Edwin Lutyens to Emily Lutyens, 14 January 1914, Papers of Edwin Lutyens at the Royal Institute of British Architects, London—which are hereafter referred to as the Lutyens Papers in this section.
121. Lockwood Kipling, *Beast and Man,* op.cit., p. 2.
122. ibid., p. 84.
123. The historians of Indian nationalism have fallen for the seductive influence of these perceptions. This is typified by the so-called Cambridge School with its complementary outposts at Sussex, Oxford and Canberra. Its principal themes and its Namierized methodology have been adopted and developed by various South-Asian Centres in the United States of America as well. Its epistemology, problematic and *raison d'etre* are certainly more sophisticated than the academic exercises at the London School of Oriental and African Studies. The tenacious pre-occupation of the London School with the 'white man's burden', and the 'gradual constitutional devolution'

of political authority to the Indians had become a tedious academic burden and it has been since ousted by a more 'credible' creed. It has been maintained in a series of researched papers, seminars, Ph. D. dissertations and a number of monographs that nationalism was a superficial veneer adopted for the sake of convenience by numerous elite-groups in a multi-racial and multi-linguistic society distinguished by its sharp vertical chasms. J. Gallaghar, the primate of the School, made no bones about his assertion that the history of Indian national movement was but a series of conflicts between traditional and modern elite-groups jostling for position and power professed by institutional changes initiated by the government. Anil Seal's *The Emergence of Indian Nationalism: Competition and Collaboration in the Later 19th Century,* Cambridge, 1968; Judith Brown's *Gandhi's Rise to Power—Indian Politics 1915–1922,* Cambridge, 1972; J.H. Broomfield's *Elite Conflict in a Plural Society—20th Century Bengal,* Berkeley, 1968; Gordon Johnson's *Provincial Politics and Indian National Congress 1880–1915,* Cambridge, 1973; F. Robinson's *Separation among Indian Muslims: The Politics of the United Provinces Muslims, 1860–1923,* Cambridge, 1974; C.J. Baker and D.A. Washbrook's *South India, 1880–1940,* Delhi, 1975; C.A. Bayly's *Local Roots of Indian Politics—Allahabad 1880–1920,* Oxford, 1975; D.A. Washbrook's *The Emergence of Provincial Politics: Madras Presidency 1870–1920,* Cambridge, 1976; and C.J. Baker's *The Politics of South India, 1920–1927,* Cambridge, 1976—have carefully contrived the story of Indian nationalism as an endless flow of elite-waves collaborating and competing with each other on the one hand and with the British government on the other. In short, national consciousness has been explained away as an elitist myth projected by different groups dressed in an attractive attire in order to ensure for themselves alluring material prizes. From this elite paradigm, our historians have concluded that in each of the regions of India there was a group with a self-conscious identity: Chitpawans in Maharashtra, Brahmins in Tamil Nadu and Bhadralok in Bengal. Anthony Low discovered in UP an elite distinguished by 'Indo-Persian Husk Culture', in D.A. Low, ed., *Soundings in Modern South-Asian History,* California, 1968. T.R. Metcalfe endowed this group with a progressive political personality with T.R. Metcalfe, *Land, Landlords and the British Raj,* Delhi, 1979; and Bernard-Cohn in J.H. Broomfield, *Mostly About Bengal,* Delhi, 1982, pp. 21–23, recommended it as a national elite!

124. Bruce Mitford, 'Causes and Effect in India', *Fortnightly Review,* 1919, vol. 112, pp. 129–38.
125. Valentine Chirol, 'Memorandum on India', op.cit., the R.T.G. Papers. Also see Valentine Chirol, *India,* London, 1926.
126. ibid.
127. T.G.P. Spear, 'Memorandum on the Basis and Structure of Indian Government', 21 January 1940, the Alexander Inglis Papers.

128. Stanley Lanepool, *Aurangzib and the Decay of the Mughal Empire*, Oxford, 1890, p.198.
129. Valentine Chirol, *India*, op.cit., p. 219; E.M. Forster, *A Passage to India*, 1961: '. . . you keep your religion, I mine. That is the best. Nothing embraces the whole of India, nothing, nothing, and that was Akbar's mistake', p. 43.
130. Otto Rothfeld I.C.S., *Indian Dust*, Oxford, 1909.
131. Lindsay Commission, *Report of the Commission on Christian Education in India*, London, 1931, esp. see 'Recent Changes Due to the Revival of Hinduism', pp. 43–45 and 'Factors which have Produced the Changes in Hinduism', pp. 45–50.
132. ibid., pp. 50, and 51.
133. Edmund Candler, *The Mantle of the East*, op.cit., pp. 29–30.
134. Lindsay Commission, *Report*, op.cit., p. 48.
135. ibid., pp. 49–50.
136. ibid., p. 51. 'Secularism is indeed the common enemy of all the religions since it demands in India, as it does elsewhere, in the name of reason and progress, that religion shall be rejected in a world where religion has no right. . . . The works of Bertrand Russell, we are told, are in constant demand in bookshops in Madras. . . Giant Pagan is indeed far from being toothless and impotent. Hinduism is far too deeply entrusted in the soul of India to be reckoned as defeated as yet. As a matter of fact, the philosophy of Vedanta and the life of secularism are perfectly natural allies. . . Both alike reject many of the values that Christianity seeks to create and preserve, and with them, therefore, Christianity can make no terms'. ibid., pp. 54–55.
137. Edmund Candler, *The Mantle of the East*, London, 1910, p. 29.
138. Lindsay Commission, *Report*, op.cit., pp. 29–30.
139. '. . . in their political attitudes, both the administration and Christian mission had become increasingly conservative; they both recognise it was by welfare service that they could command themselves to India. The rising nationalism had begun to make itself felt, stimulating the political liberalism of the educated classes into radicalism, which at the same time, was entirely successful in inhibiting the earlier tendencies of social and religious liberalism and reform. The Vedic foundation of Arya Samaj and the neo-Vedantism of Swami Vivekananda are examples of this religious reaction which now set in'. ibid., p. 34.
140. Aldous Huxley, *Jesting Pilate*, op.cit., pp. 116 and 140.
141. ibid., p.116. '. . .For, to tell the truth, I am glad to be leaving India. . . For India is depressing as no other country I have ever known. One breathes in it, not air, but dust and hopelessness. The present is unsatisfactory, the future dubious and menacing. . . . Customs and ancient superstitions are still almost as strong as they were, and after a-century-and-half of Western government, nine Indians out of ten cannot read or write and the tenth, who can, detests the Europeans who taught him. The educated and politically-

conscious profess democratic principles; but their instincts are profoundly and almost ineradicably aristocratic'. ibid., pp. 158–59.

142. G.W. Forrest, 'The Changing Scene in India', *Nineteenth Century,* May 1919, pp. 1041–52, esp. p. 1044.

143. ibid., p. 1044; also see 'The Political Situation in India', *Fortnightly Review,* 1919, pp. 742–51. The imperial perspective remained inflexible. In 1942, Lionel Howarth wrote in unambiguous terms: 'The Hindu desires by the power of the ballot box, to obtain control of the Empire of India as the inheritor of the British democratic Raj, though he has never ruled over an Empire of India in the last two thousand years, and never at all in northern India for seven hundred years. The Mohamedan says he will fight rather than agree. The question must be asked a second time: On what do we found our belief that India can be a democratic federation to be ruled by the Hindu vote? What ground have we got for thinking that India will not again break up into separate Kingdoms? What is there even in European history to suggest such a result? The American example is reverse of what we find in India. In America a homogeneous people formed a federation into which people of foreign races have been or are being assimilated. The mould was already in existence. In India we are asking for a federation while removing the mould'. Lionel Howarth, 'United India', *Nineteenth Century,* 1942, p. 235.

144. Maurice Dekobra, *Perfumed Gardens,* op.cit., p.140. 'Anyone acquainted with India, however much he might sympathise with her aspirations, could not help doubting whether self-government in this form would be attainable within a century—if indeed ever. It is not that Indians are congenitally incapable of governing themselves—any such proposition is ridiculous—but merely that they cannot govern themselves in the peculiar way which we had proposed. For it is not consonant with India's past history or the present stage of social development'. Penderel Moon, *Strangers in India,* op.cit., p.198.

145. T.G.P. Spear, 'Memorandum on the Basis and Structure of Indian Government', op.cit.

146. ibid.

147. ibid.

148. ibid.

149. ibid.

150. Maurice Gwyer, 'Memorandum of the Indian Political Situation', 20 April 1941, the Linlithgow Papers.

151. ibid.

152. ibid. In 1946, Penderel Moon felt that the destiny of India could only be realized within the traditional political system based on a deep-seated respect for hereditary authority which had been muddled by English institutions. 'The ground is already encumbered with inferior replicas of insurmountable English institutions; and there is no obvious method by

which this useless lumber can be quietly disposed of. In the immediate future we must look elsewhere for the possibility of sound development. We must look to the Native States'. 'And here,' he found, 'in the backward states, the object of so much misplaced scorn, there perhaps lies the secret of India's future and her best hopes'. Penderel Moon, *Strangers in India,* op.cit., p. 196.

153. See Katherine Mayo, 'The Widow', *Slaves of the God,* London, 1929.
154. Maud Diver, 'The Gods of the East', in Saros Cowasjee, ed., *Plain Tales from the Raj,* op. cit., p. 209; cf. also Henry Bruce, *The Bride of Shiva,* London, 1921.
155. Katherine Mayo, 'The Widow', *Slaves of the God,* op. cit.
156. Alice Perrin, 'The Centipede', in Saros Cowasjee, *Plain Tales from the Raj,* op. cit., pp. 119–26.
157. 'It has come as a shock to the general public,' Claud Hill added, 'and as a ruthless bombshell to orthodox Hinduism.' Claud Hill, *India-Stepmother,* op.cit., pp. 270–71. For a discussion on Mayo's *Mother India* from the official point of view, see ibid., 269–88.
158. Edward Thompson, *The Reconstruction of India,* London, 1930, p. 268.
159. Katherine Mayo, *Slaves of the God,* op.cit., see 'Appendix', An Extract of a review in *The New Statesman,* 16 July 1927.
160. ibid.
161. Katherine Mayo, *Mother India,* 1927, p.118.
162. W.A. Frazer, *Caste,* London, 1932.
163. ibid., pp. 263–74.
164. Rudyard Kipling and Wolcott Balestier, *The Naulakha: A Story of West and East,* London, 1952 (edn.).
165. George Orwell, 'Shooting an Elephant', *Inside the Whale and Other Essays,* London, 1980, p. 92. Even if one concedes, for the sake of argument, that both Malcolm Muggeridge and Edward M. Thomas over-simplified Orwell's *Burmese Days* (op. cit.) by asserting that Flory, the hero, was Orwell himself, one cannot withold the conclusion simply in reverence to some cultivated ambiguities that the celebrated author did not transcend the perceptions of Kipling and could rarely withdraw from Kipling's view of the Raj and its achievements. The following passage from the *Burmese Days* quoted by Goonetilleke *(Images of the Raj,* op.cit.) is self-explanatory: 'Living and working among Orientals would try the temper of a saint. And all of them, the officials particularly, knew what they were to be baited and insulted. Almost every day, when Westfield or Macgregor or even Maxwell went down the street, the High School boys, with their yellow faces—faces smooth as gold coins, full of that maddening contempt that sits so naturally on the Mongolian faces—sneered at them as they went past, sometimes hooted after them with hyena-like laughter. The life of the Anglo-Indian officials is not all jam. In comfortless camps, in sweltering offices, in gloomy *dakbungalows* smelling of dust and earth-

soil, they earn, perhaps, the right to be a little disagreeable'.

George Orwell, *Burmese Days,* 1980, p. 117. For a discussion on Malcolm Muggeridge and Edward Thomas on George Orwell, see Goonetilleke, *Images of the Raj,* op.cit., ch. iv.

Shamsul Islam saw the point when he mildly asserted that Orwell was not as big an enemy of the Raj as he is generally supposed to be. (Shamsul Islam, *Chronicles of the Raj,* op.cit., p. 84.) Both Leonard Woolf and George Orwell continued to be diffident internal critics of the Raj, while appreciating its ennobling impact. Given the opportunity they would have prayed for its permanence. This is not the role of a critic of the system. Their sporadic outbursts against the Raj are essentially schizophrenic. They were scared of their own experience but they were equally aware of the impending doom of the Raj. They shared with Kipling the faith that the tropical sun had an enervating impact on the British personnel and yet they would adhere closely to the Raj paradigms. Goonetilleke's reference to the historical perspective in terms of the ascendancy of Fascism and 'Bolshevism' and the collectivist society armed with duties and obligations and the attempts by imperialism to reform itself, etc. are fanciful disjointed thoughts or a neo-apologists' view of the Raj operating against the facts of history.

166. cf. Raymond Williams, *George Orwell,* London, 1971.
167. George Orwell, 'Shooting an Elephant', op.cit., p. 92.
168. Alice Perrin, 'The Rise of Ram Din', in Saros Cawasjee, *Stories from the Raj,* op.cit., pp. 119–29.
169. Christine Weston, 'A Game of Helma', ibid., pp. 254–59.
170. Leonard Woolf, 'Pearls and Swine', ibid., pp. 181–200.
171. ibid., p. 183.
172. ibid., p. 191.
173. Ganpat, *The Speakers in Silence,* 1921.
174. ibid.
175. George Orwell, 'Shooting an Elephant', op.cit., p. 92.
176. ibid., p.99.
177. L.H. Myers, *The Near and the Far,* London, 1940.
178. ibid.
179. L.H. Myers, *Pool of Vishnu,* London, 1940. The difference between L.H. Myers and other fiction writers on Indian themes should be emphasized. While others chose to write about India to highlight imperial perceptions, Myers made it abundantly clear that he sought to use geographical and historical material of India primarily to censure his social and material environment. And yet despite this deliberate attempt to portray contemporary history of the ascendancy of Fascism and democratic struggle against it through Indian myths and romantic history, Myers could never rise against his own passion for the brightest jewel of the Empire. cf. Inna Walter, *L.H. Myers: Myths and Symbols in His Indian Novels,* Delhi, 1984;

and for a critical appraisal, G.H. Bantock, *J.H. Myers: A Critical Study*, London, 1956, esp. pp. 253–58.

180. John Eyton, 'History From a Hill', *Dancing Fakir and Other Stories*, London, 1922, pp. 11–12.
181. John Eyton, *Dancing Fakir*, ibid., pp. 1–10.
182. John Eyton, 'The Heart to Tek Chand', ibid., pp. 11–26.
183. John Eyton, 'A Worm's Training', ibid., pp. 27–31.
184. Eyton's allegiance to Kipling cannot be minimized and the author himself acknowledged his debt to Kipling more than once. Eyton lacked Kipling's range and virtuosity, but unlike Maud Diver, he appreciated the importance of the altered political atmosphere of India during his day. He retained a subtle and sustained imperial pressure without becoming imperialism's extrovert propagandist. As a result, Eyton was more effective than Diver.
185. Hallam Tennyson, *The Dark Goddess*, London, 1947, p.125.
186. ibid., p. 139.
187. J.D. Rees, 'Indian Conditions and Indian Critics', *Fortnightly Review*, 1902, pp. 272–82.
188. ibid.
189. Arnold Lupton, *Happy India: As it Might be if Guided by Modern Science*, London, 1922.
190. ibid., chs. iii, v and xviii.
191. Eric Musaprat, *The Journey Home*, 1933, p. 82.
192. Penderel Moon, *The Future of India*, London, 1945 (edn.), p.43.
193. India League, 'Report of the Teacher's Committee of the India League', London, 18 June 1945, Papers of V.K. Krishna Menon at the Nehru Memorial Museum and Library—which are hereafter referred to as the Krishna Menon Papers in this section. One of the popular books for the children on India was the illustrated volume, *The Land of Idols or Talks with Young People About India*, London, 1895, written by Rev. John J. Pool and published by London's Missionary Society. It was an attractive volume that presented India as a land of conjurers and jugglers, enshrouded in an impenetrable mystery with idols everywhere, having 333,000,000 gods represented by innumerable shapes, a land of prostrating humanity before 'the sacred monkey', the 'Juggernaut' of Puri, seductive slippery snakes and black beauty of Krishna, whose worship often degenerated into midnight orgies; a country of untruthful and dishonest people wedded to topsy-turvy social customs and manners, and, of course, the brave young converts!
194. Rudyard Kipling, 'The Miracle of Puran Bhagat', *The Second Jungle Book*, 1920 (edn.), pp. 27–41.
195. ibid., pp. 29–30.
196. cf. Valentine Chirol, *India Old And New*, London, 1921, p. 263.
197. For 'Orientalism' in all its aspects see the monumental work, Edmund W. Said, *Orientalism*, London, 1985 (edn.). That the social mentality of the

age is conditioned by that age's social relations, is nowhere more evident than in the history of art and literature. For a detailed discussion, see Terry Eagleton, *Marxism and Literary Criticism*, London, 1985, esp. pp. 5–10.

198. ibid., p. 215. In a sense imperial culture was fashioned and defended as a variety of long term coverages against threats of self-dissolution, loss of identity, assimilation and attacks from neighbouring or native culture. It produced an image for the British which claimed a radical difference from the 'others'. The cover-ups were maintained with remarkable tenacity. The overwhelming idea was to emphasize the qualitative superiority of the imperial culture contrasting sharply to a succession of accidents and surprises representing the others. See an illuminating work, Henry Louis Gates Jr., *Black Literature and Literary Theory*, London, 1984, esp. pp. 59–79.

199. ibid., p. 203. 'Orientalism,' Said wrote, 'is a structure in the thick of an imperial contest whose dominant wing is represented and elaborated not only as scholarship but as a partisan ideology. Yet Orientalism had the contest beneath its scholarly and aesthetic idioms'. Edmund W. Said, 'Representing the Colonised', *Critical Inquiry*, Winter, 1889, p. 211.

200. Ernst Fischer, *Art Against Ideology*, London, 1969, esp. pp. 155–61; also Ernst Fischer, *The Necessity of Art: A Marxist Approach*, op.cit., pp.90–95.

Chapter III

Uncomfortable Claims: Untenable Positions

1. A British establishment in India was situated outside the old walled town. It was generally divided into two parts, the civil lines and the cantonment. The former was spaciously arranged with lots of greens between the bungalows inhabited by the *sahiblogs* and the latter was organized on severe military lines. The ruling principle was segregation. See Jan Morris and Simon Winchester, *Stones of the Empire*, op.cit., esp. pp. 89–90, 124, 169, 177 and 202–03. The Sadr and the Lalbazar grew out of the needs of the cantonment and the civil lines; see Kenneth Ballhatchet, *Race, Sex and Class in the Raj*, op.cit., esp. pp. 11—12, 18—19 and 34—38; also see Al Carthill, *Madampur*, London, 1931, pp. 41—64. For a defence of the isolation of the snooty civil lines and cantonment from the dangerous enemy, orientalism and its endemic inertia, see Al Carthill, *Madampur*, ibid., p. 86.
2. Lutyens to Emily Lutyens, 26 May 1914, the Lutyens Papers.
3. Pat Barr and Ray Desmond, *Simla, A Hill Station in British India*, op.cit.; Mollie Panter-Dones, *Ooty-Preserved: A Victorious Hill Station*, op.cit. There were many hill-stations and hence plenty of choice. About eighty stations were established by the British as retreats from the heat and cholera of the plains. 'Like meat', one of the memsahibs cribbed, 'we keep better

up here'. Some of these hill resorts were purely escapism. Simla was, however, 'the abode of the little Tin Gods' as Kipling had put it. For several months in every year it was the capital of the Raj and the embodiment of the absolute power of the viceroy. Despotic power was frankly exhibited in the life of Simla. Not to speak of the absence of the traffic on the streets, both the *baralat* and the *chotalat* were conspicuously parked on the two hillocks. There was also the imperial cathedral and the Gaiety. Together, they constituted the complex structure of an imperial hierarchy which segregated even the shopping centres. The Mal was separated from the Lower Mal and both from the *chhota bazaar*. The hill-stations espoused the desire to recreate British atmosphere with exuberance which was always alien and incompatible.

4. These exclusive clubs with daunting gateways, sentry-boxes for watchmen and stern name-plates were symbolic of the impeccable exclusiveness of the ruling class. They might have jarred the sensibility of Orwell or Forster, but they were the centres where the imperial codes of honour were formulated and upheld. They preserved the *esprit de corps* of the imperial aristocracy.
5. For the principles of political architecture and town planning of New Delhi, see the papers of Edwin Lutyens and Herbert Baker at the Royal Institute of British Architects, London. Also see, Sten Nilsson, *The New Capitals of India, Pakistan and Bangladesh,* London, 1975; Suhash Chakravarty, 'Architecture and Politics in the Construction of New Delhi', *Man and Development,* June 1985. For a sumptuous and romantic nostalgia, see Robert Grant Irving, *Indian Summer, Lutyens, Baker and Imperial Delhi,* op.cit.

   As Francis Hutchins put it, Englishmen constructed a myth of their omniscience and further cushioned it by a set of myths which presumed to describe the so-called 'real' India. This India of imperial imagination contained no element of change. Lack of cohesion rendered it vulnerable to foreign domination. Western rule, as a result, became both inevitable and desirable. See Francis G. Hutchins, *The Illusions of Permanence,* Princeton, 1967, pp. 156–57.

   The whole range of historical novels on the Indian theme stoked the self-righteous imperialism in India. These works of fiction were the result of that imperial consciousness and, in turn, they provided the emotional and material impulses for more vigorous actions and heroism. See G.D. Bearce, *British Attitudes towards India, 1784–1858,* Oxford, 1961, p. 112. The problem of 'Gorgeous East versus Land of Regrets' raised by B.J. Moore-Gilbert appears to be in real life just a pseudo question. B.J. Moore-Gilbert, *Kipling and 'Orientalism'*, London, 1986. It is true that often the sense of insecurity entertained by the small number of English families in India seemed real and this gave a fresh spurt to the problem of solidarity felt strongly by these isolated few in an alien country. But all the ideologues agreed that the Raj was a reponsibility that involved fear and suffering as well as profit, position and glory.

6. Walter Roper Lawrence, *The India We Served,* London, 1928, p. 80.
7. Samuel Sadoc, *Zarins, A Romance in India,* London, n.d.
8. ibid., p.42.
9. cf. Humphrey Trevelyan, *The India We Left,* London, 1972, p. 174.
10. Walter Roper Lawrence, *The India We Served,* op. cit., p. 83.
11. Paul Scott, *The Jewel in the Crown,* London, 1973 (edn.), pp. 14–15.
12. Edwin Lutyens to Emily Lutyens, 14 April 1912, the Lutyens Papers.
13. Percival Spear, *The Nabobs,* London, 1980 (edn.), p. 142.
14. Theatres sprang up across the wide Empire, especially in the presidency towns; touring musical companies came to India from Europe; roaming troupes of local actors took Shakespeare to the remote stations. The Gaiety Theatre at the Town Hall in Simla was patronized by the viceroy and the commander-in-chief and a select audience of a philistine society.
15. F. Yeats-Brown, *Bengal Lancer,* London, 1930, p. 9; also cf. Jon and Rumer Godden, *Two Under the Indian Sun,* London, 1966, p. 91.
16. Rudyard Kipling, 'Three and—an Extra', *Plain Tales from the Hills,* op.cit., p. 14.
17. Rudyard Kipling, 'Thrown Away', *Plain Tales from the Hills,* ibid., p. 16.
18. Rudyard Kipling, 'Two Months; June and September', *A Kipling Anthology,* op.cit., p. 9–10.
19. Strickland is a mercurial character of Kipling's official world of Simla. See Kipling, *Plain Tales from the Hills,* op.cit.; *The Life's Handicap,* op.cit.; *Land and Sea Tales,* op.cit.
20. Rudyard Kipling, 'Miss Youghal's Sais', *Plain Tales from the Hills,* ibid., pp. 27–28.
21. See for example, ibid., pp. 27–34.
22. John Masters, *To the Coral Strand,* London, 1972 (edn.).
23. Rudyard Kipling, *Kim,* op.cit.
24. T.D. Forsyth, (1827–1886): Indian civilian; commissioner of Punjab, 1860–72; visited as viceroy's agent, St. Petersburg in 1869, Yarkand in 1870 and 1873; concluded a commercial treaty with the Amir of Yarkand; obtained from the king of Burma agreement that the Karunca State should be acknowledged independent. Thomas Munro (1761–1827): Indian civilian, assisted in forming the civil administration of Baramahal, 1792–99; principal collector of the ceded districts of Hyderabad where he developed the ryotwari system of land revenue; head of a commission to reorganize the judicial and police administration of Madras Presidency, 1814; governor of Madras, 1819–1827. Charles Theophilus Metcalfe (1785–1846): Indian civilian; political officer under Lord Lake in the Mahratta War, 1804; assistant resident at Delhi, 1811–1819; resident at Hyderabad, 1820–1825; resident of Delhi, 1811–1819 and in 1825–1827; member of the supreme council, 1827–1834; lieutenant-governor, Agra, 1834; acting

governor-general, 1835–36; lieutenant-governor, North-Western Provinces, 1836–1838. Mounstuart Elphinstone (1779–1859): Indian civilian, served as agent at the Peshwa's court, Poona; resident at Nagpur; led embassy to Shah Shuja at Kabul, 1808; resident at Poona, 1810–1816; governor of Bombay, 1817–1827. See, Philip Woodruff, *The Men Who Ruled India,* vol. i, op.cit. Francis Younghusband (1863–1942): a most romantic military commander who led the mission to Lhasa in August 1904; imperialist, explorer, general and a mystic; see Peter Fleming, *Bayonets to Lahasa,* London, 1961; Peter Hopkirk, *Trespassers on the Roof of the World,* London, 1982; also see, Francis Younghusband, *The Heart of a Continent,* Hongkong 1984, and George Seaver, *Francis Younghusband: Explorer and Mystic,* London, 1952. The first Marquis of Ripon, Liberal viceroy of India, 1880–1884; see, S. Gopal, *The Viceroyalty of Lord Ripon,* Oxford, 1953.

25. Rudyard Kipling, *Kim,* op.cit.; also see, Rudyard Kipling and Wolcott Balestier, *The Naulakha: A Story of West and East,* London, 1952 (edn.) for the formless, malignant mystery of India, at once both innocent and terrible:

    This I saw when the rites were done,
    And the lamps were dead and the Gods alone,
    And the grey snake coiled on the altar stone—
    Ere I fled from a Fear that I could not see,
    And the Gods of the East made mouths at me.

26. Cunningham, *Chronicle of Dustypore,* op.cit.
27. Sydenham Clark and Michael O'Dwyer were Indian civilians and were firmly opposed to any concession to Indian nationalism. For Sydenham Clark (1848–1913): governor of Bombay, 1907–1913, see his Private Papers in British Library, London; Chakravarty, *Anatomy of the Raj,* op.cit. and the Hardinge Papers; for Michael O'Dwyer (1864–1940): governor of Punjab, 1913–1919, see *India As I Knew It: 1885–1925,* London, 1925.
28. Harcourt Montague Butler and Malcolm Hailey were able administrators with experience and known for subtle and rich texture of their minds; see Philip Woodruff, *The Men Who Ruled India,* vol. ii, op.cit. Papers of Harcourt Butler and Malcolm Hailey may be examined at the India Office Library. See W.W. Hunter, *The Indian Musalman,* London, 1971; the volumes of the Indian Gazetters prepared under his supervision and the *Rulers of India* series under Hunter's editorship as also N. Gerald Barrier, ed., *The Census in British India,* Delhi,1981. For the role of the Indian census and that of M.C.D. O'Donnell who calculated 'the number of years it would take the Hindus to all together disappear from Bengal if Muhammadens increase went on at the rate it was doing', see, ibid. pp. 91–92 and for the controversy on the Gait Circular, ibid., pp. 92–95. Dunlop Smith

virtually rendered Minto, the viceroy, a helpless victim of his own private secretary; see Martin Gilbert, *Servant of India,* London, 1966, esp. pp. 22–26. Reginald Maxwell and Maurice Hallett were the strongest men during 1942 and were primarily responsible for the suppression of the Quit India movement in U.P. and Bihar. See the papers of Dunlop Smith and Maurice Hallett at the India Office Library and those of Reginald Maxwell at the South-Asian Centre, Cambridge; also see Francis G. Hutchins, *Spontaneous Revolution,* Delhi, 1971, pp. 179–217.

29. For Reginald Craddock's role as a reactionary civil servant there is ample evidence in the Hardinge Papers and Curzon's post-viceregal papers at the India Office Library; also see Reginald Craddock, *The Dilemma in India,* op. cit. For the role of Frank Sly and Montagu Butler in manipulating the politics of Central Provinces and Berar in mid-twenties, see a cautious assessment in D.E.U. Baker, *Changing Political Leadership in an Indian Province,* Delhi, 1979. For R.F. Muddie's handling of an explosive situation in U.P. on the eve of the movement of 1942, see his carefully edited papers at the India Office Library. The papers of Haig are kept in the same library.

30. For Carmichael's governorship of Bengal, the defeat of his line and the triumph of Craddock set against a romantic Bhadralok syndrome, see J.H. Broomfield, *Elite Conflict in a Plural Society: 20th Century Bengal,* op.cit. For Hardinge's diplomatic handling of situations, see Chakravarty, *Anatomy of the Raj,* op.cit. For the support given to Baker on the gradient question by the entire ICS lobby, see the correspondence of Hailey and Keeling with Lutyens in the Lutyens Papers.

31. See for some very extrovert claims—both in Part I (Interviews with Mountbatten) and Part II (Selections of documents) in Larry Collins and Dominique Lapierre, *Mountbatten and the Partition of India March 22 August 15, 1947,* Delhi,1982. For a more rational and judicious assessment, see R.J. Moore, *Escape From Empire: The Attlee Government and the Indian Problem,* Oxford, 1983, esp. pp. 215–89.

32. Louis Broomfield, *The Rain Came,* London, 1938. It may be noted that the volume had ten impressions between February 1938 and August 1938. The vision of India that was stimulated was one of chaos and divisions and the solution that was offered was that of the Empire of England. It was constantly hammered that imperial responsibility involved both bold action undaunted by the public opinion in India or in Britain and constant sufferings and inadequate compensations for those who went over the years to the East to extend the rule of law in a land that was yet to be formally integrated into a nation. The ideal imperial missionary was one who could strike a balance between swift and sharp action and patient and persistent administrative endeavour; see Shamsul Islam, *Kipling's Law,* London, 1975.

33. Harcourt Butler to Hardinge, 3 April 1912, the Hardinge Papers; also see

for the usefulness of Jwala Prasad, F.G. Hutchins, *Spontaneous Revolution,* op.cit., pp. 194–96 especially in view of the perception that 'at the back of the mind of every Hindu officer is the anticipation, and possibly the hope, that a Congress Ministry will return to power'. ibid., p. 196.

34. See three documents: Linlithgow to Amery, 21 January 1942, pp. 44–50; 'The Indian Political Situation, Memorandum by the Secretary of State of India', 28 January 1942, pp. 81–90 and 'The Indian Political Situation, Memorandum by the Lord Privy Seal', 2 February 1942, pp. 110–12—all in N. Mansergh and E.W.R. Lumly, eds., *The Tansfer of Power,* vol. i, London, 1970.
35. David Monteath to Laithwaite, 13 July 1942, *T.O.P.*, London, 1971, vol. ii, p. 676.
36. For Winston Churchill's imperial obduracy and the so-called Churchillean negativism, see R.J. Moore, *Churchill, Cripps and India, 1939–45,* Oxford, 1971 and for Linlithgow's appreciation of the limits of Gandhi's policies and his decision to give Gandhi 'a good deal of rope', see Linlithgow to Glancy, 2 July 1942, *T.O.P.*, op.cit., vol. ii, p. 367. For Amery's close affiliation to Churchill's orthodox conservatism in Indian matters see Amery to Churchill, 13 July 1942, *T.O.P.*, p. 376, vol. ii. For an assessment of Wavell's ineffectiveness, see Larry Collins and Dominique Lapierre, *Mountbatten and the Partition of India,* op.cit.
37. For a graphic picture of the Cripps Mission, the Cripps-Johnson formula and the general excitement of the ICS for the failure of the mission, see G.C. Coupland, *Cripps Mission,* London, 1942; R.J. Moore, *Churchill, Cripps and India,* op. cit.; Horace Alexander, *India Since Cripps,* London, 1943.
38. Amery to Churchill, 13 July 1942, *T.O.P.*, vol. ii. p. 367.
39. George Orwell, *Burmese Days,* op.cit., p. 191.
40. ibid., p. 228.
41. ibid., pp. 225–42 and 244.
42. ibid., p. 136.
43. Edmund Candler, *Youth And East: An Unconventional Autobiography,* London, 1924, pp. 23–24 and 54; *The Unveiling of Lhasa,* op.cit.pp. 70–71; *A Vagabond in Asia,* London, 1900, pp. 24–26; *Sri Ram Revolutionist,* London, 1922 (edn.), pp. 306–07; *The Mantle of the East,* op.cit., pp. 6–15.
44. Lionel Curtis, 'India', n.d., circulated for the moot on 23 July 1917, the R.T.G. Papers.
45. ibid.
46. Buchan to Curtis, 2 June 1916, the R.T.G. Papers.
47. ibid.
48. ibid.
49. ibid.
50. ibid.
51. Chirol to Curtis, 3 June 1917, the R.T.G. Papers.
52. Chirol, 'Memorandum on India', August 1917, the R.T.G. Papers.

53. Chirol to Kerr, 21 November 1916, the R.T.G. Papers.
54. ibid.
55. ibid.
56. ibid.
57. Chirol to Curtis, 3 June 1917, the R.T.G. Papers.
58. Chirol to Kerr, 21 November 1916, the R.T.G. Papers.
59. Chirol to Coupland, 16 October 1916, the R.T.G. Papers.
60. ibid.
61. Chirol to Kerr, 21 November 1916, the R.T.G. Papers.
62. W.S. Marris to James Meston, 13 September 1916, the R.T.G. Papers.
63. ibid.
64. Chirol, 'Memorandum on India', July 1917, the R.T.G. Papers; also W.S. Marris to James Meston, 13 September 1916; Chirol to Curtis, 3 June 1917, the R.T.G. Papers.
65. David Lelyveld, *Aligarh's First Generation: Muslim Solidarity in British India,* Princeton, 1978, esp. pp. 300–48.
66. James Fitzjames Stephen, *Liberty, Equality, Fraternity,* London, 1974 (edn.), esp. pp. 98–99 and 183–239; John Strachey, *India,* London, 1988, pp. 359–60 and 364–66.
67. cf. Eric Stokes, *The English Utilitarian and India,* op. cit., pp. 290–322.
68. Quoted in Lelyveld, *Aligarh's First Generation,* op.cit., p. 218. Also see A.S.E.S. (Sidgwick), *Henry Sidgwick,* op.cit., p. 34; Walter Raleigh, *Laughter From a Cloud,* op.cit.; M. Holroyed, *Lytton, Strachey and Bloomsbury Group,* London, 1971.
69. David Lelyveld, *Aligarh's First Generation,* op.cit., pp. 218–19.
70. Theodore Morison, Foreword in 'An Indian Mahomedan', *British India, From Queen Elizabeth to Lord Reading,* London, 1926, pp. 11–12.
71. ibid., xiv.
72. Lelyveld, *Aligarh's First Generation,* op.cit., pp. 219–27.
73. 'A Note on The Punjab Disturbances and the Hunter Commission's Report', Stanley Reed to MacGregor, 20 February 1920, the Stanley Reed Papers.
74. ibid.
75. ibid.
76. ibid.
77. W.H. Auden, 'The End of the Empire: Partition', in Kenneth Baker, ed., *English History in Verse,* op.cit., p. 420.
78. E.M. Forster, *A Passage to India,* op.cit.
79. cf. Horace Alexander, *India Since Cripps,* London, 1943.
80. Forster's second visit coincided with the non-cooperation movement; see G.K. Das' 'A Passage to India: A socio-historical study' in John Bears', ed., *A Passage to India, Essays in Interpretation,* London, 1985, pp.1–15. E.M. Forster, *The Hill of Devi and Other Indian Writings,* London, 1983, p. 99.
81. Valentine Chirol to MacGregor, 6 April 1920, the Papers of Valentine

Chirol, at *The Times* Archives, London—which are hereafter referred to as the Chirol Papers in this section. These are remarkable documents seeking to locate a new equilibrium of relationship in the British society between the Raj and Indian nationalism from the point of view of a Liberal imperialist who had defended British alliance with Russia, apprehended the possibility of a war with Germany for over two decades and had warned against the pro-German proclivities of some officials of the foreign office, visited India numerous times, had best of relations with several viceroys, written on India from the vantage point of an uncompromising imperialist, maintained working relationship with Gokhale, raised the bogey of the 'yellow peril' and also castigated the massacre at Amritsar and urged upon the secretary of state the dire necessity of a public atonement. In contrast, see Maud Diver, *Far to Seek,* London, 1921 for her unaltered perspective and her megalomaniac arrogance. Also see Maud Diver, *Seige Perilous and Other Stories,* London, 1924.

82. Elizabeth Heine, 'Introduction' to E. M. Forster, *The Hill of Devi and Other Indian Writings* , op.cit., p. 14.
83. cf. ibid., pp. 296–97. For experiencing Hinduism in the company of Masud, see ibid., pp. 176–77 and 296–97; for the profusion of cruelty in India and Hinduism, see ibid., p. 251 and p. 263; for his inability to understand 'the Hindu Mind' and his conclusion that the Hindus 'haven't either the charm or the jollity of the Moslem', p. 275; also for 'Mr. Godbole? What a name!', ibid., p. 203.
84. E.M. Forster, *The Hill of Devi and Other Indian Writings,* op.cit., p.17. For Forster's participation in the Gokul Ashthami, ibid., pp. 60–73; for the description of Dussera, ibid., p. 86; for his impression that India was a muddle, ibid., p. 312; for his preference for Muslim ceremonies to Hindu festivals, ibid., p. 343; for his reading that there was little clear cut in India, ibid., p. 18; for his feeling that there was a total absence of democratic intimacy within the Indian people, ibid., p. 312; for his finding goddess Chamunda of Devas, 'a barbaric vermillion object, not often approached by us', ibid., p. 28; for his description of the temples at Mt. Abu as: 'They were as I expected in effect, though the arrangement surprised: standing each in a small cloister, barbaric equestrian statues of kings who made them in a vestibule. . . . The central shrine, with its cold splendour and elaborate emptiness, bored and amazed: a marvel of patience and not in bad taste. . . . Yet one didn't want to look at it. Is Indian decoration bad or ill-arranged? I cannot decide, but the eye never "dwells". . . Mist and whistling wind alarmed me,' ibid., p. 214.
85. ibid., p.16.
86. cf. Benita Parry, *Delusions and discoveries: Studies on India in the British imagination, 1880–1930*, London, 1972.
87. E.M. Forster, *A Passage to India,* op.cit.
88. In its larger sense, Liberalism is a deep-seated moral attitude which seeks

to analyse and integrate various intellectual, social, religious, political, moral and economic human relationships. Its principal postulate, the spiritual freedom of mankind, upholds a free individual conscious of his capacity for unfettered development and self-expression. It is obvious, therefore, that any attempt to exert artificial pressure or regulation on the individual, is considered as unjustifiable interference on individual's personality and initiative by Liberal ethics and politics. In the process of formulating ideals and objectives, Liberalism offered in Britain the opportunity to a particular political party for harmonious interplay of Liberal opinions on society and politics. Political Liberalism in Britain has been in touch with the past as well as future: it has been able to strike an equilibrium between Conservatism and Radicalism by recognizing the credibility of traditional institutions and the validity of reforms. By the end of the nineteenth century and more particular after the First World War, Liberalism had been, in England as elsewhere, under sustained pressures from both sides of the political spectrum, the economic democratic demands of the Left and the forces of plutocracy from the Right. So far as the brown and black colonies of the British Empire are concerned, Liberalism was a thin cheese paste spread unevenly. By the time Forster decided to come to terms with India, the Liberal discourse of the British colonial establishment had become unsure slogans, not very convincing to the ears of the Liberal spokesmen themselves. Forster's Liberalism thus could take no other form than one of evasion of fundamental issues and moral postures. His *A Passage to India,* deals with fragmented minds, mystifying muddle, uncanny questions and puts on its best argument when it states: '. . . One touch of regret—not the canny substitute but the true regret from heart—would have made him (Ronny) a different man, and the British Empire a different institution'. In his refusal to identify himself with the struggling realities of imperial India, Forster merely blots out his own social and individual face in a mystical fog of personal relationships and walks unsteadily between nothingness and nothingness; cf. Guido De Ruggiero, 'Liberalism', *Encyclopaedia of Social Science,* New York, 1935 (edn.), pp. 435–41 and Ernst Fischer, *The Necessity of Art,* op.cit. and Adolfo Sanchez Vazquez, *Art and Society,* London, 1973, pp. 157–67.

89. cf. E.M. Forster on Mt. Abu op.cit., p. 214 with Edmund Candler, *Mantle of the East,* op.cit. On 31 May 1921, E.M. Forster wrote to Lowes Dickenson: 'In fact I was coming round a little to your view of the Indian or anyhow the Hindu character—that it is unaesthetic. One is starved by the absence of beauty. The only beautiful object I can see is something no Indian has made or touched—the constellation of the Scorpion which now, hangs at night down the sky. I look forward to it as to a theatre or a picture gallery after the constant imperfections of the day'. E.M. Forster, op.cit., p. 52. Add to this Forster's sense of glory for the Raj: 'The Englishman in

India has been trained "in the fine tradition of paternal government" but unable to adjust with changing circumstances', ibid., p. 297. Forster reinforces his conviction: 'In India we have done much good and have a right', and 'our sudden withdrawal would be disastrous,' ibid., p. 343.

90. G.K. Das, 'A Passage to India' in John Bear, ed., *A Passage to India,* op.cit., p. 2.
91. Search for a human understanding between the rulers and the ruled was conditioned by what has been described as moral reluctance. cf. Adolfo Sanchez Vazquez, *Art and Society,* op.cit., pp. 9–16.
92. Andrews to Gokhale, 30 January 1914, the Gokhale Papers; Andrews to Alexander, 1 December 1924, the Menon Papers.
93. Andrews to Hardinge, 5 July 1915, the Hardinge Papers.
94. Robert Byron, *An Essay on India,* London, 1934, pp. 21–24.
95. ibid., p. 22.
96. Edward Thompson, *A Farewell to India,* London, 1931, pp.40–42.
97. ibid., p. 68.
98. ibid., p. 71.
99. ibid., p. 72.
100. ibid., p. 73.
101. ibid., p. 74–75.
102. ibid., p. 82.
103. ibid. p. 85.
104. ibid.
105. ibid., p. 93.
106. ibid., p. 120.
107. ibid., p. 141.
108. Edward Thompson, *A Letter to India,* London, 1932.
109. ibid., p. 14.
110. ibid., p. 15.
111. ibid., p. 18.
112. ibid., pp. 20–22, 26–27 and 30.
113. ibid., pp. 32 and 33–34.
114. ibid., p.40.
115. ibid.pp. 30–31.
116. In a letter to William Rothenstein of 2 April 1927 Tagore wrote: 'From your letter it is evident that you have read Thompson's book about myself. It is one of the most absurd books that I have ever read dealing with a poet's life and writings. All through his pages he has never allowed his readers to guess that he has a very imperfect knowledge of (the) Bengali language which necessarily prevents him from realizing the atmosphere of our words and therefore the colour and music and life of them. He cannot make a distinction between that which is essential and non-essential and he jumbles together details without any consideration for their significance. For those who know Bengali his presentation of the subject is too often

ludicrously disproportionate; he has been a schoolmaster in an Indian school and that comes out in his pages too often in his pompous spirit of self-confidence even in a realm where he ought to have been conscious of his limitations. The book is full of prejudices which have no foundation in fact, as for instance when he insinuates that I lack in my admiration for Shakespeare — or that I have an antipathy against Englishmen. Of course, I have my grievances against the British Government in India, but I have a genuine respect for the English character which has so often been expressed in my writings. Then again, being a Christian missionary, his training makes him incapable of understanding some of the ideas that run through my writings—like that of *Jeevan Devata,* the limited aspect of divinity which has its unique place in the individual life, contrasted to that which belongs to the universe. The God of Christianity has his special recognition as the God of humanity—in Hinduism, in our every day meditation, we try to realize his cosmic manifestation and thus free our soul from the bondage of the limitedness of the immediate; but for us he is also an individual for the individual, working out through our evolution in time, our ultimate destiny. On the whole, the author is never afraid to be unjust, and that only shows his want of respect. I am certain he would have been much more careful in his treatment if his subject were a continental poet in Europe. He ought to have realized his responsibility all the more because of the fact that there was hardly anyone in Europe who could judge his book from his own first hand knowledge. But this has only made him bold and safely dogmatic, affording him impunity when he built his conclusions upon inaccurate data. How I wish you had known Bengali!' William Radice, *Rabindranath Tagore, Selected Poems*, 1985, pp. 7–8.

117. Edward Thompson, *A Letter to India,* op.cit., pp. 37–38 and 40.
118. ibid., p. 48.
119. ibid.
120. Benthall's notings in the diary, 11 March 1940, the Benthall Papers; also see Edward Thompson, *A Letter to India,* op.cit., pp. 44 and 52–53.
121. ibid., pp. 73–74.
122. ibid., pp. 80–83.
123. ibid., pp. 81 and 102–05.
124. Edward Thompson, *The Reconstruction of India,* London, 1933 (edn.), first impression 1930.
125. ibid., pp. 56–57.
126. ibid., p. 67.
127. ibid., pp. 239 and 256.
128. Edward Thompson to Jawaharlal Nehru, 30 October 1936, Papers of Jawaharlal Nehru kept at the Nehru Memorial Museum and Library, New Delhi and which are hereafter referred to as the Nehru Papers in this section.
129. ibid.
130. Thompson to Nehru, 1 November 1936, the Nehru Papers.
131. ibid.

132. ibid.
133. Thompson to Nehru, 24 November 1936, the Nehru Papers.
134. ibid.
135. ibid.
136. ibid.
137. ibid.
138. ibid., also Thompson to Nehru, 6 December 1936, and 3 May 1937, the Nehru Papers.
139. Thompson to Nehru, 6 December 1936, the Nehru Papers.
140. ibid.
141. ibid.
142. 'Thompson on Sunderland'— a note, the Menon Papers. Also see Jabez T. Sunderland, *India in Bondage: Her Right to Freedom,* first Indian impression, 1928.
143. ibid.
144. Nehru to Thompson, 3 December 1936 and 22 April 1937.
145. Nehru to Thompson, the Edward Thompson Papers, Nehru Memorial Museum and Library.
146. F.E. Penny, *The Unlucky Mark,* London, 1909.
147. ibid., pp. 155 and 156.
148. ibid., pp. 156 and 157.
149. Lothian to Nehru, 31 December 1935, the Nehru Papers.
150. ibid.; also see Nehru to Lothian, 17 January 1936.
151. Robert Byron, *An Essay on India,* London, 1951, p. 25.
152. ibid., p. 21.
153. ibid., p. 27.
154. ibid.
155. Jane Ray, *Fascinating India,* London, 1921, p.127.
156. ibid.; also see pp. 32–41 and 64–73.
157. ibid., p.128.
158. ibid.
159. C.F. Andrews, *Zakaullah of Dilli,* London, 1913; E.M. Forster, *A Passage to India,* op.cit. and Edward Thompson, *Farewell to India,* op.cit.
160. Rudyard Kipling, 'His Chance of Life', *Plain Tales from the Hills,* op.cit., pp.77–84.
161. cf. Allen J. Greenberger, *The British Image of India, A Study in the Literature of Imperialism, 1860–1960,* London, 1969, pp. 25 and 64–65.
162. Larry Collins and Dominique Lappierre, *Mountbatten and the Partition of India March 22 August 15, 1947,* Delhi, 1982, pp. 27, 32, 60 and 103.
163. Spear's description of the Indian leaders betrays a sardonic delight that leaves a disagreeable taste behind. As a young teacher of St. Stephen's College, Delhi, Spear had come to know some of the Indian leaders then operating in the assembly chambers in Delhi under the Montford Reforms. The pen-portraits of the Indian leaders in the memoirs of this perceptive historian are startling. In sharp contrast to the impressive aristocratic

manners of Malcolm Hailey, the fluency and lucidity of Charles MacInnes and the 'jolly' good demeanour of a man like A. Muddiman, Spear dismissed Indians summarily with a jocular flourish. Thus Motilal Nehru with his powerful voice and deliberate manners is described as one with 'a sturdy built, rather portly figure clad in immaculate white' and from 'this white surround emerged a square head with a rubicund countenance'. Pandit Madan Mohan Malaviya, his slim autocratic figure and beturband head impressed our young historian but he was quick to proclaim with patronizing condescension that the Pandit was the sheer embodiment of Hindu orthodoxy. Jinnah, still fiercely nationalist, was aloof and quite having Olympian manners; but Spear thought that he was perhaps too snooty and given to survey the world with a lifeless needle. Muhammad Ali was, Spear added, a 'Maulana trapped in Congress snare'. Spear found him too suave to be sincere and too insincere to be noble and hence took an instant dislike of him. Gandhi had just emerged from his twenty-one days' fast and Spear found in C.F. Andrews an 'anxious hen hovering around sick chicken'. A prejudiced Spear decided to find the whole atmosphere around Gandhi most undemocratic. People spoke, Spear wrote, in whispers and sounds were muted. The climate, Spear remembered, 'was more of worship even than of affection and respect'. Margaret and Percival Spear, *India Remembered,* op.cit., pp. 14–15.

164. E.M. Forster, *A Passage to India,* op.cit., pp. 68–135.
165. Rudyard Kipling, 'One Viceroy Resigns', *A Kipling Anthology,* op.cit., pp. 20–21. Inscrutability was a much-advertized characteristic of India and the East in the imperial perception: '. . . Multiply/By twice the Sphinx silence / There's your East/And you're as wise as ever/So am I'. Also see Hilton Brown, *Potter's Clay: Some Stories from South India,* London, 1927, esp. p. 109.
166. Flora Annie Steel, *The Garden of Fidelity,*op.cit., pp. 130–31; also cf. E.M. Forster, *A Passage to India,* op.cit., pp. 204–05.
167. Eric Musaprat, *The Journey Home,* London, 1933, pp. 190–91.
168. Lack of comprehension created ambiguity, fluidity and a superficial freedom from hard, inconvertible facts. Thus fantasy flourished groping for its own basis in illusions away from the necessary connections with real world; cf. Christopher Caudwell, *Studies and Further Studies in a Dying Culture,* New York, 1971, pp. 183–209.
169. Jim Corbett, 'Kunwar Singh', *Jim Corbett's India, Stories Selected by R.F. Hawkins,* Delhi, 1981, pp. 11 and 12–28.
170. Flora Annie Steel, 'Shub'rat', *In the Permanent Way and Other Stories,* London, 1897, p. 1.
171. April Swayne-Thomas, *India Summer,* op.cit.; Margaret and Percival Spear, *India Remembered,* op.cit.,p. 66–67.
172. F.A. Aitken, *Behind the Bungalow,* London, 1895.
173. ibid., p. 158.
174. Alice Perrin, 'The Rise of Ram Din', Saros Cowasjee, ed., *Stories from the*

Raj, op.cit., pp. 127–34.

175. Flora Annie Steel, 'Shub'rat', *In the Permanent Way and Other Stories,* op.cit., p. 1.
176. Flora Annie Steel, 'Salt duty', *The Mercy of the Lord,* London, 1914, p. 15.
177. F.E. Penny, *The Tea Planter,* London, 1909, p. 44.
178. Alice Perrin, 'The Rise of Ram Din', op.cit.
179. Margaret and Percival Spear, *India Remembered,* op.cit.,p. 149.
180. Lockwood Kipling, *Beast and Man in India,* London 1892, pp. 132–40; also Meston to Hardinge, 31 January 1916, the Hardinge Papers; Marris to Meston, 13 September 1916, papers of Malcolm Seton at India Office Library which are hereafter referred to as the Seton Papers in this section. Also see Reginald Craddock, *The Dilemma in India,* op.cit.,pp. 25–36.
181. For the folklore of Puran Bhagat, see, 'The Miracle of Puran Bhagat' in Rudyard Kipling, *Second Jungle Book,* op.cit.
182. Malcolm Darling, *Wisdom and Waste in the Punjab Village,* London, 1924, pp. 347–48.
183. Claud H. Hill, *India-Stepmother,* London, 1929, p. 256; also, Meston's Note, 30 December 1916, James Meston Papers, India Office Library—which are hereafter referred to as the Meston Papers in this section.
184. Aldous Huxley, *Jesting Pilate,* op.cit., p. 56. For the changing perspective of the Ulama in the 18th and 19th centuries, see Barbara Daly Metcalfe, *Islamic Revival in British India: Deoband 1860–1900,* Princeton, 1982.
185. Jim Corbett, 'Loyalty', *Jim Corbett's India,* op.cit., p. 42.
186. *India. Special Number of The Times, February 1930,* London, March 1930, pp. 56–61.
187. Edmund Candler, *The Sepoy,* London, 1919 (this volume is dedicated to Valentine Chirol). For the Gurkhas, see ibid., pp. 1–25.
188. ibid.; for the Sikhs, see ibid., pp. 26–48, esp. 35–36. Candler thought that if the Rajputs had more dash than the Sikhs and thus could be trusted for taking possession of a position in an operation, the Sikh had the backbone to defend it. The Rajput, he argued on the basis of his personal experience, was dry powder like the Arabs and other products of the desert. He was inflammable. The Sikh, on the other hand, he wrote, was the son of the soil: 'He broods', but 'he is a slow fuse'. Edmund Candler, *The Mantle of Asia,* op.cit., p. 131.
189. Candler, *The Sepoy,* op.cit., pp. 49–62.
190. ibid., p. 59.
191. ibid., pp. 63–81.
192. ibid., pp. 92–95.
193. For the Jats, see Candler, ibid., pp. 115–24 and for the Marathas, ibid., pp. 104–14.
194. For the Garhwali, ibid., pp. 138–48, esp. 140 and 143.
195. For the Khataks, the Hazaras and the Santhals, ibid., pp. 149–58 and 159–69. For the Mers, the Ranghars and the Meenas etc., see ibid., pp. 181–87, 188–89, 208–16 and 217–26.

196. ibid., p. 122.

197. The imperial policy for moulding the fighting machine was quite ingenious: 'What are the elements of the follower's sang-froid?. . . In an analysis of the composition of his courage, lack of imagination would play a part, and fatalism, which become a virtue in the presence of death; but the main thing, and this explains two-thirds of his stiffening, is that it never enters his head that it is possible not to carry on with his orders', these sentiments were clotted into one — the sense of order, continuity and everything that is implied in regulation. 'These things are of the laws of necessity. He does not know it but carrying on is his gospel, philosophy and creed'. Candler, ibid., pp. 233 –34.

For the life-style of this effete aristocracy, see Thomas R. Metcalfe, *Land, Landlord and the British Raj,* op.cit., Berkeley, 1977, pp. 341–75; also see the crisis in the *sharif* culture, Lelyveld, *Aligarh's First Generation,* op.cit., pp. 92–101.

198. Maud Diver, *Royal India, A Descriptive and Historical Study of India's Fifteen Princely States,* London, 1942.

199. See, for example, R. Jeffrey, ed., *Peoples, Princes and Paramount Power: Society and Politics in Indian Princely States,* Delhi, 1978, and for a more recent romanticization of the efforts at modernization and the unfulfilled promise owing to the lapse of British paramountcy see Ian Copland, *The British Raj and the Indian Princes,* Delhi, 1982.

200. Maud Diver, *Royal India,* op.cit. For a nostalgic reminiscence of 'Ranjitsinghji of the Gown and Jack Hobbs of the Towns' see M. Ivan, 'Parker's Piece: A Sports-field of Distinction', *Cambridge Review,* June 1983.

201. 'It was John Lawrence (the tutor) who taught him (the prince) how to read and write, not only English, Hindustani but French as well. It was John Lawrence who had opened up for him the whole world, not only of the East and the West. The Englishmen, he knew now, had seen the world with detachment and without passion, not as an Englishman or as anything else, but as a man, pointing out to the Indian boy, whose world had begun and ended with the borders of the half-savage Deccan, the virtues and vices of governments and vast empires and peoples so that it became clear and simple for him to recognize what was just and good. It was John Lawrence who taught him that he was simply a man like all other men, to whom fate had brought a vast responsibility. Out of his own intelligence and goodness, John Lawrence had planted goodness and humility in the boy who one day would become the absolute ruler of twelve million people'. Broomfield, *The Rains Came,* op.cit., pp. 143–44.

202. Maud Diver, *Royal India,* op.cit. Harcourt Butler in 1930 recognized the importance of the native Indian states, 'the most picturesque part of India' and applauded this ancient indigenous system of government which survived the establishment of British dominion on the ruins of the Mughal Empire. Distinguished by persistent loyalty, these states, he argued, were the basis of British hegemony in India. Firm relationship between the states and the paramount power depended on stable treaty obligations and they

should never be transferred to any other arrangement without their expressed will and conviction. See Harcourt Butler, 'The Indian States and the Crown', *India. Special Number of The Times,* 18 February 1930, op.cit.; also see, Penderel Moon, *Strangers in India,* op.cit.,pp. 196–98.

203. Commenting on the training of the princes under the care of the British political agents and the teachers at the Mayo College, Ajmer, Candler underlined that the traditional ruling impulses and culture of the princes had been retained and was being given merely a modern and noble direction. At Mayo College, Ajmer, as elsewhere, Candler thought, British experiment had achieved its purpose. Here, 'certain solar influences are being exposed to the solvent of Western ideals, while certain natural affinities are being given free play'. Candler, *Mantle of Asia,* op.cit., pp. 53–54. The result, Candler vouched, was remarkable. 'The blazor alone was British and the colour of that was national: only the clean Conduit Street cut of it stood for the direction given to a pre-existing bias', ibid., p. 54. Indeed the players at the cricket pavilion of the College seemed to Candler to symbolize the pick of Mayo's products. The boys were not hybrid, he assured, 'but anything the more Rajputs' for the 'subtle and unconscious affining and refining processes which must result from experiments of the kind'. ibid., p. 54.

204. 'The Native Indian State', *Round Table,* 1926, op.cit.

205. Katherine Mayo, *Mother India,* London, 1927, p. 284.

206. ibid.

207. Flora Annie Steel, 'On the Second Story', *In the Permanent Way and Other Stories,* op.cit., p. 43. One cannot overlook the utter contempt shown for the educated babu. He is a liar and a coward—utterly treacherous, ridiculous, and despicable. See him portrayed thus in Flora Annie Steel's *Voices in the Night,* London, 1900; *Miss Stuart's Legacy,* London, 1893; *The Law of Threshold,* London, 1924; and 'The Reformer's Wife', *In the Guardianship of God,* London, 1900. Also see Aldous Huxley, *Jesting Pilate,* op.cit.

208. Sidney Low, *A Vision of India,* London, 1911 (edn.). The book was respectfully recommended by John Morley on 20 July 1914 as a work of proved competence; by Curzon for giving a 'striking picture of Indian life' in all its varied aspects with substantial accuracy and by Charles Crosthwaite, the lieutenant-governor of North-West Provinces as a remarkable work full of information presented in a picturesque shape on the forms and problems of Indian life.

209. Edward Thompson, *A Farewell to India,* op.cit.,p. 11. Flora Annie Steel 'On the Second Story', *In the Permanent Way and Other Stories,* op.cit. Chunnerburty is highly anglicized Bengali Brahmin in Gordan Casserly's *Elephant God,* London, 1920.

210. Sidney Low, *A Vision of India,* op.cit:, ch. xx, pp. 213–29.

211. ibid.

212. See Walter Roper Lawrence, *The India We Served,* op.cit.,pp. 163–64; Reginald Craddock, *The Dilemma of India,* op.cit.,pp. 25–26; Al Carthill, *The Lost Dominion,* London, 1924, pp. 276–78.

213. Edward Thompson, *An Indian Day,* London, 1937, first impression 1927, pp. 34 and 35–44.
214. Vernon George, *The Crown of Asia,* London, 1942. It is instructive to note that the author not only pictured India under the threat of invasion, but also wrote a thrilling tale of how a 'British Secret Agent' penetrated into the inner circles of the Sino-Japanese army and upset their plan of campaign. George asserted that it was in the interest of the British to hold India.
215. E.W. Savi, *The Devil's Playground,* London, n.d. It is a war-time story and the author missed no opportunity to expose the 'wickedness' of Gandhi. The leading Indian lady, Mrs Yusuff Ali Jan, picked on Gandhi as her target: 'The Man is acting as if he is in his dotage. With his knowledge of the world, he cannot possibly think that Hitler can be stopped by passive resistance. He must know that if Britain lost the war, India would fall like a ripe plum into Hitler's hands and who could then measure the depth of the catastrophe to us? Where would be Gandhi and Congress then? Oh. No! No Indian who is sane can willingly subscribe to abstention from cooperation in the war efforts on the side of the Empire; for we might gain our ambitions under the British government, but never under the Nazis'. p.65.
217. Charles Monoly, *Antony Vanroy,* London, 1931, p. 67.
218. E.M. Forster, *A Passage to India,* op.cit.
219. ibid., pp. 72–78.
220. Flora Annie Steel, 'Amor Vincit Omnia', *In the Permanent Way and Other Stories,* op.cit., p. 235.
221. Rudyard Kipling, 'Head of the District', *Life's Handicap,* op.cit.
222. ibid.
223. Rudyard Kipling, 'Wee Willie Winkie: An Officer and a Gentleman', in *Wee Willie Winkie and Other Stories,* London, 1951 (edn.), pp. 273–312.
224. E.M. Forster, 'India Again', *Two Cheers for Democracy,* 1971, p. 324.
225. ibid., p. 325.
226. Lionel Curtis, 'Memorandum on India', September 1917, the R.T.G. Papers; Edmund Candler, *The Mantle of the East,* op.cit.; Aldous Huxley, *Jesting Pilate,* op.cit.; Penderel Moon, *Strangers in India,* op.cit.; Claud Hill, *India-Stepmother,* op.cit.
227. Edwin Lutyens to Emily Lutyens, 14 January 1914, the Lutyens Papers.
228. Rudyard Kipling, 'The Conversion of Aurelian McGoggin', *Plain Tales from the Hills,* op.cit.,p. 107.
229. ibid., p. 108.
230. ibid.
231. Rudyard Kipling, 'The Naulakha', *A Kipling Anthology,* op.cit.,p. 17.
232. The business of the administrator was 'to obey orders and keep abreast of his files, instead of devastating the Clubs with "ism". Rudyard Kipling, 'The Conversion of Aurelian McGoggin', op.cit., p. 110.

Chapter IV

Haughty Arrogance: Recurrent Adjustments

1. Rudyard Kipling, 'The Conversion of Aurelian McGoggin', *Plain Tales from the Hills,* op.cit., p.108.
2. ibid., pp.109 and 110.
3. Rudyard Kipling, 'A Germ Destroyer', ibid., op.cit., p.122.
4. 'Minute by the Lt. Governor of Bengal on the Report of Indigo Commission', 17 December 1880, 431 of The Judicial Deptt., 1860, the Judicial Deptt. Records, National Archives of India, New Delhi. By the beginning of the 1880s, of around two hundred British born indigo planters then in India, over one half were in Bihar and the rest scattered elsewhere in Bengal and in other North Indian provinces. Three main systems of indigo cultivation were in force in the 1890s, namely the *ziraat* system of direct cultivation on factory-occupied land using the factory's hired labour, the *asamiwar* system of cultivation through factory tenants, and a voluntary agreement system utilizing the services of independent ryots and known in Bihar as the *khushki* system. The last system was favoured little by the European planters. It was the *asamiwar* system in which large-scale lawlessness and oppressive methods in the shape of extorted agreements and seizure of ploughs and cattle led to the tied indigo ryots being most abused. The government sympathized with the planters, disinclined to interfere in the planters' maltreatment of the ryot on the grounds of law and order and encouraged the formation of planters' association to look after the situation so that the atmosphere did not become too explosive. By 1905, however, king indigo was dethroned and by 1910 a number of ruined factories offered a melancholy sight. Champaran was the only flicker left of the indigo monarchy. For a general study of indigo planting, see Palit and Chowdhury, *Growth of Commercial Agriculture in Bengal 1757–1900,* Calcutta, 1910, Ch. 3; also see Raymond K. Renford, *The Non-Official British in India to 1920,* Delhi, 1987, Ch. 11.
5. John Browning, superintendent of trade, Hong Kong to Lord Dalhousie, 7 January 1857, Foreign Deptt. Secret Consultations, National Archives of India.
6. Soon after the auctioning of first eight chests of Assam Tea at Mineng Lane, London, Indian tea ceased to be a dream and became a reality. Despite temporary setbacks in 1865, the Assam region recovered soon from the crisis by 1870s and careful management brought prosperity to the industry. Individual enterpreneurs in India and Britain seized the opportunity and the government offered necessary encouragement and protection. Lonely life in wet wilderness with mosquitoes, malaria and coolie-women to provide the necessary company and an occasional get-together of other planters summed up the dehumanizing life of the planters ruling over the defence-

less and poverty-stricken labour force supplied by mushrooming labour-contractors. Labour-poaching, official collaboration and the encouragements of London's commercial and financial interests helped to create and stimulate a profitable Planter's Raj. See for details, Amalendu Guha, *From Planters Raj to Swaraj,* Delhi, 1977; W.H. Ukers, *The Romance of Tea,* New York, 1936 and P. Griffiths, *The History of Tea Industry,* London, 1977.

7. For various exploitative aggrarian systems in Indian rural life that provided the basic support to imperialism and continual movements against exploitation by peasants, see Sunil Sen, *Peasant Movements in India 1920–1950,* Delhi, 1983.
8. Rudyard Kipling, 'A Germ Destroyer', *Plain Tales From the Hills,* op.cit., p.122; Minto was almost a helpless prisoner of Dunlop Smith's efficiency. For the immense power and influence enjoyed by Dunlop Smith, see Martin Gilbert, *Servant of India,* London, 1966, pp. 22–26 and 249–53.
9. ibid., p.123. By and large, despite increasing centralization exercised by the home government over the Indian administration, the viceroy enjoyed a large measure of practical freedom both from the parliamentary criticism and the cabinet control. Besides, the relationship between the secretary of state and viceroy depended to no considerable extent upon the personal equation between the holders of the two offices. See Charles Petrie, *The Life and Letters of Austen Chamberlain, 1914–1937,* London, 1940, vol.ii, p. 31; Martin Gilbert, *Servant of India,* ibid., p. 26.
10. Rudyard Kipling, 'A Germ Destroyer', *Plain Tales From the Hills,* op.cit., p. 123.
11. Rudyard Kipling, 'The Ballad of the East and West', *A Kipling Anthology: Verse,* op.cit., p.4.
12. Rudyard Kipling, 'Beyond the Pale', *Plain Tales From The Hills,* op.cit., p. 171.
13. E.M. Forster, *A Passage to India,* op.cit., p. 161; also see 'The Unrest in India', *Quarterly Review,* 1908.
14. Benthall's entry in the diary, 5 August 1940, the Benthall Papers.
15. Reference may be made to the papers of the Round Table Group, op.cit., for the nationalist load on the official policy with regard to the Montford Reforms; also for Gandhi's impact on the British political initiatives see the instructive letter of Linlithgow to Amery, 21 January 1942, *T.O.P.* vol. 1., op.cit. and Francis G. Hutchins, *Spontaneous Revolution: The Quit India Movement,* op.cit.; D.A. Low, ed., *Congress and the Raj: Facets of the Indian Struggle, 1917–47,* London, 1977; R.J. Moore, *The Crisis of Indian Unity, 1917–1940,* London, 1974; R.J. Moore, *Churchill, Cripps and India, 1939–45,* London, 1979; B.R. Tomlinson, *The Political Economy of the Raj, 1914–1947,* London, 1979; R.J. Moore, *Escape From Empire: The Attlee Government and the Indian Problem,* Oxford, 1983.
16. Lovat Frazer, *India Under Curzon and After,* London, 1910; S. Gopal,

British Policy in India, op.cit., pp. 268–70.

17. Charles Petrie, *The Life and Letters of Austen Chamberlain,* op.cit., vol. ii, p. 97.
18. ibid., pp. 98–99. The Indian Civil Service was the vocation for gentlemen and within it there were conflicts of authority, but it was the logic of expediency and compromise that guided it. The Services had vested interests and often there was a tension between the old regime and new recruits. But if there were limits of resistance of the younger elements, there were also the attractions of the established elite. The challenge of modernity on the part of the Liberal element was met either by dignified retreat on the part of parties concerned or by careful adjustments. This was the rule of the game in this colonial autocracy. Distinguished by privileges, wealth and revering birth-rights and prepared to admit the commoners and even a few Indians, the ICS was imbued with the belief that it had, like the Crown, a special role to play in running the Empire. This basic faith sustained the traits, habits and prejudices of the English colonial nobility. cf. Jonathan Powis, *Aristocracy,* London, 1984; M.L. Brush, *The English Aristocracy: A Comparative Synthesis,* Manchester, 1984.
19. Charles Petrie, *The Life and Letters,* op.cit., p. 98.
20. ibid.
21. ibid., the Ilbert bill was introduced in the parliament during the viceroyalty of Lord Ripon with the aim of extending equal powers to the Indian and European judges. But the introduction of this bill sparked off an agitation in 1883–84 by the Europeans in India, resulting in a compromise by which the principle of racial equality, which the bill aimed to endorse, was dropped. For details, see S.Gopal, *The Viceroyalty of Lord Ripon, 1880–1884,* London, 1953, p.p. 113–66.
22. Rudyard Kipling, 'His Chance of Life', *Plain Tales from the Hills,* op.cit., p.81.
23. Linlithgow to Amery, 21 January 1942, *T.O.P.* vol i., op.cit., pp. 40–50.
24. 'The Indian Political Situation', Memorandum by Lord Privy Seal, 2 February 1942, ibid., pp. 110–12.
25. ibid.
26. ibid.
27. Geoffrey Tyson, *Danger in India,* London, 1932, pp. 1–2 and 50–66.
28. Benthall's entry in the diary, 15 August 1940, the Benthall Papers; Geoffrey Tyson, *Danger in India,*op.cit., pp. 67–85.
29. Geoffrey Tyson, *Danger in India,* ibid., p. 7.
30. ibid., pp. 7–8; also for a similar view after a decade, G.W. Tyson, *Indian Arms for Victory,* Allahabad, 1943.
31. Hilton Brown, 'India and Democracy', *Nineteenth Century,* February 1942, pp. 90–94.
32. 'India: Old and New', *Round Table,* op.cit., pp. 52–80; also Hilton Brown, 'India and Democracy', *Nineteenth Century,* op.cit., pp. 90–94.

33. 'India: Old and New', *Round Table,* op.cit., pp. 52–80.
34. Valentine Chirol, 'Memorandum on India', August 1917, the R.T.G. Papers.
35. James Meston to Lovett, 23 December 1916, the Meston Papers.
36. Marris to James Meston, 13 September 1916, the Seton Papers.
37. ibid.
38. ibid.
39. Marris to Seton, 21 November 1916, the Seton Papers.
40. ibid.
41. Marris to Meston, 13 September 1916, the Seton Papers.
42. 'Note by Claud Hill', 26 June 1917, Papers of Chelmsford, in microfilm at the Nehru Memorial Museum and Library which are hereafter referred to as the Chelmsford Papers in this section. These views were held and popularized for two decades in the official debates. See Hilton Brown, 'India and Democracy', *Nineteenth Century,* op.cit.; Hugh Molson, 'The Cripps Mission to India', *Nineteenth Century,* June 1942, pp. 255–59; W.P. Barton, 'The World War and the Problems of the Defence of India', *Quarterly Review,* January 1942, pp. 199–214; Lionel Howarth, 'United India', *Nineteenth Century,* November 1942, pp. 229–35; A Correspondent in India, 'Indian Freedom' *Fortnightly Review,* 1942, pp. 301–07; also see, Cecilie Leslie, *Goat to Kali,* London, 1942, which is a work of fiction against the background of the historical facts of India between September 1941 and 1942.
43. Butler to Wilson, 7 December 1914, Papers of Harcourt Butler, India Office Library, which are hereafter referred to as the Butler Papers in this section; Meston to Lovett, 23 December 1914, Papers of James Meston, India Office Library, which are hereafter referred to as the Meston Papers in this section.
44. A Correspondent in India, 'Indian Freedom', *Fortnightly Review,* op.cit.; also see Lionel Howarth, 'United India', *Nineteenth Century,* op.cit.
45. Hilton Brown, 'India and Democracy', *Nineteenth Century,* op.cit.
46. See for example Hugh Molson, 'The Cripps Mission to India', *Nineteenth Century,* op. cit.; W.P. Barton, 'The World War and the Problems of the Defence of India', op.cit.; William P. Barton, 'The Viceroy's Council and Indian Politics', *Fortnightly Review,* 1942, pp.109–15. Probably, some sensitive members of the imperial power-elite in India tended to visualize themselves and present the symbols of their power, wealth and privileges in terms of what their native predecessors had established as standard behavioural patterns. But even in this somewhat tortuous and farcical imitative process, they were excluded both by history and necessity of the corresponding initiatory mechanisms. One thing that they could not afford to do was to present themselves as the old nobility. Crude assertions and brutal claims became, as a result, the necessary ingredients of the official discourse of the Raj. Both newspapers and journals portrayed the different

dimensions of the dominant discourse of the Raj and often official discourses were disguised editorially. Nevertheless, they constituted a concerted positive and manipulative intervention formulating and classifying the needs and requirements of imperialism. Often, the media offered the spectacle of a vast emporium of didactic discourse and counter-discourse. Often, the very colourlessness of the emporium rendered it very seductive, making its impact almost compelling owing to its widely popular diffusion. To the parties and individuals in public life, adequately sensitised knowledge was presented as 'objective' truth and over the years British statesmen, intellectuals, thinkers and children were taught about politics, religion, economy, fine arts, philosophy and literature of India amidst a vast monumental stupidity and ignorance; cf. Richard Terdiman, *Discourse / Counter Discourse: The Theory and Practice in Nineteenth Century France,* London, 1985 and Eric, J. Hobsbawm, *Age of Revolution,* London, 1962, pp. 218–19.

47. A Correspondent of India, 'Indian Freedom', *Fortnightly Review,* op.cit.
48. ibid., p. 309; also Hugh Molson, 'The Cripps Mission to India', *Nineteenth Century,* op. cit., p. 208.
49. Lionel Howarth, 'United India', part II, *Nineteenth Century,* op.cit.
50. Hilton Brown, 'India and Democracy', *Nineteenth Century,* op. cit., p. 91.
51. Lionel Howarth, 'United India', *Nineteenth Century,* op.cit.; also see George Schuster and Guy Wint, *India and Democracy,* op.cit.,pp. 57–65.
52. W.P. Barton, 'The Deadlock in India and the Indian States', *Quarterly Review,* July 1943, pp. 16–27.
53. Lord Willingdon, 'Speech at the East India Association', *Asiatic Review,* October 1941; also see, *Quarterly Review,* June 1941, p. 273.
54. W.P. Barton, 'The Deadlock in India and the Indian States', op.cit.
55. ibid.
56. ibid.
57. ibid.
58. George Dunbar, *India at War: A Record and Review: 1939–1940,* London, 1941, pp. 36–45; the gradual transformation of Leonard Woolf during his colonial career in Ceylon into an anti-imperialist spokesman is instructive and the story of this remarkable metamorphosis has been recalled by many including Goonetilleke, see D.C.R.A. Goonetilleke, *Images of the Raj,* op.cit., p. 58. It is, however, not difficult to locate that an element of racist paternalism lingered on in Woolf's sensibility despite superficial conversion. Leonard retained a firm faith that the subject people would be best served by the administration of the western educators. The programme of fostering colonial self-government, he thought, could only be achieved through the imperial structure. He detested the colonisers but admired the civil servants. He protested against the loss of sovereignty of the native community but at the same time applauded the extension of *Pax Britannica* which checked the speculative tyranny of the private companies. For a

sensitive Leonard Woolf it might not have been agreeable to be considered by the highly accomplished Tamil association of Jaffna as a 'superior breed' with a riding whip to assert the white man's burden, but it was more traumatic for him to discover that in the poor district of Hambantota he merely invited the hatred of the local population for pursuing official orders to quarantine draught animals. 'For I have no more desire to be God than one of his victims'. See Leonard Woolf, *Growing: An Autobiography of the Years 1904–1911*, London, 1967 (edn.), pp.113–14 and 187–94. True, there was an aesthetic alienation of Woolf from imperialism and this sentiment is pellucid and persistent in all his works on the East especially so in his novel, *The Village in the Jungle*, London, 1966, (edn.). But it is significant to note that this alienation was an instinctive and emotional protest and not a rational and well-grounded repudiation of imperialism. He was appalled by his own perception that white men lived, at worst, alienated, grotesque lives in Ceylon as elsewhere in the Raj, whereas the Sinhalese, Tamils and Moors were in perfect harmony with their environment. All the same he was equally convinced of the blessings of a rational imperial government and that its injunctions, with occasional personal lapses, were conducive to the welfare of the people. Operating amidst a dull, superstitious, ignorant, fatalist and poor world, Woolf was inclined to agree with Orwell that the determined English officer was bound to be authoritarian and that futility was inevitable in the jumble of seperations of the East.

59. ibid.; also see Verney Lovett, 'Indian Politics, 1940–41', *Quarterly Review*, June 1941, pp. 256–73.
60. Edward Thompson, *A Letter From India*, op.cit.; also see Valentine Chirol, 'Indian Problem', 4 October 1928, *The Times Literary Supplement*, London.
61. Robert Byron, *An Essay on Indian Question*, op.cit.
62. Edward Thompson, *Reconstruction of India*, op.cit.
63. Verney Lovett, 'Indian Politics, 1940–41', op. cit.
64. ibid.
65. Lionel Howarth, 'United India', *Nineteenth Century*, op.cit.
66. Hilton Brown, 'India and Democracy', *Nineteenth Century*, op.cit.
67. Hamish Blair, *1957*, London, 1929.
68. Hamish Blair, *Governor Hardy*, London, 1931.
69. John Masters, *To the Coral Strand*, op.cit., p. 157.
70. Cunningham, *Chronicle of Dustypore*, op.cit.
71. ibid.
72. Al Carthill, *Madampur*, London, 1931, p. 39.
73. ibid., pp. 39–40 and 326–27.
74. Charles Petrei, *The Life and Letters of Austen Chamberlain*, op.cit., vol.ii, p. 380.
75. ibid.

76. George Schuster and Guy Wint, *India and Democracy,* op.cit.,p. 57.
77. cf. Edward Thompson, *The Reconstruction of India,* op.cit.,pp. 259–66; also see E.M. Forster, *A Passage to India,* op.cit.,p. 93.
78. F. Yeats-Brown, *Bengal Lancer,* London 1930, p. 122.
79. Edward Thompson, *Farewell to India,* op.cit., p. 24.
80. E.M. Forster, *A Passage to India,* op.cit., p. 108.
81. John Masters, *Bhawani Junction,* London, 1954, p. 152. The imperial pride survived the Raj, see Masters, *Thunder at Sunset,* London, 1974, and Jon Godden, *The Peacock,* London, 1954.
82. S. Chakravarty, *Anatomy of the Raj,* op.cit.,p. 103.
83. Hardinge to Carmichael, 10 January 1913, the Hardinge Papers.
84. S. Chakravarty, *Anatomy of the Raj,* op.cit.,pp. 95–106.
85. ibid., pp. 107–10.
86. Culled from David Page, *Prelude to Partition,* Delhi, 1980, pp.73–140. The Raj manoeuvred the political situation in such a way as to make the communal question a matter of calculation of the imperial high policy. And it was primarily done for the sake of the self-interest of the few thousand Europeans who ruled the vast continent. The situation demanded constant watchfulness and manipulation. See ibid., p.263.
87. Maurice Hallett to Linlithgow, 16 June 1942, *T.O.P.,* London, 1971, vol. ii, pp. 220–22.
88. ibid
89. ibid., p. 221.
90. ibid.
91. ibid. 'The Muslims are undoubtedly the strongest and the best organised minority community in India. Though treated by Sir Stafford Cripps with far greater respect than other organisations, the Muslim League felt that whatever might be their answer to the British offer, a final decision would rest wholly and solely on the manners in which the Congress reacted. This accounts for the reply of the Muslim League, refusing the offer, being delayed till the Congress refusal was in Sir Stafford Cripps' hand'.
92. The Revd. J. McKenzie to Linlithgow, 29 December 1942, *T.O.P.*, vol. i. op.cit., pp. 172–75.
93. 'It is not only Congress leaders who have been influencing the students in this way. I have reason to believe that in many Colleges influences are at work, even from the side of the teachers, that are leading to hatred and contempt of the British. . . There is among the students very little political thinking, and very little orderly discussion of political questions, but one is conscious of the existence of a great store of violent emotion which can be drawn upon and exploited by designing people. Argument has been given place to angry assertion and ridicule. It is surprising and distressing to find that this spirit has spread even to circles that one has accustomed to think as temperate and loyal'. ibid., p. 173; also see M. Hallett to Linlithgow, 16 June 1942, *T.O.P.*, op.cit., vol.ii, p. 222.

94. Sharaf Athar Ali to P.C. Joshi, 17 May 1942 (intercepted) *T.O.P.*, vol. ii, pp. 128–132; A. Hope to Linlithgow, 23 July 1942. *T.O.P.*, op.cit., vol. ii, pp. 441–44; R. Lumley to Linlithgow, 24 April 1942, *T.O.P.*, op.cit., vol. i, pp. 846–47.
95. Maurice Hallett to Linlithgow, 16 June 1943, *T.O.P.*, op.cit., vol. ii, p. 222.
96. For Roosevelt's plan for the solution of Indian problem, see Note by Graham Spry of an interview with the President, 15 May 1942, *T.O.P.*, op.cit., vol. ii, pp. 89–92; G.S. Bajpai to the Government of India, 17 July 1942, *T.O.P.*, vol. ii, pp. 401–02; R. Campbell to A. Cadogan, 5 August 1942, *T.O.P.*, vol. ii, pp. 579–80; Linlithgow to Amery 12 July 1942, *T.O.P.*, op.cit., vol. ii, pp. 426–28; Linlithgow to Amery, 21 September 1942, *T.O.P.*, op.cit., vol. ii, pp. 1003–05; 'India as factor in Anglo-American relations', *T.O.P.*, vol. ii, pp. 471–73.
97. Linlithgow to Amery, 1 February 1943, *T.O.P.*, vol. iii, pp. 568–69. 'Meanwhile I have discussed with Hallett and find him very strongly in favour of my own earlier view from which as you know I have never wavered that Gandhi, if he desired to do so, should be allowed on his own responsibility to starve to death. I have now thought it well to consult all Governors again as to the reactions to allowing him to fast unto death in confinement, releasing him when in immediate danger to death, or cat and mouse. . . .' The policy meant releasing Gandhi as soon as his life was in danger in order to avoid the risk of his dying as a state prisoner. Under the plan, if after release, Gandhi abandoned his fast and recovered his health, he would again be arrested unless he publicly denounced any intention of promoting a mass movement. See Linlithgow to Amery, 2 February 1943, *T.O.P.*, op.cit., vol. iii, pp. 570–71.

    In 1928 senior industrial and trade union leaders held joint discussions with a view to promoting industrial cooperation and efficiency. This 'cooperative' spirit came to be known as Mond-Turneism after the leaders of the two delegations to the discussions — Sir Alfred Mond representing the industrial houses and Ben Turner leading the trade unions. For details see Henry Pelling, *A History of British Trade Unionism*, London, 1963, pp. 187–90.
98. Jon Clark, Margot Heinemann, David Margolies and Carole Snee, eds., *Culture and Crisis in Britain in the Thirties*, London, 1979, esp. pp. 13–36.
99. ibid., pp. 16–22; also see Robin Skelton, ed., *Poetry of the Thirties*, 1965, pp. 13–38.
100. V.K. Krishna Menon, 'Note on the Round Table Conferences', 13 May 1934, the Menon Papers.
101. ibid.
102. ibid.
103. ibid.
104. ibid.
105. ibid.

106. *The Islington Gazette,* 8 December 1931, the Menon Papers.
107. ibid.; also see the reply by J.W. Poynter in *The Islington Gazette,* 11 December 1931, the Menon Papers.
108. Laurence Housman to Krishna Menon, 9 January 1932, the Menon Papers.
109. ibid.
110. Revd. F. Arthur Wenyon to Barbara Macnamara, 10 February 1932, the Menon Papers.
111. ibid.
112. Minutes of a discussion with George Lansbury, April 1932, the Menon Papers.
113. ibid.
114. Minutes of a 'Reception of Mahatma Gandhi at Mr Horrabin's House', 3 December 1931, the Menon Papers.
115. ibid., pp. 2–4 and 17.
116. ibid., p. 12.
117. ibid., pp. 27–28.
118. ibid., pp. 6–8.
119. ibid., p. 9.
120. Harold J. Laski, 'India at the Crossroads', n.d., the Menon Papers.
121. ibid., p. 1.
122. ibid., pp. 2–3.
123. ibid., p. 3.
124. ibid.
125. ibid.
126. ibid.
127. ibid., p. 7.
128. ibid.
129. ibid., pp. 5–6
130. ibid., p. 21.
131. ibid., p. 19.
132. ibid., p. 20.
133. ibid., pp. 20–21.
134. It may be instructive to examine the position of the die-hard imperialists in relation to India in the early 1930s in Lilian A. Underhill's *Liberty For India,* London, 1932.
135. Minutes of a 'Reception of Gandhi at Mr Horrabin's House', op.cit.,p. 14.
136. ibid.
137. ibid.
138. ibid.
139. A small collection of the papers of Horace Alexander is kept in the Nehru Memorial Museum and Library. Although the collection is by no means exhaustive, the correspondence of C.F. Andrews and Agatha Harrison are revealing and informative which hereafter are referred to as the Alexander Papers in this section.

140. Horace G. Alexander, 'Friends and India', 2 January 1942, issued by *The Friends Committee,* the Alexander Papers.
141. See, the Alexander Papers.
142. Horace Alexander, 'Friends and India', op. cit.
143. Horace Alexander, 'India', *New Statesman and Nation,* 14 April 1934, the Alexander Papers.
144. See Horace Alexander, *India Since Cripps,* op.cit.
145. Horace Alexander, 'Jawaharlal Nehru, A Study', *The Friends,* 14 February 1936, the Alexander Papers.
146. Horace Alexander, 'Friends and India', op.cit.
147. ibid.
148. Agatha Harrison to Horace Alexander, 3 September 1931, the Alexander Papers.
149. 'India and the World Peace', summary of a talk given by C.F. Andrews before the American Friends Service Committee in Philadelphia, 5 December 1929, the Alexander Papers.
150. ibid.
151. ibid.
152. ibid.
153. ibid.
154. Wedgwood Benn to Horace Alexander, 23 January 1931, the Alexander Papers.
155. Private Secretary, Viceroy of India to Horace Alexander, 18 October 1931, the Alexander Papers.
156. C.F. Andrews to Ramsay MacDonald, 24 June 1931, the Alexander Papers.
157. ibid.
158. ibid.
159. ibid.
160. ibid.
161. ibid.
162. ibid.
163. ibid.; also see C.F. Andrews to Mahatma Gandhi, 26 June 1931, the Alexander Papers.
164. Alexander to Andrews, 25 November 1931, the Alexander Papers.
165. Agatha Harrison to Horace Alexander, 20 November 1931, the Alexander Papers.
166. Alexander to Andrews, 26 November 1931, the Alexander Papers.
167. Agatha Harrison to Horace Alexander, 9 December 1931, the Alexander Papers.
168. Malcolm MacDonald to Horace Alexander, 4 December 1931, the Alexander Papers.
169. ibid.
170. ibid.
171. Malcolm MacDonald to Horace Alexander, 10 December 1931, the

Alexander Papers.

172. Irwin to Horace Alexander, 18 December 1931, the Alexander Papers.
173. Irwin to Horace Alexander, 2 February 1932, the Alexander Papers.
174. Agatha Harrison to Horace Alexander, April 1932, the Alexander Papers.
175. ibid.
176. ibid.
177. ibid.
178. ibid.
179. Agatha Harrison to Horace Alexander, March 1932, the Alexander Papers.
180. ibid.
181. Agatha Harrison to Horace Alexander, 7 March 1932, the Alexander Papers.
182. ibid.
183. ibid.
184. ibid.
185. Agatha Harrison to Horace Alexander, 26 March 1932, the Alexander Papers.
186. ibid.
187. ibid.
188. Agatha Harrison to Horace Alexander, April 1933, the Alexander Papers.
189. ibid.
190. Agatha Harrison to Horace Alexander, April 1932, the Alexander Papers.
191. ibid.
192. ibid.
193. ibid.
194. Agatha Harrison to Horace Alexander, September 1932, the Alexander Papers.
195. Agatha Harrison to Horace Alexander, 13–14 September 1932 and Agatha Harrison to Horace Alexander, 18 September 1932, the Alexander Papers.
196. Agatha Harrison to Horace Alexander, 24 September 1932, the Alexander Papers.
197. ibid.
198. Agatha Harrison to Horace Alexander, September 1932, the Alexander Papers.
199. Agatha Harrison to Horace Alexander, 24 September 1932, the Alexander Papers.
200. ibid.
201. Agatha Harrison to Horace Alexander, April 1933, the Alexander Papers.
202. ibid.
203. ibid.
204. ibid.
205. ibid.
206. Agatha Harrison to C.F. Andrews and Horace Alexander, May 1933, the Alexander Papers.

207. Agatha Harrison to Horace Alexander, 11 May 1933, the Alexander Papers.
208. ibid.
209. ibid.
210. Agatha Harrison to Horace Alexander, 9 June 1934, the Alexander Papers.
211. ibid.
212. ibid.; Reporting on the tangle between the Government of India and the Congress regarding the plague situation in Borsad, Agatha wrote in September 1935 to Mahadev Desai: '. . . I must say that when I got that Borsad material, and copied it, I felt that neither the Government nor the Congress came out well in what was said. It is all so tragic. It showed of course the gulf that exists between them both—and in a way, how each tries to score off the other. It all seemed as though in the midst of the conflicting opinion, the main issue—that of human need might be lost sight of by both sides in the controversy. . .' Agatha Harrison to Horace Alexander, 14 October 1935, the Alexander Papers. In another letter in October 1935, Agatha wrote that she felt Nehrū discounted the importance of the efforts at conciliation and would have 'shut the door' and in yet another letter in October 1935, she wrote: 'Fancy J.N. and Masani thinking that I had in mind the discussion of "amiable trivialities"! I don't think that either of them were being very imaginative'. On 30 March 1935, the letter of Agatha Harrison to Horace Alexander laid bare the sharp differences of opinion between Polak and Agatha. In view of the realities of the situation, Agatha pointed out: 'Whereas as I see it, we have a responsibility in trying to find out what we can do. Bearing in mind the fact that some of us have a human touch with men like Nehru and the Mahatma—and that they trust us. . . it may be necessary to say something to them. You will have seen Mr Gandhi's interview with the *Daily Herald* correspondent. I'm pondering on a cable to him—that might run something like this — "You will find a more excellent way than the sword."' the Alexander Papers.
213. Agatha Harrison to Horace Alexander, 1 February 1934, the Alexander Papers.
214. Agatha Harrison to Carl Heath and Horace Alexander, 15 January 1931, the Alexander Papers.
215. ibid; also for the suspicion caused by Menon as Jawaharlal Nehru's agent in London, Agatha Harrison to Horace Alexander, 9 February 1936, the Alexander Papers.
216. Agatha Harrison to Horace Alexander, 9 February 1936, the Alexander Papers.
217. Agatha Harrison to Horace Alexander, April 1934, the Alexander Papers.
218. ibid.
219. Irwin to Horace Alexander, 10 August 1941, the Alexander Papers.
220. Horace Alexander to Irwin, 18 August 1941, the Alexander Papers.
221. Irwin to Horace Alexander, 3 September 1941, the Alexander Papers.

222. Reginald Coupland, *Cripps Mission,* London, 1943; Reginald Coupland, *Indian Politics,* London, 1943, pp. 285–87; also Reginald Coupland to Horace Alexander, 14 May 1943, the Alexander Papers.
223. David Owen to Horace Alexander, 17 January 1944; Agatha Harrison to Horace Alexander, 28 January 1944, both in the Alexander Papers.
224. For the apprehension of Gandhi's loneliness, see Agatha Harrison to Horace Alexander, 10 June 1937, the Alexander Papers.
225. Even as early as 1937, they had been drifting away from *The Friends,* see Agatha Harrison to Horace Alexander, 10 June 1937, the Alexander Papers.
226. ibid.
227. ibid. Agatha Harrison to Horace Alexander, 17 January 1944, the Alexander Papers; also see an interesting letter on Indian politics by T.G. Spear to Horace Alexander, 17 April 1935, the Alexander Papers.
228. Horace Alexander to Agatha Harrison, 19 September 1943, the Alexander Papers.
229. 'Private Discussion Meeting held on 9 March 1944', Speaker: Horace Alexander, in the presence of Sir Frederick Whyte, A. Yusuf Ali, Lionel Aird, Lady Barlow, Sir William Barton, Sir Frank Brown, A.H. Byrt, Lt. John Cartland, Sir John Claque, Sir Malcolm Darling, Miss Agatha Harrison, A.V. Hodson, Col. D.J.P. Kelly, A.D.K. Owen, Dr Alice Pennell, Sir John Pratt, Miss C.G.K. Scovell, Robert Stokes, Miss Mary Trevelyan, S.H. Wood, Hon. H.A. Wyndham, Miss Margaret Cleeve, Mrs Margaret Cornell, E. Penderel Moon etc. The Alexander Papers.
230. ibid.
231. ibid.
232. ibid.
233. ibid.
234. ibid.
235. ibid.
236. ibid.
237. ibid.
238. ibid.
239. ibid.
240. ibid.
241. ibid.
242. ibid.
243. For the impact of 'Churchillism' and its impact on British policy from 1939 to 1945, see a readable and densely documented work, R.J. Moore, *Churchill, Cripps and India, 1939–1945*, London, 1979.
244. J.H. Muirhead, 'What Imperialism Means', *Fortnightly Review,* August 1900, pp. 177–87.
245. ibid., p. 184.
246. ibid ; also see 'The Ethics of the Empire', *Round Table,* June 1918, pp.

448–501.

247. J.H. Muirhead, 'What Imperialism Means', op.cit.
248. ibid.
249. ibid.
250. Charles Petrie, *The Life and Letters of Austen Chamberlain,* op.cit.,p. 40.
251. Also see Penderel Moon, *Strangers in India,* op.cit., pp. 89–90.
252. Suhash Chakravarty, *Anatomy of the Raj,* op.cit., pp. 112–113.
253. J.H. Muirhead, 'What Imperialism Means', op.cit.
254. Rudyard Kipling, 'Lipeth', *Plain Tales from the Hills,* op.cit., pp. 1–22; F.F. Sherwood, 'The Conversion of Allah Ditta', *Five Indian Tales,* London, 1925, pp. 139–60.
255. F.F. Sherwood, 'A Pair of Cuff-Links', ibid., pp. 47–68.
256. F.F. Sherwood, 'Nathu Chamar', ibid., pp. 71–111.
257. F.F. Sherwood, 'De Profundis', ibid., pp. 15–44.
258. 'The Ethics of Empire', *Round Table,* op.cit.
259. S. Chakravarty, *Anatomy of the Raj,* pp. 111–14.
260. See *The Report of the Lindsay Commission,* op.cit.; also see 'Minutes of the Governing Body', St. Stephen's College 1935–36 Records, St. Stephen's College, Delhi, Courtesy, Dr John Hala.
261. Victor Dane, *Naked Ascetic,* London, 1933, p. 241.
262. Edmund Candler, *Sri Ram Revolutionist: A Transcript From Life, 1907—1910,* London, 1912.
263. ibid., pp. 3, 12, 36, 37, 86, 87 and 88.
264. ibid., pp. 306–08.
265. ibid., pp. 294–96.
266. F.E. Penny, *A Love Tangle,* London, 1916, p. 101.
267. 'Oriental instinct and European training were like oil and water; they succeeded in mingling no better than those two inimical elements. East was distinct and separate even in its most infinitesimal form'. ibid. p. 87.

Chapter V

In Retrospect

1. The most sympathetic, though somewhat extravagant interpretation of the Indian resurgence by a Western observer can be seen in Romain Rolland *The Life of Ramakrishna,* Calcutta, 1929 esp. sections entitled, 'To My Western Reader', pp. 4–14; 'The Builders of Unity: Ram Mohan Roy, Devendranath Tagore, Kesab Chandra Sen, Dayananda', pp. 92–145 and 'Ramakrishna and the Great Shepherd of India', pp. 147–70; for the impact of the movement in the fields of literature and painting, see some interesting insights in the extremely readable volume, James H. Cousins, *The Renaissance in India,* Madras, 1918. The significant feature of the perspective of the author is that he did not deal with his Indian theme 'as

retrospective and finished but as a contemporary phenomenon and, therefore, happily incomplete'.

2. For the myopic imperial vision and fragmented Indian images, see *Report of the Commission on Christian Education in India,* op.cit., pp. 43–50. cf. Cecilie Leslie, *Goat to Kali,* op. cit., for the social, cultural and intellectual portrayal of modern India between 1941–1942 in conformity with imperial perceptions; for the 'perplexing' eternal 'paradoxes' of India, see Edmund Taylor, *Richer By Asia,* London, 1948.
3. *Report of the Commission on Christian Education in India,* op.cit., pp. 54–55.
4. Stanley Jones, *The Christ of the Indian Road,* London, 1925.
5. ibid., pp. 6–7. Strangely enough, even the potential similarities between European and non-European responses to Christian ethics were dismissed as irrational and unfounded. The imperial mind questioned the traditional Christian belief in the spiritual equality of white and non-white people. Ronny of *A Passage to India* approved of religion 'as long as it endorsed the National Anthem, but he objected when it attempted to influence his life'. He declined to entertain his mother's old-fashioned arguments that 'God has put us on the earth to love our neighbours and to show it, and He is omnipresent, even in India, to see how we are succeeding'. E.M. Forster, *A Passage to India,* op.cit., p.51. Imperialism implanted a profound antipathy towards the black race. The native converts' ideas of Christianity were made to appear fairly hollow and their attraction to Church too materialistic. These nominal Christians, it was added, were worse than the outright heathens and avowed 'scoffers' and 'sceptics'. There was a widespread suspicion of the futility of marginal conversion. As the enthusiasms of evangelical circles at home waned, both government and missionaries in India were dovetailed in an integrated imperial assault. The missionaries became involved in the power structure of the colonial situation and found it difficult to distinguish between Christianity and culture. See 'Contact between Settlers and Native People', in A. Lemen and N.C. Pollack, *Studies in Overseas Settlement and Population,* London, 1980, pp. 81–102; *Report of the Commission on Christian Education in India,* op.cit. Also see William Robinson, *By Temple Shrine and Lotus Pool,* op.cit., for the advocacy of uncompromising opposition to Hinduism, its deceptive 'reforms' and its professed goals. 'Take it how you may, call it all you will—high, low, new, old, pure or impure, worship or pure intelligence or worship of all that is vile, you find Hinduism illusive as the mirage of an African desert, yet as ponderable as the solid earth', ibid., p. 49. Robinson repudiated all attempts to accommodate reformed and eclectic Hinduism.
6. Stanley Jones, *The Christ of the Indian Road,* op.cit., pp. 207–08.
7. ibid.
8. Orientalism, as Edward W. Said put it, served over two centuries the

ideological demands of imperialism. As an influential political and academic tradition, it inherited a weighty legacy. Under this somewhat nebulous idiom, stressed by military adventures, natural historians, commercial enterprises, official despatches, travellers, exotic adventures, fiction writers, there developed a powerful doctrine that fashioned the trends of Europe's imperial discourse. Its primary function was to emphasize the nuances of a mysterious and unpredictable Oriental character, the absoluteness of Oriental despotism, the grossness of Oriental sensuality, the queer absence of rationality in Oriental imagination, the profusion of decoration in the Oriental art and the inert immobility of Oriental social stability. The Eastern world was seething with incoherent power, unorganized intelligence and sudden violent eruptions. Sylvain Levy, the president of the Society Asiatique between 1928–1935, with all his expressed humanity and compassion for the fellow Asiatics, counselled patient endeavour on the part of the West as a superior civilization and advised it not to push the East on to a crisis point owing to inherent jealousy and rancour. T.E. Lawrence thought that as a White expert he could assume the role of an Oriental prophet giving shape to the upsurge in the new Asia. The Arabs of Duncan MacDonald and the Indians of Rudyard Kipling were the 'childish primitives', while the Westernized ones were obstinate Orientals involved in a great conspiracy against the Western supremacy much before the task of reconstruction was complete. To Chirol and most of the European experts on Orientalism, there was no room for rapprochement between the white West and the coloured East, while Curzon, Cromer and Lugard, spoke in the same imperial lingua franca and upheld resolutely the undisturbed rule of the West over the East. The establishment of the School of Oriental and African Studies was hailed by Curzon as the necessary furniture of the Empire; see, Edward W. Said, *Orientalism,* op.cit.; Evelyn Baring Cromer, *Modern Egypt,* London, 1908; George Nathaniel Curzon, *Subjects of the Day: Being a Selection of Speeches and Writing,* op.cit.; David Garnett, *The Letters of T.E. Lawrence of Arabia,* London, 1938; Valentine Chirol, *The Occident and the Orient,* Chicago, 1924; Alan Sandison, *The Wheel of Empire: A Study of Imperial Idea in Some Late Nineteenth and Early Twentieth Century Fictions,* New York, 1967.

9. For the impact of the doctrine of Orientalism on the Marxist concept of the Asiatic mode of production, see Bryan S. Turner, *Marx and the end of Orientalism,* London, 1978.
10. Edward W. Said, *Orientalism,* op.cit., pp. 39–40, 45–49, 227–30, 269–70 and 300–09; also see Bryan S. Turner, *Marx and the End of Orientalism,* op.cit., pp. 82–83.
11. For Marx's formulation of the Asiatic mode of production, see Karl Marx, *A Contribution to the Critique of Political Economy,* Moscow, 1970, p. 21; *Capital,* Moscow, 1954, vol. i, pp. 79–80; *The First Indian War of Independence,* Moscow n.d., pp. 16, 33, and 161–63.

12. Hegel's *Phenomenology of Spirit,* translated by A.V. Miller with an analysis of the text and foreword by J.N. Findlay, Oxford, 1979, pp. 104–38.
13. 'Independence and Dependence of Social Consciousness: Lordship and Bondage', ibid., pp. 111–19. For Hegel's idea of the dreaming, unregulated fancy of the Hindu mind, lack of objectivity in the Hindu culture, its inability to comprehend its own individuality, its wild frenzy of sensuous excesses, the typical form of Hindu pantheism of imagination and not of thought, the irrationality of Hindu aesthetics, the immeasurable extension of Hindu images, the inflated enormity of Hindu religious forms reflecting a certain feeling of uncanniness, excesses and unstable movements despite some elements of tenderness, see Partha Mitter, *Much Maligned Monsters, History of European Reaction to Indian Art,* Oxford, 1977, pp. 208–20. For Christian-heathen and civil-savage dichotomies in the colonial societies, see the stimulating work, George M. Fredrickson, *White Supremacy: A Comparative Study in American and South African History,* Oxford, 1981, op.cit., pp. 98–99.
14. James Mill, *The History of British India,* London, 1820, vol. ii, p.135; also see J.S. Mill, *Autobiography,* Harold J. Laski, ed., London, 1949, pp. 23–24.
15. James Mill, *History,* op.cit., pp. 137, 166–67, 186 and 195.
16. See G.C. Trevelyan, *Life and Letters of Lord Macaulay,* London 1908; James Mill, *The History of British India,* esp. vol. ii, pp. 120–80 op.cit.; J.S. Mill, *Autobiography,* op.cit.; James Fitzjames Stephen, *Liberty, Equality and Fraternity,* London, 1874; also see the remarkable synthesis in Eric Stokes, 'The Utilitarian Legacy', *English Utilitarians and India,* op.cit., pp. 234–322.
17. L. Stephen, *Life of Sir James Fitzjames Stephen,* London, 1895; also see James Fitzjames Stephen, *Liberty, Equality and Fraternity,* op.cit., as the basic statement of imperialism in India. The syntax of the imperial prose in India was candid and unambiguous: 'It is essentially an absolute government, founded, not on consent, but on conquest. It does not represent the native principles of life or of government, and it can never do so until it represents heathenism and barbarism. It represents a belligerent civilisation, and no anomaly can be more striking or so dangerous, as its administration by men, who being at the head of a Government founded upon conquest, implying at every point the superiority of the conquering race ... shrink from the open, uncompromising, straightforward assertion of it, seek to apologise for their own position, and refuse, from whatever cause, to uphold and support it'. James Fitzjames Stephen, quoted in Eric Stokes', *The English Utilitarians and India,* op.cit., p. 288.
18. cf. Eric Stokes, *The English Utilitarians and India,* ibid., pp. 234–322.
19. Francis G. Hutchins, *Spontaneous Revolution,* op.cit., pp. 179–217.
20. 'This peace (the pax-Romena) actually was, and the more highly educated

Romans must have seen that it was about to become, the mother of laws, institutions of all kinds, under which our characters have been moulded. The Roman law, at that period as clumsy as the English law is at present, but nearly as rich, sagacious and vigorous, was taking root in all parts of the world under the protection of Roman armed force, and all the arts of life, literature, philosophy and art were growing by its side. An Englishman must have a cold heart and a dull imagination who cannot understand how the consciousness of this affected a Roman governor. I do not envy the Englishman whose heart does not beat high as he looks at the scarred and shattered walls of Delhi or at the Union Jack flying from the fort of Lahore'. James Fitzjames Stephen, *Liberty, Equality and Fraternity,* op.cit., pp. 98–99.

21. V.G. Kiernan, *Marxism and Imperialism,* London, 1968, pp. 37–64.
22. cf. Jeffrey Richards, *Visions of Yesterday,* London, 1934. The author provides a full survey of all the imperial films, particularly those of Hollywood.
23. cf. Heins Gollwitzer, *Europe in the Age of Imperialism 1880–1914,* op.cit., pp. 41, 49 and 65; C. Northcote Parkinson, *East and West,* London, 1963, pp. 151–55.
24. Eric Stokes, *The English Utilitarians and India,* op.cit., pp. 309–10; cf. Edward W. Said on Eric Stokes in *Orientalism*, op.cit., pp. 212–18.
25. Penderel Moon, *The Future of India,* London, 1945, pp. 56–57.
26. Agatha Harrison to Horace Alexander, 19 September 1944, the Alexander Papers.
27. Larry Collins and Dominique Lapierre, *Mounbatten and the Partition of India, March 22 August 15 1947,* Delhi, 1981, op.cit., pp. 13–14.
28. William Paton, 'Britain and India', *The Christian News-Letter,* London, September 1943, the Menon Papers; also see, Paul Scott, *The Jewel in the Crown,* London, 1975 (edn.), p. 10.
29. Harold J. Laski, 'Speech at the Birthday Celebration of Jawaharlal Nehru, India League 14 November 1945', encl. S.J. Mason, chief editor, Reuters to V.K. Krishna Menon, 15 November 1945, the Menon Papers.
30. ibid.
31. V.P. Menon, *The Story of the Integration of the Indian States,* Delhi, 1969 (edn.), pp. 59–79.
32. This image has been etched by his biographers; see R. Hough, *Mountbatten: The Hero of Our Time,* London, 1980 and Larry Collins and Dominique Lapierre, *Mountbatten and the Partition of India,* op.cit.
33. Collins and Lapierre, *Mountbatten and the Partition of India,* ibid., pp. 97–98.
34. ibid., pp. 99–102; R.J. Moore, *Escape from Empire,* op.cit., pp. 234–59.
35. Collins and Lapierre, *Mountbatten and the Partition of India,* op.cit. For the criticisms by Jawaharlal Nehru, M.A. Jinnah and Vallabhbhai Patel of the failure of callous and incompetent British officials to check massacre,

looting and arson in Punjab, see 'Viceroy's Personal Reports, Report No. 10. June 28, 1947,' pp. 128–30 and for the official attitudes and reactions, 'Memorandum by the Governor of the Punjab on the Main Criticisms against the Punjab Government for the handling of the Current disturbances', 8 August 1947, pp. 130–38, ibid.

36. ibid., p. 137; also pp. 131–35.
37. Larry Collins and Dominique Lapierre, *Freedom at Midnight,* op.cit., p. 314; cf. John Masters, *To The Coral Strand,* op.cit. pp. 108–10 for Rodney's recall by admiring Indians as a comparable wishful thinking. 'I got out of your damned way. I left you to run the bloody country', a proud Rodney exclaimed, 'as best as you could, and even then, you had to send for me when you came across something you didn't understand.' ibid., p. 108.
38. ibid., pp. 214–15; also John Masters, *Pilgrim Son: A Personal Odyssey,* London, 1973, pp. 11, 27 and 47.
39. John Masters, *To The Coral Strand,* op.cit., pp. 215.
40. Paul Scott, *The Jewel in the Crown,* op.cit., p. 473.
41. ibid. And what terrified Lady Manners most was '. . . the thought that gradually, when the splendours of civilised divorce and protestations continuing as good friends are worked out, the real animus will emerge . . . I mean of course the dislike and fear that exists between the black and white . . . I suppose everything gets stripped down to that, in the end, because that is the last division of all, isn't it? The colour of skin, I mean; not dying'. pp. 476–77.
42. Paul Scott, *The Jewel in the Crown,* ibid., p. 473; also cf. Gomathi Narayan, *The Sahib and the Natives, A Study in Guilt and Pride in Indo-Anglian and Anglo-Indian Novels,* Delhi, 1986, p. 99.
43. Christine Weston, *Indigo*, London, 1944, p. 299.
44. Jon Godden, *The Peacock,* London, 1950, pp. 19–96.
45. Paul Scott, *An Alien Sky,* London, 1979, pp. 24–26; also see John Masters, *Pilgrim Son: A Personal Odyssey,* op.cit., p. 27.
46. 'The most common currency of our Indian associations appears in the surviving fragments of our inheritance from Kipling. Of the 181 individuals interviewed for the study, 69 spontaneously mentioned Kipling as a source of the early impressions relating to India, and it seems reasonable to guess that many more would have recalled him if specifically jogged on the point. It became clear in any case that Kipling's India was still part of the mental baggage carried about by a great many Americans of youthful maturity or order'. Harold R. Issacs, *Images of Asia, American Views of China and India,* New York, 1972 (edn.), p.24. Viewed superficially, the image was that of a fabulous India. But primarily it was that of the very benighted heathen Hindu with sacred cows, mobs of religious fanatics hurling themselves into the Ganga, naked ascetics, fakirs, the burning ghats, the blood-thirsty *Kali,* multi-headed gods, obscene Hindu sculp-

tures, phallic symbols, erotic carvings, lesser breeds, faceless crowd, conquered and prostrated people, villainous souls and dark skinned ruffians. The anarchic nature of human libido, however, created serious problems for the guardians of ethnic boundaries and privileges. Both officials and writers endeavoured to create the myth of sexual insecurity of the English ladies in India, as in Africa and elsewhere in lonely district outposts. The memsahib was always prepared, it was maintained, to face any native's assault with a loaded revolver in her pouch. Hutchins concludes that this fear of sexual assault from the subjects was 'the result of the influence of revulsion and fear, shame and insecurity, of the attempt to justify dislike and defensiveness by the perception of an imagined threat, in other words, of changes in British attitudes for which Indians could scarcely be held responsible'. Francis Hutchins, *The Illusion of Permanence,* Princeton, 1967, p.71; also see for this 'prurient fantasy', Benita Parry, *Delusions and discoveries: Studies on India in the British imagination, 1880–1930,* London, 1972, p.98. See for the 'Prospero complex', O. Mannoni, *Prospero and Calliban: The Psychology of Colonization,* Pamela Powesland, trans., London, 1956, p.110; E.M. Forster, *A Passage to India*; Maud Diver, *Desmond's Daughter*; John Masters, *To The Coral Strand* ; Paul Scott, *The Jewel in the Crown* ; Rumer Godden, *Kingfisher's Catch Fire*; Cecilie Leslie, *Goat to Kali* ; and almost everyone who wrote on India shared this distorted colonial psychology of the Kipling-hunted exclusive clubs of the Raj.

47. Philip Woodruff, *The Wild Sweet Witch,* London, 1947.
48. ibid.
49. ibid.
50. Dennis Gray Stoll, *The Dove Found No Rest,* London, 1955, pp.173 and 205.
51. Rumer Godden, *Kingfishers Catch Fire,* London, 1953. For Rumer Godden India was still 'a muddle' that defied definition or comprehension.
52. cf. Philip Woodruff, *Call the Next Witness,* London, 1945.
53. Mary Margaret Kaye, *Shadow of the Moon,* London, 1953, see p. 331.
54. T.W. Simeon, *The Mask of a Lion,* London, 1952.
55. Rumer Godden, *Black Narcissus,* London, 1939.
56. Philip Woodruff, *The Island of Chamba,* London, 1950. 'India's going to be Hindu; make no mistake about it. . . Well, how can Hindu India tolerate an island only seventy miles from her rule as an independent state by Muslim? . . .' Hindu India, Woodruff was at pains to emphasize, had desperate and dangerous ideas about a Muslim India recalling the memories of Czechoslovakia and Poland. Philip Mason was bitter, pugnacious and vituperative. The image that was sought to be projected had been nurtured over years. India was still, mysterious, chaotic, unfathomable, incorrigible, essentially undemocratic, racially and religiously compartmentalized, and yet seductive. Thus a pure murder story based on trial and

evidence was turned into an imperial discourse by Philip Woodruff. His hero, Christopher, was overwhelmed by the sudden despair of his work, a contempt for the sand of his daily ploughing, and a baffled feeling that he was on a surface beneath which he could not see, playing always with guesses which he could never know with certainty. Personally he longed for England; he wanted to deal with people who would say what they thought and who would not be the slaves of passion and intrigues and he wanted to feel beneath his feet a soil that was friendly to man. Philip Woodruff, *Call the Next Witness,* op.cit., pp. 217–18. Also see Pamela Hinkinson, *Indian Harvest,* London, 1941 and Babbot (Isobel Abbot), *Indian Interval,* London, 1960.

57. cf. Iain Wright, 'F.R. Leavis, The Scrutiny Movement And The Crisis' in Jon Clark etc., ed., *Culture and Crisis in Britain in the 30s,* op.cit., pp. 37–65; Oswald Sprengler, *Decline of the West,* C.F. Atkinson (trans.) 2 vols. (1926–29); E.H. Goddard and P.A. Gibbon, *Civilisation or Civilisations: An Essay in the Sprenglerian Philosophy of History,* London, 1926, pp. 2–4. and F.R. Leavis, *D.H. Lawrence,* Cambridge, 1930, pp. 27–28 for the continued faith in the possibilities of a creative future also Jon and Rumer Godden, *Two Under the Indian Sun,* p. 307, London, 1966.

58. Quoted in Q.D. Leavis, 'Abinger Harvest, by E.M. Forster' in *A Selection from Scrutiny Compiled by F.R. Leavis,* Cambridge, 1968, vol. ii, pp. 134–38.

59. ibid., p. 137.

60. cf. 'Why can't we be friends now?' said the other, holding him affectionatley, 'It's what I want. It's what you want.' But the horses didn't want it—they swerved apart; the earth didn't want it, sending up rocks through which riders must pass single file; the temples, the tanks, the jails, the palace, the birds, the carrion, the Guest House, that came into view as they issued from the gap and saw Mau beneath: they didn't want it, they said in their hundred voices, 'No, not yet', and the sky said, 'No, not there.' E.M. Forster, *A Passage to India,* op.cit., p. 316. Forster like his Liberal fellow-travellers was unable to affirm categorically that 'we should give up control' or to assert, 'no, we shall hold on regardless.' As Edward W. Said conceptualized, the 'self-conscious contemplative passivity' of Forster was formed into 'paralysed gestures of aestheticized powerlessness.' Thus despite the record of colonial exploitation and the consciousness of that experience, Forster could neither recommend decolonization nor its continuity. 'No, not yet, not here,' is all Forster can muster by way of resolution. See Edward W. Said, 'Representing the Colonized: Anthropology's Interlocutors', *Critical Inquiry,* 1989, pp. 205–25.

61. cf. R.G. Coupland, *The Future of India,* London, 1943; also see Harry J. Greenwell, *Storm over India,* London, 1933.

62. Horace Alexander, *India Since Cripps,* op.cit.

63. Paul Scott, *The Jewel in the Crown,* op.cit., pp. 44 and 45–46.

64. ibid., p. 73.
65. *Condition of India*—Being the Report of the Delegation sent to India by the India League in 1932, London, n.d., pp. 383–403.
66. Quoted in John M. Mackenzie, *Propaganda and the Empire*, op.cit., p. 40. Nostalgia, patriotic sketches and imperial myths of the popular songs of pre-Second World War days continued to impassion popular theatre. There was much wishful thinking and a good deal of make-believe: There are enemies around us who are jealous of our fame / We have made a mighty Empire and they'd like to do the same. Oblivious of the massive fall out of the end of the Raj, popular audience of the provinces were still fond of singing: And we mean to be the top dog still / Bow-Wow / Yes, we mean to be the top dog still. In this strange requiem of the Raj, even the cultured society joined its voice. Class distinction was blurred as queen Victoria hailed 'the Mother of the Empires', pronounced that 'the hand that rocks the cradle is the hand that wrecks the world', and still continued to believe that from New Zealand to Bangkok via Bermuda and Malta, 'Chips of the Grand and Old Block' ruled and would once again rule. The date of this national excitement fell much after 15 August 1947. See Gyles Brandreth, *I Scream for Ice Cream; Pearls from the Pantomimes*, London, 1947, pp. 49–50, 58–59 and 79–81.
67. Paul Scott, *The Towers of Silence*, London, 1973.
68. Jon Stallworthy, 'Epilogue to An Empire 1600-1900'; Baker, *English History in Verse*, op.cit., pp. 423–24.
69. Noel Coward, 'I Wonder What Happened to Him', ibid., pp. 421–22.
70. Jon Stallworthy, 'Epilogue', op.cit.
71. ibid.
72. cf. Harry Politt, *Serving My Time*, London, 1940; and William Gallacher *Revolt on the Clyde*, London, 1936.

Biographical Notes

Alexander, Horace Gundry (1893–1989): British historian; author; spokesman of Friends of India; close to Gandhi; associated with the Indian Conciliation Group; leader of Friend's Ambulance Unit in India, 1943.

Allen, Reginald Clifford (1889–1939): British Labour politician; general manager, *Daily Citizen,* 1911–15; director, *Daily Herald,* 1925–30; supported the 'national' Labour Group.

Ambedkar, Bhimrao Ramji (1891–1956): Indian statesman; led the depressed classes; attended the Round Table Conferences, 1930–32; joined the Viceroy's Executive Council, 1942; one of the architects of India's republican constitution.

Amery, Leopold Charles Maurice Stennett (1873–1955): British statesman; colonial secretary, 1924–29; dominion secretary, 1925–29; secretary of state for India, 1940–45; a founder of the Empire Parliamentary Association; a member of Rhodes trustee, 1919–55.

Andrews, Charles F. (1871–1940): Anglican priest of the Cambridge Brotherhood, Delhi; close associate of both Mahatma Gandhi and Rabindranath Tagore.

Ansari, M.A. (1880–1936): Indian nationalist leader from U.P.; medical practitioner, Delhi; president, the Muslim League, 1918, the National Congress, 1927 and the All Parties Conference, 1928; participated in the Civil Disobedience Movement.

Asquith, Henry Herbert (1852–1928): British statesman; joined the Liberal Imperial Group during the South African War, 1899–1902; prime minister, 1908–1916; key figure in constitutional controversy of 1909–11.

Attlee, Clement Richard (1883–1967): British statesman; deputy leader, parliamentary Labour Party, 1931; leader of the same, 1931–45; prime minister, 1945–51.

Auckland, Eden George, first Earl of (1784–1849): British statesman and governor-general of India, 1836–42.

Auden, Wystan Hugh (1907–1973): English poet, dramatist, librettist and essayist.

Austin, Alfred (1835–1967): English poet laureate.

Baden-Powell, Robert Stephenson Smyth (1857–1941): British army general;

participated in India (1876), Zululand (1888), Ashanti (1895–96) and Matabaland (1896) campaigns; held Mefaking during its long siege (1899–1900); founder of Boy Scout and Girl Guide movement.

Bajaj, Jamnalal (1889–1942): Indian cotton merchant; banker; Congressman and close associate of the Mahatma.

Baker, Herbert (1862–1946): British architect; joined Milner's kindergarten; built government buildings at Pretoria; collaborated with Edwin Lutyens in New Delhi; other works include India House and South Africa House in London and Rhodes House in Oxford.

Baldwin, Stanley (1867–1947): British statesman; prime minister in 1923, 1924–29 and 1935–37; member of the MacDonald's national government, 1931–35; supported the Government of India Bill 1935; target of Harold Rothermere, William Beaverbrook and Winston Churchill for being inadequate in the Empire free-trade movement and for supporting 'dominion status' for India.

Benthall, Edwin Charles (1893–1961): Senior Partner of Bird & Co; appointed by the ministry of economic warfare, Britain, 1940–42; close adviser to the Government of India; member of the Viceroy's Executive Council, 1942–45.

Bentinck, William Henry Cavendish (1774–1839): British statesman; governor-general of Bengal, 1828–33 and governor-general of India, 1933–35; known for his enlightened administration.

Besant, Annie (1847–1933): Theosophist, educationist and Indian nationalist leader.

Beveridge, William Henry (1879–1963): British social reformer and economist; his 'Beveridge Plan' became the blue print for the welfare state legislation of 1944–48.

Bhopal, Hamidlullah, Nawab of (1894–1960): Indian prince; Chancellor, Chamber of Princes, 1931–32 and 1944–47; a delegate to the Round Table Conference, 1930; negotiated to safeguard princes' rights; subsequently, advocated division of India into Hindustan, Pakistan and Rajasthan.

Bikaner, Ganga Singh Bahadur (1880–1940): Indian prince; educated at Mayo College, Ajmer; Chancellor, Chamber of Princes, 1921–1924; attended the Round Table Conferences, 1930–31; supported All India Federation.

Birla, G.D. (1894–1983): Indian commercial and industrial magnate; president of the Federation of Indian Chambers of Committee and Industry, 1929; a close associate of Gandhi.

Brailsford, H.N. (1873–1958): British journalist and a committed socialist; editor, *New Leader*, 1922–26; wrote regularly in *New Statesman and Nation.*

Butler, Montagu Sherard Dawes (1873–1952): Member of the Indian Civil Service; secretary, Government of India; governor, Central Provinces, 1925.

Butler, Spencer Harcourt (1869–1938): Member of the Indian Civil Service; secretary, foreign department, 1907–10; in charge of education, 1910–15; lieutenant-governor United Provinces, 1918–21; governor, United Provinces, 1921–23.

Campbell-Bannerman, Henry (1836–1908): British statesman; served in the administration of Gladstone and Rosebery, 1892–95; leader of the Liberal Party in the House of Commons, 1899; opposed Joseph Chamberlain's South African policy of enforcing unconditional surrender of the Boers as a method of barbarism; prime minister, 1905–08.

Candler, Edmund (1874–1926): British author; the writings of Kipling and the sacrifice of John Nicholson inspired his Indian career; taught at Darjeeling and Patiala; appointed director of publicity to the Punjab government and was awarded Commander of the British Empire ; his works expressing sharp animosity towards Indian nationalism, especially his work *Sri Ram* which created much stir in England.

Carlyle, Robert Warran (1859–1934): Member of the Indian Civil Service; scholar; Member of the Governor-General's Council, 1910—15.

Carlyle, Thomas (1795–1881): British essayist; historian and man of letters.

Carmichael, Thomas David Gibson (1859–1926): British colonial administrator; governor of Victoria, Australia 1908–11 and of Bengal 1912–17; art connoisseur.

Cecil, James Edward Herbert Gascoyne (1861–1947): British Conservative statesman; leader of the House of Lords, 1925–29; of the opposition of the Lords, 1929–31; sharply opposed to the Government of India Bill, 1935; president of the National Union of Conservative and Unionist Associations, 1942–45.

Cecil, Robert Arthur Talbot Gascoyne, third Earl of Salisbury (1830–1903): British Conservative statesman; prime minister and foreign secretary, 1885–86.

Chamberlain, Austen (1863–1937): British statesman; Liberal-unionist chancellor of exchequer, 1903–05; secretary of state, 1915; Conservative leader, 1921; foreign secretary, 1924–29; secured signature of the Locarno Pact, 1925; awarded the Nobel peace prize, 1925.

Chamberlain, Joseph (1836–1914): British statesman; imperialist colonial secretary.

Chelmsford, Thesiger Frederick John Napier, first Viscount (1863–1933): British viceroy of India, 1916–21.

Cherwell, Viscount (1886–1957): British scientist and politician; personal scientific adviser to British prime minister in the Second World War.

Chirol, Ignatius Valentine (1852–1927): Traveller, journalist and author; in charge of *The Times* foreign department, 1896–1912; expert on imperial and far-eastern affairs of the foreign office; member of the Royal Commission on Indian Public Services, 1912–14; visited India seventeen times; wrote extensively on India with official authority.

Churchill, Winston L.S. (1874–1965): Conservative leader of the British nation; prime minister, 1940–45, 1951–55; organized British victory in the Second World War; die-hard imperialist; opposed to any concession to India.

Clark, George Sydenham (1848–1913): Administrator; governor of Bombay, 1907–1913.

Cotton, Henry (1845–1915): Member of the Indian Civil Service, 1867–1902; president, Indian Congress, 1904; M.P. 1906–10.

Coupland, Reginald (1884–1952): Historian; Beit professor of colonial history, Oxford; visited India with the Cripps' Mission 1942; wrote on Indian problems and politics.

Craddock, Reginald Henry (1864–1937): Member of the Indian Civil Service; home member, Viceroy's Council 1912–17; lieutenant-governor, Burma, 1917–22; Conservative M.P. ; known for his hostility against Indian aspirations.

Crewe-Milnes, *Robert Offley Ashburton,* Marquis of Crewe (1858–1945): British Liberal politician, secretary of state for India, 1910–15.

Cripps, Richard, Stafford (1889–1952): British Christian Socialist and distinguished member of the Labour Party; known for his Mission to India, 1942 and also for his participation in the Cabinet Mission, 1946.

Croft, Henry Page (1881–1947): British politician; formed a strong imperialist 'National Party', 1917–22; returning to Conservative fold agitated for tariffs and against the Indian self-government; joint parliamentary under-secretary, 1940–45.

Crozier, William Percival (1879–1944): Journalist; joined the *Manchester Guardian,* editor, 1932–44; had extensive contact with Indian Liberals through B. Shiva Rao.

Curtis, Lionel George (1872–1955): Public servant and subsequently, Beit lecturer on colonial history, Oxford; as head of the Milner's Kindergarten prepared the Salbourne Memorandum, 1901; founder of the Round Table Group, 1910; joined constitution discussion in India, 1916–17; brought about the foundation of the Royal Institute of International Affairs, 1920–21.

Curzon, George Nathaniel (1859–1925): Conservative British politician; a leading authority on Asian affairs; viceroy of India 1895–1905; adopted adventurous policy in Tibet and Persian Gulf; held *durbar* in Delhi, 1903; secured partition of Bengal, 1905; a leading spokesman of the Empire in the House of Lords; member of cabinet, 1915 and 1916.

Darling, Malcolm Lyall (1890–1950): Member of the Indian Civil Service; chief financial commissioner, 1936–39; Indian editor, the B.B.C., 1939–44.

Darwin, Charles Robert (1809–1882): British naturalist; author of the significant and influential work, *Origin of Species,* London, 1959.

Das, Chittaranjan (1870–1925): Nationalist leader; president, Indian National Congress, 1922; founder, Swaraj Party; popularly known as Deshbandhu.

Dawson, George Geoffry (1874–1944): British journalist and editor, *The Times,* 1912–19 and 1923–41; especially intimate with Baldwin whose Indian policy he supported.

Dickinson, G. Lowes (1862–1932): British humanist; historian and philosopher.

Digby, K.M. (1800–1880): British miscellaneous writer; author of *The Broad Stone of Honour,* 1824 and other works on the emotional aspects of Catholicism.

Dilke, Charles Wentworth (1843–1911): British politician and the author of the influential works, *Greater Britain,* 1868 and *Problems of Greater Britain,* 1890.

Disraeli, Benjamin (1804–1881): British statesman and man of letters; prime minister of England, 1868 and 1874–80.

Diver, Maud (1875–1945): British author; born in India in a family having long connections with the country; wrote romantic novels on the British in India and also on the Indian princes; a life-long friend of Mrs Fleming, Rudyard Kipling's sister.

Duff, Alexander (1806–1876): British missionary; opened a school at Calcutta, 1830; encouraged by Bentinck; defended the cause of English education in India in opposition to the 'orientalists'.

Duncan, Jonathan (1755–1811): Evangelist resident of Benaras, 1788 and governor of Bombay, 1795–1811.

Dyer, Reginald Edward Harry (1864–1927): British general; ordered the massacre at the Jallianwala Bagh, Amritsar, 1919; resigned from Indian services, 1920.

Ellenborough, Edward Law (1790–1871): British colonial administrator; governor-general of India, 1942–44.

Elliot, Gilbert John Murray Kynynmond, fourth Earl of Minto (1845–1914): British statesman; viceroy of India, 1905–10.

Elphinstone, M.S. (1779–1859): British colonial administrator; famous for his enlightened government of Bombay and Deccan.

Eyton, John : British author and popular writer on Indian themes in the 1920s with Kipling as his model ; works include *Bulbulla* , 1928 and *The Dancing Fakir and Other Stories,* 1922.

Faizul-Huq, A.K. (1873–1962): Indian nationalist; chief minister of Bengal, 1937–43.

Fisher, H.A.L. (1856–1940): British historian; statesman; member of the Royal Commission on Public Services in India, 1912–17.

Fitzgerald, Edward (1809–1883): English translator of Omar Khayyam; poet; intimate friend of Tennyson and Carlyle; reinforced the traditions of chivalry.

Foot, Isaac (1888–1960): British politician; Liberal M. P., 1922–24 and 1929–35; member of the Round Table Conferences and the Joint Select Committee.

Forster, Edward Morgan (1879–1970): British novelist and man of letters; one of the Bloomsbury group; visited India in 1912 and revisited in 1921; worked out in his *A Passage to India* the rubrics of personal relationships between human beings irrespective of political and social differences.

Frere, Henry Bartle Edward (1815–1884): British colonial administrator; served in India and South Africa; governor of Bombay, 1862–67; high commissioner of South Africa, 1877–80.

Froude, James Anthony (1818–1894): British historian and man of letters; an associate of Carlyle; interested in imperial and colonial affairs; most significant work, *Oceana or England and her Colonies,* 1886.

Fuller, Joseph Bampfylde (1854–1935): British colonial administrator; chief commissioner, Assam, 1902–1905; lieutenant-governor, East Bengal and Assam, 1905.

Gallacher, William (1881–1965): British politician; intimately involved with

British working class movement; Communist M.P., 1935–50.

Gandhi, Mohandas Karamchand (1869–1948): Indian national leader; organized non-violent movements against British imperialism; insisted on the supremacy of means over ends; hailed by his countrymen as the Mahatma.

Godden, Jon (1906–1984): British novelist; brought up in India; important works on India include *Peacock*.

Godden, Rumer : British novelist writing on Indian themes; brought up in India; the most important works are *The River* and *The Black Narcissus*.

Gordon, Charles George (1833–1885): Legendary British army general of the Empire; participated in various encounters in Turkey, Africa, India and China; killed in the operation against Mahdi in Sudan.

Grant, Robert (1779–1839): Governor of Bombay, 1834–38.

Green, T.H (1836–1886): British idealist philosopher.

Grigg, Edward William Macleay, first Baron of Altricham (1879–1955): British administrator, politician, joint-editor, *Round Table,* 1913; editor, *National Review,* 1948–55; Conservative M.P., 1933–45; parliamentary secretary, 1940–42; minister resident, Middle East 1944–45.

Gwyer, Maurice Linford (1878–1952): Jurist; chief justice of India; president of the Federal Court, 1937–43.

Haggard, Henry Rider (1856–1925): British novelist; with special interest in rural England, agriculture, adventure and the romantic concept of the Empire.

Haig, Harry Graham (1881–1956): Member of the Indian Civil Service; governor of the United Provinces, 1934–39.

Hailey, William Malcolm (1872–1969): Member of the Indian Civil Service; governor of the Punjab 1924–48; of the United Provinces 1928–34; chairman of the School of Oriental and African Studies since 1941.

Hallett, Maurice Garnier (1883–1969): Member of the Indian Civil Service; governor of the United Provinces, 1939–44.

Hardinge, Charles, Hardinge of Penshurst (1858–1944): British diplomat; viceroy of India, 1910–16.

Harrison, Agatha: Secretary, The India Conciliation Group formed in 1931 by the Society of Friends.

Havelock, Henry (1795–1857): British army general; during the Revolt of 1857 commanded a column which recaptured Kanpur; with Outram's reinforcement affected the first relief of Lucknow; with Colin Campbell offered the second relief in November 1857; Campbell completed the work of retribution.

Heath, Carl: Chairman, India Conciliation Group.

Hegel, Georg Wilhelm Friedrich (1770–1831): Most significant idealist philosopher of Europe in the nineteenth century, left a profound impact.

Hoare, Samuel Viscount Templewood (1880–1959): British statesman; secretary of state for India, 1931–35; a principal witness before the Joint Select Committee on Indian constitution, 1933–34; foreign secretary 1935; resigned on the Abyssinian issue in December 1935.

Hope, James Fitzalan, first Baron of Rankeillour (1870–1949): British politician; chairman of the Ways and Means Committee of the Commons and deputy speaker, 1921–24 and 1924–29; prominent Roman Catholic layman.

Housman, Laurence (1865–1959): Writer; art critic; playwright; pioneer feminist; pacifist and socialist.

Hugh, Graham (1848–1938): British newspaper proprietor; protectionist and imperialist.

Hunter, W.W. (1840–1900): Member of the Indian Civil Service; from 1869 to 1881 supervised and helped the compilation of the statistical survey of the Raj; after retirement, wrote *History of British India* (II. Vols.) and a much acclaimed novel, *The Old Missionary,* 1895, apart from writing for the *Contemporary Review.*

Huxley, Aldous Leonard (1894–1963): British writer and man of letters; works include essays and travel books.

Hyndman, Henry Mayers (1842–1921): Socialist leader of Britain; took lead in forming the Social Democratic Federation, 1881; left the British Socialist Party and formed the National Socialist Party, 1916; wrote several books defending political Marxism and two volumes of autobiographical works.

Irwin, Lord Edward Frederick Lindlay Wood, first earl of Halifax (1881–1959): Later Viscount of Halifax; British statesman; viceroy of India, 1926–31; applauded for an attempt at a reconciliation with India.

Jayakar, M.R. (1876–1948): Bombay lawyer; Swarajist politician; M.L.C., 1923–25, Bombay.

Jinnah, Muhammed Ali (1876–1948):Bombay lawyer and politician; withdrew support for Gandhi and Congress during non-cooperation; leader of Pakistan movement; governor-general of Pakistan, 1947–48.

Kaye, Mary Margaret : British author, born and lived most of her life in India; descendant of Major Edward Kaye who commanded the battery at the siege of Delhi and of Sir William Kaye, the author of a history of the uprising.

Kerr, Philip Henry (1882–1940): British journalist and politician; founder and first editor, *The Round Table,* 1910–16; member of Milner Kindergarten; private secretary to Llyod George, 1902–09.

Khan, Abdul Gaffar (1890–1988): Indian nationalist leader of the North-West Frontier; organized the Khudai Khitmatgar movement; participated in the campaigns of the Indian National Congress during the freedom movement; popularly known as Frontier Gandhi.

Khan, Syed Ahmed (1817–1898): Indian nationalist; served East India Company; founder of the Aligarh movement; member, Imperial Legislative Council, 1878–83.

Kinsley, Charles (1819–1875): British author; professor of Modern History at Cambridge, 1960–69.

Kipling, Rudyard (1865–1936): British author; joined staff of *Lahore Civil and Military Gazette,* 1882; noted for his stories, poems and novels dwelling on the theme of the imperial race doing justice and upholding law.

Kunzru, Pandit Hirday Nath (1887–1978): Member of the Indian National

Congress; actively associated with Congress until the Liberals seceded in 1918; President of the All-India Liberal Federation; member, United Provinces Legislative Council.

Lansbury, George (1859–1940): Christian Socialist and pacifist of Britain; led the Labour Party after the formation of MacDonald's national government; resigned in 1935 on the question of sanction against Italy for its invasion of Ethiopia.

Laski, Harold Joseph (1893–1950): British political theorist; professor of political science 1925–50; rejected the pluralist theory of state and moved closer to Marxism; chairman of the Labour Party and the chief target of the Conservative election campaign.

Lawrence, John (1811–1879): British civil servant in India; served the East India Company from 1829–78; viceroy of India, 1864–69.

Layton, Walter Thomas (1884–1966): British economist; newspaper proprietor; editor, the *Economist,* 1922–38; chairman, *The News Chronicle,* 1930–31 and the *Star,* 1936–35.

Lindsay, Alexander Dunlop (1879–1952): Scholar, master at Balliol, 1924—49; welcomed the opening of Oxford to wider social classes; his democratic theories were an outcome of his Christian beliefs; adviser on education to the Labour Party; chairman, Committee of Protestant Colleges in India, 1930.

Linlithgow, Alexander John Hope (1887–1952): Viceroy of India 1936–43.

Lloyd George, David (1863–1945): Liberal prime minister of Britain who led a coalition government in 1932.

Lothian, Lord (1882–1940): British statesman; under secretary for India, 1932; chairman, Indian Franchise Commission, 1932.

Luce, Mrs Henry Robinson (Clare Boothe): British playwright, columnist and author; member, House of the Representatives, U.S. Congress, 1943–46.

Lugard, Frederick John Dealty (1858–1945): British soldier, administrator and author; served in Sudan (1885), Burma (1886) and Uganda (1890); governor of Nigeria, 1912–14; governor-general of Nigeria, 1914–19; author of the influential book,*The Rise of East African Empire,* (II. Vols.).

Lutyens, Edwin Landseer (1869–1944): British architect; built series of romantic country homes in England, 1889–1909; architect of New Delhi.

Lyall, Alfred (1835–1911): Indian administrator and writer; foreign secretary, government of India, 1878–1881; lieutenant-governor of the United Provinces, 1882–87.

Lytton, Edward Robert Bulwer, Earl of Lytton (1831–1891): British diplomat and poet; viceroy of India, 1876–80.

MacDonald, James Ramsay (1866–1937): British labour leader; prime minister, 1924 and 1929–35.

MacDonald, Malcolm (1901–1981): British politician; under-secretary for the dominions, 1931–35.

Malaviya, Madan Mohan (1861–1946): Indian politician; founder and vice-chancellor of the Benaras Hindu University; Congressman; president, All-India

Hindu Mahasabha, 1923, 1924 and 1936.

Marris, William Sinclair (1873–1945): Member of the Indian Civil Service; intimately associated with Milner's Kindergarten and member of the Round Table Group; governor of Assam, 1921–22; of the United Provinces, 1922–27.

Martin, Basil Kingsley (1897–1969): British journalist and editor; lead-writer, *Manchester Guardian*, 1927–30; editor, *New Statesman, New Statesman and Nation*, 1931–60; co-founder with W.H. Robson of the *Political Quarterly*.

Mason, Philip : Member of the Indian Civil Service, 1928–47; preferred to write on India under the pseudonym, Philip Woodruff; apart from *The Men Who Ruled India*, (II. Vols.) wrote several novels including, *The Island of Chamba* and *The Wild Sweet Witch*.

Masters, John : British author of novels on Indian themes; born in a family that served the Raj for generations; left in utter frustration after India's independence, for the US; concentrated on the glories and pride of the Raj.

Maxwell, Reginald Maitland (1882–1967): Member of the Indian Civil Service; member of the Viceroy's Executive Council 1938–44 and advisor; secretary of state for India, 1944–45.

Mayers, Leopold H. (1881–1944): British novelist; wrote four philosophical novels set in the India of 1929 to 1940, republished collectively as *The Near and the Far*, 1943.

Mayo, Katherine (1868–1940): British author of the controversial book, *Mother India*, 1927.

Mayo, Richard Southwell Bourke, the sixth Earl of Mayo (1882–72): British statesman; viceroy of India assassinated at Port Blair.

Menon, V.K. Krishna (1895–1974): Indian nationalist; secretary, India League, 1927–44.

Meston, James (1865–1943): British civil servant who served under the Raj; lieutenant-governor, United Provinces, 1912–18; an associate of Lionel Curtis and his group.

Mill, James (1773–1836): Utilitarian philosopher; promulgator of Benthamism in England; wrote the *History of India*, (VI Vols.), 1818.

Mill, John Stuart (1806–1873): Philosopher, devoted his life to the humanizing and widening of the Utilitarian School.

Mohammad Ali Mohammad, Raja of Mahmudabad (1889–1931): Indian politician; member U.P. legislature, 1908–09 and of the governor-general's council 1907–20; president, All India Muslim League, 1915–19 and of the British India Association, 1917–21.

Molesworth, George Nobel (1890–1968): General in the British Indian army; deputy chief of general staff, India 1941–42; secretary, military department, India Office, 1943–44.

Montagu, E.S. (1879–1924): British statesman; Liberal M.P., 1906–22; secretary of state for India, 1917–22.

Monteath, David Taylor (1887–1961): British statesman; permanent under-secretary of state for India, 1942–45.

Montgomery, Robert (1809–1887): British administrator; served under the Raj as commissioner, Lahore Division, 1849; chief commissioner, Oudh, 1858; lieutenant-governor, 1859–65; member of the council of state for India, 1868.

Mookerjee, Syama Prasad (1901–1953): Indian politician and statesman; president, Hindu Mahasabha, 1943–44; finance minister, Bengal, 1941.

Moon, Penderel: Member of the Indian Civil Service, 1929–44.

Morley, John (1838–1923): British Liberal politician and man of letters; editor *Fortnightly Review;* secretary of state for India, 1905–15.

Morison, Theodore (1863–1936): Educationist and writer; professor, Anglo-Oriental college at Aligarh, 1899 and later the principal of this college, 1899–1905; member, Council of India, 1906–16.

Mountbatten, Louis Francis Albert Victor Nicholas (1900–1979): British statesman; viceroy of India, March 1947–August 1947; governor-general of India, 15 August 1947–21 June 1948.

Muir, John Ramsay Bryce (1872–1941): British historian and politician; Liberal M.P., 1923–24; chairman, Liberal Party, 1931–33; president, National Liberal Federation, 1933–36.

Mundy, Talbot (1874–1965): British author; worked in the Baroda state; travelled extensively; settled in the US; wrote some books on India.

Nazim-ud-Din, Kwaja (1894–1964): Indian politician and statesman; member of the Indian Muslim League; chief minister, Bengal, 1943.

Newbolt, Henry John (1862–1938): Poet and man of letters; upheld faith in Christianity.

Nicholson, John (1821–1857): British general; commanded the storming party in the assault on Delhi, 1857 and was killed; a legendary figure.

O'Dwyer, Michael Francis (1864–1940): British administrator; lieutenant-governor, Punjab, 1913–20.

Orwell, George (1903–1950): British author, man of letters and a socialist; born in India; worked in the imperial police force in Burma, 1922–27; wrote his experiences in *Burmese Days* and *Shooting the Elephant and Other Essays*.

Parkin, George Robert (1846–1922): British educationist and imperialist; first organizing secretary of Rhodes Scholarships; settled permanently in England, 1902; his works include *Imperial Federation*, 1892.

Paton, William (1886–1943): British Presbyterian minister and secretary of the International Missionary Council; secretary, National Christian Council of India, Burma and Ceylon, 1921–27; editor, *The International Review of Missions*, 1927-43.

Pearson, Karl (1857–1936): British academic mathematician and biologist whose enthusiasm for the Darwinian theory of evolution by natural selection never flagged.

Perrin, Alice (1867–1934): British author; wrote novels based on her own experience and those of her family in India.

Polak, H : British associate of Gandhi from his days in South Africa; member of the Conciliation Group.

Pollitt, Harry (1890–1960): British Communist leader; active in voicing his opposition to the First World War; participated in 'Hands off Russia' movement after the Russian revolution; founder member of the Communist Party of Great Britain; general secretary of the same, 1929–56 with a short interval; sought to expand the Communist Party's influence and was responsible for the Communist Party's production of 'The British Road to Socialism.'

Rajagopalachari, Chakravarti (1879–1972): Prominent Indian nationalist; Liberal politician ; differed with Gandhi on many occasions ; chief minister of Madras, 1937–39; member, Governor's Executive Council, 1946–47; first Indian governor-general of India, 1948–50.

Reading, Lord (1860–1935): British politician and statesman; Liberal M.P., 1904–13; chief justice, England, 1913; viceroy of India, 1921–26.

Reed, Herbert Stanley (1872–1959): British journalist; correspondent of *The Times* and *Daily Chronicle,* 1897–1907 and editor *The Times of India,* 1907–14; director of publicity of Government of India, 1914–18.

Rhodes, Cecil John (1853–1903): British imperialist; cotton planter in Natal, 1870; moved to Orange Free State on the discovery of diamonds, 1871; had commanding shares in Kimberley diamond fields; prime minister of the Cape, 1890–96; resigned after the failure of the Jameson Raid.

Risley, Herbert Hope (1851–1911): Member of the Indian Civil Service; census commissioner, 1879; director of ethnography for India, 1901.

Roberts, Frederick Sleigh (1832–1914): British general; served in India, 1857–58; in Abyssinia 1868; marched from Kabul to Kandhar, 1879–80; Commander-in-Chief in India, 1880–93; advocated forward policy against Russia in Asia; appointed supreme command in South Africa, 1899. For his views, see *Forty-one years in India,* 1897.

Robertson, George Scott (1848–1907): Anglo-Indian administrator; entered Indian Medical Service, 1878; political agent, Gilgit, 1889 and 1899; Liberal M.P., 1906.

Robinson, George F. Samuel, Marquis of Ripon (1877–1909): British statesman; Liberal viceroy of India, 1880–84.

Rolland, Romain (1866–1944): French novelist and sociological writer.

Rothermere, Viscount, Harold Sidney Harmsworth (1868–1940): British secretary for air, 1917–18; director of propaganda to neutral countries, 1918; took over the *Daily Mail* on his brother's death.

Roy, B.C. (1882–1962): Indian academician and politician; vice-chancellor, Calcutta University, 1942–44; also member of the National Congress Working Committee ; chief minister of West Bengal after independence.

Roy, M.N. (1887–1954): Leading member of the International Communist movement; left Communist movement to start his Radical Humanist Group; was affiliated to the Left Front of the Indian national movement since mid-thirties.

Ruskin, John (1819–1900): British author, artist and reformer; his work *Seven Lamps of Architecture* had considerable influence on the Gothic revival of his time.

Sankey, John (1866–1948): British statesman; Lord chancellor, 1929–35;

chairman, Imperial Relations Committee, and of Federal Structure Committee of the Indian Round Table Conferences.

Sapru, Tej Bahadur (1875–1949): Prominent advocate and Liberal politician; member, U.P. legislative council, 1913–16; of the Imperial Legislative Council, 1915–20; law member of the Viceroy's Executive Council, 1920–23; attended the Round Table Conferences.

Sastri, V.S. Srinivasa (1869–1946): Liberal politician; president, Servants of India Society, 1915–27; represented India at various imperial assemblies.

Savi, E.W. (1865–1954): British author; wrote over a hundred novels after she returned to England following a long active association with India.

Scott, Paul (1920–1978): British author; served the army in India and Malaya from 1940–46; subsequently, between 1960 to the end of his life, wrote thirteen distinguished novels including the well-acclaimed *The Raj Quartet*.

Schuster, George Ernst (1869–1936): British politician; finance member of the Viceroy's Executive Council, 1928–38; Liberal Member of Parliament, 1940–1944.

Seeley, John Robert (1834–1895): English historian of the British Empire, author of *The Expansion of England*.

Sidgwick, Henry (1837–1900): English philosopher; noted for his theories concerning ethics.

Simon, John (1873–1954): Liberal politician and lawyer; chairman, Indian Statutory Commission, 1927–30.

Sitwell, Francis Osbert (1892–1929): British author; writer of novels, short stories, poems including highly-acclaimed autobiographical works.

Smith, Frederick Edwin, first Earl of Birkenhead (1872–1930): British lawyer and politician; secretary of state, 1924–28.

Smuts, Jan Christian (1870–1950): South African general and politician; fought against Britain in the Boer War, 1899–1902; prime minister, Union of South Africa, 1919–29 and 1939–48; member of the War Cabinet, 1917–19; chancellor of Cambridge University, 1948–50.

Snow, Charles Prestwich (1846–1952): British journalist; editor, *The Manchester Guardian,* 1872–1929; raised the paper to a leading place as a moral force in world politics.

Sprengler, Oswald (1880–1937): German philosopher; his *Decline of the West* (II. Vols.) on the decay of the Western civilization had a far-reaching impact.

Srivastava, Jwala Prasad (1889–1954): Member of the civil defence, and the Viceroy's Executive Council, 1942–43.

Steed, Henry Wickham (1871–1956): British journalist; editor of *The Times* , 1919 ; head of the foreign department; intensely imperialistic.

Steel, Flora Annie (1847–1927): British author; often compared to Kipling; married a member of the ICS; stayed in India till 1889; wrote a number of volumes on Indian folklore; also wrote short stories, biographical fiction on the Indian princes and novels; known for her fiction set against the Revolt of 1857,*On The Face Of the Waters*.

Stephen, James Fitzjames (1829–1894): British judge and diplomat; intimate with Froude and Carlyle; legal member of the Council of India, 1869–72; defended Lytton's Indian policy, 1877–80.

Stoll, Dennis Grey: British composer, writer on music; wrote serveral novels including *The Dove Found No Rest.*

Strachey, John (1823–1900): British statesman; member of the Governor-General's Council, 1868; lieutenant-governor, North-West Province, 1894–96; published *India*, 1888.

Suhrawardy, Huseyn Shaheed (1893–1963): Indian politician and statesman; minister in charge of civil supplies in the Bengal government, 1943.

Tagore, Rabindranath (1861–1941): Indian writer, poet, educationist and artist; founder of the international school at Shantiniketan; awarded the Nobel Prize for literature in 1919.

Temple, Richard (1826–1902): British administrator in India; worked with John Lawrence in Punjab and James Wilson in Bihar; lieutenant-governor, Bengal, 1874–77; governor, Bombay, 1877–80; published works include *India in 1880* and *Men and Events of My Times.*

Thompson, Edward John (1886–1946): Served as an educational missionary in Bengal; special correspondent of the *Manchester Guardian;* intimately known to the leaders of the Indian National Congress including Tagore and Gandhi; wrote on British Indian history including some novels reflecting the aspirations, frustrations and tensions of India in search of her identity, and a critical work on Tagore.

Wavell, Archibald Percival (1883–1950): British administrator on Allenby's staff, 1918 and commander-in-chief, Middle East, 1939–41, India, 1941–43; supreme commander, South-West Pacific, 1942; viceroy of India, 1943–47.

Wedderburn, William (1838–1918): Member of the Indian Civil Service; retired in 1887; formed the Indian Parliamentary Committee in 1893; presided over the twenty-fifth session of the Indian National Congress, 1910; chairman, the British Committee of the Congress, 1889–1918.

Weston, Christine : British author; born and lived in India for several years.

Willingdon, Lord (1866–1941): British statesman; Liberal M.P., 1900–1910; governor of Bombay, 1913–18; viceroy of India, 1931–36.

Woolf, Leonard (1880–1969): British author and man of letters; served the government of Ceylon from 1910 for about ten years; turned anti-imperialist; wrote his autobiography, *The Village in the Jungle* and later published his diaries about his experiences in Ceylon.

Wrench, John Evelyn Leslie (1882–1966): Founder of the Royal Overseas League and the English-Speaking Union; editor, the *Spectator*, 1925–32; senior trustee, Cecil Rhodes Memorial Foundation.

Index

T

V

W

Y